American

Culture

Between

the Wars

American

Culture

Between

the Wars

**REVISIONARY
MODERNISM &
POSTMODERN
CRITIQUE**

Walter

Kalaidjian

 COLUMBIA UNIVERSITY PRESS NEW YORK

Columbia University Press
New York   Chichester, West Sussex

Copyright © 1993 Columbia University Press
All rights reserved

Library of Congress Cataloging-in-Publication Data
Kalaidjian, Walter S. 1952–
    American culture between the wars : revisionary modernism and postmodern
critique / Walter Kalaidjian.
      p.   cm.
    Includes bibliographical references and index.
    ISSN 0-231-08279-9 (cloth).—ISBN 0-231-06279-7 (pbk.)
    1. Arts and society—United States—History—20th century. 2. Feminism and the
arts—United States. 3. Afro-American arts. 4. Avant-garde (Aesthetics)—United
States—History—20th century. 5. Literature and society—United States—History—
20th century.
    I. Title.
NX180.S6K32   1993
700'.1'09097309041 = dc20   93-15213

∞

Casebound editions of Columbia University Press books are printed on permanent and
durable acid-free paper.

Printed in the United States of America
C 10 9 8 7 6 5 4 3 2 1

For Emily, Willa, Andrew, and Ted

Contents

Illustrations   ix

Acknowledgments   xv

Introduction: The Vision Thing   1

   The Twilight of High Modernism   1
   The Historical Avant-Garde   5
   Revolution and Social Modernization   8
   Political Critique in Postmodern Culture   14

1. Revisionary Modernism   19

   Transnational America   19
   The Constructivist Moment   28
   Articulating the Masses   35
   Communal Forms and the JRC   47

2. War of Position and the Old Left   59

    Subculture in The Depression Era   59
    Harlem Partisans   66
    Artists in Uniform   105
    The Guerrilla Aesthetics of Diego Rivera   109
    Fordism and Americanism   122
    Left Androcentrism and the Male Dynamo   138

3. The Feminist Vanguard in the Popular Front   160

    Muriel Rukeyser and the Poetics of Specific Critique   160
    Rereading "The Book of the Dead"   165
    The Visual Culture of the New Deal   175

4. Transpersonal Poetics   188

    $L=A=N=G=U=A=G=E$ Writing and the
       Historical Avant-Gardes   188
    Kenneth Fearing's Textual Recodings   199

5. The New Times of Postmodernity   211

    From Spectacle to Simulation   211
    The Regime of Signs: Matt Mullican   222
    Tactics of Intervention: Barbara Kruger, Jenny Holzer,
       and Nancy Spero   225
    Soliciting Censorship: Hans Haacke   244

Epilogue: Acting Up   252

    Notes   265
    Picture Credits   305
    Index   307

Illustrations

0.1. Hans Haacke, "The Vision Thing." Announcement card for April 1992 exhibition.   xviii

1.1. Alice Beach Winter. "Why Must I Work?" *The Masses* (May 1912).   22

1.2. Robert Minor, "Your Honor, this woman gave birth to a naked child!" *The Masses* (September 1915)   23

1.3. Henry Glintenkamp, "Physically Fit," *The Masses* (October 1917).   25

1.4. Art Young, "Having Their Fling," *The Masses* (September 1917).   26

photo insert   *following page 46*

1.5. El Lissitzky, "Drive Red wedges into White troops!" Poster.

1.6. Vladimir Mayakovsky and Aleksandr Rodchenko, advertisement for GUM Department Store (1923).

1.7. Vladimir Mayakovsky and Aleksandr Rodchenko, advertisement for Red October biscuits (1923).

1.8. Aleksandr Rodchenko, advertisement for books (1929).

1.9. Vladimir Mayakovsky and Aleksandr Rodchenko, Poster for Rezinotrest (1923).

1.10. Vladimir Mayakovsky, series of candy wrappers (1924).

1.11. Export packagings with English texts (no date).

1.12. Poster depicting project for new *Isvestia* building (1925).

1.13. Aleksandr Rodchenko, catalogue cover for Soviet section of International Exhibition of Decorative Arts (1925).

1.14. El Lissitzky, front cover of *Veshch* (1922).

1.15. Louis Lozowick, *New York* (1925). Lithograph.   41

1.16. Louis Lozowick, *Tanks #1* (1929). Lithograph.   42

1.17. Louis Lozowick, *Brooklyn Bridge* (1930). Lithograph.   43

1.18. Louis Lozowick, *Strike Scene* (1934). Lithograph.   44

1.19. Louis Lozowick, *Thanksgiving Dinner* (1938). Lithograph.   45

1.20. Louis Lozowick, ad for New Masses Ball, *New Masses* (December 1928).   49

1.21. Robert Edmond Jones, poster for the Paterson Strike Pageant (1913).   50

2.1. William Siegel, "The White Bourgeois Version of the Negro—as the White Worker Knows Him," *New Masses* (May 1930).   64

2.2. Aaron Douglas, study for *Aspects of Negro Life: An Idyll of the Deep South* (1934).   66

2.3. Winold Reiss, "African Phantasy: Awakening," *The New Negro* (1925).   67

2.4. Miguel Covarrubias, "Orchestra" (1927).   68

2.5. Miguel Covarrubias, "Flapper" (1927).   69

2.6. Miguel Covarrubias, "Couple Dancing" (1927).   70

2.7. Bruce Nugent, "Drawing for Mulattoes—Number 2" (1927).   71

2.8. Bruce Nugent, "Drawing for Mulattoes—Number 3" (1927).   72

2.9. Bruce Nugent, cover illustration *Opportunity* (October 1925).   73

2.10. Aaron Douglas, advertisement for *Nigger Heaven* (1926).   74

2.11. W. B. Williams, "When They Get Together They'll Dump Us Off!!" *The Messenger* (August 1919).   76

2.12. Trademark of the National Association for the Promotion of Labor Unionism Among Negroes, *The Messenger* (1929)   76

2.13. "Following the Advice of the 'Old Crowd' Negro," *The Messenger* (September 1919).   77

2.14 "The 'New Crowd Negro' Making America Safe For Himself," *The Messenger* (September 1919).   78

2.15. Cover illustration for *The Messenger* (December 1921).   79

2.16. Charles Cullen, untitled illustration in Charles S. Johnson, *Ebony and Topaz* (1927).   80

2.17. Charles Cullen, untitled illustration in Charles S. Johnson, *Ebony and Topaz* (1927).   81

2.18. Allan Randall Freelon, "Hail Negro Youth," *Black Opals* (Spring 1927).   82

2.19. Winold Reiss, "The Brown Madonna," *The New Negro* (1925).   85

2.20. Winold Reiss, "Portrait Sketch: Elise Johnson McDougald," *The New Negro* (1925).   90

2.21. Bruce Nugent, "Drawing," *Fire!!* (1926).   92

2.22. Bruce Nugent, "Carus," *Beyond Where the Stars Stood Still.*   93

2.23. Charles Cullen, "Tableau," *Color* (1927).   94

2.24. Samuel Leibowitz, Communist International Labor Defenders attorney, with Scottsboro boys in Decatur, Alabama.   98

2.25. Hugo Gellert, "The Face of the NAACP, with the arms of the bosses," *New Masses* (February 1932).   100

2.26. Cover of the *The Crisis* (April 1932).   101

2.27. Diego Rivera, *The Making of a Fresco, Showing the Building of a City* (April–June 1931).   114

2.28. Diego Rivera, *Detroit Industry,* fresco, south wall (May 1932–March 13, 1933).   116

2.29. Diego Rivera, *Detroit Industry*. Fresco, north wall (May 1932–March 13, 1933).   117

2.30. William Siegel, untitled cartoon of Edsel Ford, *New Masses* (May 1932).   119

2.31. Diego Rivera, *Man, Controller of the Universe.*   121

2.32. E. Haldeman-Julius, "I Will 'Fordize' the Magazine Field Too!" *Broom* (1923).   127

2.33. William Siegel, "Bigger and Better Belles Lettres," *New Masses* (October 1929).   131

2.34/2.35. Fred Ellis, "Two Civilizations," *New Masses* (June 1933).   133

2.36/2.37. Hugo Gellert, untitled lithograph of factory owner and Soviet worker.   135

2.38. William Gropper, "Defend the Soviet Union," *New Masses* (May 1932).   136

2.39. "Release All Class War Prisoners!" *Labor Defender* (June 1930).   137

2.40. Hugo Gellert, lithograph of prison handshake.   137

2.41. Anton Refrigier, "Subway Model Sketch" (1939).   139

2.42. Hugo Gellert, cover illustration, *The Liberator* (March 1918).   140

2.43. Hugo Gellert, lithograph of V. I. Lenin.   142

2.44. Hugo Gellert, "Good News!" *New Masses* (March 1934).   143

2.45. Hugo Gellert, lithograph of machine strangling worker.   144

2.46. Hugo Gellert, lithograph of two nude workers with sledge-hammers.   145

2.47. Hugo Gellert, lithograph of two workers with tools.   146

2.48. Enrico Prampolini, "The Aesthetic of the Machine and Mechanical Introspection in Art," *Broom* (October 1922).   148

2.49. Louis Lozowick, *Machine Ornament 2* (1927).   149

3.1. Lucienne Bloch, "Childhood," fresco (1935).   177

3.2. Marion Greenwood standing on scaffold before *Blueprint for Living* (1940).   178

3.3. Marion Greenwood seated on scaffold before *Blueprint for Living* (1940).   180

3.4. Marion Greenwood, detail from *Blueprint for Living* (1940).   180

3.5. Walter Quirt, *The Pursuit of Happiness* (1937).   181

3.6. Vertis Hayes, *Growth of Medicine* (1937).   182

3.7. Eitaro Ishijaki, "Emancipation of the Negro Slaves," detail from *The Civil War* (no date).   182

3.8. Michael Newell, *Evolution of Western Civilization* (1938).   183

3.9. Diego Rivera. *Allegory of California* (1931).   185

3.10. Edna Hershman, *Recreational Activities* (detail) (1937).   186

4.1. William Gropper, "Join the Maroons," *New Masses* (April 1927).   206

4.2. Sue Coe, *War Train* (1986).   207

4.3. Ilona Granet, *Bums Bomb* (1982).   208

5.1. Matt Mullican, "Untitled" (1982).   223

photo insert   *following page 222*

5.2. Barbara Kruger, "Your body is a battleground" (1989).

5.3. Barbara Kruger, "You are an experiment in terror" (1983).

5.4. Barbara Kruger, "We won't play nature to your culture" (1983).

5.5. Barbara Kruger, "We are being made spectacles of" (1983).

5.6. Barbara Kruger, "You construct intricate rituals which allow you to touch the skin of other men" (1983).

5.7. Jenny Holzer, selections from the "Survival" series (1984).

5.8. Jenny Holzer, *Private Property Created Crime* (1982).

5.9. Jenny Holzer, *Protect Me From What I Want* (1986).

5.10. Jenny Holzer, *Money Creates Taste* (1986).

5.11. Jenny Holzer, *Under a Rock* (1987).

5.12. Nancy Spero, *Codex Artaud XVII* (detail) (1971–72).

5.13. Nancy Spero, *Codex Artaud IV* (detail) (1972).

5.14. Nancy Spero, *Let the Priests Tremble* (detail) (1984).

5.15. Nancy Spero, *Sheela and the Dildo Dancer* (detail) (1987).

5.16. Hans Haacke, *Taking Stock* (unfinished) (1983-84).

5.17. Hans Haacke, *On Social Grease,* Plaque 6.

5.18. Hans Haacke, *The Chase Advantage* (1976).

5.19. Hans Haacke, *The Chase Advantage* (detail) (1976).

5.20. Hans Haacke, *A Breed Apart* (1978).

5.21. Hans Haacke, *The Right to Life* (1979).

5.22. Adrian Piper, *Vanilla Nightmares #8* (1986).

E.1. Judy Baca, *The Great Wall of Los Angeles* (detail: "Division of the Barrios") (1983).

E.2. Judy Baca, *The Great Wall of Los Angeles* (detail: "1940s: We Fight Fascism at Home and Abroad") (1981).

E.3. Greenpeace Garbage Barge Protest, banner on New York City garbage barge (1987).

E.4. Suzanne Lacy and Leslie Labowitz, *In Mourning and In Rage* (1977).

E.5. Suzanne Lacy, *The Crystal Quilt* (1987).

E.6. Suzanne Lacy, "Model For Elements in Public Art" (1988).   257

photo insert   *following page 238*

E.7. Matt Herron, "Rock Hudson Panel" of *The Quilt* (1987).

E.8. Matt Herron, The NAMES Project, *The Quilt* (1987).

E.9. Gran Fury, "New York Crimes" (1989).

E.10. Gran Fury. "Read My Lips (boys)" (1988).

Acknowledgments

Several individuals and institutions gave me direction and support for my research and writing of *American Culture Between the Wars,* without whose assistance this book would have been unthinkable. To begin with, I am grateful to the American Council of Learned Societies for a Senior Fellowship during 1989–90, which allowed me time to draft portions of the text. The National Endowment for the Humanities provided a travel grant to the Sukov Collection of Little Magazines in 1988 at the University of Wisconsin Library, as well as a 1989 Summer Stipend and fellowship at Harvard University's Institute for the Study of Avant-Gardes. At Harvard, I received helpful criticism on portions of the manuscript from Alice Jardine and Susan Suleiman.

In revising the text I had useful advice from Vincent Leitch, Cary Nelson, John Carlos Rowe, and Alan Wald. Several colleagues offered productive responses to papers I delivered at the Modern Language Association (1989, 1990, and 1992), American Studies Association (1990), College English Association (1990), and Mainstream(s) and Margins Conference (1992). Portions of this book have been published in *American Literary History* (Summer 1991), *Cultural Critique* (Winter 1992), and

Postmodern Culture (May 1992). Finally, I gratefully acknowledge permission to quote from Bruce Andrews, "While," copyright © 1987 Roof Books; Alan Davies, "Shared Sentences," copyright © 1987 Roof Books; Fanny Howe, excerpt from *Introduction to the World,* copyright © 1986 The Figures.

Revisionary Modernism and Postmodern Critique

0.1. Hans Haacke, "The Vision Thing." Red, white, and blue announcement card for April 1992 exhibition at the John Weber Gallery, New York City.

Introduction: The Vision Thing

The Twilight of High Modernism

In the reception of American modernism there is surely no lack of histories, no shortage of master narratives, willing to hail the age as belonging to this or that author, school, or movement. To take only one example, Marjorie Perloff's polemical query in her 1982 essay "Pound/Stevens: whose era?" underscores the motivated, not disinterested, politics at work in every act of cultural historicism.[1] Alluding to Hugh Kenner's monument to antiquarian historicism *The Pound Era* (1971), Perloff wages mental warfare with Harold Bloom's campaign for the "Age of Stevens." But more to the point, this very staging of modernism through the clash between two "great" white patriarchs is symptomatic of how criticism exploits historical framing to prop up disciplinary authority, institutional force, and canonical power.

On both axes of the Pound/Stevens divide, each suasive version of literary modernism rests on a rigorous account of familiar and obscure facts, dates, primary documents, biographical anecdotes, key textual revisions—everything that goes into the makeup of empiricist historiography. Viewed through the lens of contemporary theory, such acts of historical explanation are regarded as inescapable, interpretive occasions. Each one, that is, shapes as much as reflects the period it narrates. For any normative history, argues Hayden White, entails a metahistorical framework in at least three ways: *aesthetically,* in its choice of narrative style and plot; *epistemologically,* in its explanatory paradigm; and *ethically,* in its ideological stance toward the past.[2] Metahistory happens, moreover, in the tasks of sorting out, defining, clarifying, and explicating past events because meaning as such is never given, or simply found, but is produced out of the vital dialectic between consciousness, mediated by language, and the world. In rereading historical texts, metahistorism is critical, rather than impartial, in teasing out what White describes as "the tropological wager buried at the heart of their strategies of explanation, emplotment, and ideological implication" (T, 74).

Not just a supplement to past accounts of American literary history, *American Culture Between the Wars* intervenes precisely in the "tropological wager" underwriting the discursive field of modernist canonicity. Postwar scholarship on high modernism has largely silenced the century's complex and contentious social context. So strictly has this repression been maintained that, according to Cary Nelson, "we no longer know the history of the poetry of the first half of this century; most of us, moreover, do not know that the knowledge is gone."[3] This lapse of cultural memory persists, arguably, through the canon's incredibly narrow focus on a select group of seminal careers. Such reigning tropes of individual talent have served to fix, regulate, and police modernism's unsettled social text, crosscut as it is by a plurality of transnational, racial, sexual, and class representations.[4] The *figure*head of the author as valorized "agent," to borrow from Kenneth Burke's grammatical pentad, has overshadowed the material "scene" of twentieth-century cultural production in the United States.[5]

In resisting this tendency, *American Culture Between the Wars* builds on the project of textual studies which, as Robert Scholes defines it, moves beyond the limited, disciplinary boundaries of "literature" to investigate "[a]ll kinds of texts, visual as well as verbal, polemical as well as seductive."[6] My reading of the expanded cultural field of American modernism actually reverses a set of oppositions that have served within canonical institutions to privilege the literary over the social, aesthetics over politics, formalism over popular culture, and domestic nationalism over global multiculturism. Moving on into the twenty-first century, it is not just the monuments to "heroes" like Vladimir Lenin that have been hammered to the ground. The same demolition job, as Fredric Jameson reminds us, is also being carried out on the godfathers of literary modernism, whose canon "in the very middle of the debate on its existence, begins furiously to melt away, leaving a great rubble pile of mass culture and all kinds of noncanonical and commercial literature behind it."[7] While the spread of a more democratic field of cultural representation is to be welcomed, the "anything goes" version of postmodern euphoria reflects what Jameson describes as "an age that has forgotten how to think historically in the first place" (P, ix). The impasse of such ahistoricism, however, marks a limit to Jameson's own version of postmodernism. For in theorizing the cultural logic of the postwar decades, Jameson forgets our moment's relation to the diverse social text of the interbellum avant-gardes.[8]

Nevertheless, twentieth-century America does possess a particular history of cultural critique. This avant-garde praxis comes from the politicized coupling of image and text, art and journalism, poetry and visual agitation. The conjuncture of popular culture and left politics, as you find it in America's little magazines between the wars, fostered an alternative discourse of racial, sexual, class, and transnational experience. My project in *American Culture Between the Wars* not only delves into this radical tradition but also considers how it lives on (albeit in dramatically altered forms) within today's spectacle of commodity culture. In this vein, I examine postmodern strategies of critique that, like their precursors in the historical avant-gardes, also mix high and low, formalism and populism, museum culture and everyday life through the progressive fusion of text and image. But equally important, such postmodern inmixing—as you find it, say, in Hans Haacke's exposés of British Leyland's South African labor practices or American Cyanamid's policies on female sterilization—advances the avant-garde critique of social relations by *articulating* the glossy, postmodern look of the commodity form to advanced capitalism's repressed, and often scandalous, modes of commodity production.[9] Contrary to the Frankfurt School scorn for popular forms of entertainment, one of the political lessons of American modernism is that cultural critique must engage in what Antonio Gramsci called a "war of position" within, not outside, today's conglomerate mass media.[10]

American Culture Between the Wars reads the historical avant-gardes through postmodernity and vice versa so as to question each moment's ideological limits against a wider social background. Briefly, as a period term the historical avant-garde designates both the formalist and politicized aesthetic schools and movements that once flourished between the world wars.[11] It covers the Italian Futurism of F. T. Marinetti; Russian Cubofuturism, Constructivism, and other aesthetic movements within the Soviet "living factory of the human mind"; the dadaist scenes in Zurich

(1915–20), New York (1915–20), Berlin (1918–23), and Paris (1919–22); the cinematic montage of Serge Eisenstein; the camera work of Alfred Steiglitz and the collaborative aesthetics of the New York-based 291 gallery circle generally; the Harlem Renaissance; literary imagism, vorticism, and surrealism; various other experimental modernist aesthetics showcased in such internationalist little magazines as *Blast, Broom,* and *transition*; and the more populist writings and visual arts that emerged from American journals like *The Masses, Liberator, New Masses,* and *Partisan Review,* among countless others.

Until recently, however, the diversity of this cultural production has been overshadowed by the more sanitized canon of high modernism. The academy's classic definition of "high" or "great" culture—the domain of its "intellectual and especially artistic activity"—is founded on a logic that denies another cultural model: what Raymond Williams has described in terms of "a particular way of life, whether of a people, a period or a group."[12] My strategy in *American Culture Between the Wars* is to call this difference into crisis, to unravel conventional distinctions between the aesthetic and the social—distinctions that, as Pierre Bourdieu has argued, serve to fetishize the former by repressing the latter.[13]

In particular, my book's cultural critique is lodged against high modernism's pledge of allegiance to a transhistorical canon, founded on the subordination of gender, race, and class differences to what T. S. Eliot idealized as the universal "mind of Europe."[14] From the Vietnam era onward, various new social movements have refused to salute the latter's mainly Caucasian and androcentric outlook. Institutionalized in the postwar academy, museum culture, gallery market, and publishing industry, the traditional canon has resisted and obscured the experience of women, ethnic and racial minorities, lesbians and gay men, as well as other subcultural and proletarianized groups. Beyond the authoritarian politics of high modernism, we still lack an understanding of the multiple audiences, plural subject positions, and socioaesthetic alliances that made up the historical avant-gardes in the United States. Although George Bush trivialized the heritage of radical democracy as "the vision thing" during his 1992 reelection bid for the presidency (figure 1), it nevertheless represents all of us who have passed through America's social precincts of class oppression, racial bigotry, xenophobia, and sexism.

What deserves sustained attention today is the link between postmodernity's cultural pluralism and the historical avant-gardes' own critical adventurousness—something Jean-François Lyotard has described as a "long, obstinate and highly responsible investigation of the presuppositions implied in modernity," a kind of Freudian *Durcharbeitung* ("working through") "operated by modernity on itself."[15] A postmodern reading of American high modernism, I argue, would not simply challenge its elite, canonical figures but, just as crucial, recover the *inter*national context of America's avant-gardes. Such an approach would interrogate what Homi K. Bhabha has theorized as "the traditional authority of those national objects of knowledge—Tradition, People, the Reason of State, High Culture."[16] A revisionary modernism would undertake the polemical tasks of debating and contesting such tropes of nationality and aesthetic formalism. Moreover, this new map of modernity would shift the boundaries of critical reception that have segregated the interbellum avant-gardes in the United States from contemporaneous transnational, African-American, feminist, and proletarian traditions of cultural critique.

In reviving the still obscure figures of America's historical avant-gardes, we would profit from following Gerald Graff's caveat against reproducing traditional models of coverage that contain art and literature's social text within the academy.[17] A more productive project would set overlooked talents of the interbellum decades into dialogue with cultural activists and collectives of our own moment. Such an exchange would negotiate between, on the one hand, the kind of populist aesthetics that reached fruition during the Great Depression and, on the other hand, a poststructuralist understanding of language, subjectivity, and the latter's ideological investments in discursive form. What emerges from this crossing of the historical avant-gardes and postmodernism is something that has long eluded the postwar academic canon: a postindividualistic solidarity among sexual, racial, class, and ethnic subject positions, at once formally sophisticated and critically responsive to America's cultural diversity.[18]

The Historical Avant-Gardes

As the theorists of the Frankfurt School of Social Research observed, the historical avant-gardes expressed art's contradictory negotiation of the new industrial forces and techniques of mechanical reproduction, big-city life, and the triumph of bourgeois values in the social field. The aesthetic dimension's remove from what Habermas has described as "the possessive-individualistic, achievement- and advantage-oriented life style of the bourgeoisie"[19] offered, according to Adorno, a refuge of *negation* against the alienating economic, social, and cultural advances of consumer capitalism. Valorizing the critical distance of the autonomous art work, Adorno was less sanguine than, say, Walter Benjamin about the political resources of dadaism, film, and the mechanical reproduction of cultural texts. One of Benjamin's central theses, of course, argued that film, as a mass-mediated aesthetic, reconciles elite and popular culture, art's critical and affective registers, the difficulty of Picasso and the "visual enjoyment" of Charlie Chaplin.

But taking issue with Benjamin's belief that "with regard to the screen, the critical and receptive attitudes of the public coincide," Adorno argued that such cinematic fusions of high- and lowbrow aesthetics, on the contrary, "bear the stigmata of capitalism. . . . Both are torn halves of an integral freedom, to which however they do not add up."[20] In his 1936 response to Benjamin, Adorno remained suspicious, given the growing popularity of German National Socialism, of a certain romantic "blind confidence in the spontaneous power of the proletariat in the historical process—a proletariat which is itself a product of bourgeois society" (AP, 123).[21] Against the avant-garde intervention into mass culture—which he viewed as already appropriated by the commodity form, totalitarian propaganda, advertising, and kitsch—Adorno sought to debunk capital's cultural logic through the austere negations of Beckett, Kafka, and Schönberg, among others.

In the postwar era, however, Herbert Marcuse questioned whether Adorno's cloistral version of aesthetic autonomy (contained as it was in the "affirmative" canon of the postwar Academy) actually hastened rather than resisted the spread of consumer society. The utopian imagination, he argued, simply lacked any real social force when cast into aesthetic registers divorced from the more prosaic struggles of everyday life.[22] Following Marcuse's late attempts to secularize Frankfurt School aesthetics, Peter Bürger's influential study, *Theory of the Avant-Garde* (1974), also advanced Walter Benjamin's push for political critique within the new mass media of commodity culture. In particular, Bürger investigated the avant-gardes' attack on "institution art."[23] Building on aestheticism's rebellion against the utilitarian values and academic styles of the Victorian scene, the avant-gardes, Bürger held, unmasked art's shaping role in culture, laying bare its local habitats and commercial economy.

While the aesthetic gambit of the historical avant-gardes failed politically to co-opt consumer culture,[24] their postwar legacy survives in what Bürger describes as the "neo-avant-gardiste" happenings and pop aesthetics of the 1960s. In Bürger's view, this work marks the failure of the avant-gardes insofar as it "institutionalizes the *avant-garde as art* and thus negates genuinely avant-gardist intentions" (TA, 58). Differing from Bürger's rather pessimistic take on the socioaesthetic limits of the sixties, my argument in *American Culture Between the Wars* links the radical praxis of the historical avant-gardes to the more recent and more politically inflected aesthetics of the post-Vietnam era. In particular, I glean a critical, rather than affirmative, dimension within contemporary culture of the last two decades. This politicized postmodernism challenges art's institutional place within the museum and gallery markets, the academy, the state, and multinational corporate interests.

Bürger's focus on the avant-gardes' negation of bourgeois aesthetics, nevertheless, sheds light on the continuing tendency to repress a given text's worldly social life. Indeed, from this vantage point, the move to simply ignore a work's transaction with material culture appears not so much a "natural" as an ideological gesture. Today, however, any textual praxis that would lay claim to powers of cultural critique is inescapably tied to the mixed status and fate of the historical avant-gardes. On the one hand, the avant-garde assault on aesthetic autonomy has uncovered the institutional networks of production, marketing, and distribution that mediate "great" art and literature. But on the other hand, twentieth-century history has repeatedly testified to the failed legacy of *littérature engagé* in its attempts to foment decisive social change either within the commodity forms of American consumer culture or against the bureaucratic state capitalism that, until the 1990s, propped up the Soviet bloc. In our postmodern moment, where the once-shocking gestures of aesthetic protest (dadaist, constructivist, surrealist, vorticist, and the rest) have all been played out—have become merely historical—the antiaesthetic stance risks a certain nostalgia. All too often, it assumes a *camp,* not revolutionary, posture, stylized for consumption by the market spaces of the gallery, museum, academic lecture and television talk show circuits, and the other organs of today's conglomerate media. Nevertheless, it is precisely within the recent technologies of communication, which have led to what Hans Magnus Enzensberger has called the "industrialization of the mind," that postmodern aesthetics must negotiate communal representations, infiltrating popular flows of entertainment in an oppositional "war of position."[25]

Postmodernism's doubled-edged chance for commodification *and* critique is bound up with the historical avant-gardes' own clash with what Andreas Huyssen has called the "great divide" cleaving high from popular culture, art from politics, and the aesthetic sublime from its social foundations. However cogent in its analysis of European aesthetics, Huyssen's map of postmodernity in the United States rests on a debatable account of how the avant-gardes traveled from the Continent to America. While the fin-de-siècle critique of "institution art" was lodged against the European hegemony of high aesthetics—reproduced as they were in an elite network of salons, galleries, museums, concert halls, and opera houses— such a movement, Huyssen claims, failed to develop in the United States precisely because America lacked a dominant high culture to begin with. Aside from the marginal presence of New York Dada, the avant-garde attempt to wed art and life, for Huyssen, did not migrate to America until the 1960s "in the form of happenings, pop vernacular, psychedelic art, acid rock, alternative and street theater" (AGD, 193). Such subversive forms expressed populist antagonisms to the 1950s' version of high modern formalism based in the abstract expressionism of the New York art scene, in the New Criticism of the burgeoning postwar academy, and in the elite canons merchandised through the conglomerate press market.

Periodizing the American avant-gardes in the 1960s, however, leads Huyssen to elide key transnational connections joining the historical avant-gardes in Europe and Russia to the interbellum scene in the United States. "The absence of an indigenous American avant-garde in the classical European sense, say in the 1920s," he argues, "forty years later, benefited the postmodernists' claim to novelty in their struggle against the entrenched traditions of modernism" (167). Yet in valorizing the 1960s as the avant-garde moment in the United States, Huyssen appears unaware of precursor traditions in America that likewise sought to bridge the "great divide" between high and mass culture. In fact, avant-garde critique was not so much absent in the American context as it was repressed in its subsequent reception. European, Soviet, and native aesthetic traditions, imbricated as they were in domestic little magazines of the 1920s and 1930s, afforded a rich terrain for the avant-garde fusion of life and art in the United States.

Revolution and Social Modernization

American Culture Between the Wars offers a revisionary account of this neglected cultural history. My study of the American avant-gardes cuts across the grain of canonical modernism through rereading the very figures that it has erased, through asking tough questions of how a work's intrinsic form inscribes extrinsic politics, and through unsettling traditional distinctions that privilege formalism over socioaesthetic diversity. To begin with, my opening chapter retrieves the *inter*national dimension of the American avant-gardes. Here I compare the aesthetic theory and cultural initiatives of the Russian avant-gardes with their counterparts in the United

States. But unlike past readings that have contained the Futurists within the formal registers of high modernism, I lay out an alternative, and hitherto repressed, version of the American reception of Soviet Constructivism.[26] Specifically, I examine how this utopian moment was fueled by a discourse of resistance to class oppression. In particular, I revisit the battle against authoritarian politics and aesthetic elitism waged in the pages of America's little magazines between the world wars.

Popularized in such journals as *Anvil, Blues, Broom, Contact, Contempo, The Crisis, Dynamo, Fire!!, Hound and Horn, Laughing Horse, The Liberator, The Masses, New Masses, Opportunity, Others, The Rebel Poet, Secession,* and *transition,* the American tradition of critique between the wars nurtured a revolutionary textual praxis. This new cultural force aspired to the avant-garde transformation of everyday life in its internationalist scope; its diversity of gender, racial, and class perspectives; its contentious mix of Greenwich Village bohemianism and Washington Square socialism; and its blend of high and populist styles. From this collaborative setting, as well as from the period's theoretical manifestoes and populist verse forms, I glean a poetics whose reliance on mass recitation and chant forms foregrounds the ways in which poetry is mediated by group praxis. This alternative theory of verse writing's dialogic form and communal reception differs significantly both from the impersonal poetics of high modernism—which rests on the individual talent's dealings with a transhistorical canon—and from the kind of lyric solipsism that reigns over postwar confessional verse. Both of these latter aesthetic ideologies, installed as they are in the postwar academy, have eclipsed the more socially progressive bases and material settings of cultural production that thrived in America between the wars.[27]

Building on chapter 1's retrieval of the American avant-gardes, my second chapter considers both the resources and limits of the cultural tasks undertaken by the domestic Old Left. On the one hand, the progressive, subcultural enclaves afforded by organizations like the John Reed Clubs and their publication organs provided a valued entré for marginalized urban artists such as, say, Richard Wright in Chicago, Langston Hughes in Harlem, and Edwin Rolfe in Manhattan, as well as rural and regional authors like H. H. Lewis in Missouri and Joseph Kalar in northern Minnesota. Similarly, within the editorial circles of, say, *The Liberator* and *New Masses,* such mentoring figures as Joseph Freeman, Mike Gold, and Claude McKay, offered rich opportunities for proletcult writers like Sol Funaroff and Herman Spector, as well as "third generation" poets, notably Kenneth Fearing. The iconography and poetic imagery of heroic communism and socialist realism often debunked with elegance and wit the reign of monopoly capitalism in the United States. Such Soviet-inspired styles were successfully employed in key interruptions of high modernist discourse as in Sol Funaroff's "What the Thunder Said: A Fire Sermon." Writing against Eliot's monarchist Anglo-Catholicism, Funaroff reinterprets the modern waste land from an internationalist, working-class vantage point.

On the other hand, the autocratic world outlook coming from Moscow, especially during the Comintern's so-called Third Period of the late 1920s and early 1930s, just as often stifled and disaffected potential talents in the liberal and African-American communities. The reduction of classism and economism that plagued Second International thinking led leftist artists and writers in America to mimic Soviet-style proletcult. The Old Left's admittedly limited aesthetic range provided precious little ideological terrain on which to recruit the American masses, swayed as they were by a burgeoning pop culture industry. As I detail in chapter 2, this failure to communicate a politics of cultural enunciation is underscored in the CPUSA's vexed relationship with the African-American community.

While the communist International Labor Defense Fund was mounting its heroic defense of the Scottsboro Boys in 1931, *New Masses* launched its Third Period push to discredit the vernacular culture of the Harlem Renaissance and thus subordinate its nativist, African-American discourse to an imported, Soviet-American semiology. This Party-orchestrated campaign culminated in the crackdown on Harlem's black coalition politics in 1933. Following this centrist strategy, however, the CPUSA lost a valuable opportunity to empower what Houston Baker would later theorize as the transgressive text of signifying, black maroonage.[28] Contradicting today's tendency to simply collapse gender, race, and class relations into a seamless political trinity, the rhetoric of their actual clash in the United States arrives as a sobering testament to historical division. "Negro landlords," charged Mike Gold in 1933, "shoot down Negro tenants, with the aid of white police. White bosses shoot down white workers. In the New York garment strike, Jewish bosses kill and maim Jewish workers by the aid of Italian gangsters and Irish cops. There is NO RACE in the class war."[29] Such an alien, and alienating, discourse—laced as it is with racial, anti-Semitic, and ethnic stereotypes—nevertheless offers an arresting caveat against any easy affiliation across cultural differences.

My second chapter rereads the classist representations of the Third Period aesthetic in America not so much as celebrations of a nascent working-class revolution but more as compensatory symptoms of its loss to the advent of Fordism and Americanism that cast the industrial die for what Guy Debord and Jean Baudrillard would later describe as a global postwar order of spectacular simulation. In migrating to the United States, Soviet-style proletcult encountered a hyperreal culture industry, whose entrenched bases in Hollywood, Tin Pan Alley, and Madison Avenue had effectively colonized mass society for commodity consumption. Like their counterparts in the formalist tradition of high culture—examined in the recent work of Andreas Huyssen and Janice Radway—American prole- tarian artists and writers also reacted against this bourgeoning new con- sumer society through a tropology of rigid, male gender codes. Yet such androcentric signs and symbols had limited purchase on the social diversity of actual men and women in the United States.[30] American proletcult's own phallocentric imagery of a largely white, masculine prowess can be reread, symptomatically, as a denial of the spreading cultural logic of con- sumerism that went hand-in-hand with the new Fordist techniques of mechanical reproduction.

For Antonio Gramsci, of course, Fordism marked a crucial turning point in the progress of advanced capitalism, one that demanded a radical rethinking of both Second International economism and the cultural pol- itics of vanguard Leninism. More powerful than either the legacy of the Soviet Revolution or the rise of Italian fascism, Ford's new industrial mode of production stood, according to Gramsci, as "the biggest collective effort to date to create, with unprecedented speed, and with a consciousness of purpose unmatched in history, a new type of worker and of man."[31] What was revolutionary about Ford's approach was its adaptation of Frederick W. Taylor's time and motion studies to the semi-automatic production line. This technical regime, in Gramsci's account, reduced workers to replaceable cyborgs within a production process driven by capital and managed by a new administrative class.[32]

But equally important, the gigantic scale of Ford's mechanical infra- structure, documented in Diego Rivera's expansive *Detroit Industry* murals of River Rouge, was also very costly to maintain. Consequently, it demanded not only a speed-up in the labor process but also a reliable market for its mass products. Ford's decisive advance lay in researching and surveillancing workers' habits of consumption as part of his productive calculus.[33] By targeting the domestic arenas and personal enclaves of con- sumption, he hastened the commodity form's penetration of everyday life, thereby setting the foundation for the postwar consumer society. Signifi- cantly, the Fordist apparatus coupled a revolutionary principle of mech- anization with a managerial strategy of planned consumption. Buttressed by the pervasive spectacle of advertising, Fordism, according to Michel Aglietta:

> marks a new state in the regulation of capitalism, the regime of intensive accumulation in which the capitalist class seeks overall management of the production of wage-labour by the close articulation of relations of production with the commodity relations in which the wage earners purchase their means of consumption. Fordism is thus the principle of *an articulation between process of production and mode of consumption.*[34]

For all its talent, wit, and incisive polemics, American proletcult lacked a popular strategy for dealing with what Gramsci theorized at the time as advanced capitalism's mode of consumption.[35] The depression era left simply could not keep pace with this new cultural logic, whose nuanced and stylized play of ideological representation seduced the popular desires of working men and women for consumption in excess of their class roles.

In fact, it was not until the Popular Front campaign of the mid-thirties that the CPUSA actively enlisted fellow travelers and liberal allies against the rise of European fascism. Only then did the Old Left begin to compete with the commodity form on its own representational terrain. Such depression era critiques of advanced capitalism, however, came as too little and too late in the United States. As I argue in my second chapter, the left's failure to mount what Gramsci described as a nuanced "war of position" within the nascent consumer society of the 1920s reaches a crisis stage during the censorship of Diego Rivera by the Rockefellers in 1932. Unable, finally, to forge cultural alliances across the gulf of Comintern classism and economism, the domestic Old Left succumbed to capital's hegemonic domination of everyday life. The now largely forgotten experience of the depression era is, nevertheless, crucial to contemporary debate over the cultural politics of postmodern representation.

Although mediated by the theoretical revolution of recent decades, the embattled aesthetic positions within the so-called New Left and post-Marxist camps rest on the interbellum clash over Marxism's base/superstructure binarism. Today's cultural politics in large part replay the Depression-era struggle between party vanguardism and emergent democratic movements. However nuanced and updated with the poststructuralist focus on discourse in Derrida, Lacan, and Wittgenstein, the critique in the work of Ernesto Laclau and Chantal Mouffe of scientific Leninism and its autocratic politics draws on the Gramscian watershed of the 1930s. Lodged against the economism of the Second International, Gramsci's attack on party bureaucracy insightfully credited ideology as a material force. It is ideology, Laclau and Mouffe argue, "embodied in institutions and apparatuses, which welds together a historical bloc around a number of basic articulatory principles" (HSS, 67).

Insofar as this neo-Gramscian theory advances the discursive nature of hegemony, it strikes a postmodern blow against Communist orthodoxy. Releasing the Gramscian notion of hegemony from the essentialism of Gramsci's own residual class privilege, Laclau and Mouffe deny any natural, or unmediated, representations of class identity and class interests. Instead, with the poststructuralist recognition that "the so-called 'representation' modifies the nature of what is represented" (HSS, 58), Marxism's orthodox privileging of economic base over ideology is decisively reversed. Here, "the identity of classes is transformed by the hegemonic tasks" (HSS, 58) of articulating social relations and subject positions within multiple and competing discursive fields beyond the more narrowly construed antagonisms of class struggle.

Supplementing the materialist focus on class domination in the labor process, Laclau and Mouffe ramify the postmodern job of political critique to consider a broader spectrum of "discursive conditions for the emergence of a collective action, directed towards struggling against inequalities and challenging relations of subordination . . . to identify the conditions in which a relation of subordination becomes a relation of oppression, and thereby constitutes itself into the site of an antagonism" (HSS, 153). Such discursive antagonisms underwrite a range of new social movements on the part of, say: women against capitalist patriarchy; African-Americans and Native Americans against Caucasian stereotyping and white racial privilege; ecological activists against environmental degradation; gays and lesbians against compulsory heterosexuality; community artists against urban gentrification; coalitions of children, the homeless, and the handicapped against cuts to social support services; people with AIDS (PWAs) against pharmaceutical giants like Burroughs Wellcome. Not surprisingly, such departures from party vanguardism have been stigmatized by neo-Leninist ideologues as "a capitalist politics of pure irrational spontaneity," its followers anathematized as "anti-communist" dupes to social fascism.[36]

Predictably, such tags and charges have simply recycled the Comintern's assault on the anti-Stalinist left and depression era fellow-travelers, who likewise forswore the party's hidebound bureaucracy. The post-Soviet split within the CPUSA between old-line Marxist-Leninists like Gus Hall and revisionary Communists like Angela Davis and Herbert Aptheker play out this same divide. Even in the 1990s, despite the fall of the Soviet Union, vanguard party bureaucrats in America still ignored Davis' call for "rigorous self-evaluation, radical restructuring, and democratic renewal" and instead fell back on old clichés, stereotyping their critics as "traitors to the working class."[37] Similarly, the depression era attempt to ramify a leftist hegemony—to fashion diverse subject positions across a range of Popular Front struggles beyond proletcult—was also strongly resisted in the mid-1930s. The hostile reception that greeted Kenneth Burke's 1935 American Writers' Congress speech, embracing popular rather than proletarian symbols of agitation, remains one of America's most memorable episodes of party parochialism. But the lambasting of Diego Rivera as a Trotskyite "prostitute" and bashing of Muriel Rukeyser as a bourgeois "poster girl" also stand out as scandalous instances of Communist xenophobia and Old Left chauvinism.[38] It is an irony of history that during these very years Antonio Gramsci was theorizing the need for a "war of position" within advanced capitalism from precisely the same American context whose native left, meanwhile, looked to the outdated and outmaneuvered signs of frontal revolution imported from the Soviet Union.

The broadening of cultural representation during the Popular Front years proved salutary, I argue in my third chapter, in dislodging the text of proletcult, particularly in Rukeyser's work at mid-decade. Her documentation of abusive mining practices in West Virginia exceeded the Third Period critique of monopoly capitalism by addressing the concrete conditions and forms that social domination takes in women's experience. The force of Rukeyser's feminist advance against, on the right, the then nascent formalism of American New Criticism and, on the left, the class and economic reduction of Third Period vanguardism, can be gauged precisely from their mutual resistance to the revolutionary signifying practice she mounts in "The Book of the Dead." The harsh and often sexist critical reception of her Popular Front poetics is symptomatic of what from the hindsight of Foucauldian theory we can now reread as the universalizing bias both on the left and right against the kind of *specific* institutional critique that shapes Rukeyser's documentary long poem.

Political Critique in Postmodern Culture

Surveying the rift that divides the historical avant-gardes from postmodernity, my final chapters locate common ideological ground between, on the one hand, Benjamin's and Brecht's theories of avant-garde intervention in popular culture and, on the other hand, poststructuralist strategies of subverting the dominant codes and technical habitus of today's information society. In chapter 4, I link the collaborative publishing networks and the recent critiques of private lyricism, expressive poetics, and the author function undertaken by the $L=A=N=G=U=A=G=E$ writers to the group solidarity and communal aesthetics of their avant-garde counterparts of the depression era. In particular, Kenneth Fearing's satiric recodings of American advertising, popular journalism, bureaucratic state rhetoric, and business jargon look forward to $L=A=N=G=U=A=G=E$ writing's textual interruptions of the linguistic habits and verbal conventions reproduced throughout the discourses of consumer society.

In this vein, my fifth chapter investigates the collaborative aesthetics employed in the new social movements of the post-Vietnam era, including the interventionist visual art of Hans Haacke, Jenny Holzer, Barbara Kruger, Mike Mullican, Adrienne Piper, and Nancy Spero. What these postmodern cultural praxes share with the historical avant-gardes is the latter's subversive deployment of image and text. But just as importantly, they advance the avant-gardes' interrogation of institution art—something Henry Sayre has described as "an apparently recalcitrant set of assumptions, shared by mainstream museums, galleries, magazines, publishers, and funding agencies, about what constitutes a 'work' of art."[39] Over against the formalist tradition of modernism, promulgated by Clement Greenberg, Michael Fried, and Barbara Rose, on the one hand, and affirmative postmodernism on the other, Sayre theorizes an undecidable aesthetics of *performance*. Reflecting the poststructuralist revolution of the 1980s, Sayre argues that much of contemporary art enacts the "condition of contingency, multiplicity, and polyvocality which dominates the postmodern scene. If pluralism can be defined as the many possible, but more or less equal, 'solutions' which arise in answer to a particular aesthetic situation or crisis, undecidability is the condition of conflict and contradiction which presents no possible 'solution' or resolution" (OP, xiii).

Similarly, each of the contemporary collectives and single artists that I discuss in *American Culture Between the Wars* taps the aesthetic possibilities of postmodern contingency—positioned here, however, within the more specific context of capital's current legitimation crisis. Today, the cultural contradictions of Fordism reflect a productive regime that, since the 1920s, has depended on the spread of consumption throughout the entire fabric of everyday life. In the planned economy of the postwar era, consumer society has been underwritten by mounting concessions to labor. These negotiations have extended the wage relation to include unemployment insurance, accident benefits, social security and pension funds, minimum wage standards, affirmative action guidelines for redressing discriminatory hiring and compensation practices, along with a host of other private and governmental services and social guarantees. Such concessions are, of course, expensive in terms of the restraints they place on capital accumulation. Today, the high price of an ever-widening socialization of consumption is coupled with late Fordist labor processes defined by costly outlays for robotics and automated transfer lines that require longer production runs and larger commodity batches. In this milieu, the crisis of advanced capitalism erupts where the expense of production simply outpaces society's consumptive limit.

Neo-Fordism describes capital's contemporary strategy, faced with this dilemma, for deterritorializing its older, modern industrial order.[40] In the postwar decades, the centrally administered production line is dispersed into more autonomous, self-regulating groups reterritorialized into a labor process relying on information exchange, data analysis, and the proliferation of specialized discourses. This Neo-Fordist regime lowers the costs of collective consumption in the relatively privileged and metropolitan sectors of the economy. Yet it nevertheless breeds unique forms of proletarianization, social antagonism, and political resistance throughout the so-called new-world enterprise culture. Building on the Foucauldian thesis that strategies of power generate micropolitical tactics and flows of resistance, Michel de Certeau has analyzed the acts of subversion that workers and consumers employ in negotiating the postmodern condition. Despite new techniques of worker surveillance (like key-stroke monitoring in computerized data entry), job resistances—in the forms of, say, a worker's tactic of stealing time, outright property theft, as well as neo-Luddite tactics of sabotaging the "electronic sweatshop" of postindustrial labor processes—persist as blockages, rupturings, and rechannelings of mainstream flows of capital accumulation.

A further challenge to the regime of Neo-Fordism stems from the growing competition among capitals in today's volatile, transnational environment. Here, shifting market flows and changing consumer styles are spurred on by technological advances in mass telecommunications. Such a dynamic consumer economy has fostered a new galaxy of subcultural groups demanding specialized representations, concessions, benefits, and social guarantees. "Interpellated as equals in their capacity as consumers," argue Chantal Mouffe and Ernesto Laclau, "ever more numerous groups are impelled to reject the real inequalities which continue to exist" (HSS, 164). The sheer economic pressure to occupy new consumer niches across national, ethnic, race, gender, and class lines has fueled the demand for democratic revolution throughout a range of sociopolitical struggles over minority and women's rights, gay liberation, the environment, disarmament, animal liberation, the rights of children and the elderly, and other grass-root campaigns. Faced with these new social movements, global capital can only transcend the emergent demands of such subcultural groups by becoming something other than itself.[41] The return to old-style repression and modernist authoritarianism, however, seems unlikely in the face of postmodernism's reigning standard of common sense. For Neo-Fordist ideology itself depends on the consumer's unfettered, but individualized, pursuit of the commodity form.

The most dramatic sign of this new democratic consumerism is, perhaps, the fin-de-siècle fall of the Soviet Union. After seven decades of Communist misrule, the Soviet experiment in socialism lies, like the Berlin Wall, in the rubble of the past. The push for glasnost, perestroika, and de-Stalinization during the Gorbachev era not only redrew the map of Eastern Europe and unraveled the Soviet Union as such, but equally important, opened the closeted text of state socialism for all the world to read. What that legacy bears out is the grim quip told in post-revolutionary Slovakia on what distinguishes capitalism from communism: in the former system, as the joke goes, "man exploits man" whereas in the latter "it's the other way around."[42]

The collapse of the Soviet Union, however, does not necessarily betoken a decisive setback for progressive critique in the United States. Since the 1939 Hitler-Stalin pact, state-administered Communism has served to discredit rather than to advance the idea of a feasible socialism. But more to the point, from the October Revolution onward, the Soviet Union held sway in America not so much as a social reality, but more as a overdetermined symbol. For the Old Left, it stood as the Promised Land of industry, proletarian empowerment, and democratic freedoms. American proletcult idealized the Soviet experiment as a futurist utopia released from the grip of necessity. On the right, the specter of global communism projected onto the USSR supported a longstanding repression of radical democracy: reaching back to the Palmer Raids of the 1920s; underwriting the Truman Doctrine of Containment of World Communism (1947); justifying the Red Scare and McCarthy hearings of the 1950s; escalating the nuclear arms race of the cold war; provoking America's misadventure in Vietnam; deflecting national attention from the CIA's covert arms deals with the Nicaraguan contras; and rationalizing U.S. intervention in Grenada. Bereft of the USSR as bête noire and global menace, the conservative right is now hard pressed to defend bloated Pentagon budgets, a patriarchal military establishment, and an impoverished domestic agenda. Today, this legitimation crisis presents an opportunity for progressive, cultural intervention.

"The 1990s," the New Times Project predicted at the close of the '80s, "will see myriad political and social struggles. But in essence they will come down to a single question: on whose terms will this new era be moulded?"[43] Moving into the twenty-first century, my epilogue takes up this challenge. Here I consider the resources of site-specific, cultural critique that targets public institutions for radical democratic change. Such institutional protest emerges from new antagonisms to dominant forms of subordination, often staged through the very spectacles and popular entertainment flows that we associate with the conglomerate media. Such populist interventions, as you find them, say, in Gran Fury's slick AIDS visuals or in Suzanne Lacy's feminist media events occupy the margins of the postmodern scene. They agitate along the fault lines and zones of stress that fissure the mainstream myths, icons, and imaginary representations which legitimate advanced capitalism. Contrary to Jameson's claim that the smooth, visual regulation of postmodernism's glossy surface renders oppositional critique "uncool,"[44] today's wholesale destruction of the environment, government inaction in the face of a relentless AIDS epidemic, outright gay-bashing, transnational systems of advanced proletarianization, the global oppression of women, men and women's unpaid labor in the domestic sphere, the degradation of minorities to what Cornel West has described as the *walking nihilism* of inner city ghetto life,[45] expanding militarism and conventional arms proliferation all open outrageous, postmodern breaches in the administered facade of the so-called "new world order." Such glaring signs of multicultural contradictions, ecological erosions, fiscal irrationalities, persistent sexual inequities and blatant harassment, as well as myriad other forms of social barbarism and waste, nevertheless, offer fresh terrains on which to debate, subvert, and displace the dominant representations shaping today's postmodern society.

1. Revisionary Modernism

Transnational America

Heralding in 1916 a "Trans-National America," the young radical intellectual Randolph Bourne looked forward to our own social diversity in the post-Vietnam era. Bourne's protest against the "Anglo-Saxoning" of American culture would be sharply debated in the 1920s between such high modernists as William Carlos Williams and T. S. Eliot. But Bourne's focus on the clash of values dividing the "individualistic" leanings of old-line New England from the collective allegiances of America's new immigrant masses would be repressed in the subsequent reception of the modern canon. "The older generation," he wrote, "can never understand that superb loyalty which is loyalty to a community—a loyalty which, paradoxical as it may seem, nourishes the true social personality in proportion as the individual sense is lessened."[1] Self-reliance's cultural antagonism to the social personality would set the stage for ideological conflict throughout the interbellum years. Yet it is only now, in the post-Reagan/Bush era, that this quarrel has emerged once again as a pressing issue in reconstructing American cultural history.

Today's postmodern recovery of radical democracy marks the limit of high modernism by repudiating the latter's ahistorical formalism; its privileged position in museum culture, the gallery market, and the academy; its autonomy from everyday life; and its valorization of the individual talent. In contrast, America's communal tradition of revisionary critique was forged from a populist, *inter*national social text. During the interbellum decades in the United States, the shaping role of transnationalism in American poetics, the visual arts, and mass culture reflected underlying demographic forces in the makeup of social modernism. At the heart of America's bustling industrial scene, New York boasted, by the 1910s, a population of some five million city dwellers, 40 percent of whom were first generation émigrés. It was these new masses of working men and women that Bourne welcomed on the eve of the Soviet revolution in "Trans-National America."

Bourne's campaign for a transnational mass culture opposed the old-line, Brahmin class of New England intellectuals who, under the guise of melting-pot rhetoric, sought to assimilate societal differences to the ideological regimes of Americanism and what would soon emerge as the dominant productive order of Fordism in the 1920s.[2] The alternative, transnational alliances of the 1910s, joined as they were to the struggle for labor rights by the Industrial Workers of the World (IWW), led writers, artists, and intellectuals like Bourne beyond the more narrowly conceived interests of nationalism, especially as they hastened American entry into the First World War. The strategy here called for linking the international diversity of the new American masses to the antiwar movement of the 1910s. A year after his "Trans-National America" essay, Bourne pointed out in "The War and Intellectuals" that class allegiances cut across national boundaries in the "Great War." American monopolists, he observed, supported militarism in seeking to profiteer from the small entrepeneurs, farm laborers, and factory workers who would actually go into battle against their class counterparts in Europe. Bourne's antiwar polemic was tied to the struggle for radical democracy on behalf of labor, "the oppressed masses and excluded races at home" (HLR, 215). But it also emerged from the turbulent milieu that spawned the American Union Against Militarism. The campaign against America's participation in World War I carried out by intellectuals like Bourne, as well as Max and Crystal Eastman, Winthrop D. Lange, Paul V. Kellogg, Amos Pinchot, and others was not only waged in the streets but popularized in such publications as *The Masses*.

Not unlike *Craftsman, Comrade, International Socialist Review, Coming Nation, Mother Earth,* and *New York Call, The Masses* remains at once the most distinguished and controversial of the socialist little magazines of its day. *The Masses* was originally launched as a muck-raking publication by Piet Vlag in 1911. After a year of meagre subscriptions, the journal suspended publication until Max Eastman rejuvenated it in 1912. "Our magazine provided for the first time in America," he noted, "a meeting ground for revolutionary labor and the radical intelligentsia. It acquired, in spite of its gay laughter, the character of a crusade."[3] Under Eastman's direction, *The Masses* offered a lively forum for the kind of eclectic salon culture that could be found, say, at the Rand School or Ferrer Center, and in the studio parties hosted by Mabel Dodge, Alyse Gregory, and Gertrude Vanderbilt Whitney. At any of these get-togethers, wrote Dodge, one would come upon "Socialists, Trade-Unionists, Anarchists, Suffragists, Poets, Relations, Lawyers, Murderers, 'Old Friends,' Psycho-analysts, IWWs, Single Taxers, Birth Controlists, Newspapermen, Artists, Modern-Artists, Club Women, Woman's-place-is-in-the-home Women, Clergymen, and just plain men."[4] Eastman allied himself with such collaborators as Randolph Bourne, Stuart Davis, Floyd Dell, Mabel Dodge, Hugo Gellert, Emma Goldman, Amy Lowell, Robert Minor, John Reed, Boardman Robinson, Carl Sandburg, Mary Heaton Vorse, and Art Young, among others. Moreover, Eastman forged durable links to the IWW, the women's movement, Greenwich Village bohemia, and other avant-garde subcultures that together provided the journal with a diversified, popular constituency.

The Masses gave radical authors and artists a venue for publishing material that was otherwise too controversial to place in contemporaneous journals. Many of the reform issues represented in *The Masses* would later be enacted into laws that we take for granted today: the income tax, women's suffrage, child labor legislation, worker's compensation, minimum wage rates, and the eight-hour day. Alice Beach Winter's cover "Why Must I Work?" for the May 1912 issue recalled Lewis Hine's famous 1908 portrait of Sadie Feifer, a ten-year-old spinner in a North Carolina cotton mill (figure 1.1). Such arresting images exposed the scandal of the estimated 1.7 million children under sixteen who by the turn of the century were employed in Southern mills, New England factories, and on farms nationwide. The class tyranny of child labor was subversively exposed in Sarah Cleghorn's lyric "Golf Links"—later collected in Marcus Graham's *An Anthology of Revolutionary Poetry* (1929):

The Golf Links lie so near the mill
That almost every day
The laboring children can look out
And see the men at play.[5]

In addition to championing children's rights, *The Masses* also addressed a range of feminist issues pertaining to women's experience and the politics of sexual difference, ranging from women's suffrage and economic justice to more taboo social topics such as prostitution, venereal disease, birth control, and free love. These weighty issues, however, were often lightened through the comic caricatures of artists like Robert Minor. Debunking Victorian intolerance for sex education and "family limita-

1.1. Alice Beach Winter, "Why Must I Work?" *The Masses* (May 1912).

1.2. Robert Minor, "Your Honor, this woman gave birth to a naked child." *The Masses* (September 1915).

tion," his 1915 cartoon for the September issue of *The Masses* lampooned Anthony Comstock, president of the puritanical New York Society for the Prevention of Vice. Comstock is here depicted as an irate prosecutor who drags a mother before the bar with the absurd indictment that "Your Honor, this Woman gave birth to a naked child!" (figure 1.2).[6]

Not surprisingly, such pointed cultural critiques ran certain political and, eventually, legal risks. Because of its provocative stances, *The Masses* lost access to the Canadian mails, distributors in Boston and Philadelphia, the Columbia University library and bookstore, and other vital outlets. By adopting polemical, antiwar stances, the journal entered into legal battles with the Associated Press, the New York Society for the Suppression of Vice, as well as Ward and Gow (a New York-based magazine distributor). These clashes culminated in the celebrated lawsuit *United States v. Eastman et al.* of 1918. Offended by *The Masses*'s satiric gibes at American militarism in cartoons, poetry, and editorials, the Wilson administration conspired to shut down the magazine under the newly legislated Espionage Act of 1917. This law empowered the Postmaster General to deny use of the mails to any material that, in his opinion, promoted treason or insurrection against the laws of the United States.

Accordingly, Postmaster General Albert S. Burleson of Texas stripped *The Masses* of its mailing privileges in August that same year on the grounds that its editors were fomenting seditious viewpoints and draft resistance through the pacifist cartoons of Henry Glintenkamp, Boardman Robinson, and Art Young; in articles by Eastman and Dell; and through Josephine Bell's verse tribute to Emma Goldman and Alexander Berkman, who, she wrote:

> Are in prison tonight,
> But they have made themselves elemental force
> Like the water that climbs down rocks,
> Like the wind in the leaves:
> Like the gentle night that holds us:
> They are working on our destinies:
> They are forging the love of nations.[7]

However harmless such lyricism seems today, it nevertheless constituted grounds for national sedition in 1917. The American Union Against Militarism's pacificist agenda was eloquently captured in Henry Glintenkamp's cartoon "Physically Fit," published in the October 1917 issue of *The Masses* (figure 1.3). Offered as evidence in *The Masses* trial, *Physically Fit* alludes to contemporaneous exposés of the military's bulk ordering of coffins during the First World War. Similarly, Art Young's "Having Their Fling"—another of the works cited by the Postmaster General—lampooned the business side of the Great War as it filled the coffers of editors, capitalists, politicians, and the clergy alike (figure 1.4).

As "Having Their Fling" suggests, the antiwar protest of *The Masses* rested on international socialism's position that global conflict served mainly to advance the business interests of monopoly capitalism and the profits that trickled down to its ideological institutions. With little share of this wealth, workers had nothing to gain from war regardless of the national outcome. They would be better served by building a transnational class solidarity. In repudiating American jingoism, Randolph Bourne anathematized its "patriotic" call for war as a thin disguise masking underlying commercial interests. His critique indicted the telling hypocrisy of American pleas for social justice abroad but not on the domestic front:

> Numbers of intelligent people who had never been stirred by the horrors of capitalistic peace at home were shaken out of their slumber by the horrors of war in Belgium. Never having felt responsibility for labor wars and oppressed masses and excluded races at home, they had a large fund of idle emotional capital to invest in the oppressed nationalities and

ravaged villages of Europe. Hearts that had felt only ugly contempt for democratic strivings at home beat in tune with the struggle for freedom abroad. (HLR, 215)

Bourne's allusion to the "ugly contempt for democratic strivings" on the domestic front referred, in part, to the harassment and repression of *The Masses* promulgated by the Wilson administration. Those eventually brought to trial in 1918 for conspiring to obstruct conscription included Josephine Bell, Floyd Dell, Max Eastman, Henry Glintenkamp, John Reed, Merrill Rogers, and Art Young.

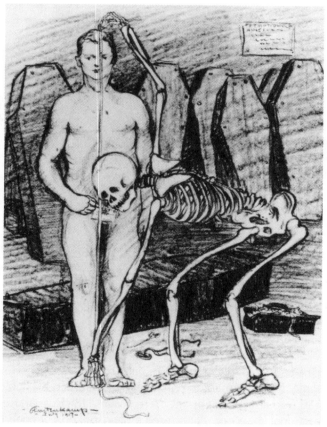

1.3. Henry Glintenkamp, "Physically Fit." *The Masses* (October 1917).

1.4. Art Young, "Having Their Fling." *The Masses* (September 1917).

Agitating in the courtroom, however, the defendants turned the trial into a political spectacle. They exploited this media event to advertise variously the causes of free expression, pacifism, feminism, socialism, and class struggle. Max Eastman, in particular, orchestrated his defense so as to broadcast populist stances on the "Great War," the Russian Revolution, and international socialism. He offered a plainspoken but cogent distinction between, on the one hand, America's supposed political liberties and, on the other hand, its real limits on economic freedom and individual expression. Socialists, he claimed, do not consider the vote as a guarantee; rather, "they think that democracy will begin when the people rule in industry as well as in politics. And they believe that true liberty involves the right to work and to possess all that you produce by doing your work."[8] Grounding his argument in a distinctively American tradition of pacifism, Eastman adopted the same stance against conscription that his family ancestor Daniel Webster had taken a century earlier. This nativist oratory went far in dispelling the district attorney's strategy of maligning him as a Bolshevik. With a split jury, the court declared a mistrial.

The spectacle of government censorship and the general curtailment of civil liberties thrown up by *The Masses* trial—coupled with the heady currents of proletarian uprising witnessed in John Reed's reports from St. Petersburg—fomented leftist sympathy for the Russian Revolution. In 1917, it sparked the imagination of young intellectuals like Joseph Freeman. "The overthrow of the Czar in February, 1917," Freeman recalled of his student days at Columbia University, "filled us with joy" (AT, 91). Conversely, the suppression of *The Masses* seemed to mark the nadir of American civil liberties. "We had become so identified in our own minds with the magazine," he wrote, "that . . . to kill *The Masses* was to kill our real university" (AT, 101). Thus it was the Russian experiment in socialism that gave hope and inspiration to a generation of American students, who were witnessing state repression of First Amendment guarantees in the United States. One month before the October uprising, Randolph Bourne had written in the September entry of his war diary that for the "young men and women" of America, "the real arena lies in the international class-struggle, rather than in the competition of artificial national units. They are watching to see what the Russian socialists are going to do for the world, not what the timorous capitalistic American democracy may be planning" (HLR, 232–33). Bourne and his colleagues did not have to wait very long to witness what the Russians would "do for the world." The following year Lenin's *Letter to the American Workingmen* was passed from Bolshevik courier Michael Borodin to Carl Sandburg. The Illinois Poet Laureate in turn smuggled it into the United States for publication in Max Eastman's *The Liberator* (1918), the successor to *The Masses*.[9]

Inspired by such charismatic and vanguardist revolutionaries as Lenin and Trotsky, American intellectuals like Lincoln Steffens (following the lead of his protégé, John Reed), Robert Minor, and Max Eastman soon made the pilgrimage to the Soviet New Jerusalem. Upon his return from having toured Russia in 1918 for the Bullitt commission on post-revolutionary conditions, Steffens summed up the era's utopian investment in the new socialist state: "I have been over into the future," he declared, "and it works."[10] The artistic milieu that Steffens and the American sculptor Jo Davidson witnessed for the Bullitt commission was soon popularized by Floyd Dell in his review of *Education and Art in Soviet Russia,* an anthology of reports on Soviet cultural programs that included an introductory essay by Max Eastman. Throughout the next decade, figures such as John Dos Passos, Joseph Freeman, Mike Gold, William Gropper, Bill Haywood, Ernest Hemingway, Josephine Herbst, Joshua Kunitz, Claude McKay, Scott Nearing, William Saroyan, Anna Louise Strong, Edmund Wilson, and countless others set out for the promised land of social revolution. Once there, Americans not only witnessed the birth of a new political order. But equally important, they also found a vital and sophisticated aesthetic scene informed by the most advanced trends in French neo-impressionism, symbolism, Fauvism, Italian futurism, and international dadaist styles.

The Constructivist Moment

The Russian avant-gardes had emerged during the prior two decades in revolt against both the Western academic tradition of neo-classical easel painting centered in the Imperial Academy of Fine Arts in St. Petersburg and the more provincial heritage of icon painting in Moscow.[11] In the 1910s, the mingling of traditional peasant arts such as wood block prints (luboks), fiber arts, primitive sculpture and other native crafts with fin de siècle and art nouveau styles was reflected in Sergei Diaghilev's noted journal *Mir iskusstva* (The World of Art), which promoted a cosmopolitan blend of formalism, symbolism, and subjectivism. Diaghilev also sponsored gallery shows of Russian artists like Lev Bakst, Alexander Benois, Sergei Chekhonin, and Konstantin Somov, in exhibitions with Continental counterparts such as Degas and Monet in both Russia and Paris. These shows stimulated patronage and a burgeoning art market especially in Moscow. Here major collectors like Sergei Shchukin and Ivan Morosov speculated in the impressionist, post-impressionist, fauve, post-fauve, and cubist works on view at the Salons des Independants and Salons d'Automne. Through such acquisitions, Russian artists were exposed to extensive collections of works by Manet, Fantin-Latour, Pissarro, Renois, Degas, Monet, Van Gogh, Gauguin, Matisse, Cezanne, and Picasso. Influenced by these Continental artists as well as the symbolist painter Viktor Borisov-Musatov, a new group of Russian artists, represented in the

"Crimson Rose" show of 1904 and later the "Blue Rose" exhibition of 1907, began to feature such intrinsic aesthetic qualities as rhythm, color, tension, and mass that heralded the techniques of the pre-revolutionary avant-gardes.[12] By 1910, Mikhail Larionov, Natalia Goncharova, and Aristarkh Lentulov advanced the neoprimitivist tendencies of the "Blue Rose" toward a cubist attention to geometric precision in line and plane. Significantly, Marinetti's "Futurist Manifesto," that had appeared as early as 1909 in Russia, inspired Larionov and Goncharova the following year to fuse futurism with Eastern motifs in the Russian Cubofuturism and rayonism of "The Donkey's Tail" group.[13] The important "Exhibition of Painting. 1915" in Moscow showcased a fabulous array of avant-gardes that included works by David and Vladimir Burliak, Marc Chagall, Goncharova, Kandinsky, Larionov, as well as two figures that would soon dominate the Russian pre-revolutionary avant-gardes: Kazimir Malevich, the founder of the suprematist movement, and Vladimir Tatlin, the leading proponent of Constructivism.

Having made a pilgrimage to Paris in 1913 to work with Picasso, Tatlin advanced Picasso's cubist constructions of *objets trouvés* toward a bolder, three-dimensional sculpting of real space with glass, iron grill, tin, plaster, and other industrial materials. At its most ambitious, Tatlin's work would eventually aspire in the post-revolutionary period toward an architectural Constructivism, notably in his famous design for a "Monument to the Third International," a gigantic glass and metal tower spiraling to more than double the height of the Empire State Building. Significantly, Malevich's 1915 manifesto "From Cubism and Futurism to Suprematism: The New Painterly Realism" reflected on the emergence of the avant-gardes from the rapid technological change of social modernization: "The new life of iron and the machine, the roar of motor cars, the brilliance of electric lights, the growling of propellers."[14] Like the futurists, Malevich celebrated the new productive forces unleashed by industrial capitalism as they fragmented fin-de-siècle Victorian culture, dispersing its bourgeois social order and conventions along new pathways of speedy interchange and violent transformation. He welcomed the chance to shrug off the painterly vestiges of academic classicism, bourgeois realism, and subjective aestheticism. "Any hewn pentagon or hexagon," he irreverently declared, "would have been a greater work of sculpture than the Venus de Milo or David" (AR, 123).

The futurists' dynamic disruption of the old representational values in art, Malevich contended, prefigured his own even more abstract tenets of Suprematism.[15] His new austere style, showcased in his thirty-five contributions to the "0.10" exhibition of 1915, was elegant testimony to the painter's innovative passage beyond Futurism in his minimalist use of a primary, cubofuturist color palette—black, white, red, yellow, and green— and simple geometrical shapes—square, rectangle, triangle. Compositions such as *Black Square* (1913), *Black Circle* (1913), *Black Square and Red Square* (1913), *House Under Construction* (1914–1915) made up the basic language of Suprematism. But it grew more complex, in color shading and dynamic vectoring of geometrical elements, eventually realizing three-dimensional spaces in Malevich's projects of the 1920s—*Planits* and *Arkhitektonics*. By thus welcoming the new currents of social modernization, Malevich, Tatlin, and contemporaneous exhibitors of Russian Cubofuturism and Rayonism played vangardist roles in the aesthetic dimension that foresaw radical social change in the post-revolutionary period—the era of so-called "heroic" communism.[16]

The formal innovations of the Russian avant-gardes presaged the disruptive shifts in traditional life style, customs, and habits of perception brought on by industrial modernism. Yet the futurist dictum that "Art is a part of Life!" would be staged, in the post-revolutionary years, on a grander scale than anyone could foresee *avant le guerre*. To begin with, the Revolution swept aside the bourgeois patronage system that had sustained the *World of Art* and other avant-garde scenes. Overseen by Anatolii Lunacharsky, cultural life was conducted under the state auspices of People's Commisariat for Enlightenment (Narkompros). This agency supported such leftist tendencies as Altman's Communist Futurism (Komfut) and Aleksandr Bogdanov's Proletarian Culture Organization (Proletkult), Narkompros' Visual Arts Section (IZO), and the Institute of Artistic Culture (Inkhuk). Moreover, as part of this new state administration of the arts, the traditional bastions of academic classicism were revamped and infused with the nascent Russian avant-gardes. Only a year after the Revolution, the august St. Petersburg Academy was disbanded and replaced by the Petrograd and Free Art Educational Studios (Pekgoskhuma). Similarly, the Moscow Institute of Painting, Sculpture, and Architecture merged with the Stroganov Art School under Tatlin's direction and were reformed as the Free State Art Studios (Svomas).

The cultural power bestowed by the new state institutions on artists and writers of the Revolution permitted them to advance their vanguardist roles, heretofore confined to the aesthetic dimension, now into a wider sociopolitical field. Kandinsky, for example, assumed leadership of Inkhuk in Moscow (1920), with Tatlin and Punin overseeing the Petrograd division (Ikhk) and Malevich directing a branch in Vitebsk. The utopian hope for this new rapprochement between art and life was eloquently captured in Vladimir Mayakovsky's 1918 address "Shrine or Factory?" delivered at a mass meeting held in Petrograd's Winter Palace: "Art must not be concentrated in dead shrines called museums," he declared. "It must be spread everywhere—on the streets, in the trams, factories, workshops, and in workers' homes."[17] Coinciding with the avant-garde's desire to infuse itself throughout proletarian culture was the state's mutual need for mass cultural propaganda in combating the triple peril of civil war, foreign intervention, and a faltering economy weakened by Polish and Baltic blockades.

Faced with these challenges to the Revolution, leftist painters and illustrators employed graphic arts techniques based in the compositional designs and color palette of Cubofuturism and Suprematism to advertise the ideology of domestic solidarity. Under such sponsoring state offices as the Russian Telegraph Agency (ROSTA), artists and writers joined forces to broadcast, through posters and window art, the ideological signs of revolution to a wide popular constituency. "Window ROSTA was a fantastic thing," wrote Mayakovsky. "It meant telegraphed news immediately translated into posters and decrees into slogans."[18] In fact, poster art was disseminated in such high volume that during the Defense Week of 1919 alone, according to *Pravda* reports of the time, the Moscow Committee of the Russian CP published over 375,000 posters for display on walls, trams, and other public spaces.[19] Such visual art was not only distributed locally but traversed the length and breadth of the country on agitational trains and steamships. Bedecked with cubofuturist, rayonist, and suprematist styles fused with folk elements and cartoon art, these traveling revolutionary signs boosted Soviet resolve on the several fronts of the Civil War during the days of "heroic" communism. Significantly, it is precisely in this moment's special play of revolutionary and counterrevolutionary forces—aristocracy vs. peasantry, bourgeois vs. proletariat, Red Army vs. White army, personal privilege vs. collective will—that the traditional barriers separating high art from everyday life, artist from audience, formalism from politics, the avant-gardes from mass culture were surmounted.

The historical urgency of the times took the visual arts into politicized registers, especially so in the work of Eliezer Lissitzky. Trained as an engineer at the Technische Hochschule, Darmstadt, Lissitzky experimented with typographical and architectural design, collaborating in 1917 with Marc Chagall on illustrations of Hebraic texts. The following year Lissitzky assumed a professorial post in Vitebsk where Chagall served as director of the Vitebsk School of Art. Although Lissitzky had followed the current trends of blending Cubofuturism and peasant *lubok* prints, it was not until the following year at the Tenth State Exhibition that he was exposed to Malevich's suprematist art. Lissitzky's work adopted Suprematism's compositional techniques but added a narrative dimension to Malevich's aesthetic, advancing it into new, politicized registers, as in his 1920 poster "Drive Red Wedges into White Troops!" (figure 1.5). (Figures 1.5–1.14 are in a photo insert following p. 46.) Intervening in the period's Civil War between the Red and White armies, Lissitzky's striking color lithograph appropriated Suprematism's pure geometrical forms—here triangles, circles, and rectangles—along with its minimalist use of red, white, and black hues, in a simple but elegant narrative strategy summed up in the title's polemical slogan. Out of the Revolution's particular historicity, artists like Lissitzky imported narrative and representational elements into the formal techniques of Suprematism.

What distinguishes the political avant-gardes, in figures such as Lissitzky, Mayakovsky, Rodchenko, and other Constructivists, is precisely such dialectical negotiations between the formal advances of modernist aesthetics and the dynamic conditions of collective reception and mass distribution unique to their revolutionary moment. The period of heroic communism—with its civil wars, foreign adventurism, and dire economic threats—gave the avant-gardes a large audience receptive to the signs of futurist utopia. In the urban centers, theater sets (co-designed by Natan Altman, Ovan Puni, Zhenia Bogoslavskaya, Malevich, and Tatlin) showcased the ideological signs of revolution in performance productions scripted by poets and dramatists such as Mayakovsky and Vsevelod Meyerhold.[20] During and shortly after the 1917 Revolution, similar enclaves of avant-garde cross-fertilization could be found in Moscow's Cafè Pittoresque: a theater club, conceived in 1917 by Tatlin, Alexander Rodchenko, and Georgy Yakulov that hosted readings by Khlebnikov, Kruchenikh, Mayakovsky, and others amidst the moment's latest constructivist decor. Empowered by the Revolution, these kinds of collaborative performance art reached epic scale in Natan Altman's 1918 futurist celebration of the October Revolution in Petrograd's Winter Palace, and again two years later in an epic recreation of "The Storming of the Winter Palace," involving a cast of over 8,000 citizens and troops.

The Russian avant-gardes had begun as a disavowal of academic formalism—witnessed, for example, in the collaborative manifesto *A Slap in the Face of Public Taste* (1912). Suddenly, the movement spawned by painters and poets David Burliak, Vladimir Mayakovsky, Benedikt Livshits, and Victor Khlebnikov was released from the bohemian cafes, eso-teric art leagues, and obscure galleries now to negotiate audiences in mass registers of nationwide broadcast and distribution. Meanwhile, proletcult ideologues such as Osip Brik boldly claimed a vanguardist role for the futurists in *designing* social change. "Factories, industrial plants, work-shops," he declared in the 1918 inaugural issue of *Iskusstvo kommuny* (Art of the Commune) "are waiting for artists to come to them, to give them designs for new and unprecedented objects."[21] Brik's call for cultural intervention at the heart of society's productive forces polarized the already conflicted avant-gardes. On the one hand, figures like Kandinsky and Chagall veered away from the moment's extrinsic demands into neo-romantic expressivity. Tellingly, both eventually left for Europe. Pursuing an inward emigration, Malevich steeped himself in the intrinsic values of self-referential formalism. On the other hand, Tatlin, Rodchenko, Lis-sitzky, and the Obmochu group broke out of the confining space of the easel. Instead, they began to work with industrial materials in three-dimen-sional sculptural and architectonic forms. These avant-gardists forwarded the Constructivist principles promoted by proletcult critics such as Brik and Alexei Gan and exhibited in gallery shows like the 1920 Society of Young Artists exhibition (Obmokhu) and "5 × 5 = 25" show of 1921. Not insignificantly, the Russian avant-gardes employed industrial design principles and processes of mass production to contest both the master-piece status of the individual art work and the role of the individual auteur under affirmative bourgeois culture.

"Technique and industry have confronted art," wrote Varvara Stepa-nova, "with the problem of construction as an active process, and not a contemplative reflection. The 'sanctity' of a work as a single entity is destroyed."[22] Indeed, figures like Tatlin, Liubov Popva, and Varvara not only theorized such a deauraticization of the art object but actually went to work in factories such as Petrograd's Lessner metallurgical plant and Moscow's Tsindel textile mills. The Constructivists' campaign to inject art into life benefited from the institutional backing of Narkompros head Lunacharsky. Not unlike the managers of the American culture industry, Lunacharsky insisted that "particular attention must be given to the devel-opment of mass taste and artistic creativity by introducing art into every-day life and into industrial production at large."[23]

Thus, the particular historicity of the nascent Soviet state—its unique negotiation of institutional power and cultural transformation—allowed the Russian avant-gardes to supplant the high modernist impasse of paint-erly values with equally sophisticated, but less cloistral, aesthetic strategies.

Appropriating Suprematism's concern for line, color, and geometrical plane, Russian Constructivists such as Lissitzky, Rodchenko, the Stenberg brothers, and Tatlin went beyond formalism to consider the viewer's response to sculptural forms in real space. Moreover, under pressure from the turbulent, post-revolutionary period, their anticipation of social reception as part of a work's constructive process led to a new rapprochement between formalism and agitation. This theoretical leap from faktura to factography permitted the political avant-gardes to migrate, quite dramatically in the space of a few years, from the formal "laboratory" of intrinsic experimentation into the broader cultural registers of mass spectacle.[24]

Yet in the more prosperous decade of the 1920s, rapid changes in both technology and new Soviet economic policies presented unique hurdles to securing popular investment in the Revolution. Such challenges compelled the avant-gardes to pay attention, not just to aesthetic production but to shifting tastes and trends in consumption. In 1921, while the Bolsheviks were mopping up the remnants of the contra-revolutionary White Army, Lenin unveiled his New Economic Policy (NEP). This plan allowed for limited free enterprise as a way of injecting the flagging Soviet economy with a dose of entrepreneurial stimulation. Suddenly the avant-gardes were competing with capital itself for the hearts and minds of the Russian masses, now in hot pursuit of the new fashions, goods, and consumer durables of a burgeoning commodity culture.

In this dawning era of technological change, mass advertising flourished through the new techniques of mechanical reproduction in typography, graphic design, and photomontage. Exploiting these innovative productive forces, however, a new class of nouveau-riche *neppies* quickly imported the signs of bourgeois affluence, cabaret culture, and conspicuous consumption from the West. This conjuncture linked the advance of technological reproduction with the NEP's entrepreneurial drive. But more to the point, it forced the avant-gardes to compete in the shaping of popular culture. In his 1923 essay "Agitation and Advertisement," Mayakovsky urged his colleagues to "Give advertising some thought!" Advertising, as "commercial agitation," he held, serves the same end in the market place as propaganda in revolutionary struggle. "It is the weapon which is born of competition. . . . We cannot leave this weapon," he concluded, "this agitation on behalf of trade, in the hands of the NEP-men."[25]

Agitating within the spectacle of a burgeoning Soviet consumer society, Mayakovsky joined forces with Constructivist artist and head of the Institute of Artistic Culture (Inkhuk) Alexander Rodchenko from 1923 to 1925

---

under the title of "Reklam-konstruktor" (Advertisement-constructor). Rodchenko teamed up with Mayakovsky in formatting the poet's terse slogans and ad pitch techniques. Their collaboration reached fruition in the striking typographical arrangements and stunning visual lay-outs of their ROSTA window artistry. This working partnership of painter and poet translated the suprematist style of clean lines, simple geometrical planes, and a primary color palette into agitational designs for the Soviet mass market economy. Their ads promoted the agricultural commodities of Mosselprom, the rubber goods of Rezinotrest, Crimean cigarettes, and so on. Such sophisticated ad campaigns both spurred consumer demand for state products and spread the ideological signs of proletarian revolution (figures 1.6–1.9).

Rodchenko, Mayakovsky and other "Left Front" Constructivists (Anton Lavinskii, Konstantin Medunetskii, Vladimier and Georgii Stenberg, and Varvara Stepanova) designed newspaper and poster ads for a complete gamut of consumer goods—from cooking oil to tires, biscuits to galoshes, and pacifiers to "home-study" text books. But they also intervened in the spectacular circulation of the consumer goods themselves: designing agitational formats for book jackets, calendars and other "giveaways," cigarette packaging, chocolate and caramel wrappers, and trademark labels (figures 1.10–1.11). The Constructivists' fusion of avant-garde aesthetics with the everyday products of kitsch culture aimed to outrun the commodity form on its own ground and thereby fuse consumer demands and popular satisfactions with the aims and ideals of the proletarian revolution. As Yakov Chernikhov would later assert at the end of the decade, "Constructivism can, and must, take into consideration all the concrete needs of contemporary life and must answer in full the needs of the mass consumer, the collective 'customer'—the people."[26]

Articulating the Masses

Such was the scene of rapprochement between the avant-gardes and mass culture that greeted a generation of American expatriates as tourists of the Revolution in the 1920s. Like their Russian counterparts, artists and writers in the United States had also moved leftward, inspired by the Soviet Revolution and chastened the following year by *The Masses* trials. The radical coalition of bohemians and leftist partisans that made up the editorial circle of *The Masses* was revived in 1918 as *The Liberator*. In the post-revolutionary period it kept an American audience abreast of developments in the USSR through on-the-scene reports by Max Eastman,

John Reed, Claude McKay, John Dos Passos, and Anna Louise Strong to some 60,000 subscribers.

The Liberator's pro-Soviet stance was institutionalized in 1922 when the journal moved to the Workers' Party headquarters, under the executive editorial leadership of Joseph Freeman, a key player in this merger as well as in the formation of New Masses four years later. In 1917 Freeman had befriended Randolph Bourne, Kenneth Burke, Matthew Josephson, and Richard McKeon at Columbia University. Here he was exposed to the socialist tutelage of expelled Columbia professors J. M. Cattrell and Henry Wadsworth Longfellow Dana. Fresh from having penned the prospectus of New Masses for its major sponsor, the Garland Fund, Freeman in May 1926 expatriated to Russia, where his colleague Mike Gold had recently spent the summer a year earlier. Gold's 1921 manifesto "Towards Proletarian Literature," written under his real name Irwin Granich for The Liberator (which he was co-editing at the time with Claude McKay) had established him as the strongest American proponent of the kind of working-class cultural hegemony that in the Soviet Union was being theorized by A. A. Bogdanov and administered by Lunacharsky.

Although appointed to The Liberator staff by Max Eastman, Gold repudiated Eastman's divorce of social change from personal creativity, set forth in his preface, "American Ideals of Poetry," to Eastman's The Colors of Life (1918).[27] There, Eastman admitted the necessity for social reform. But he added the caveat that never as poet had he discovered his "undivided being there." "I have found that rather in individual experience," he confessed, "and in those moments of energetic idleness when the life of universal nature seemed to come to its bloom of realization in my consciousness" (CL, 13). Rejecting Eastman's mystified lyricism, Gold displaced the self's ontological privilege in favor of the more vital expressivity of the masses. In this respect, Gold followed the contemporaneous doctrine of the Soviet Proletarian Cultural and Educational organization (Proletcult). "For the old artist," wrote Bogdanov in 1920, "originality is the expression of the independent value of his 'I,' the means of his own exaltation; for the new artist, originality denotes a profound and broad comprehension of the collective experience."[28]

Unlike Eastman, who viewed Soviet-style proletcult as a "crude humiliation of arts and letters,"[29] Gold idealized the social changes he witnessed in Russia. "The Social Revolution of today," he insisted, "is not the mere political movement artists despise it as. It is Life at its fullest and noblest. It is the religion of the masses, articulate at last."[30] Gold's vision of an articulate masses, however idealized in his 1921 essay, was exactly what he claimed to have witnessed at mid-decade in the fusion of Russian futurism and Soviet popular culture:

> All the young writers have been influenced by the powerful Futurist school, which before the war had so heroically claimed the Machine Age for art. The futurists were the readiest to accept the Revolution, and their writers and artists are national figures now in Soviet Russia. Every newspaper cartoon, every book cover decoration, every new building, statue, monument, factory, textile design, moving picture, poem, story and symphony, has been affected by futurist theory and practice. This is one of the enormous surprises and revelations that come to the writer who visits Russia today.[31]

The broad distribution of the political avant-gardes that Gold found in Soviet society made America's cloistral literary culture, by comparison, seem hopelessly severed from the people. "Carl Sandburg sells some two thousand copies of his poems here," the editor complained, "but Mayakovsky, a futurist writing the most modern and complex rhythms, sells three million books in Soviet Russia" (ANC, 130).

Gold's focus on literature's institutional base was similarly reflected in Joseph Freeman's analysis of the increased Soviet publishing runs of the post-revolutionary period. "An important aspect of the popularization of culture among the masses of the Soviet Union," he would later report in *Voices of October* (1930), "is the wide distribution of books."[32] Like Gold, Freeman was impressed with both the quantity and quality of Soviet publishing which had boosted literary production from an estimated 34,600 titles and 133,500,000 copies in 1912 to about 115,500 titles and 212,000,000 copies a decade into the post-revolutionary period. Of the some 2,000 Soviet publishing outlets, the major houses, such as the Moscow Worker, Educational Worker, Land and Factory, the State Medical Publishing House, New Village, State Publishing House (GOSIZDAT), and Proletariat, did not confine their distribution to the cities, but aggressively marketed texts in a national network of over 6,000 book stalls and 4,000 books shops in small towns, villages, and hamlets (VO, 22).

In affirming Gold's ideal of an *articulate,* rather than a merely indoctrinated, masses Freeman praised "two unique Communist institutions: the worker-peasant correspondent and the wall newspaper, both of which permit the masses of the population to voice their thoughts in the most direct manner" (VO, 25). These two forms of local reporting served to broadcast everyday life in the factory, farm, and office. They acted variously, Freeman argued, as forums for showcasing proletarian aesthetics, as journalistic vehicles for ongoing workplace reform and as checks against bureaucratization, inefficiency, and exploitation of the people. Noting the some 250,000 worker and peasant correspondents, Freeman approvingly quoted from Lenin's plan to "Give the workers a greater possibility . . . to write about everything, as much as possible about their daily life, their interests, their work" (VO, 25). Freeman's crusade for the worker-correspondent was no doubt spurred by Soviet popular ads promoting the new communications media that he might have viewed while an expatriate in Russia. A 1925 subscription poster for *Izvestiia,* for example, linked the ideal of a literate masses to the goal of social modernization captured in the constructivist tower for the Izvestiia building in downtown Moscow (figure 1.12). Tellingly, this utopian symbol of the future, like Tatlin's "Monument to the Third International," never got off the drawing board.

By unsettling the traditional separation of the reader and writer under the bourgeois press, Freeman's analysis looked forward to Walter Benjamin's seminal essay "The Artist as Producer" (1934). There Benjamin would likewise theorize the Soviet press as a collaborative "theater of literary confusion."[33] Freeman's review of the various aesthetic trends and groups in both pre- and post-revolutionary Russia, balanced art's vanguard revolutionary role against its subordination to mass interests and popular satisfactions. He welcomed the advanced aesthetics that emerged from avant-garde enclaves like Moscow's Domino cafe and in such futurist organs as *Art of the Commune* and *Artistic Work in Industry.* But Freeman also maintained that "every movement in the Soviet arts lived or died by the supreme test as to whether or not it had anything to offer to the new social order" (VO, 32).

During the 1920s, such aesthetic pragmatism, for Freeman, did not yet entail the kind of repression that would culminate in the 1934 First All-Union Writers' Conference proclamation of "socialist realism" as the official Soviet style. Indeed, the Political Bureau of the Communist Party in its 1924 Resolution on Literature, Freeman argued, had recommended openness in fostering proletarian culture's popular underpinnings. State Communism should support the heritage of traditional art and literature as well as the creative contributions of fellow-travelers. "The Party should declare itself," the resolution concluded, "in favor of the free competition of various groups and tendencies in the field of literature. Any other solution to the question would be quasi-bureaucratic."[34] As a Comintern translator, Freeman had witnessed the fierce clash of wills between Stalin and Trotsky in the Throne Room of the Kremlin, and he occasionally saw portents of Stalinism in the officious bureaucrats of the Central Committee. Yet in the mid-1920s, he was more impressed by the heady atmosphere that he imbibed from the Revolution's writers, artists, playwrights, and cinematographers such as Eisenstein, Mayakovsky, and Meyerhold.

For his part, Max Eastman deflated Freeman's idealized hopes for post-revolutionary culture. *Voices of October,* Eastman charged, was sheer agitprop and distorted its actual historical context. "That book, *Voices of October,*" he observed, "with its wonder story by Joseph Freeman of a 'tremendous growth' of proletarian literature . . . appeared at the exact mathematical center of the time now officially conceded to be one in which the political inquisition was so rabid that loyal revolutionists dared not even discuss whether a work of art possessed talent or not, or so much as mention the question of form above a whisper!"[35] Not only did Freeman and his co-authors, Louis Lozowick and Joshua Kunitz, smooth over the real political struggles and social clash in the Soviet Union, but they lionized the leaders of the October Revolution as themselves sophisticated proponents of the arts. Just as Mike Gold had praised Trotsky for being "as universal as Leonardo da Vinci" (ANC, 131), so Louis Lozowick could boast that:

> Lunacharsky acted as guide to Russian immigrants through the Louvre and Trotsky wrote on Meunier years before they became respectively Soviet Commissars of Education and of War. Intellectuals in the vanguard of the Russian revolutionary movement were as a rule well-versed in the classics and abreast of contemporary philosophy, art and literature. They always recognized the paramount importance of culture in the social transformation which was their goal.[36]

In imitating such charismatic revolutionaries, leftist expatriates like Freeman, Gold, Lozowick, and Kunitz viewed themselves, upon their return to the US, as vanguardist mentors for younger American artists and writers.

Louis Lozowick, for example, played a key internationalist role in the transatlantic circulation of suprematist and constructivist styles exhibited in Moscow, Berlin, and Paris in the mid-twenties (figure 1.13). Five years before his Soviet collaborations with Joseph Freeman on *Voices of October,* Lozowick had been influenced by his personal association with El Lissitzky. In 1922, when the West hosted constructivist aesthetics in Berlin (figure 1.14), Lozowick was exhibiting with El Lissitzky in Dusseldorf. Significantly, both Malevich's suprematist emphasis on the "pure" aesthetic values of line, plane, and geometrical form as well as Lissitzky's fascination with machine imagery and mechanical ornamentation left their mark on

Lozowick's cubofuturist style in the 1920s. Throughout the next two years, the American artist would serve as an intellectual broker of the Russian avant-gardes. In particular, Lozowick published his own translations of Russian poets, reviewed such shows as the Berlin Constructivist exhibition, and reported on Soviet projects like Tatlin's proposed "Monument to the Third International" in *Broom*. Returning to New York in 1924, Lozowick continued to popularize the Russian avant-gardes. Here he published essays for *The Menorah Journal* on Marc Chagall, El Lissitzky, and the Moscow Jewish State Theater, as well as occasional pieces for the *Nation* and *The Union Bulletin*, among other journals. His lectures on the Soviet avant-gardes for the Societe Anonyme were published as a collection of essays entitled *Modern Russian Art* (1925). Moreover, his notoriety as an artist and art critic led to his participation on the executive board of *New Masses* in 1926.

What is notable about Lozowick, beyond his role as an intellectual envoy for the Russian avant-gardes, was his successful fusion of suprematist and constructivist principles on the one hand with America's industrial landscape on the other: New York skyscrapers and urban street scenes, Minnesota grain elevators, Montana copper mines, Seattle lumber yards, and New Jersey blast furnaces. "The dominant trend in America of today," he wrote for the 1927 *Machine Age Exposition:*

> beneath all the apparent chaos and confusion, is towards order and organization which find their outward sign and symbol in the rigid geometry of the American city: in the verticals of its smoke stacks, in the parallels of its car tracks, the squares of its streets, the cubes of its factories, the arc of its bridges, the cylinders of its gas tanks.[37]

Lozowick's early lithograph of *New York* (1926) blends basic geometrical elements in the constructivist manner, tending toward a more dynamic, futuristic composition of space on the right-hand axis of the work (figure 1.15). His later industrial subjects such as *Tanks #1,* however, demonstrate a greater formal commitment to the "pure" geometrical elements of the cone, circle, triangle, and rectangle that he viewed as the foundational order underlying the urban spectacle (figure 1.16). Similarly, the dominant vertical lines and perspectival deployment of receding trapezoidal spaces in *Brooklyn Bridge*—winner of the 1931 Mary S. Collins Prize for Best Lithograph in Philadelphia's Third Exhibition of American Lithography—features a similar attention to geometric form (figure 1.17). In the mid-1930s, however, Lozowick's lithographic designs would become increasingly politicized in their narrative content: as in his antiwar

1.15. Louis Lozowick, *New York* (1925). Lithograph.

portrait of a disabled veteran selling flowers on Wall Street in *Buy a Poppy* (1934); his depiction of a workers' walkout in Strike Scene (1934) (figure 1.18); his image of a violent clash between laborers and police in *Tear Gas* (1934); his disturbing self-portrait in *Lynching* (1936); and his pathetic scene of a depression era soup kitchen in *Thanksgiving Dinner* (1938) (figure 1.19).

Just as Lozowick popularized the Constructivist and Suprematist styles in American lithography, Joseph Freeman championed the post-revolutionary avant-gardes in American letters. Even before he met Trotsky and Lunacharsky, Freeman had in the early 1920s become something of a cultural commissar for the new generation of poets that would emerge from the Dynamo group a decade later. In 1924 he, along with Mike Gold, was leading poetry writing workshops under the auspices of the

1.16. Louis Lozowick, *Tanks #1* (1929). Lithograph.

Workers' School. These classes profoundly shaped the formative careers of such figures as Edwin Rolfe. "Some of us," Rolfe would later write, "took Michael Gold's 'Writers' Workshop' class at the old Workers' School on East Fourteenth Street":

> We studied journalism and had fragmentary talks with Joseph Freeman. . . . Talking, lecturing, writing, they kept their ideas and convic-

tions alive and growing when all others descended into bogs, were side tracked, or deserted. It was Joseph Freeman who finally showed some of us our real direction, our real goal. . . . "Stop thinking of yourselves," he said, "as poets who are also revolutionists or as revolutionists who are also poets. Remember that you are *revolutionary poets*."[38]

Such collective settings of creative writing were further inspired by cultural exchanges with Soviet envoys. Vladimir Mayakovsky, for example, toured

1.17. Louis Lozowick, *Brooklyn Bridge* (1930). Lithograph.

1.18. Louis Lozowick, *Strike Scene* (1934). Lithograph.

the New York literary scene in 1925. "How is it," he asked Joseph Freeman at the time, "that these so-called revolutionary writers of America
have no organization of their own? . . . You should have an association
of proletarian writers. We have several of them in our country, the
German comrades have them, other countries have them too" (AT, 372).

The next year, Gold and Freeman took up Mayakovsky's challenge.
Along with several members of the Workers Drama League, they
attempted to form an American Proletarian Artist and Writers League.
The proposed league received a sympathetic response from such liberal
fellow-travelers as Van Wyck Brooks, Floyd Dell, Langston Hughes, Hor-

ace Kallen, Lola Ridge, and others. But it was not until the founding of *New Masses* that the inner circle of left New York intellectuals, writers, and artists found themselves, under the leadership of Joseph Freeman, Hugo Gellert, and Mike Gold, joined to an emerging cultural hegemony. In its internationalist scope; its diversity of gender, racial, and class perspectives; and its blend of high, avant-garde, and populist styles, this new conjuncture offered a progressive alternative to liberal journals like *The New Republic*.

One index of the cultural power that *New Masses* commanded was its distinguished staff of contributing editors. Its roster of notables reads like

1.19. Louis Lozowick, *Thanksgiving Dinner*
(1938). Lithograph.

a "Who's Who" of New York intellectual life between the wars: Sherwood Anderson, Van Wyck Brooks, Stuart Chase, Stuart Davis, Adolph Dehn, Floyd Dell, Max Eastman, Waldo Frank, Arturo Giovanitti, Susan Glaspell, Claude McKay, Lewis Mumford, Eugene O'Neill, Elmer Rice, Lola Ridge, Boardman Robinson, Carl Sandburg, Upton Sinclair, Genevieve Taggard, Jean Toomer, Louis Untermeyer, Mary Heaton Vorse, Edmund Wilson, Jr., Robert Wolf, and Art Young, among others. *New Masses'* first two issues alone featured the feminist poetics of Babette Deutsch, winner of that year's "Nation" Poetry Prize; the modernist poetics of Robinson Jeffers, Alfred Kreymborg, and William Carlos Williams; modern short fiction by D. H. Lawrence; the cubofuturist artwork of David Burliak, Stuart Davis, and Louis Lozowick; commentary by Egmont Arens, John Dos Passos, and Leon Trotsky; and satiric cartoon art of Hugo Gellert, William Gropper, Otto Soglow, and Art Young.

But equally important, *New Masses* offered a populist forum for showcasing unknown talent and otherwise marginalized feminist, minority, ethnic, and proletarian constituencies. *New Masses* actively solicited its readership's input on format, aesthetic styles, social content, and political perspectives. It followed the kind of dispersed network of worker correspondents that its editors found so appealing in the Soviet cultural revolution. "We would like to fill a page," they declared,

> with letters from all over the country telling of industries, occupations, changing social customs, the daily work and play of Americans everywhere. We see this as a possible feature—a monthly mosaic of American life, in which the tragedy and comedy, the hopes and dreams of the most obscure American mill town or cross roads village will be chronicled with as much respect and sympathy by our correspondents as if they were reporting the political or artistic events of a European capital.[39]

Such respect for regional and class diversity was not divorced, as it later became in the postwar canon of high modernism, from the internationalist and cosmopolitan avant-gardes in Berlin, Moscow, New York, and Paris.

Two years later, on the eve of the 1929 stock market crash, Mike Gold and Hugo Gellert revived the, by then, financially ailing *New Masses*. Delving into the obscure subcultures of working-class America, Gold and Gellert eschewed the kind of Greenwich Village bohemianism that had lingered on from the days of *The Liberator*. Instead, they revamped the magazine to reflect the kind of proletarian populism featured in Soviet journalism. In its June 1928 issue the newly launched magazine advertised

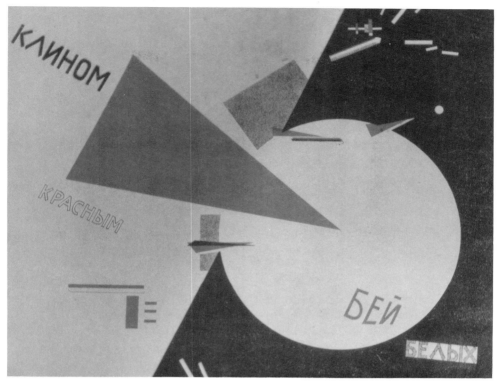

1.5. El Lissitzky, "Drive Red wedges into White troops!" Poster.

1.6. Vladimir Mayakovsky text /
Aleksandr Rodchenko design,
''Seize this lifebelt!
Everything for Everyone.
High Quality and cheap!
Take it from us on the highest authority!''
(1923). Newspaper advertisement
for the State Department Store,
GUM, on Red Square.

1.7. Vladimir Mayakovsky text / Aleksandr Rodchenko design, "I Eat Biscuits from the Red October Factory. I Buy Them Only From Mosselprom" (1923). Newspaper advertisement.

1.8. Aleksandr Rodchenko, advertising poster for books (1925). Reconstruction by Varvara Rodchenko.

1.10. Vladimir Mayakovsky, "Landowners soon disposed of Vrangel—They pushed him into the Black Sea" (1924). Series of wrappers for KRASNOARMEISKAIA ZVEZDA (Red Army Star). Caramels with texts and designs by Mayakovsky.

1.9. Vladimir Mayakovsky text / Aleksandr Rodchenko design, "There are not and have never been any better dummies. They are ready for sucking till you reach old age. Sold Everywhere" Rezinotrest, the State Trust of the Rubber Industry.

1.11. Anonymous (no date). Export packagings with English text, featuring the Soviet icebreaker *Krassin* (or *Krasin*), which became famous internationally and at home for its rescue of the Swedish Arctic expedition led by Nobel.

1.12. "1926 Subscriptions Have Opened for the Daily Paper *Izvestiia*, the Weekly *Krasnaia Niva* (Red Cornfield) and the Monthly *Novyi Mir* (New World)." Poster (1925) depicting the project for the new *Izvestia* building.

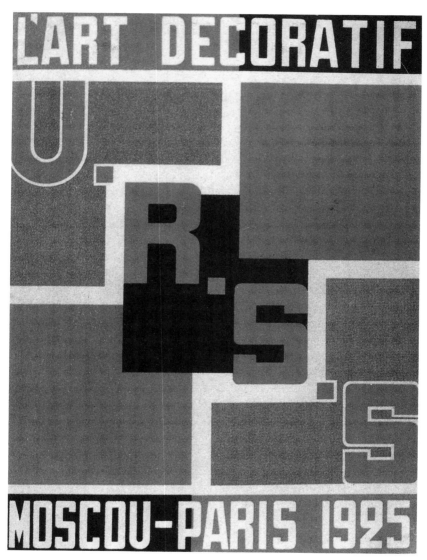

1.13. Aleksandr Rodchenko, front cover of the catalogue, *L'Art décoratif U.R.S.S. Moscou—Paris 1925,* for the Soviet section of the 1925 International Exhibition of Decorative Arts, Paris.

1.14. El Lissitzky,
front cover of
the journal *Veshch*
(The Object) (1922), which
El Lissitzky published
with Ilia Ehrenburg.

its break with the liberal publishing scene and boldly solicited an alternative constituency. "The *New Masses* does not compete," they declared, "with the *Mercury*, the *Nation*, the *New Republic* or any other magazine. It is unique. It takes a chance. It is the voice of the lowbrow, the failure, the rebel, the boy worker, the factory poet, the tenant farmer, the poorhouse philosopher, the men and women at the bottom."[40] Gold espoused the constructivist drive to deliver art to the heart of the forces of production, sending out a call the next month for worker correspondents. As editor, he invited "Strike stories, prison stories, work stories . . . The poetry of steel workers."[41]

Communal Forms and the JRC

The following year, in imitation of such Soviet cultural organizations as the Moscow-based Proletarian Artists and Writers League, the *New Masses* editorial staff founded a New York culture club of some fifty members, named after the Harvard alumnus and posthumous saint of the Soviet Revolution, John Reed. Gold's manifesto "A New Program for Writers" publicized the goals of the Club's literary wing. In it, Gold called for "a national corps of writers" not unlike the Soviet network of worker correspondents that he and Freeman witnessed in the mid-1920s. "Instead of having a board of contributing editors made up of those vague, rootless people known as writers," Gold declared, "we will have a staff of industrial correspondents."[42] Soon such cities as Chicago, Cleveland, Detroit, Philadelphia, and Seattle boasted affiliates with cadres of some fifty cultural activists each. Shortly before their liquidation in 1935, when proletcult aesthetics were officially scrapped in favor of the Popular Front drive against fascism, the clubs comprised thirty chapters with a national membership of over 1200.[43] Most were organized into subcommittees specializing in the fine arts, drama, film and photography, dance, and music. But the clubs also spliced traditional aesthetics with the politics of everyday life. They sponsored mass pageants, guerrilla theater, classical and jazz concerts, art and photography exhibitions, poetry readings, and lectures. The John Reed Clubs agitated in such marginal cultural registers on behalf of women, minority and ethnic groups, senior citizens, aliens, strikers, the unemployed, and the homeless.

What an American proletariat culture might have actually looked like can be gleaned from the variety of activities sponsored not only by the John Reed Clubs but also by such groups as the Workers International Relief organization and the Workers Cultural Federation. To peruse the monthly Workers' Art columns in *New Masses* and the numerous JRC journals of the '30s (such as Detroit's *The New Force,* Grand Rapids' *The Cauldron,* Indianapolis' *Midland Left,* Hollywood's *The Partisan,* Chicago's *Left Front,* New York's *Partisan Review,* and Philadelphia's *Red Pen*) is to be struck by the uncanny hybrid of revolutionary agit-prop and middle-brow Americana that made up these enclaves of depression era leftist culture. One reads here, for example, of the Red Dancers' call for male partners to join in their mass pageant *The Belt Goes Red* for the Lenin Memorial Meeting at Madison Square Garden. Cosmopolitan visuals by Louis Lozowick advertised fund raisers like the annual *New Masses* Ball, inviting one and all to "Come to the Big Red Carnival" for hot jazz, dancing, and costume contests (figure 1.20). Chapter fund drives mirrored those of their all-American counterparts such as the Shriners, Elks, or Lions. Detroit teenagers, for example, sold *New Masses* subscriptions to support the Michigan district's Hunger Strike and march on the capital. In Philadelphia, boosters aided the Unemployed Councils' march on the Lloyd Committee of city charity. Contradicting the low-brow stereotypes that critics such as Irving Howe have projected onto these groups, the midwestern John Reed Club concert ensembles included members of the Cleveland Symphony Orchestra. Nevertheless, it is true that most of the clubs' cultural activities were agitational, such as those of the Red Pioneer Children's Orchestra of Chicago that performed at labor picnics and demonstrations on the campuses of the University of Chicago, Northwestern, and Loyola. Now long forgotten, a Detroit pageant *Undesirables* (1931)—one of the countless depression era agit-spectacles—comprised a cast of 600 held at the Olympia Auditorium demonstration against the Cheeney Alien Registration bill. That same year, the Dramatic Section of the Workers Cultural Federation (Dramsec) staged an agitprop production during a picnic of the Trade Union Unity League in Pleasant Bay Park, organized, directed, and written collaboratelly by the Workers Laboratory Theatre, the Prolet-Buehne (German) and Artef (Yiddish) groups, members of the International Workers Order, Hungarian Workers Dramatic Club, Young Communist League, International Labor Defense and Women's Councils. Part of a left tradition that reached back to the I.W.W. Paterson Strike Pageant of 1913 (figure 1.21), Dramsec organized agitational guerrilla theater groups among striking Pennsylvania coal strikers, Paterson silk workers, and their children.

Among America's mixed bag of proletarian subcultures, the most prolific was the New York charter of the John Reed Club. Its artists' wing pursued such collaborative works as the spectacular painting "American

NEW MASSES BALL

Come to the Big Red Carnival
━━Chunks of Whirling Fun!
Come and Sing with Us Folks
━━and Dance with us till 3 A. M.
Come Expecting a Lot, Because
━━You'll Get a Lot!

There'll be a Jazz Band
━━Hot and Blue!
There'll be Costumes,
━━Crazy and Gay!
You'll be There, We'll be There
━━and how We'll Dance!

DEC. 7 FRI.
WEBSTER HALL
119 EAST 11th STREET, NEW YORK

TICKETS ON SALE AT *New Masses Office*,
39 Union Square (Phone Reservations accepted until the last minute—Algonquin
4445); *Rand School*, 7 East 15th St.;
Workers Book Shop, 28 Union Sq.; *New
Playwrights Theatre*, 133 W. 14th St.

Buy Your Tickets in
━━Advance for $1.50!
Buy Your Tickets or
━━You'll Pay $3.00 at Door!
In either Case You'll
━━Get Your Money's Worth!

1.20. Louis Lozowick, ad for the *New Masses* Ball
(December 1928).

Today'' entered as a group project in the 1932 Annual Exhibition of Independent Artists, Grand Central Palace. Moreover, under the auspices of its artists' committee, Walter Quirt—who would go on to establish his reputation as a noted social-surrealist muralist for the WPA and later an art professor at the University of Minnesota—administered a program to supply brochures and color posters to labor organizations and other revolutionary groups. In addition to sponsoring symposia on modern and revolutionary art that featured speakers such as Louis Lozowick, the New York chapter curated exhibitions of revolutionary drawings, paintings, photography, and lithographs that toured the country. In exporting these

1.21. Robert Edmond Jones, poster for the
Paterson Strike Pageant (1913).

local and domestic initiatives, the New York members invited their counterparts in Germany to submit material as part of an international art competition for a traveling exhibition in New York and the USSR. They called for artworks which would reflect the Comintern's Third Period agenda lodged against lynchings, unemployment, national oppression, international imperialism, and fascism.

In league with the International Union of Revolutionary Writers, the writers' wing of the New York JRC called for contributions of proletarian fiction, poetry, and drama for translation and publication in Germany and the Soviet Union. In addition, the club served as a public forum for literary exchange through hosting local debates and panel discussions with the New Masses Club. The New York JRC also sponsored global conferences like the convention of international revolutionary writers at the Workers School that included 61 delegates from the Yiddish proletarian writers (Proletpen), the Hungarian Proletarian Writers and Workers Correspondents, and Workers Cultural Federation. New York chapter members also worked closely with allied organizations such as the Film and Photo League of the Workers International Relief (WIR), distributing revolutionary films of Sovkino and the German WIR (Prometheus and Weltfilm)—including *10 Days that Shook the World, Cannons or Tractors, Storm Over Asia, Old and New,* and *Volga to Gastonia.* Similarly, the New York JRC and WIR held exhibits, organized protests against Hollywood's ethnic and racial stereotyping, and offered classes in cinematography, photography, and film criticism.

The group solidarity afforded by these cultural enclaves fostered the conviction that the creative act was never wholly personal but mediated by the kind of communal experience encountered daily through the JRC programs, on the editorial boards of little magazines, in classes and social events held at the Workers' School and the party headquarters on Union Square, and, more prosaically, in the period's street demonstrations, breadlines, and Hoovervilles. The collective agency that these group settings promoted drew inspiration from the avant-garde generation of World War One. Beginning with such precursors as Randolph Bourne and the other young radicals of his generation who worked on little magazines like *The Masses,* America's historical avant-gardes regarded groups, rather than individuals, as the productive sources of literary expression. "From this standpoint," wrote Bourne in his farewell editorial in *The Seven Arts,* "we looked upon art as a sharing of life, a communism of experience and vision, a spiritual root of nationalism and internationalism."[44] That Bourne's communal credo seems so radically distanced from our present aesthetic milieu stems, in part, from the academic formation of literary modernism.

The reigning narratives of the postwar academy, especially those of New Criticism, repressed such collaborative impulses in an attempt to move American culture into formal registers where intrinsic aesthetic discipline, not social change, would shape modern poetics. Canonical studies of the early twentieth century—such as, say, Hugh Kenner's *The Pound Era* (1971)—typically stressed the high modernist consensus that emerged from the aesthetics of literary imagism and vorticism in the work of Crane, Eliot, H. D., Moore, Pound, Stevens, and Williams. Similarly, even later, cross-disciplinary studies such as Sanford Schwartz's *The Matrix of Modernism* (1985), were often disabled by this same formalist impasse.[45] By the end of the 1980s, the issues at stake in analyzing the politics of modern poetry were cogently theorized in Cary Nelson's *Repression and Recovery: Modern American Poetry and the Politics of Cultural Memory* (1989). But beyond these accounts, we still lack a sustained reading of the ways in which modernist poetics both overtly intervened in the wider sociopolitical field of the interbellum decades and anticipated the contemporary critique of postmodernity. A thoroughgoing cultural, rather than literary, history of this period would consider how art and literature participated in, rather than transcended, the worldly, social transactions of the age.

Modern writers, in fact, often found themselves coming together to address pressing political issues, where they in turn discovered common sources of revolutionary aesthetics. Figures such as Ralph Cheney, Jack Conroy, H. H. Lewis, Norman Macleod, and Lucia Trent, for example, were drawn into group solidarity not just at the level of a formalist aesthetic consensus but, equally important, through the political turmoil thrown up by the 1920–27 Sacco and Vanzetti trial and execution. In protesting this domestic trauma, they edited the 1928 anthology *American Arraigned!* Not insignificantly, this effort further led to the annual *Unrest* anthologies of 1929–31 and the founding of such little magazines as *The Rebel Poet* (1931) and *Contempo* (1932). Collaborative publishing, the Rebel Poets proclaimed in their 1931 "Manifesto," "broke the way for the international recognition of our fellowship as the militant voice of class-conscious poets, poetry lovers, and writers everywhere."[46] These politicized efforts also shaped such alternative anthologies as *An Anthology of Revolutionary Poetry* (1929), *Poems of Justice* (1929), *The Red Harvest* (1930), *We Gather Strength* (1933), *Banners of Brotherhood* (1933), and *Proletarian Literature in the United States* (1935), among others.

Group collections did not so much serve to promote poets as individual talents for the conglomerate and academic book markets, as most anthologies do today. Instead, they were deployed as counterstatements to what Lucia Trent and Ralph Cheney described as the poetic "star system." "Cooperative anthologies," they wrote, "are the poets' logical answer to the public's neglect to buy other anthologies. They are the best antidote to the star system. There should be more co-operation among poets, not less."[47] Isidor Schneider made essentially the same point about activist publishing in his *New Republic* review of *We Gather Strength,* presenting Sol Funaroff, Joseph Kalar, Edwin Rolfe, and Herman Spector as "four young writers who are building their careers as poets outside the capitalist publishing apparatus. . . . They are not only creating a revolutionary poetry but gathering together what will probably be the most responsible and satisfying audience poetry can hope for in our time."[48] Not incidentally, this interbellum critique of poetry's institutional settings was also tied—in the writing of Cheney, Gold, Trent, and Schneider—to a transpersonal theory of poetry, one that differed from the impersonal poetics of high modernism.

Eliot, Pound, and Stevens, of course, were also engaged in such collective movements as literary imagism and vorticism. And these movements were also influenced by contemporaneous advances in the visual arts and promoted through the same collaborative scene of little magazines shaping the work of their "leftist" counterparts. Yet the high modernists limited theories of literary production to, in Eliot's and Pound's case, the individual talent's engagement with an idealized canon, and in Stevens' the poet's "noble" rage to order the age's forces of phenomenological and sociocultural violence. In their subsequent reception, the struggle over which of these literary "fathers" should be assigned the paternity rights to the modern era is a telling symptom of such *auteurism*.[49]

In the postwar epoch, the persistence of the single author as the ground for contemporary poetry's institutional formation is patent both in the "subjective" and confessional schools. More broadly, such possessive individualism underwrites the hierarchy of literary careerism that presides over formalist verse and the antiacademic "poetry of revolt." But in the prewar decades things were otherwise. Repudiating the private sensibility of the lyric self, Isidor Schneider held, for example, that "poetry is, by its nature, a social art. . . . It was only under capitalism," he said, "that poetry attempting to adapt itself, began to attempt individualistic forms, especially the lyric."[50] Similarly, Lucia Trent and Ralph Cheney assumed that "poetry is older than prose, just as communal consciousness is older than any refinement of individual psychology. . . . In other words, the chorus is older than the lyric."[51]

Choral forms, what Mike Gold welcomed in *New Masses* as "mass recitation" poems, frequently staged protests against such major political scandals as the Sacco and Vanzetti execution and Scottsboro trial. "Mass recitation," Gold theorized, "is group art; any outcropping of individualism would ruin it in production."[52] In publishing his "Scottsboro Boys Chant" in *The Rebel Poet,* Jack Haynes explained that "mass chants," while they ought to eschew free verse, should also avoid lapsing into sheer doggerel. Hayes' chant alternates choral refrains with topical allusions to labor struggles so as to foment unrest. The textual power of these prole-tarian verses stems from the impassioned cadences of the protest march rap, cut and mixed with picket line chants:

> Innocent men, innocent men
> They shall not burn them down there in the pen
> White men, red men, yellow men, black
> Workers sweat and die, bosses get the jack
> In Harlan, Kentucky or Imperial Valley
> Where conditions are bad in this land of the free
> Framed workers burn in a chair, or drop hard to hang
> Scottsboro, Scottsboro, Scottsboro boys.
> . . . . .
> Innocent men, innocent men
> They shall not burn them down there in the pen
> Protest, protest, not a minute too soon
> For no crime at all, they shall not burn next June
> Bourgeois plot wars to bring back good times
> Death stares us in the face in our soup lines
> Down with the frameups, down with war
> Capitalist bosses, you have gone too far.
> Scottsboro, Scottsboro, Scottsboro boys.[53]

Released from any monolithic, working-class identity, the more demo-cratic rhetoric of Haynes' chant crosses racial, regional, as well as class differences. A similar appeal to cultural diversity marks the poetic nexus of class, race, and gender representations in "A Negro Mother to Her Child":

> Quit yo' wailin' honey bo'
> 'Taint no use to cry
> Rubbernipple, mammy's breast
> Both am gone bone dry.
> Daddy is a bolshevik
> Locked up in de pen
> Didn' rob nor didn' steal
> Led de workin' men.
> What's de use mah tellin' you
> Silly li'l lamb
> Gon'ter git it straight some day
> When you is a man.
> Wisht ah had a sea o' milk

Mek you strong an' soun'
Daddy's waitin' til you come
Brek dat prison down.[54]

During the Roaring Twenties, James Weldon Johnson and Countée Cullen had questioned the political value of black vernacular expression, tied as it was to the denigrating stereotypes of the minstrel tradition. Nevertheless, "A Negro Mother" productively grafts the African-American folk idiom to international class revolution. Not unlike the progressive recovery of black vernacular in the poetics of, say, Sterling Brown, this dialect verse, however, did not appear in any of the standard black press organs of the day such as *Crisis* or *Opportunity*. As Cary Nelson points out in *Repression and Recovery*, it was originally published in *The Daily Worker* (1930) and later featured on the August 1932 cover of the internationalist journal *The Rebel Poet* beside Olga Monus' "Southern Silhouette," an arresting block print of a black lynching. Cultural difference is thus not only inscribed in the verbal and thematic elements of the work but also marks its publication history.

But what may be even more unsettling for many of us today, the poem was actually penned by V. J. Jerome, a white writer who was the Communist Party's "commissar of culture" throughout the depression years. It is true that in an earlier moment of the postwar era—for writers, say, of the 1960s' Black Aesthetic movement—such interracial crossings might have been rebuffed and indicted for their stereotyping and paternalism. Indeed, it is not hard to imagine these charges being leveled against Jerome by essentialist feminism of that period. It would be a mistake to discount essentialist groups shaped by particular genealogies of oppression—such as those, say, of radical feminist circles, black cultural nationalism, or the Native American Indian Movement (AIM). Nevertheless, we must also credit the recent theoretical advance, in Werner Sollors' words, "beyond ethnicity."[55] Instead of regarding the languages of cultural difference as belonging solely to lines of racial, ethnic, or biological descent, a postmodern take on these versions of essentialism would rearticulate them to a democratic plurality of subject positions and discursive sites, where none would reduce subjectivity to a fixed identity.

In this vein, the historical avant-gardes anticipate our own tentative negotiations with verbal forms that cut across the cultural boundaries dividing us by race, class, and gender. Significantly, these communal forms— linked as they were to such mass movements for social change—appealed to a diversified audience that was nevertheless joined in what, for us in the post-Reagan/Bush years, recedes as a lost horizon of alliance politics. We need to resist the familiar critical tendency that simply dismisses proletarian poetry *tout court* as a dogmatic expression of party doctrine—an assumption seldom tested through sustained close readings of the period's actual verse. A more productive approach to this material would consider how depression-era poetry actually functioned as a potent catalyst for changing views of self and society in the rhetoric of criticism, radical journalism, and other, nonliterary texts.

Reviewing Edwin Rolfe's 1936 Dynamo Press volume *To My Contemporaries* for *New Masses,* Joseph Freeman found strong poems that prompted his theoretical claims for the transpersonal foundations of poetic form. Freeman's critical assertion that the "individualist concept of the artist as a free agent . . . is doomed to disappear with the passing of individualist civilization"[56] followed from Rolfe's "Credo" that:

> To welcome multitudes—the miracle of deeds
> performed in unison—the mind
> must renounce the fiction of the self
> and its vainglory. It must pierce
> the dreamplate of its solitude, the fallacy
> of its omnipotence, the fairytale
> aprilfools recurring every day
> in speeches of professors and politicians.
> It must learn
> the wisdom and strength and the togetherness
> of bodies phalanxed in a common cause,
> of fists tight-clenched around a crimson banner
> flying in the wind above a final, fierce
> life-and-death fight against a common foe.[57]

Most readers today will no doubt find these lines troubling in the way they lend themselves to the kind of vulgar Marxism that marks Freeman's review. His faith in the imminent "passing of individualist civilization" reflects the historical assumptions of such Second International theorists as Karl Kautsky and George Plekhanov. Reducing the material forces of ideology to mere expressions of underlying economic infrastructures, this brand of Marxism posited "inexorable laws" of historical determination that would necessarily culminate in the triumph of proletarian revolution. Thus preparing for the inevitable, this orthodoxy espoused a unified and static working class identity. Such a strategy, of course, proved reactionary as it both ignored cultural difference and impeded political intervention in what was viewed as the natural unfolding of certain economic truths.

But moving beyond the political impasse of Communist orthodoxy, the role Rolfe assigns to consciousness in "Credo" is less mimetic than deconstructive. On the one hand, to inaugurate revolutionary modes of collective public life, the "mind" must aggressively "pierce / the dreamplate of its solitude"—the Romantic poetics of sincerity that would later dominate postwar confessional verse.[58] Yet on the other hand, this active, theoretical agency simultaneously deflates "the fallacy / of its omnipotence": what Jean Francois Lyotard would later critique from the vantage point of postmodernity as the tyranny of Enlightenment master narratives, including those that, following orthodox Marxism, would idealize the proletariat as the universal subject of history.[59] The poem's "credo" cuts both ways: at once asserting and placing *sous rature* the poet's faith in political commitment. The poem does express the period's Popular Front solidarity against the peril of fascism. Yet it also passionately affirms the poet's power to critique the ideological "dreamplate" of political discourse. Admittedly, the radically utopian and communal impulses inscribed here, and that everywhere mark proletarian poetics, make alien and unsettling claims on us at first. Few of us who read recent American verse will feel entirely comfortable with following Rolfe in simply giving up the "fiction of the self." But this very resistance to embracing "the togetherness / of bodies phalanxed in a common cause" points symptomatically to the personal bias of postwar confessionalism whose residual power still dominates poetry's contemporary milieu. Subjective autonomy and lyric personalism, however valorized in the postwar era, for Rolfe's generation seemed an illusory, and dangerous, luxury. Disengaged from political struggle, it could have actually jeopardized the Free World's resistance to the onslaught of Nazism. Reading the poem against its own historical moment, we may begin to see how our own contemporary allegiance to possessive individualism is not so much a "natural" as it is a historically contingent credo.

What a closer attention to the social contexts both of this body of literature and its reception serves to demonstrate, then, is that our own assessment of a work's literary significance does not necessarily rest on universal foundations of aesthetic judgment. On the contrary, as we move back and forth between the pre- and postwar periods, such sharp disagreements concerning poetry's formal resources and pragmatic functions, clearly show that whatever standards of taste and distinction we import into our readings of poetry are subject necessarily to certain contingencies of value.[60] The shock of radical difference that we confront in proletcult verse—a difference that violates nearly everything we have been disciplined to expect from poetry—highlights how our personal reading habits are themselves not just "normative" but always already positioned in relation to particular critical genealogies—always already mediated, that is, by our own immersion in history.

2. War of Position and the Old Left

Subculture in the Depression Era

However committed to social change in the United States, the Old Left effort to transplant Soviet-style proletcult onto American soil proved a gross miscalculation. To begin with, any chance of forging a broad coalition of fellow travelers and progressive intellectuals was unlikely given the dogma of capital's so-called Third Period, declared at the Comintern's 1928 Sixth World Congress. There, Bukharin in a report entitled "The International Situation and the Tasks of the Comintern," divided postrevolutionary history into three stages. The initial period, lasting from 1917 through the 1923 defeat of Germany, he characterized as an "acute revolutionary crisis." The next five years showed a "partial stabilization of capitalism." Finally, the current (third) period was marked by capital's temporary spread but would culminate in a "great collapse" and "final catastrophe."[1] Exploiting his own version of the Third Period theory, Stalin stepped up Soviet collectivization of industry and agriculture, while he isolated Bukharin, Trotsky, and social democracy in general.

In the mid-1920s Stalin already had employed his doctrine of "socialism in one country" to anathematize Trotsky, who was committed to "permanent revolution" worldwide. In carrying out a relentless campaign for power, Stalin had pressured Trotsky to resign as Commissar of War in 1925. In the next four years, Stalin exiled Trotsky from the Politburo (1926), the Communist Party (1927), and the Soviet Union (1929). In keeping with his global political philosophy, Trotsky advocated internationalist styles of experimental modernism, which he had valorized over proletcult in *Literature and Revolution* (1923). Consequently, his expulsion from Russia cleared the way for more parochial and nationalist expressions of what Stalin would later dub in 1932 as "socialist realism."[2]

Comintern ideologues, meanwhile, believing in the imminent decline and breakup of capitalism worldwide, redoubled the push for class struggle so as to fragment the bourgeois hegemony and thereby hasten the so-called dictatorship of the proletariat. At the same time, the Third Period strategy called for a "United Front From Below" with alliances to the African-American community, socialist unions, and labor parties at the rank-and-file level.[3] In line with this new doctrine, the 1930 Kharkov Second World Plenum of the International Bureau of Revolutionary Literature (IBRL), the governing organ of the International Union of Revolutionary Writers (IURW), charged American Delegates from *New Masses* and the New York John Reed Club—Fred Ellis, Michael Gold, William Gropper, Joshua Kunitz, A. B. Magil, and Harry Potamkin—with the task of making *New Masses* "the cultural organ of the class-conscious workers and revolutionary intellectuals in the U.S. country."[4] The following year, the IURW further prodded the editorial board of *New Masses* toward the Third Period position in its "Resolution on the Work of New Masses for 1931." In it, the IURW faulted the magazine with having failed to mount a forceful defense of the Soviet Union, Latin America, and African-Americans at home. More troubling, the journal had sacrificed revolutionary content for "[a]esthetic innovations and experiments in form together with a fetishistic approach to capitalist technique and its underestimation of the consciousness and militancy of the revolutionary movement." Finally, the board had failed to create "a wide worker-correspondents movement."[5] The Third Period strategy of stepping up the ideological spread of proletcult, however insistent, only served to isolate the already marginal factions of working-class artists and writers in the United States.

Soviet pressure during the early 1930s simply drove America's own nativist left away from the mainstream into the obscure margins of a proletarian *subculture*. The alternative life styles and group solidarity fostered within working-class culture clubs like the John Reed network, the Workers International Relief (W.I.R.), Workers Cultural Federation, and other groups rested on a contradictory semiotics that conveyed both identity *and* difference. Drawing from the native traditions of dissent in *The Masses, The Liberator, The Daily Worker,* and other radical journals, America's proletarian subculture signaled a communicative *difference* from the dominant ideological signs of American commodity culture. This differential group outlook was signified through two discursive modes. The first derived from collective rituals of cultural *transgression* that served to estrange the dominant, representational norms "naturalizing" everyday life. Proletcult art, poetry, theater, posters, and cartoons defamiliarized America's valorized stereotypes, employing satire, parody, and black humor to unmask such conventional values as capitalist philanthropy, entrepreneurship, upward mobility, and affluence.

Shaped as it was by the post-revolutionary semiotics of the Russian avant-gardes, American proletcult expressed in what were transgressive, unspeakable, or tabooed icons under capitalism—in, say, a Red Banner or a raised fist, in the stylized presentation of hammers, sickles, wrenches, and all manner of working-class tools and factory gear—a bricolaged, subcultural *homology.*[6] Like the later, postwar youth subcultures analyzed by the Birmingham Center for Contemporary Cultural Studies, proletarian clubs of the Great Depression era served to cement members into a unified, group identity through their distinctive emblems; codes of dress, jargon, and mannerisms; social protocols, rituals, and rites of passage.[7] In the absence of the deep structural changes to the reign of capital predicted by Third Period orthodoxy, proletcult expressed a utopian, not material, resolution to the plight of labor in depression era America. As a form of *symbolic* resistance, proletarian culture was doomed to fail in the United States for at least two reasons. Not only did American proletcult lack the kind of institutional base that its Soviet counterpart enjoyed, but its imported images, styles, and subcultural signs cut against the vernacular grain of nativist popular culture so that it often simply repulsed noninitiates.

One such moment is memorably dramatized in Richard Wright's well-known account of his stint in the Chicago John Reed Club. It was not just Communist economic theory, its view of trade unionism, or even the intrigue of local party politics that claimed Wright's allegiance. What arrested him was socialism's seductive semiotics—its polemical discourse coupled with a striking visual iconography—that he gleaned from the copies of JRC journals such as *Anvil, Left Front, Midland Left, The New Force, Partisan Review,* and *Red Pen,* given to him by fellow club members. "The revolutionary words leaped from the printed page," he recalled, "and struck me with tremendous force. . . . It seemed to me that here at last, in the realm of revolutionary expression, Negro experience could find a home, a functioning value and role."[8]

But the same revolutionary signs and symbols that enchanted him, were anathema to the unconverted—to (in Wright's account of the following, heated encounter) the poet's mother:

She hobbled to the bed on her crippled legs and picked up a copy of the *Masses* that carried a lurid May Day cartoon. She adjusted her glasses and peered at it for a long time.

"My God in heaven," she breathed in horror.

"What's the matter, Mama?"

"What is this?" she asked, extending the magazine to me, pointing to the cover. "What's wrong with that man?"

With my mother standing at my side, lending me her eyes, I stared at a cartoon drawn by a Communist artist; it was the figure of a worker clad in ragged overalls and holding aloft a red banner. The man's eyes bulged; his mouth gaped as wide as his face; his teeth showed; the muscles of his neck were like ropes. Following the man was a horde of nondescript men, women, and children, waving clubs, stones and pitchforks.

"What are those people going to do?" my mother asked.

"I don't know," I hedged.

"Are these Communist magazines?"

"Yes."

"And do they want people to act like this?"

"Well—" I hesitated. My mother's face showed disgust and moral loathing. She was a gentle woman. Her ideal was Christ upon the cross. How could I tell her that the Communist party wanted her to march in the streets, chanting, singing?

"What do Communists think people are?" she asked.

"They don't quite mean what you see there," I said, fumbling with my words.

"Then what do they mean?"

"This is symbolic," I said.

"Then why don't they speak out what they mean?"

"Maybe they don't know how."

"Then why do they print this stuff?"

"They don't quite know how to appeal to people yet," I admitted, wondering whom I could convince of this if I could not convince my mother.

"That picture's enough to drive a body crazy," she said, dropping the magazine, turning to leave, then pausing at the door. "You're not getting mixed up with those people?"

"I'm just reading, Mama," I dodged. (GF, 119–20)

In this dramatic clash of readings, Wright's defensive hedging and dodging of his mother's probing, albeit plainspoken, reaction to party ideology is a telling symptom of the Old Left's failure to appeal to the everyday people it claimed to champion. Although he was aggressively lobbied by a Comintern that was poorly represented in the African-American community, Wright could not deal with the daily paranoia of party investigations and Kafkaesque trials that splintered the Chicago John Reed Club. Indeed, it would not be long before Wright's own psychic negotiation of his double role as black poet and party ideologue would unravel, leading to his own denunciation and expulsion.

Part of the Comintern's problem in recruiting African-Americans like Wright lay in its denial of the long-standing vernacular traditions native to the black community. Repudiating the funky heritage of urban ghetto life—what Ishmael Reed, following James Weldon Johnson, would later celebrate in *Mumbo Jumbo* as the text of Jes' Grew[9]—the party was decidedly inept in finessing the pitfalls of proletcult dogmatism. Even in such progressive, black strongholds as Harlem, fewer than five percent of even the committed Communist African-Americans regularly attended party-sponsored rallies, marches, fraternal organizations, culture clubs, Communist summer camps and resorts—this in a region where the party had forged durable links to some 2,000 black Communists in its defense of the Scottsboro Boys (despite its clash with the NAACP) and through other Popular Front activities such as the Workers Alliance, and party-affiliated tenants' organizations.[10] "The persistence of [black] membership turnover, even in periods without major controversy," according to Mark Naison, "suggests that obstacles to the party's success were deep-rooted and structural" (CH, 283).[11] Thus, Wright's quick conversion to, and rapid exile from, the Chicago branch of the CPUSA was not a unique but representative disaffection. In fact, the John Reed Clubs, as Wright described them, were torn by racial tensions. The kind of ideological battles among party members and fellow-travelers that he witnessed on a daily basis eroded any chance of group consensus among their various other constituencies divided as they were along ethnic, race, gender, and class lines.

It is true that the CPUSA productively exposed denigrating stereotypes of blacks and aggressively championed racial justice. But even though it hosted any number of African-American cultural events, the party also fundamentally misread the distinctive, vernacular signs of black expression in the United States.[12] This paradox marks a good deal of Old Left representations of black Americans but is especially patent in a cartoon that William Siegel published in the May 1930 issue of *New Masses* (figure 2.1). As the caption explains, Siegel offers two contradictory versions of the African-American community: "the white bourgeois version of the Negro" vs. "as the white worker knows him." However well intended, Siegel's visual rendering of these representational differences actually served to perpetuate both racist and classist assumptions about blacks. Siegel's leftist reduction of the black aesthetic, nevertheless, appealed to the CP leadership as evidenced, two months later, in his sanitized portrait of "Negro Workers" that was showcased on the cover of the July 1930 *New Masses*.

In both plates of the May issue cartoon the power of defining the cultural roles available to blacks belongs to a foregrounded pair of white viewers. Thus the shift in class representation is, nonetheless, framed by a distanced (hence privileged) Caucasian gaze—one that interprets, and thereby fixes, African-American identity. The ideological limits of Siegel's

2.1. William Siegel, "The White Bourgeois Version of the Negro—as the White Worker Knows Him," *New Masses* (May 1930).

unconscious racial framing are plain to see in the second panel which, however much it liberates blacks from both rural and urban stereotypes, also expunges the distinctive, vernacular nuances of the slave songs, black sermon, African ritual performance, blues, and jazz culture that have historically empowered black Americans with their own distinctive interpretive community. While Siegel's cartoon reduces the political subtext of biblical slave songs to sheer caricature, James Weldon Johnson, as early as 1922, had clearly identified the biblical story of Moses and the Hebrew Exodus as a trope for liberation in African-American slave songs.

Five years later, in *God's Trombones* (1927), Johnson would theorize the black preacher as a source of consolation and political solidarity for displaced slaves in the antebellum South. "It was through him," Johnson wrote, "that the people of diverse languages and customs who were brought here from diverse parts of Africa and thrown into slavery were given their first sense of unity and solidarity."[13] Johnson's focus on antebellum sermon as a discourse of black "unity and solidarity" was visually underscored by Aaron Douglas' illustrations. These original images transcoded Biblical typology to a stylized African-American iconography of exodus from the chains of Southern bondage. The recovery of black sermon in Johnson's "Let My People Go" presented less a theological than a materialist reading of Israel's oppressed class role, "working without money and without price":

> Four hundred years
> They'd held them down in Egypt land.
> Held them under the driver's lash,
> Working without money and without price.
> And it might have been Pharaoh's wife that said:
> "Pharaoh—look what you've done.
> You let those Hebrew Children go,
> And who's going to serve us now?
> Who's going to make our bricks and mortar?
> Who's going to plant and plow our corn?
> Who's going to get up in the chill of the morning?
> And who's going to work in the blazing sun?
> Pharaoh, tell me that!" (God's Trombones, 50)

In contrast to this liberatory narrative, Siegel reads the Hebrew exodus as a symptom of religious false consciousness. He drains this folk tradition of any political effectivity, linking it instead to the racist stereotypes of the black minstrel tradition: the surreal world of Jim Crow, Zeb Coon, Amos an' Andy, plantation medleys and "August hams."

2.2. Aaron Douglas, study for *Aspects of Negro Life: An Idyll of the Deep South* (1934).

Even a decade later, Lawrence Gellert would similarly lambaste the black Southern preacher in *New Masses* as "a pompous, fat-headed, blow-hard parasite, prating meaningless platitudes about 'de Lawd an' his By an' By Kingdom.' But for himself on earth in the meanwhile he reserves the best house in the community."[14] Not only does Siegel misunderstand the social text of black sermon, but his cavalier parody of African worship and its ritual artifacts fails to grasp the subcultural resources latent in the ritual mask. Henry Louis Gates, Jr., for example, reads the figure of the African mask as a trope that mediates white and black cultural boundaries: "the verbal sign of the mask of blackness that demarcates the boundary between the white linguistic realm and the black, two domains that exist side by side in homonymic relation signified by the very concept of Signification."[15] Such a double strategy can also be seen at work in Douglas' visual textuality which imports vernacular signs of African ancestry into an American context (figure 2.2). To its credit, *New Masses* productively laid bare the violence of depression era lynchings and represented blacks as responsible and constructive workers. Nevertheless, as Siegel's work shows, it failed to credit African-Americans either with their own nativist traditions or a capacity to assume vanguardist roles in forging a revisionary socialist culture.

Harlem Partisans

Siegel's cartoon of black America, read as a cultural rather than an aesthetic document, marks a key moment of party repression—one that aimed to reverse what the Harvard Rhode Scholar and cultural scion of the New Negro movement, Alain Leroy Locke had described in "1928: A Retrospective Review," as the peak in the "flood tide of the present Negrophile movement."[16] Locke was referring, of course, to the Roaring Twenties' so-called renaissance in African-American cultural expression celebrated in the salons, cabarets, and lecture halls of Harlem, Durham, Washington, D.C., Atlanta, Hampton, Nashville, and Lincoln. The white urban dilettantes in Siegel's first panel caricature a somewhat decadent, bourgeois fascination with the kind of black subculture depicted, say, in Winold Reiss' exotic fantasies on African themes (figure 2.3) or Miguel Covarrubias' depictions of Harlem cabaret life (figures 2.4–2.6). A more

2.3. Winold Reiss, "African Phantasy Awakening," *The New Negro* (1925).

2.4. Miguel Covarrubias, "Orchestra" (1927).

stylized inmixing of primitive African and flapper motifs marked Bruce Nugent's interracial images of the urban mulatto (figures 2.7 and 2.8). Celebrating this popular icon of the twenties (figure 2.9), Nugent recodes what was a conflicted figure of racial "passing" and black "double-consciousness" into a more subversive, cosmopolitan sign.

Such subcultural representations were popularized for mainstream readerships in Carl Van Vechten's *Nigger Heaven* (1926) and Claude McKay's *Home to Harlem* (1928). In the mid-1920s, Van Vechten, *the* major white promoter of the Harlem Renaissance had capitalized on the uptown exoticism of black cabaret life in a best seller that eventually sold over 100,000 copies. Dubbed the first "Negrotarian" by Zora Neale Hurston, Van Vechten had been introduced to the Harlem intelligentsia by the NAACP officer Walter White. In time, he became something of a middle-man in marketing African-American literature to the white literary establishment. Van Vechten contributed to the surge of interest in black culture at the mid-decade by publishing over a dozen articles and reviews of jazz and blues artists, black theater, and African-American literature in such journals as *Vanity Fair, Theatre Magazine* and *The Crisis*. But he also operated behind the scenes as a broker of black literature, promoting and reprinting James Weldon Johnson's *Autobiography of an Ex-Coloured Man* (1926) and securing publication for Langston Hughes' first two volumes of verse *The Weary Blues* (1926) and *Fine Clothes to a Jew* (1927) with Alfred A. Knopf.[17]

The New York salon parties that Carl and Fania Van Vechten hosted at their West Side apartment offered a setting where white and black, high and low, elite and popular talents could come together. Here the likes of George Gershwin could rub shoulders with, say, Bessie Smith at integrated soirées that on any given night might host such notables as Tallulah Bank-

2.5. Miguel Covarrubias, ''Flapper'' (1927).

2.6. Miguel Covarrubias, "Couple
Dancing" (1927).

head, Paul Robeson, Theodore Dreiser, James Weldon Johnson, Adele
Astaire, Langston Hughes, Ethel Waters, F. Scott Fitzgerald, Countée Cullen, Elinor Wylie, Rudolph Valentino, Zora Neale Hurston, Salvadore Dali,
H. L. Mencken, Walter White, Louis Untermeyer, and Helena Rubenstein,
among countless others.[18] It was this crossover audience that Alfred A.
Knopf hoped to solicit in promoting *Nigger Heaven* in the leading black
and white journals of its moment. Knopf advertised the book, with accompanying visual designs by Aaron Douglas, in such venues as *The Ameri-*

can *Mercury* and the *New York Herald Tribune,* with the hook of offering Caucasian readers a "fascinating drama that takes place in the gallery of the vast theatre of New York—from which the white world below can be seen, but which it cannot see."[19] Drawing from the black slang term for a theatre balcony's "nigger heaven," Knopf's visual layout, originally planned to be run in white journals, solicits the same subliminal voyeurism that positions Siegel's Caucasian subjects as consumers and viewers of the African-American spectacle (figure 2.10).

As a white representation of Harlem subculture, *Nigger Heaven* remains pertinent to today's struggle over the body of black aesthetics, especially in

2.7. Bruce Nugent, "Drawing for Mulattoes—Number 2" (1927).

2.8. Bruce Nugent, "Drawing for Mulattoes—
Number 3" (1927).

OPPORTUNITY
JOURNAL OF NEGRO LIFE

The Vanishing Mulatto The Virgin Islands

Tulsa and the Business League   A Pushkin Poem

Contest Announcement

OCTOBER
1   9   2   5

15 CENTS
the copy

2.9. Bruce Nugent, cover illustration for
Opportunity (October 1925).

the drama of racial politics that marks the book's critical reception. Because
Van Vechten portrayed not just the black exotica of Harlem cabaret life,
but also the old-line "high yellow" intelligentsia of "Sugar Hill," Robert
Bone would credit him some three decades later with having "created a
sympathetic audience for the serious treatment of Negro subjects."[20] But
writing after the black aesthetic movement, David Lewis anathematized the
book in the 1980s. Lewis claimed that "[f]rom the point of view of racial
uplift, *Nigger Heaven* was a colossal fraud; . . . the depiction of the Talented Tenth in high baroque," he charged, "barely muffled the throb of
the tom-tom" (188). This postwar interpretive clash repeats the mixed
reception the novel met within the Harlem community of the 1920s.

2.10. Aaron Douglas, advertisement for *Nigger Heaven* (1926).

Purveying "one damned orgy after another," *Nigger Heaven* for W. E. B. Du Bois, pales in comparison with Langston Hughes' socially committed portrait of black jazz clubs: "Both Langston Hughes and Carl Van Vechten know Harlem cabarets; but it is Hughes who whispers, 'One said he heard the jazz band sob / When the little dawn was grey.' Van Vechten never heard a sob in a cabaret. All he hears is noise and brawling."[21] More indebted to Van Vechten than Du Bois, however, James Weldon Johnson defended the novel's titillating exoticism through the clever argument that it "set off in sharper relief the decent, cultured, intellectual life of Negro Harlem." Of greater historical interest, perhaps, is the racist tendencies that *Nigger Heaven* elicited in its Caucasian reception. While Johnson argued that *Nigger Heaven* was "the most revealing,

significant and powerful novel based exclusively on Negro life yet written,"
it did tend to perpetuate black stereotyping in the responses of notable
white critics that, however well intended, nevertheless projected primordial "blood and soil" roles on blacks.[22] In portraying black subculture as
a corrective to the waste land of modernism, such readings not infre-
quently reduced Harlem's cosmopolitan milieu to primitivist stereotyping.
Where color was at issue, as socially committed a critic as, say, Max Eastman could lapse into a sheer infantilization of racial difference, depicting
ahistorical and idealized black subjects as "earth's own children, whom
the brooding sun / Has warmed with color, / Who through life's drama
dance and run."[23]

Despite the often eroticized, utopian, and ahistorical reductions of the
Harlem Renaissance by a number of white readers, black authors seldom
lost sight of what was at stake politically in forging a bold new African-
American society.

Harlem's cultural revolution actually rested on earlier, materialist readings of the "new negro," theorized by among others, A. Philip Randolph
and Chandler Owen, the editors of *The Messenger,* a black socialist magazine that would operate from 1925 through 1928 as the house organ
of the Brotherhood of Sleeping Car Porters. From its inception in 1917,
The Messenger tended to subordinate racial autonomy to an integrated
working-class strategy (figure 2.11) and later, trade unionism (figure 2.12).
Nevertheless, signs of the "new negro" began to emerge in its numbers
of the late 1910s. In a September 1919 *Messenger* cartoon, the Soviet
example of militant revolution, coupled with the violent machinery of
modern futurism, encoded the "new negro" as a figure who parted company with the accommodating politics of the "old crowd" negro. Instead,
the "new crowd negro" actively resisted America's entrenched racism
through heroic acts of what Stokeley Carmichael and the Black Panther
Party would endorse in the mid-1960s as black power (figures 2.13–2.14).
The following year in an editorial entitled "The New Negro—What Is
He?" Randolph and Owen answered the question in terms of the "political, economic, and social" aims of black emancipation. Linking the "new
negro" cause to transnational and working-class movements for social
liberation as in, say, "the right of Russia to self determination" (74), *The
Messenger* editors articulated the "new negro" to "all other forward, progressive groups and movements—after the great world war. He is the
product of the same world-wide forces that have brought into being the
great liberal and radical movements that are now seizing the reins of political, economic, and social power in all of the civilized countries of the

2.11. W. B. Williams, "When They Get Together They'll Dump Us
Off!!" *The Messenger* (August 1919).

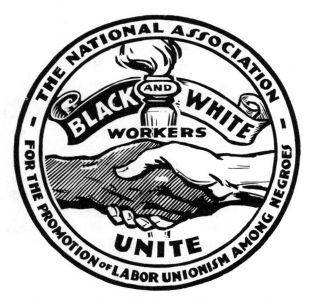

2.12. Trademark of the National Association for
the Promotion of Labor Unionism Among
Negroes, *The Messenger* (1922).

FOLLOWING THE ADVICE OF THE "OLD CROWD" NEGRO

2.13. "Following the Advice of the 'Old Crowd' Negro," *The Messenger* (September 1919).

world'' (74). Unlike the 1920s' highly stylized iconography of urban black sophistication, *The Messenger*'s depiction of black emancipation borrowed from the kind of socialist and proletarian imagery popularized in *The Masses* and *The Liberator* (figure 2.15).

In recoding and refining this class-based version of the "new negro," the socioaesthetic gambit of Harlem's black intelligensia of the 1920s looked forward to the post-Marxist take on ideology's material powers of representation to effect social change. "The status of the Negro in the United States," wrote James Weldon Johnson in his classic preface to *The Book of American Negro Poetry* (1922), "is more a question of national mental attitude toward the race than of actual conditions. And nothing will do more to change that mental attitude and raise his status than a demonstration of intellectual parity by the Negro through the production of literature and art."[24] Although the black exodus to Harlem and the subsequent flourishing of the "new negro" renaissance has been variously read as a flight from the material ravages of rural crop failures, Southern lynching, and the Ku Klux Klan, the proponents of "renaissan-

THE "NEW CROWD NEGRO" MAKING AMERICA SAFE FOR HIMSELF

2.14. "The 'New Crowd Negro' Making America Safe For
Himself," *The Messenger* (September 1919).

cism" in the 1920s sought to subordinate such social and economic
causes to the cultural forces of Harlem's emergent aesthetic ideology.

What were drawing the black masses to Manhattan's new "race capital," according to Alain Locke, was not so much the postwar surge in
Northern manufacturing, but was "to be explained primarily in terms of
a new vision of opportunity."[25] That ambitious "new vision" inscribes
much of the utopian iconography of the Renaissance as in, say, Charles
Cullen's illustrations of uplifted black figures that strain toward a hopeful
vista of dawning new prospects (figures 2.16 and 2.17). A similar optimism also marks Allan Randall Freelon's cover design for the inaugural
1927 issue of *Black Opals* (figure 2.18). This youthful illustration com-
plements the cultural agenda of the Philadelphia-based little magazine
which embodied, according to its editors Arthur Fauset and Gwendolyn
Bennett, "the embryonic outpourings of aspiring young Negroes."[26] Yet
what increased New York's African-American population over 250%
between 1910 and 1930 was not just Harlem's modernist semiosis but

attractive Northern wages that were more than twice as high as those in the South.[27]

Actually, most black workers were employed—reported Charles S. Johnson in his "Black Workers and the City" essay for the *Survey Graphic*—in "blind alley" jobs. According to Johnson's figures taken from the 1920 Census, some 24,528 African-American men made a living in New York as porters, waiters, chauffeurs, elevator operators, janitors, and so on, but only 56 blacks were apprenticed to skilled labor. Similarly

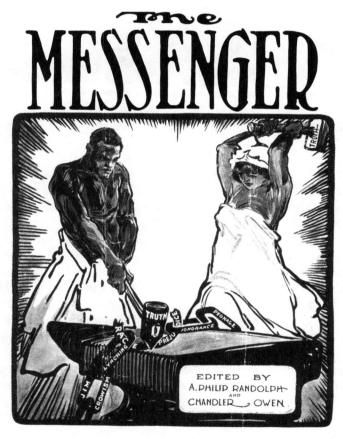

Harding at Birmingham

2.15. Cover illustration for *The Messenger* (December 1921).

2.16. Charles Cullen, untitled illustration in Charles S. Johnson, *Ebony and Topaz* (1927).

24,438 or 60 percent of black women in New York worked as servants to whites. While blacks swelled the ranks of chauffeurs, garment workers, and longshoremen throughout the 1910s, labor unions proved a hurdle to black employment. "One feels tempted to inquire," Johnson concluded, "of the 'workers' friend,' the unions, why those trades in which these unions are well organized have not shown equivalent increases in Negro workers. Ten years added but 18 brick masons, 81 painters, 16 plasterers and 42 plumbers."[28] Not just another '20s boom town, Harlem found itself on the cutting edge of America's racial paradox where visions of social betterment collided head on with persistent discrimination in the professions and skilled labor. Consequently it offered, according to Locke, a "laboratory of a great race-welding," where "a transformed and transforming psychology permeates the masses" (Locke, 7). Economic empowerment, according to Locke and his colleagues, was a necessary but hardly a sufficient impetus for social change.

Small pockets of entrepreneurial success—as in, say, Durham's prosperous North Carolina Mutual Life Insurance Company and its Mechanics and Farmers Bank—coupled with growing black enclaves in the professions and academy were sowing the seeds for the growth of an African-American bourgeoisie. This new class strategy, however, had failed to link up with a mass base in the labor movement due largely to a relentless torrent of racist state propaganda. Contributing to *The New Negro* on the theme of "labor in the shadows," Du Bois noted that the main impediment to international solidarity among workers and Pan-Africanists was "white capital," which by "segregating colored labor in just those parts of the world where it can be most easily exploited" had undermined organized trade unions.[29] Significantly in Du Bois' reading, it is the force of racial propaganda installed throughout the modern culture industry, that drives home capital's global wedge against labor. The "propaganda of poet and novelist," he wrote, "the uncanny welter of romance, the half knowledge of scientists, the pseudo-science of statesmen—all these,

2.17. Charles Cullen, untitled illustration in Charles S. Johnson, *Ebony and Topaz* (1927).

2.18. Allan Randall Freelon, "Hail Negro
Youth," cover illustration for *Black
Opals* (Spring 1927).

united in the myth of mass inferiority of most men, have built a wall which
many centuries will not break down" (407). In glossing Claude McKay's
recent sojourns in Russia, Du Bois noted (with some regret) that it was the
Soviet Union, and not the United States, which "has been seeking a *rapprochement* with colored labor" (408).

Writing to the left of Du Bois' liberal position, a younger colleague in
the Pan-Africanist movement C. L. R. James would, at the end of the
next decade, reflect back on the revolutionary symbolism of literary Garveyism, the blues, jazz, and Harlem cabaret life as symptoms of a black
counter-offensive to the relentless cultural subordination of African-Americans to the Caucasian norm. "The main organs of publicity," he
observed, "are in the hands of the whites":

The millions who watch the films always see Negroes shining shoes or doing menial work, singing or dancing. Of the thousands of Negro professional men, of the nearly two hundred Negro universities and colleges in America which give degrees in every branch of learning, and are run predominantly by Negro professors, of this the American capitalist takes good care that nothing appears on the screen.

Thus the American Negro, literate, Westernized, and American almost from the foundation of America, suffers from his humiliations and discriminations to a degree that few whites and even many non-American Negroes can ever understand. The jazz and gaiety of the American Negro are a semi-conscious reaction to the fundamental sorrow of the race.[30]

In James' reading, it was Marcus Garvey who most successfully mounted a popular counteroffensive to the dominant signs of white propaganda. Tapping black resentment from America's longstanding tradition of racial discrimination, Garvey exploited African-Americans' anger upon returning to a Jim Crow society after their heroic service in World War I, symbolized in the first American award of France's coveted Croix-de-Guerre to a black veteran.

Organized in 1914, Garvey's Universal Negro Improvement Association (UNIA) provided the institutional vehicle for sponsoring the arts, poetry, oratory, and debates all devoted to a Pan-African agenda. Garvey himself was invited to America by Booker T. Washington, where he undertook a lecture tour in 1916, agitating on behalf of an African homeland. By the end of the decade Garvey had been catapulted to national attention through his arrest for having libeled the assistant district attorney of New York. Meanwhile, his program for African self-determination was widely popularized by the UNIA's house organ *The Negro World,* whose international circulation to some 200,000 subscribers—twice the peak sales of the NAACP's *The Crisis*—made it the most widely read African-American journal of its day. Garvey galvanized the international black community through his charismatic leadership, his bold separatist agenda, and his espousal of a "Negro capitalism." Yet despite the power of a broad base of popular support running into the millions, Garvey's horrendous political misadventures and business failures—symbolized in his badly mismanaged Black Star steamship line and outrageous collaboration with the Ku Klux Klan to deport blacks to Africa—led such major African-American journals as *The Messenger,* Chicago *Defender* and *The Crisis* to join in a 1923 "Garvey Must Go Campaign."

Beyond the many absurdities of Garvey's political regime, Garveyism, as an ideological discourse, showed Locke and the rest of the "new negro" leadership that the popular appeal of Pan-Africanism was indeed widespread. "In a real sense," Locke would theorize two years later, "it is the rank and file who are leading and the leaders who are following" (NN, 7).[31] Garveyism proved that the rhetoric of race experience had tremendous potential for fusing the Pan-African "rank and file" to a political bloc whose solidarity cut across national boundaries. Instead of putting the stereotypes of black exoticism, the minstrel tradition, and folk vernacular on display for the white gaze, Locke and the other self-styled "new negroes" (Countée Cullen, Jessie Faucet, Rudolph Fisher, Angelina Weld Grimké, Langston Hughes, Zora Neale Hurston, Georgia Douglas Johnson, Claude McKay, Bruce Nugent, Willis Richardson, Anne Spencer, and Jean Toomer, among others) sought to articulate traditional African-American folk signs and cultural tropes not just to an emerging black bourgeoisie but to the broader struggle for black labor privileges, women's empowerment, and gay rights.

The foundational text of the Harlem Renaissance, *The New Negro* (1925) featured contributions not only on the African heritage in American art, music, dance, fiction, drama, and poetry, but also sociological readings of the rising black bourgeoisie and professional classes, Pan-African labor, and the African-American women's movement. The anthology's discursive strategy sought to reverse the imagery, signs, and symbols of racial oppression into figures of Pan-African empowerment. Its revolutionary, signifying task was, as Locke described it, "to convert a defensive into an offensive position, a handicap into an incentive" (11).[32] In fulfilling James Weldon Johnson's belief that "the world does not know that a people is great until that people produces great literature and art" (ANP, 9), Locke sought to reposition the African and vernacular traces of the black aesthetic from America's denigrated margins to its mainstream. His mission was to inscribe "a new figure on the national canvas" (ix) and to promote a "culturally articulate" (ix) black vanguard. *The New Negro*'s cultural task of serving as midwife to a new generation of African-American talent was eloquently captured in Weinold Reiss' frontispiece illustration, "The Brown Madonna" (figure 2.19).

Reflecting back on Johnson's agenda to legitimate black aesthetics on a par with high Western culture, Henry Louis Gates, Jr. would later deem the New Negroes' fixation on their Caucasian reception "a trap." The result, he concluded in the 1980s, was simply that "many of these poets borrowed with very little modification the forms of white poetry. Far too

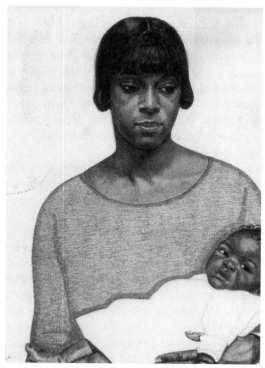

2.19. Winold Reiss, "The Brown Madonna."
Pastel frontispiece for *The New Negro*
(1925).

often, their models were not of the first order; these black mockingbirds
did not supersede the creations of their borrowed forms."[33] Such a dismissal, however, coming as it does after the flourishing of a vernacular
black aesthetic movement in the 1960s and its subsequent inroads into
African-American studies in the postwar academy, tends to minimize the
more limited range of options open to the New Negroes. In fact, Gates'
reading gives short shrift to what they actually achieved in terms of nur-
turing a new tradition of black formalism: one that would reach fruition a
generation later in such figures as Gwendolyn Brooks. When we begin to
read the Harlem Renaissance against the grain of its own historical limits
and beneath the mask of its formalist makeup, its revolutionary force
endures as a productive resource for the contemporary task of fashioning
revisionary black subject positions.

"Our poets," Locke noted in what remains a decisive break with America's dominant racial discourse of stereotype and caricature, "have now stopped speaking for the Negro—they speak as Negroes" (48). To speak as a Negro, however, did not stop at popularizing Harlem cabaret life, nor did it aim merely to establish an academic enclave of black experimental modernism. More to the point, the new negro intervention in American culture certainly did not mean repressing class and gender representations in the name of aesthetic formalism. Daring to "speak as Negroes," Locke and his colleagues boldly collaged African and vernacular traditions with revisionary gender roles. They forged radical subject positions that would not be revived again en masse until the black, feminist, and gay revolutions in postwar American culture.

Spearheading social change in the aesthetic dimension, the "new negroes" outran the acceptable range of cultural representation permitted blacks in the 1920s. Not incidentally, this younger generation of outspoken black talent elicited a telling conservatism both on the right from black Victorians like Benjamin Brawley and on the left from proletcult ideologues such as Mike Gold. "If Mr. Locke's thesis is insisted on too much," Du Bois warned, "it is going to turn the Negro renaissance into decadence."[34] Beyond the tendency toward aestheticism—something Du Bois consistently derided—several of the New Negro luminaries entertained a fresh eroticism in their work that reflected their gay, lesbian, and bisexual life-styles. Wallace Thurman, Bruce Nugent, Countée Cullen, Alaine Locke, Alice Dunbar-Nelson and Angelina Weld Grimké, as Gloria Hull and Maureen Honey have argued, led the way in fostering the period's explicitly eroticized—and often same sex—themes and images.[35]

The "new negro" generation challenged Du Bois' liberal caveat against Harlem decadence from two fronts: working both within the black aesthetic canon and on its radical avant-garde. The former strategy shaped Countée Cullen's 1927 anthology *Caroling Dusk,* while the latter underwrote Wallace Thurmon's shortlived, but widely provocative, journal *Fire!!: A Quarterly Devoted to the Younger Negro Artists* (1926). In his "Foreword" to *Caroling Dusk,* Cullen rather self-consciously positioned his text within an authoritative African-American literary continuity by citing its foundational precursors, including James Weldon Johnson's inaugural volume *The Book of American Negro Poetry* (1922), as well as Robert Kerlin's *Negro Poets and Their Poems* (1923), and Newman Ivey White's *An Anthology of Verse by American Negroes* (1924). Cullen's tactic was to popularize new black talents by joining them to a reputable body of "modern Negro poets already established and acknowledged, by virtue of their seniority and published books, as worthy practitioners of their art."[36] Thus, he linked Dunbar's dialect poetry and Johnson's sermon forms to Helene Johnson's "colloquial verses" and Hughes' blues lyrics, while noting Sterling Brown's fusion of vernacular idiom with sonnet forms.

Cullen revised somewhat the task of the black artist as James Weldon Johnson had defined it five years earlier. "What the colored poet in the United States needs to do," Johnson had argued, "is something like what Synge did for the Irish" (ANP, 40). Cullen, however, parted company with Johnson's nationalist paradigm as an inadequate, ideological limit to the emerging diversity of the new black canon. He resisted any "attempt to corral the outbursts of the ebony muse into some definite mold to which all poetry by Negroes will conform" (xi). In this vein, Cullen foregrounded the role of black authors in advancing experimental modernism and the international avant-gardes. As examples, he cited Jessie Fauset's debts to the Sorbonne and Lewis Alexander's reliance on tanka and haiku forms. But equally important, Cullen shrewdly articulated Anne Spencer's "cool precision" to the new wave of imagist poetics, popularized in America by Amy Lowell. Differing from the often phallocentric bent of high modernists like Ezra Pound, Cullen, as a black bisexual editor, was open to the revisionary gender roles inscribed in the poetry of Alice Dunbar-Nelson, Angelina Weld Grimké, and Gladys May Casely Hayford. He not only promoted art that challenged stereotypical relations between the races but published works that subverted Victorian sexual norms.

Grimké's sensual celebrations of nature in "Greenness," for example, projected the polymorphous sexuality of Whitman's *Leaves of Grass* into lesbian registers. Separated at birth from her mother, it is not surprising that Grimké would encode her longing for "little leaves" of grass through a libidinal economy based on the infant's pre-Oedipal bond to the maternal body: "Is not each leaf," she muses, "a cool green hand, / Is not each blade of grass a mothering green finger, / Hushing the heart that beats and beats and beats?" (CD, 37). Adopting a male persona, her portrait "A Mona Lisa" delves more explicitly into the eroticized territory of the feminine unconscious:

> I should like to creep
> Through the long brown grasses
>   That are your lashes;
> I should like to poise
>   On the very brink
> Of the leaf-brown pools
>   that are your shadowed eyes;

I should like to cleave
    Without sound,
Their glimmering waters,
    Their unrippled waters,
I should like to sink down
    And down
        And down. . . .
            And deeply drown. (CD, 42–43)

Grimké's passionate regression into a psychic landscape of feminine otherness looks forward to the recovery of the pre-oedipal domain of maternal sensuality, theorized by such psychoanalytic French feminists as Julia Kristeva, Luce Irigaray, and Hélène Cixous, and such America lesbian writers as Adrienne Rich. As Henry Louis Gates, Jr., has noted, in contrasting the Harlem Renaissance with black postmodernism, the writing of the 1920s seems somewhat flawed by today's standards in its mannered romanticism and stilted formalism.[37] Nevertheless, it would seem more productive to regard such renaissance styles of black feminism, I would argue, not so much in terms of their aesthetic limits as of their cultural difference. Crediting this difference would instead read Harlem's somewhat mannered presentation of female eroticism as a forerunner to the bolder stylistics of *l'écriture féminine:* a poetics that, according to Julia Kristeva, breaches the repressive formalism of *symbolic* discourse with the libidinal pulsations and sensuous textuality of the *semiotique*.[38]

That African-American women writers of the renaissance, like their postwar counterparts, deployed black feminist poetics as politicized interventions into Harlem's racial and sexual status quo was explicitly theorized by, among others, Gladys May Casely Hayford. Like Grimké, Hayford also adopted a male subject position to embrace a revisionary image of feminine desire:

Into my hands she cometh, and the lightning of my
    desire
Flashes and leaps about her, more subtle than Heaven's
    fire;
The lightning's in love with you darling; it is loving
    you so much,
That its warm electricity in you pulses where I may
    touch.
        . . . . .
I sometimes wonder, beloved, when I drink from life's
    proffered bowl,

> Whether there's thunder hidden in the innermost parts
> of your soul. (CD, 199)

Such erotic lyricism, however, was also tied, in Hayford's theoretical writings, to the cultural task of emancipating the black body from the stigmatized codes of white America. In her biographical statement for *Caroling Dusk,* Hayford adopts James Weldon Johnson's earlier mission of correcting the stereotype of racial inferiority in the aesthetic dimension. "By twenty," she wrote, "I had the firm conviction that I was meant to write for Africa. . . . to show those who are prejudiced against colour, that we deny inferiority to them, spiritually, intellectually, and morally" (CD, 196). But unlike Johnson, who legitimated black art through its masterpiece status, Hayford turned to the immediacy of the embodied life to release racial difference from the denigrating signs of white oppression.

Looking forward to the '60s slogan "black is beautiful," Hayford's task, as she described it, was to depict "the beautiful points of Negro physique, texture of skin, beauty of hair, soft sweetness of eyes, charm of curves, so that none should think it a shame to be black, but rather a glorious adventure" (CD, 197). A similar agenda can be gleaned in the visual attention that Winold Reiss pays to the cosmopolitan emergence of Harlem womanhood in, say, his stunning portrait of Elise Johnson McDougald (figure 2.20). However ignored today, McDougald herself remains an important precursor of black feminist theory. In particular, her contribution to Alain Locke's March 1925 *Survey Graphic* issue, "The Double Task: The Struggle of Negro Women for Sex and Race Emancipation"— later reprinted as "The Task of Negro Womanhood" in *The New Negro*— lays out a devastating analysis of African-American women's dual oppression in their racial and sexual lives. "We find the Negro woman," she declared, "figuratively, struck in the face daily by contempt from the world about her" (NN, 382):

> She is conscious that what is left of chivalry is not directed toward her. She realizes that the ideals of beauty, built up in the fine arts, exclude her almost entirely. Instead, the grotesque Aunt Jemimas of street-car advertisements proclaim only an ability to serve, without grace or loveliness. (NN, 369–70)

Supplementing her critique of such denigrating media stereotypes, McDougald documented the various class positions black women occupied in the New York labor market. But she also noted the progressive solidarity afforded by women's groups like Harlem's Utility Club, Utopia

2.20. Winold Reiss, "Portrait Sketch: Elise
Johnson McDougald." Pastel
illustration in *The New Negro* (1925).

Neighborhood, Semper Fidelius, and the Colored Branch of the YWCA.
Looking ahead to contemporary black feminist critique, she linked African-American women's oppression in the public sphere to their subordination to black patriarchy in the nuclear household. Of Harlem's husbands
and fathers, she wrote, "Their baffled and suppressed desires to determine
their economic life are manifested in overbearing domination at home.
Working mothers are unable to instill different ideals in their sons. Conditions change slowly" (NN, 380).

Such social inertia not only impeded the agenda of black feminism, but
also resisted the new identity politics of African-American gay and lesbian
activism. In the mid-'20s, the cultural task of eroticizing black subject posi-

tions was taken into contested registers in the controversial aesthetic politics of the *Fire!!* editorial circle: Wallace Thurman, Gwendolyn Bennet, Richard Bruce (Bruce Nugent), John Davis, Aaron Douglas, Langston Hughes, and Zora Neale Hurston. Not unlike such avant-garde counterparts as Vladimir Mayakovsky, David Burliak, and Victor Khlebikov, who advertised their Russian Futurism as "A Slap in the Face of Public Taste"—the *Fire!!* editors were deliberately provocative. They sought, in Langston Hughes' recollections to "*épater le bourgeois,* to burn up a lot of the old stereotyped Uncle Tom ideas of the past."[39] Reflecting back on the journal's inflammatory conception, Bruce Nugent has recounted that "Wally [Thurman] and I thought that the magazine would get bigger sales if it was banned in Boston. So we flipped a coin to see who wrote bannable material. The only two things we could think of that were bannable were a story about prostitution or about homosexuality."[40] In the end, they featured both themes in Gwendolyn Bennet's "Wedding Day" (a conflicted interracial romance between an expatriate black boxer and a white American prostitute in Paris) and in "Smoke, Lilies, and Jade," an excerpt from Nugent's novel-in-progress.

Nugent's contribution featured an explicit, interracial love scene between Alex, a black male artist and Beauty, his white, gay lover who resembles a figure from a Langston Hughes lyric:

> Somewhat like Ariel
> Somewhat like Puck
> Somewhat like a gutter boy
> Who loves to play in Muck.[41]

In an erotic dream sequence, Beauty merges with a female character Melva to become an androgyne, embodying both masculine contours and feminized lines:

> . . . Beauty . . . Melva . . . Beauty . . . Melva . . . Alex slept . . . and dreamed. . . . he was in a field . . . a field of blue smoke and black poppies and red calla lilies . . . he was searching . . . on his hands and knees . . . searching . . . among black poppies and red calla lilies . . . he was searching pushed aside poppy stems . . . and saw two strong white legs . . . dancer's legs . . . the contours pleased him . . . his eyes wandered . . . on past the muscular hocks to the firm white thighs . . . the rounded buttocks . . . then the lithe narrow waist . . . strong torso and broad deep chest . . . the heavy shoulders . . . the graceful muscled neck . . . squared chin and quizzical lips . . . grecian nose with its temperamental nostrils.
>
> (37)

The libidinal economy of Nugent's stylistic elisions and repetitions borrowed from modernist stream of consciousness. This reverie, in particular, aids in interpreting the exotic, sexually ambiguous figure in Nugent's accompanying drawing to Bennet's "Wedding Day," *Fire!!*'s other intentionally provocative contribution (figure 2.21).

Nugent's penchant for depicting interracial gay affairs also is plain to see in "Beyond Where the Stars Stood Still," his little-known recasting of the Christian nativity story. This version focuses on Caspar, the twenty-year-old King of Ethiopia, and his quest to celebrate the birth of the Messiah. Along the way, Nugent recounts his meetings with Melchior, Shah of Persia, and Balthasar, King of Sheba. But instead of dramatizing the nativity scene as such, Nugent follows these three wise men to King Her-

2.21. Bruce Nugent, "Drawing." Woodcut
illustration in *Fire!!* (1926).

CARUS

2.22. Bruce Nugent, "Carus." Illustration in
Beyond Where the Stars Stood Still.

od's court, where the narrative lavishes an erotic, visual attention on the
tyrant's page, Carus (figure 2.22): "He was fourteen, and fabulously white,
with long green eyes and carefully tangled auburn curls. His eyebrows had
been shaved and others drawn with an up-slanting line of indigo."[42] The
story climaxes with Carus' decision to betray Herod, to lead the wise men
to Bethlehem, and to confess his love for Caspar, the young black King
of Ethiopia. Intervening in this way, Nugent goes to the heart of the Christian mythos, recoding its foundational nativity narrative to reflect a same-
sex relationship between men. Although the mainstream criticism has
until recently tended to closet such same-sex representations, it is clear
that Nugent intended his performative act of coming out as a gay artist to
be an indispensable dimension of his aesthetic strategy.[43] More to the
point, in challenging the cultural norm of what Adrienne Rich defines as

compulsory heterosexuality, Nugent anticipates the gay performative speech acts of such contemporary gay art collectives as Gran Fury, Wave Three, and Little Elvis of ACT UP and Queer Nation. Here, the aesthetic object is radically dilated beyond its formal framing and disciplinary purity to "come out" as a spectacular display.

Not unlike Nugent's work, the collaborations of Countée Cullen and Charles Cullen had also suggested such interracial, homoerotic relationships in, say, "Tableau" from *Color* (see figure 2.23). There, Charles Cullen's intimate portrait—suggesting homoerotic bonding—illustrates Countée Cullen's bold image of a male couple "Locked arm in arm" as it cuts against the grain of social convention. The poem throws into sharp tension the idealized figure of the two boys—"The golden splendor of the day, / The sable pride of night"—against a provincial backdrop, where:

> From lowered blinds the dark folk stare,
> And here the fair folk talk,
> Indignant that these two should dare
> In unison to walk.[44]

However alienated from the closeted silent majority of both "dark folk" and "fair folk," the same sex, interracial couple foregrounded here nevertheless asserts a queer performative act whose utopian mix of image and text serves to decenter the heterosexist mainstream divided as it is by race, gender, and class.

Fire!! not only escalated the political stakes of such revisionary, same-sex relationships, but the volume's polemical thrust was driven home in the final commentary on the "Intelligentsia" by Arthur Huff Fauset and Thurman's column "Fire Burns." Fauset's witty jibes relied on the discur-

2.23. Charles Cullen, "Tableau." Illustration in *Color* (1927).

sive resources of the vernacular tradition to signify on both old-line Victorians and left-wing ideologues alike.[45] While praising authentic, vanguard intellectuals like Sinclair Lewis, Dreiser, Mencken, and Shaw, Fauset anathematized their literary sycophants, "prostrated at the altar of Liberalism" (46). The black community owed them about as much as "a Negro slave owes to Georgia" (45); their contribution to social change was "as negligible as gin at a Methodist picnic" (45). "These are the folk," Fauset quipped, "who talk Bolshevism in their parlors and wouldn't go to Russia if it were placed, like milk for cats, in saucers on their doorsteps" (46). Thurman's commentary further aligned his aesthetic with that of Carl Van Vechten, whom he had defended that previous September in a review of *Nigger Heaven* for *The Messenger*.[46]

The cultural radicalism of this avant-garde wing of the Harlem Renaissance drew heated attacks and counterstatements that year, notably from Benjamin Brawley's review of "The Negro Literary Renaissance" in *The Southern Workman,* as well as from George Schuyler, Mike Gold, and Langston Hughes in the *Nation.* Invoking the entrepreneurial rhetoric of Booker T. Washington, Brawley repressed explicit mention of *Fire!!*'s controversial homoeroticism. Instead, he assaulted Nugent's contribution on stylistic grounds. A latter-day Victorian, Brawley had little use for modern vers libre, jazz, and blues ballads. Instead, he preferred Gray's "Elegy" and Lowell's "The Vision of Sir Launfal" to black vernacular verse. The young renaissance writers, he concluded, in flirting with "sordid, unpleasant, or forbidden themes," had turned "away from anything that looked like good honest work in order to loaf and to call oneself an artist."[47]

George Schuyler, co-editor of *The Messenger,* the socialist outlet for the Brotherhood of Sleeping Car Porters, assailed "renaissancism" on essentialist grounds. Schuyler argued that in elevating regional folk traditions to cultural universals the "new negroes" had not so much valorized black aesthetic expression as reinforced artificial differences among the races—stereotypes that played into the hands of reactionary whites:

> Because a few writers with a paucity of themes have seized upon imbecilities of the Negro rustics and clowns and palmed them off as authentic and characteristic Aframerican behavior, the common notion that the black American is so "different" from his white neighbor has gained wide currency. The mere mention of the word "Negro" conjures up in the average white American's mind a composite stereotype of Bert Williams, Aunt Jemima, Uncle Tom, Jack Johnson, Florian Slappey, and the various monstrosities scrawled by the cartoonists.[48]

Schuyler's dismissal of black sermons, spirituals, blues, and jazz traditions as legitimate subjects for modern art repeated James Weldon Johnson's earlier reservations about black folk materials, especially the limited expressive range of negro dialect, which is, he held, "an instrument with but two full stops, humor and pathos." But whereas Johnson offered a more nuanced distinction between minstrel stereotypes and the original folk motifs in the work of Langston Hughes, Sterling Brown, and Aaron Douglas, among others, Schuyler repudiated this heritage *tout court* as "negro-art hokum."[49]

The following month, Mike Gold drove Schuyler's critique further to the left, subordinating racial difference, predictably, to class solidarity against capital: "We Negroes, Jews, Germans, Chinese, Anglo-Saxons are all part of America, for better or worse. . . . the only real division is that of economic classes."[50] After lecturing Langston Hughes about slumming with "white dilettantes" in Harlem nightclubs, Gold advised the new black intellectuals to "leave the cabarets of the jaded dilettantes and the colleges of the middle-class strivers, and help the mass of their brothers in the economic fight" (WBF, 37). But in his eagerness to subordinate Harlem's emergent black aesthetic to the discourse of class struggle, Gold ignored the proletarian portraits and themes already depicted in Hughes' renaissance poetry. If Gold had listened more closely to the vernacular of *Fire!!*'s "Elevator Boy," he might have heard a worker's tirade against alienated labor:

> Maybe no luck for a long time.
> Only the elevators
> Goin' up an' down,
> Up an' down,
> Or somebody else's shoes
> To shine,
> Or greasy pots in a dirty kitchen.
> I been runnin this
> Elevator too long.
> Guess I'll quit now. (*Fire!!*, 20)

Instead, Gold left the reception of such working-class poetics to Victorian-minded critics like Benjamin Brawley, who could only parrot the accommodationist rhetoric of Booker T. Washington, declaring "that no one with such a job should leave it until he is reasonably sure of getting something better" (Brawley, 179).

For his part, Hughes argued in his definitive aesthetic manifesto of the

1920s "The Negro Artist and the Racial Mountain" (1926) that the denial of race experience whether in the name of bourgeois respectability or in service to class solidarity simply repressed cultural difference. In this essay, Hughes held up for sustained critique the psychic "desire to pour racial individuality into the mold of American standardization, and to be as little Negro and as much American as possible."[51] Racial assimilation, in his view, served the class strategy of dividing bourgeois, and often "high yellow," African-Americans from the black masses. In America, he observed, signs of affluent class privilege imbricated with Caucasian culture—"years of study under white teachers, a life-time of white books, pictures, and papers, and white manners, morals, and Puritan standards" (694)—led "high class" blacks to serve what Du Bois called "white capital."

Not insignificantly, the vernacular recovery of black jazz, the blues, slave songs, and other linguistic, pictorial, and musical tropes in the work of Winold Reiss, Aaron Douglas, Jean Toomer, Paul Robeson, and the other proponents of the Harlem Renaissance functioned as a counterdiscourse, albeit patronized and popularized by white benefactors, that beat out a "tom-tom of revolt against weariness in a white world, a world of subway trains, and work, work, work" (694). In the mid-1920s, Hughes' materialist espousal of the longstanding, vernacular traditions of America's black subculture far exceeded Gold's or Brawley's more narrowly aestheticized and classist readings of African-American culture. Yet a decade after the emergence of the New Negro, Aaron Douglas would report on the dismal state of race and modern aesthetics at New York's American Artists Congress. "In the Metropolitan Museum of Art," he declared, "there is a room devoted to modern American masters. Not one Negro face is represented." Moreover, Aaron deplored the social realism of the 1930s, which erased the distinctive vernacular traces of African-American culture in its own way. "It is when we come to revolutionary art," he held, "that we find the Negro sincerely represented, but here the portrayal is too frequently automatic, perfunctory and arbitrary. He becomes a kind of proletarian prop, a symbol, vague and abstract."[52]

The situation of the black cultural activist in the 1930s was doubly challenged by contradictory racial and class tensions. These divisions were occasioned in part by the trial of the Scottsboro boys, which pitted the NAACP against the party-sponsored International Labor Defenders (ILD). In 1931, nine black youths were arrested on the trumped-up charge of raping two white girls, Victoria Price and Ruby Bates, aboard a freight train in Alabama. As it happened, physical evidence offered by medical examiners at the time actually refuted this charge; moreover, testifying under oath, Bates would later recant the whole story as a lie in 1933. In its own moment, the Scottsboro trial remains as powerful a national symbol of America's institutional racism as the Rodney King trial of the 1990s (figure 2.24).[53]

Disregarding the evidence, Alabama juries and state officials refused to acquit or pardon the boys in trials through 1937, when four were set free. But it would not be until 1950 that Andrew Wright, the last of the innocent Scottsboro nine, would be paroled. Part of what was at stake in the trial was the issue of who would represent the interests of the black underclass:

2.24. Samuel Leibowitz, Communist International Labor
Defenders attorney, with Scottsboro boys in
Decatur, Alabama.

the Northern left of the CPUSA or the Southern black mandarins of the NAACP's "talented tenth." For his part, NAACP Executive Secretary Walter White was reluctant in the early spring of 1931 to identify his black bourgeois organization with a gang of alleged rapists. Beating the NAACP to the punch, the ILD lobbied the boys' parents and secured the right to serve as legal representatives for the nine defendants. Throughout the Third Period, the two organizations used the trial to wage a propaganda war as much against each other as the state of Alabama.

At a June 7 meeting of Chattanooga's Ministers' Alliance, the NAACP's Field Secretary William Pickens assailed the ILD, charging "their chief aim is communistic propaganda, and that the plight of these youths is only a vehicle for that propaganda . . . I even suspect," he continued, "that it is their feeling that if justice should miscarry or if the boys should be lynched, it would further play into their hands and give them material for still more sensational propaganda among the more ignorant of the colored population" (S, 85). Rebutting such attacks in *New Masses,* Eugene Gordon lampooned the NAACP as "the Nicest Association for the Advantage of Certain Persons." Meanwhile, the *Daily Worker* allowed as how Wilkens "toured the South in order to ingratiate the NAACP with the Ku Klux Klan." In the *Worker*'s hyperbolic rhetoric, Wilkens "grovelled before the white master and in whining 'admissions' did all that he could to deliver the nine innocent boys to the hangman of Alabama."[54] This inflammatory caricature was popularized the following year by such visual artists as Hugo Gellert, whose *New Masses* cartoon— "The Face of the NAACP, with the arms of the bosses" (figure 2.25)— stigmatized the NAACP as a front for white power interests.

In an effort to shore up its own authority and to contain black communism, the NAACP in the spring of 1932 ran two issues in its house organ, *The Crisis,* featuring the position statements of several African-American editors (figure 2.26). This strategy, however, was only partly successful as more than one editor noted the party's leading role in fighting against Jim Crow restrictions in jury selection, union memberships, housing, access to medical care, and so on. Although these social justice initiatives could not be denied, admitted P. B. Young of the *Norfolk Journal and Guide,* the "blood and thunder" appeals to "revolution" and "mass action" would not appeal to most African-Americans.[55] While social change was being shaped internally in Russia, argued J. Alston Atkins of the *Houston Informer,* "In the life of the American Negro every expression which is labeled 'Communism' is for the most part both planned and worked from without" (*Crisis,* 118). Soviet-style representations, accord-

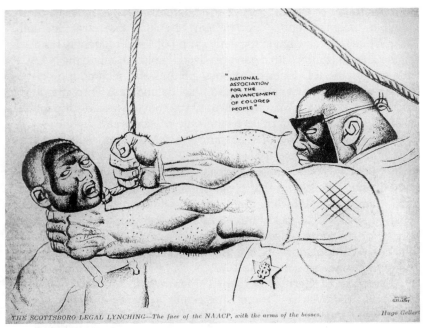

THE SCOTTSBORO LEGAL LYNCHING—The face of the NAACP, with the arms of the bosses.   Hugo Gellert

2.25. Hugo Gellert, "The Face of the NAACP, with the arms of the bosses," *New Masses* (February 1932).

ing to E. Washington Rhodes of the *Philadelphia Tribune,* went against the grain of the "peculiar love which Negroes have for America and American institutions" (*Crisis,* 118). For his part, Frank M. Davis of the *Atlanta World* was concerned that communist agitation, especially in the South, would only prompt a reactionary white backlash. These pragmatic reservations were underscored, however, by a more fundamental, class bias against communist ideology.

Despite the appeal of racial equality held out by the CPUSA, the NAACP's "talented tenth" resisted the party's challenge to their own possessive individualism and class privilege. "Communism," wrote Roscoe Dunjee of Oklahoma's *Black Dispatch,* "as a political and economic theory, does not meet and join fully with my ideal notion of government. . . . To my way of seeing things, individualism, with its street addresses and titles to property, is the proven pavement to all sound, economic progress."[56] It was within such a divisive political setting that Langston Hughes undertook a class-based poetics that nevertheless carried forward the racial agenda of the Harlem Renaissance. While reading at Tuskegee in January 1932, Hughes traveled to nearby Kilby Prison to meet the Scottsboro nine. There on death row, within a stone's throw of the electric chair, Hughes tried to lift the spirit of the Scottsboro boys by reading them his ironic, blues-based verse.

To his credit, Hughes would finesse throughout the 1930s the reduction of socialist realism, publishing politicized verse spliced with the nuanced vernacular signs of the twenties-style black aesthetic. His pragmatic negotiations with proletcult were deemed to be so politically correct that by the close of the decade Mike Gold would devote a preface to his black comrade's volume *A New Song* (1938). But much earlier, at the time of his break with patron Charlotte Mason (the infamous "god-

APRIL, 1932   FIFTEEN CENTS THE COPY

THE CRISIS

Reg. U. S. Pat. Off.

Afro-American

Journal & Guide

Amsterdam News

7 NEGRO EDITORS on COMMUNISM

GEORGE WASHINGTON

Philad'a Tribune

Informer

Atlanta World

Houston Defender

2.26. Cover of the *The Crisis* (April 1932).

mother" of protégés Richmond Barthé, Aaron Douglas, Zora Neale Hurston, Hall Johnson, Alain Locke, Claude McKay, and Louise Thompson), Hughes would employ black dialect in the compressed, blues lyricism of "Park Bench" to anathematize New York's gross class inequities:

> I live on a park bench,
> You, Park Avenue.
> Hell of a distance
> Between us two.
>
> I beg a dime for dinner—
> You got a butler and maid.
> But I'm wakin' up!
> Say, ain't you afraid
>
> That I might, just maybe,
> In a year or two,
> Move on over
> To Park Avenue?[57]

Writing in such leftist journals of the 1930s as *Contempo,* the *Daily Worker, International Literature, New Masses,* and *Partisan* (and allied with Harlem intellectuals and artists like Aaron Douglas, Louise Thompson, Augusta Savage, and Romeo Beardon in Marxist-led cultural organizations such as the Vanguard group), Hughes would exploit the figurative language of the blues vernacular to personify revolutionary social change as a "best friend":

> Good morning, Revolution:
>   You're the very best friend
>   I ever had.
> We gonna pal around together from now on.
> Say, listen, Revolution:
>
> You know, the boss where I used to work,
> The guy that gimme the air to cut down expenses,
> he wrote a long letter to the papers about you:
> Said you was a trouble maker, an alien enemy,
> In other words a son-of-a-bitch.
> He called up the police
> And told 'em to watch out for a guy
> Named Revolution.[58]

In "Good Morning, Revolution" Hughes splices such blues masterworks as Leadbelly's "Good Morning Blues" with the provocative rhetoric of revolutionary proletcult. Standard academic criticism has often sought to valorize black authors such as Langston Hughes and Sterling A. Brown on the basis of how they "elevate" the blues idiom through figurative artifice. All too often, this kind of reception has contained Hughes' vernacular critique of depression era capitalism in depoliticized readings of the poet's existential angst.[59]

In the academy, canonical readings have shored up earlier attempts to legitimate the universal aesthetic value of black literature. James Weldon Johnson, for example, sought to place black aesthetics on a par with the "masterpieces" of Western humanist culture, out of the faith that "No people that has produced great literature and art has ever been looked upon by the world as distinctly inferior" (ANP, 9). Academia's sanitized reception of Hughes as the idealized "poet laureate" of black folk culture was buttressed by the poet's own forced disavowal of his depression era allegiances when he was threatened with blacklisting by Joseph McCarthy's Senate Committee on Government Operations.[60] Another way critics have of repressing Hughes' partisan verse dismisses its alleged outworn topicality, that it lacks what David Hume described as "durable admiration." Thus, Raymond Smith claims that "Many of his poems, written in hasty response to some event reported in yesterday's newspaper, for example, have badly dated."[61] Ironically, the critical valuation of Hughes' canonical status rests not so much on any universal standard of aesthetic taste as on the historical repression of his politically charged career.

Rereading this body of work, however, against our century's largely unchanged social text of international racism and class exploitation, the oppression of black labor depicted in Hughes' early verse remains as pertinent now in the late twentieth century as it was in his 1928 contribution to *The Crisis,* "Johannesburg Mines":

> In the Johannesburg mines
> There are 240,000 natives working.
>
> What kind of poem
> Would you make out of that?
>
> 240,000 natives working
> In the Johannesburg mines. (GMR, 10)

The antipoetic strategy of "Johannesburg Mines" is designed to demystify the reader's investment in literary formalism. But Hughes' politicized verse often employs the same formal presentation of Whitmanesque anaphora, cut and mixed with Pan-African imagery, that established his canonical stature in such notable works as "The Negro Speaks of Rivers." Tellingly, however, it is only when such literary techniques voice the theme of internationalist class struggle that canonical readers reject them for having failed the test of time. Nevertheless, when we turn to, say, Hughes' Whitmanesque contributions to a 1932 volume of *The Negro Worker,* and read there of capital's global exploitation of Third World subalterns, the poet's depression era crossing of race and class critique assumes even greater authority and social urgency after six decades of "The Same":

It is the same everywhere for me:
On the docks at Sierra Leone,
In the cotton fields of Alabama,
In the diamond mines of Kimberley
On the coffee hills of Haiti
The banana lands of Central America,
The streets of Harlem,
And the cities of Morocco and Tripol.

Black:
Exploited, beaten, and robbed,
Shot and killed.
Blood running into

DOLLARS
POUNDS
FRANCS
PESETAS
LIRE

For the wealth of the exploiters—
Blood that never comes back to me again.
Better that my blood
Runs into the deep channels of Revolution,
Runs into the strong hands of Revolution. (GMR, 9)

In rejecting the vernacular tradition as a bourgeois hindrance to black class consciousness, leftist intellectuals like Mike Gold lost a valuable opportunity to enlist the native signs of black America for social change. Even when Hughes closed ranks with Gold and the party, he never lost sight of race as a foundational category of cultural critique. Hughes' anticipation of postwar black cultural nationalism, however, was lost on Gold's classism, which led him to the patronizing conclusion that "If Negroes think they can build up some special racial culture in this huge America, they are either optimists or are blinded by race patriotism" (WBF, 37).

Artists in Uniform

Such parochial economism not only undermined cultural inroads to the black community, but alienated potential allies in the anti-Stalinist left as well. The Comintern's mixed signals regarding the role of so-called fellow travelers remains one of its more lasting failures in building a durable political consensus in America. By at once recruiting and repudiating intellectuals who espoused proletarian values, the party bureaucracy lost the chance for cultural rapprochement on the left in the Third Period. Reflecting party divisions, the editorial board of *New Masses* was conflicted throughout the early 1930s in just how to carry out the vexed Comintern tasks of both soliciting and purging itself of such progressive gadflies as Max Eastman and V. F. Calverton.

The rift dividing revolutionary from bourgeois intellectuals grew apace in 1932 with the "Draft Manifesto of John Reed Clubs" presented by the New York Chapter to the Chicago National Conference of John Reed Clubs that May. In following the Third Period position on capitalism's imminent demise, the manifesto dutifully anathematized bourgeois culture in the United States. Specifically, it lodged the sweeping charge that

> most of the American writers who have developed in the past fifteen years betray the cynicism and despair of capitalist values. The movies are a vast corrupt commercial enterprise, turning out infantile entertainment or crude propaganda for the profit of stockholders. Philosophy has become mystical and idealist. Science goes in for godseeking. Painting loses itself in abstractions or trivialities.[62]

This unstinting denunciation of modernism echoed the earlier statement of the WCF entitled "Art is a Weapon: Program of the Workers Cultural Federation." "The most cursory glance at American cultural institutions," it maintained, "will reveal them at once as instruments of capitalist domination."[63] Beyond registering these kinds of complaints, however, such JRC and WCF tracts offered little in the way of theoretical strategies for intervening in the new visual culture of mechanical reproduction. Unlike, say, Walter Benjamin's sophisticated readings of film and mass spectacle, Third Period proletcult deplored American pop culture *tout court* as the decadent expression of monopoly capital.

By so delimiting the field of cultural intervention, proletarian writers allowed themselves precious little terrain on which to negotiate alternative representations of American society. To make matters worse, the Comintern's 1927 repudiation of Trotsky, who, only a year earlier, had served as a powerful intellectual role model for American leftists like Mike Gold, fomented internal party dissension and paranoia, culminating in *Partisan Review*'s anti-Stalinist split a decade later.[64] Perhaps the two most celebrated American victims to the Third Period's anti-Trotskyite campaign were V. F. Calverton, editor of *The Modern Quarterly,* and Max Eastman who, as late as 1928, remained on the editorial board of *New Masses.* Both socialists, however, were singled out for their anti-Stalinist dissent by the IURW in its "Resolution on the Work of the *New Masses* for 1931." In this white paper the Comintern scolded the magazine for having "showed manifestations of 'rotten liberalism' expressed both in the failure to carry out systematic work in exposing social-fascism as a whole, and in keeping silent about the treacherous role of a number of social-fascist ideologues who have formerly been closely connected with the magazine (Max Eastman, V. F. Calverton)."[65]

These reprimands mounted in 1932 with A. Elistratova's *International Literature* critique that came at the same time as the dismantling of the Russian Association of Proletarian Writers (RAAP) in preparation two years later for the First All-Union Writers' Conference proclamation of socialist realism as the official cultural style of the Soviet Union.[66] Falling in line with the Comintern's left turn, *New Masses* purged both Calverton and Eastman in its January 1933 issue to which Eastman replied in his stinging tirade of "Artists in Uniform" in Calverton's *The Modern Monthly* the following August.[67] There Eastman ridiculed Soviet proletcult values that, he held, have led to an

> obsequious and almost obscene lowering of the standards of the creative mind, of which that Kharkov congress and the whole subsequent record of the International Union of Proletarian Writers forms a picture. It is a picture of sacerdotal bigotry on the one side and sacrosanctimonious prostration to the priesthood, the repositories of the sacred dogma— sacred just so long as it is backed up by the secular, armed and priest-employing power—on the other.[68]

Joshua Kunitz, in turn, gibed that Eastman "expounds the pale, escapist, art-for-art's sake aesthetic typical of the tired petty-bourgeois radical who stands bewildered amidst the deafening clashes of the opposing worlds."[69]

Such combative posturing not only divided intellectuals like Kunitz and Eastman but also severed potential alliances among the proletarian writers themselves as in the conflict that split the "Rebel Poets, an Internationale of Song." Writers like Ralph Cheney, Jack Conroy, H. H. Lewis, Norman Macleod, and Lucia Trent had come together in solidarity to protest the

1920–27 Sacco and Vanzetti trial and execution. The fruit of their collaboration, a collective anthology *American Arraigned!* (1928), marked a productive, utopian moment in American literary history, captured in Ralph Cheney and Lucia Trent's credo that "We suggest as the modern seven wonders"

> the increasing recognition that equal unrestricted opportunity belongs to all individuals of all races and creeds, or lack of creed; the labor movement; the rising opposition to violence and murder, whether they be expressed in lynching, capital punishment, or war; the emancipation of women; modern psychology and the extensions of consciousness; birth control; and the development of machinery to lessen labor and increase production. The poet who cannot find inspiration in these wonders is . . . in short, no real poet.[70]

Reaching out to a broad constituency that included not only labor but also women and all "races and creeds," Cheney and Trent anticipated in 1929 the Comintern movement beyond its classist Third Period stances of 1928–33 toward the 1935 Popular Front strategy of soliciting fellow-travelers and "the people" at large into a broad, antifascist alliance.

Yet by May 1933—with the advent of Jack Conroy's new journal *Anvil,* the successor to *The Rebel Poet*—the consensus of communists, socialists, anarchists, and other nonaffiliated proletarian poets that unified the Rebel Poets group had crumbled under party pressure. *Anvil's* inaugural issue gave front-page coverage to Cheney's and Conroy's mutually antagonistic position statements. Although Cheney sought to downplay his break with the new journal's left turn toward communism, Conroy considered it a "retreat" from political commitment. "I cannot think," Conroy wrote, "that the polite evasions used by Cheney to mollify timorous readers have any positive effect in bringing about and fostering a revolutionary literary movement—rather they help to nullify its beginnings."[71]

Although it is not surprising that leftist writers such as Sol Funaroff, Mike Gold, Joseph Kalar, and Herman Spector would distance themselves from cultural elitists like Eliot and Pound, it is remarkable that they would go out of their way to rebuff potential allies such as William Carlos Williams and Marxist colleagues in the Objectivist camp like Charles Reznikoff and Louis Zukofsky. Reviewing Reznikoff's *Jerusalem "The Golden"* and *Testimony* in *Dynamo,* Herman Spector branded Reznikoff with the stigma of aestheticism, charging him with expressing a "limited world view" that failed to engage the moral and political urgencies of the moment. Such shortcomings left him particularly susceptible to an enervating pessimism in the face of history: "The fatal defect of the objectivist theory," Spector concluded, "is that it identifies life with capitalism, and so assumes that the world is merely a wasteland. The logical consequent is a fruitless negativism."[72] Writing under the pseudonym of Charles Henry Newman, Sol Funaroff charged Williams with the same narrow sensibility that was, he asserted, inadequate to the breadth and depth of contemporary social life. By focusing on the "radiant gist" of minute particulars, Williams, according to Funaroff, lost sight of panoramic social forces. "He carves cameos," Funaroff charged, "where the proportions of a Michael Angelo are needed. He paints miniatures where murals are required" (SMP, 29).

Some journals solicited just this kind of contestation as in M. A. Abernethy and A. J. Buttitta's editorial policy statement for *Contempo:* "Being an asylum for authors wherein they may, like editors, enjoy the privileges of free speech, our pages have been marked by polemic. CONTEMPO ENCOURAGES LITERARY CONTROVERSY."[73] A telling exposé of the remarkable divisiveness, endemic to leftist literary circles during these years was Herbert Solow's 1938 retrospective for *Partisan Review.* Solow laid out the various political fates of writers who had contributed to *New Masses* in its inaugural year. His statistics documented how the Old Left devoured its own intellectual progeny. Of the 150 writers who had published 268 pieces from 1926–27, seventeen of the most prolific (contributing 53 items or 19%) had been officially blacklisted as anti-Stalinist "enemies of the people." Out of another 34 writers contributing 81 items (33%), five had been purged—Leon Trotsky, Edmund Wilson, V. F. Calverton, Travers Clements, Arnold Roller—with another three (C. E. S. Wood, Witter Bynner, and Waldo Frank) held in suspicion. Of a remaining core of ten writers, two—Max Eastman and James Rorty—had been exiled, while John Dos Passos was on his way to the same fate.[74] In a similar study, Irving Howe noted that half of the twenty-one editors and authors that had published five or more pieces for *New Masses* in 1937 had similarly been reviled as "enemies of the people."[75]

Seldom, however, was this contentious milieu inscribed in the actual verse of the period, which tended toward an idealized, utopian representation of politics. Nevertheless, in a 1934 poem published in *Dynamo,* Joseph Freeman (whose *American Testament* was yanked out of circulation following a Comintern directive)[76] reflects on the sharp contradiction between the hope for party unity and despair from its violent machinations:

To all the skies in every land,
The banner of revolt unfurled,
The worker with his iron hand
Crushes the rotten empires of the world;

Another age shall come, a life
Of work and wisdom, love and art;
Meantime a comrade slips a knife
Into your full and unsuspecting heart.

On the bright rim of worlds unborn
Dark seas of monstrous passion hiss;
Cain's bloodstained fingers greet the morn,
Judas moists his lips for the fatal kiss.[77]

More revealing as a cultural document of the times than as memorable poetry, Freeman's verse often wavers, as it does here, between an unshakable faith in the proletarian ideal and plaguing doubts about revolutionary realpolitik. In these lines, such ambivalence is inscribed through a utopian vision, shattered by a biblical typology of betrayal and fratricide.

The Guerrilla Aesthetics of Diego Rivera

While Freeman narrowly escaped the party's public denunciation, what remains the most glaring case of a major fellow traveler sacrificed to such political infighting is Diego Rivera's blacklisting at the 1928 Kharkov conference. Rivera's own turn toward a class-based aesthetic reached back to the previous decade when, following the failure of the Mexican revolution, he traveled to Paris in 1919 to study Neo-Impressionism, Cubism, and Futurism. There, Ilya Ehrenbourg, a special envoy of the new Soviet government, invited Rivera, along with Lezier and Picasso, to collaborate in Moscow with the Russian avant-gardes on advancing proletarian art. However frustrated by the Russian bureaucracy, it was nonetheless out of this post-revolutionary experience that Rivera theorized a sophisticated, class-based aesthetic—one which, resting on the collaborative framework of muralist art, would break through the limits both of academic and cubo-futurist versions of easel painting. The following year, Rivera traveled to Italy to study fresco techniques and by 1921 had returned to his native state to spearhead a revival of the guild spirit in Mexican mural decoration. Arriving in Mexico after fourteen years, Rivera found a conservative patronage system that not only withheld support from the avant-gardes, but ingrained in young artists "a cult of individual eccentricity," the idea, as he described it, "that the artist is an entity distinct from the human world . . . mysteriously set apart from the community."[78]

Rivera himself was no stranger to the exacting discipline of aesthetic formalism. In Italy he had steeped himself in the Renaissance tradition of fresco art and in Paris had mastered the intrinsic techniques of Neo-Impressionism and Cubism. Yet as a Marxist, he also resisted any divorce of aesthetic conventions from the social and economic conditions of their emergence. Genuine aesthetics, he thought, should depict the lived reality of the moment, not its transcendence. What made for "great" art, he believed, was a blend of formal craft and an active contact with the world. Every powerful artist, according to Rivera, has inescapably served as a propagandist for a particular world outlook. Just as Giotto was an apologist for the Franciscan resistance to feudal domination, and just as Bruegel was a propagandist for the Dutch bourgeoisie against aristocratic oppression, so Rivera championed the labor of proletarian culture to break out of fin de siècle aestheticism. While seemingly apolitical, the nineteenth-century theory of "pure" painterly values and its culmination in the art-for-art's-sake movement, for Rivera, were tied to conservative cult values that invested art with a specious, mystified aura. They gave easel painting "the legend of its intangible, sacrosanct, and mysterious character which makes art aloof and inaccessible to the masses."[79] The doctrine of "pure" art served politically to fetishize aesthetic style as an object of exchange value for the bourgeois art market: "to limit the possessors of art, to make art into a kind of stock exchange commodity manufactured by the artist, bought and sold on the stock exchange, subject to the speculative rise and fall which any commercialized thing is subject to in stock exchange manipulations" (RS, 52).

Repudiating both aesthetic commodification and the cult of the individual painter, Rivera espoused cooperative craft syndicates that would release art for the masses. Inevitably, his campaign to return art to the life of the people clashed with the privileged institution of easel painting, tied as it was to the market values shaping personal collections, exclusive galleries, and private museums. Nevertheless, through commissions from Mexican Minister of Education José Vasconcelos, Rivera was successful in organizing a collective labor union of painters that undertook collaborative mural projects for the amphitheater of the National University's Preparatory School and the Ministry of Education building. Benefiting from such colleagues as Xavier Guerrero, José Clemente Orozco, and David Alfara Siquieros, Rivera fused Cubofuturism with the ancient pictorial styles of Aztec wall decoration. Despite the hostile reception he received in Mexico from journalists, conservative politicians, and the art establishment, Rivera and his guild syndicates attracted international attention. John Dos Passos, for example, after viewing Rivera's murals in Mexico City, published an admiring review in the March 1927 issue of *New Masses*. Unlike the New York art world that offered merely "A few private sensations and experiments framed and exhibited here and there, a few watercolors like Marins, and a lot of warmed-over truck, leavings of European fads," Rivera's art he proclaimed, amounted to "a challenge shouted in the face of the rest of the world."[80]

It was the Soviet Union that, welcoming this challenge, invited the muralist that same year to attend the celebrations of the Tenth Anniversary of the October Revolution. Visiting Russia for a second time, Rivera was so impressed with the festivities he witnessed in Red Square that he composed forty-five watercolor and pencil sketches, later incorporated into his famous Radio City mural. Meanwhile, his fame had preceded him in Soviet art circles and it was not long before he was commissioned by Lunacharsky to undertake a fresco as a preliminary test to a more significant contract for the newly constructed V. I. Lenin Library.[81] It was at this time that Rivera became embroiled once again in a heated cultural tug-of-war. As a participant in the agitprop group *Octobre*—a collaborative experiment in adapting muralist techniques to the expanded field of Soviet public spectacle—Rivera was soon caught up in the struggle between contending factions of the Russian futurists and socialist realists. Rivera viewed the latter movement as a reactionary revival of Russian classicism, anathematizing it as "the most abject and shameless academic tradition of the bureaucracy of Czarist Russia."[82] "In place of the Czar," he charged, "they painted Lenin; in place of a battle in the Crimean War they painted a battle of the Red Army of the Soviet Union" (WAF, 275).

This unflinching critique of Russian easel painting coupled with Rivera's personal clash with the artists assigned to him and, more seriously, his political resistance to the rise of Stalinism, together led to his abrupt departure in the spring of 1928 under the pretext of managing the Workers and Peasants Bloc in its bid for office in the upcoming Mexican presidential campaign. Owing to his continued critique of Soviet socialist realism, Rivera found himself the following year tried and expelled from the party on the trumped up charge of undermining the Mexican CP in his government post as Director of the School of Plastic Arts. After his expulsion from the party, Rivera quickly fell out of favor with his traditional base of support in the United States.

New Masses had featured reproductions of Rivera's work in the 1920s with favorable reviews by John Dos Passos (1927) and Myron Chaffee Myron (1929). But with the February 1932 publication of Robert Evan's essay "Painting and Politics: The Case of Diego Rivera," its position on the Mexican muralist echoed the Comintern's charge that he had abandoned the party and was complicit in the counterrevolutionary repression of Ramon P. Negri. Even worse, Evans charged, to cover his tracks Rivera went on to advertise himself as a Trotskyite in a belated attempt to masquerade as a progressive artist: "The Trotskyist label left Rivera free to pose as a 'revolutionary' painter while glorifying Mexican chauvinism on the wall of the National Palace and accepting commissions from the wealthy American bourgeoisie he once so savagely caricatured."[83] Falling in step with the party line, the New York John Reed Club soon disavowed Rivera, apologized for having mistakenly invited him to speak to the New York chapter, and gave back Rivera's $100 donation to the club, "with which he hoped to buy himself that revolutionary cloak which he needs to serve his capitalist masters effectively."[84]

Unbeknownst to the New York John Reed Club rank and file, the speaking engagement was actually a setup, according to Albert Halper's eyewitness account. High officials of the party headquarters on 13th Street in league with *Daily Worker* editor Bill Dunne, had planned in advance to blackball the guest speaker at the meeting. After Rivera's inspiring speech, party officials rose from all parts of the lecture hall to denounce him. In a carefully orchestrated attack, they excoriated the artist, charging that he was merely an opportunist who had betrayed the Revolution to paint Trotskyite murals for capitalist bosses like the Fords and Rockefellers. Meanwhile, the majority of the audience, who had attended the talk out of respect for the Mexican revolutionary, were understandably stunned. But all quickly accepted the party agenda succumbing, in Halper's rendering, to a kind of mob psychology. "It was the first character assassination I had witnessed," Halper recalled, "and it was a most thorough job. Because of the obedient silence of those in the hall who did not participate in the attack, I knew that they, who had come to admire and pay homage to this talented man, now began to revile him in their thoughts."[85] The same party charges were later leveled against Rivera in *Art Front,* where Mary Randolph accused him of toning down his work's political content in order to preserve patronage. Rivera, she bluntly charged, is "a willing prostitute who makes his work pay."[86]

However much the left would try to besmirch the muralist, the sheer cultural power of his work for the National Palace soon brought him major commissions from another quarter—the newly formed Mexican Arts

Association, a prestigious American conglomerate headed by John D. Rockefeller, Jr. Soon Rivera was offered a single artist retrospective show at the recently opened Museum of Modern Art. This would be Rivera's American entré to the most important and hotly contested commissions of his career. Thus, having lost his base of support in the party, and black-listed as a Trotskyite, Rivera nevertheless embarked in the struggle for proletarian art underwritten, paradoxically, by the financial elite of the New York art market.

Such a dubious position necessitated a nuanced and more cunning aesthetic politics—a practice that would lead Rivera to agitate from within the bourgeois patronage network as a kind of double agent. "It was in the quality of a guerrilla fighter then," he wrote in V. F. Calverton's *The Modern Quarterly,* "that I came to the United States." "My munitions," he boasted, "are the walls, the colors, and the money necessary to feed myself so that I may continue to work" (RS, 56).

Rivera's American tenure followed, in the content of his mural work, an increasingly politicized trajectory that would erupt finally in what remains the most scandalous public clash over patronage ever witnessed in the United States. Beyond the apolitical frescos he undertook for the Luncheon Club of the San Francisco Stock Exchange and the home of Mrs. Sigmund Stern, his California School of Fine Arts mural (now San Francisco Art Institute) *The Making of a Fresco, Showing the Building of a City* (1931) boldly showcased the kind of constructivist values Rivera had endorsed in 1928 as a cofounder of *October, Association of Artistic Labor* in Russia. A cosignatory of the group's inaugural declaration, Rivera pledged himself to the principle that working-class culture "must overcome individualistic and commercial relationships, which have dominated art up until now."[87] Thus, as a self-professed guerrilla muralist, Rivera exploited the California School of Fine Arts commission to represent art's institutional base as such.

The post-individualistic credo espoused in the *October* manifesto was, for Rivera, not simply theoretical rhetoric but something he inscribed in the very content of the California fresco itself (figure 2.27). Briefly, the work depicts a muralist syndicate on a high scaffold painting the monumental figure of a worker at the controls of modern technology. In Rivera's compositional design, the scaffold divides the picture into a triptych. Flanking the central image of the muralists on the left are similar, collaborative images of iron forgers and a sculpting guild that wield power chisels driven by a foregrounded compressed air machine. On the right panel Rivera depicts architects, draftsmen, metal workers, and riveters that

2.27. Diego Rivera, *The Making of a Fresco, Showing the Building of a City* (April–June 1931).

together are erecting a skyscraper set off against the backdrop of a futuristic cityscape. Thus, the central portrait of the muralist syndicate, imbricated as it is in a more panoramic vision of industrial labor, decisively releases the aesthetic act into collective registers of transpersonal creativity beyond bourgeois solipsism.

Rivera's tribute to working-class values, while relatively uncontested in the California paintings, would later launch him into a national controversy over his 1933 *Detroit Industry* mural. Based on the contacts Rivera had made with Dr. W. R. Valentiner and Edgar P. Richardson, and with the backing of Dwight Morrow, the muralist was approached by the Detroit Arts Commission in 1931 to undertake a major fresco for the inner court of the Detroit Institute of Art. Now at the height of his prestige (reflected in his 1931 MOMA single artist show), Rivera eagerly accepted this new assignment. Its subject, the historical development of Detroit's technological heritage, appealed to his constructivist goal of meshing art with the new productive forces of advanced industrial society. Much has been made over the fact that Rivera extensively toured the Ford River Rouge, Parke-Davis Chemical, Chrysler, Michigan Alkali, and other plants for nearly three months before actually beginning to paint the factory scenes of the Detroit mural in July 1932. Rivera himself regarded his careful preparation as a tribute to the exacting science and discipline of the new technologies that, he fully expected, would pass to the proletariat as its rightful class inheritance.

But beyond his obvious fascination with machinery, Rivera considered the Detroit commission as a valuable opportunity to test the pragmatic evolution of his craft—a socioaesthetic praxis that he had built from the ground up as a dialectical transaction with the people. In Mexico he had begun to experiment with the popular effects of his work on the peasantry. "But it was urgently necessary for me," he later explained, "to continue it in a highly industrialized country. . . . [O]nly by testing the action and reaction between my painting and great masses of industrial workers could I take the next step towards my central objective—that of learning to produce painting for the working masses of the city and country."[88] In his MOMA show the previous year, he had reached into such mass registers of exposure, with over 31,000 paid admissions to his exhibition in just the first two weeks.[89] Now in Detroit, Rivera would celebrate what were the world's most advanced industrial techniques in automotive design, assembly-line production, aeronautics, chemistry, and pharmaceutics—techniques that he viewed, like the Russian Constructivists, as themselves the collective artistic expressions of proletarian culture.

Paying tribute to these "dynamic productive sculptures which are the mechanical masterpieces of the factories" (PA, 19), Rivera viewed his own aesthetic role as itself part of a more global, geopolitical mythology wedding Northern technology to the cultural roots of primordial, South American cultures. The *Detroit Industry* fresco reflected this cosmology. The East Wall's earth symbols of ecological fertility and organic fruition complemented the West Wall's depiction of advanced aeronautics and the modern commerce route linking the agricultural South (figure 2.28) to the industrial North (figure 2.29). Similarly, monumental nudes representing the four races—black, red, yellow, and white—hold the earth's raw materials. These figures are juxtaposed with the then state-of-the-art factory machines and the most minutely detailed processes of metal smelting, rolling, and casting; motor assembly; body welding, painting and finishing at the River Rouge plant. Believing that proletarian art should benefit from a traditional range of formal techniques, Rivera grafted pre-Columbian representations of such Aztec gods as Coatlicue onto the South Wall's monumental fender stamping press.[90] Moreover, he employed Renaissance nativity motifs to depict the North Wall's modern vaccination scene. Drawing from the formal resources of the modern aesthetic revolution, Rivera borrowed the techniques of Italian Futurism to convey the dynamic energies and fast-paced regimen of assembly line production. Here the cubist accentuation of line, plane, and oblique geometrical composition, stylizes the sheer complexity of visual information within the fresco's panorama of collaborative tasks.

Rivera's formal eclecticism made for an elegant and forceful tribute to

2.28. Diego Rivera, *Detroit Industry*. Fresco, south wall (May 1932–March 1933). Detroit Institute of Arts.

2.29. Diego Rivera, *Detroit Industry*. Fresco, north wall (May 1932–
March 1933). Detroit Institute of Arts.

the Detroit working class. Yet to be commissioned under the patronage
of Edsel Ford, as Rivera was for about ten months from May 1932
onwards, was regarded as particularly heinous by the left community,
given the infamous Ford River Rouge massacre that previous March.
Domestic automakers had witnessed a steady decline in average yearly
income from $1,639 in 1929 to $757 in 1931, not to mention deep
layoffs and factory speed-ups. In the year Rivera worked for the Fords, an
estimated 10,000 children were to be seen huddled everyday in Detroit
bread lines. Responding to such dire conditions, a group of some 5,000
Ford workers, Communists, and their families organized a March 7 hunger
march to proceed from Detroit to the Dearborn plant site. Here a committee would present a list of eleven demands to Ford, dealing with job
conditions, health benefits, coal allowances, home loans, and so on.[91]

At the Dearborn city line, they were met by Charles W. Slamer, acting
chief of police and his deputies. According to reports at the time, Slamer
"called out, asking who their leaders were. A chorus of voices replied,
'We are all leaders' " (Sugar, 334). Marching peaceably through police
tear gas and water cannons, the protesters were finally met with small

arms and machine-gun fire at the gates of River Rouge, where four of their number succumbed to mortal injuries. While up to 100 protesters suffered bullet wounds, not one of the police was shot in return. As part of its coverage of this national tragedy, New Masses published an "Open Letter to Edsel Ford" from an unemployed Ford worker and brother of one of the wounded. "You," he charged Ford, "a patron of the arts, a pillar of the Episcopal Church, stood on the bridge at the Rouge plant and saw four workers killed and over twenty wounded. You did not lift a hand to stop . . . the massacre."[92] In May—the same month that Rivera began his Detroit Industry fresco (whose South Wall would commemorate the patronage of Edsel Ford)—New Masses carried William Siegel's stinging cartoon of the wealthy auto magnate brandishing a smoking machine gun over the slumped figure of a slain protester (figure 2.30).

As controversial as Rivera's commission was on the left, the Detroit fresco was similarly attacked by the right. In particular, its proletarian content incensed conservative civic and church ideologues. Here indeed, Rivera had before him all the volatile elements he could ever want for conducting a proper experiment in the mass effects of muralist agitprop. Rivera's gloss on the iconography of the Holy Family in his vaccination panel was particularly offensive to the Episcopal and Catholic clergy that lobbied Councilman William P. Bradley and the Detroit News. Both demanded that the "paintings be washed from the walls" while Assistant Corporation Counsel John Atkinson charged the Detroit Art Commission with funding public obscenity.[93] Counterefforts were launched by the People's Museum Association in league with Unitarian churchmen such as Augustus P. Reccord. But more encouraging than these symptoms of his artwork's growing political force was the broad popular support Rivera enjoyed from the masses of working people who rushed to his defense. Some twelve-thousand workers joined in a united front that delivered a resolution to Detroit's mayor. Their statement warned that they would defend the murals by whatever means necessary. For his part, Rivera found in Detroit's conjuncture of working-class solidarity and conservative reaction an iron-clad confirmation that he had arrived at an aesthetics of revolutionary power. His craft now functioned, he was convinced, as a potent catalyst for social agitation.

On the heels of his Detroit victory, Rivera went directly to work on an even more challenging project that would lead his heretofore successful guerrilla art tactics into a political cul-de-sac. Early in 1933, Rivera had contracted with the Rockefeller dynasty to paint three large panels in the lobby of the RCA Building in Rockefeller Center on a theme that sparked

2.30. William Siegel, untitled cartoon of
Edsel Ford, *New Masses* (May
1932).

the muralist's utopian imagination: "Man at the Crossroads Looking with
Uncertainty but with Hope and High Vision to the Choosing of a Course
Leading to a New and Better Future." Rivera understood the title as a
choice between modernity's two dominant modes of production—
between capitalism and socialism. "The crossed roads," as far as he was
concerned, "were the individualist, capitalist order on the one hand, and

the collectivist, socialist order on the other; and Man, the Producer, in his triple personality of worker, farmer, and soldier stood at their intersection" (PA, 21). Faithful to his vocation as a guerrilla muralist, Rivera solicited the Rockefeller proposition not only because the theme was one that intrigued him but it offered even bigger laboratory conditions for refining the powers of proletarian art.

From the very beginning, Rivera's aesthetic was rigorously site specific. The cosmopolitan space of Radio City, as the name implied, would allow him to shape the political signs of the times and deliver them to a larger audience than any of his prior commissions. "A work of art is true," Rivera wrote of the muralist's craft,

> only if its function is realized in harmony with the building or room for which it has been created. . . . when at Rockefeller Center in New York I painted the naked and objective truth about the essential factors of social strife, and included a portrait of Lenin, I did so because Rockefeller Center is a group of public buildings open to all the inhabitants of the city and containing theaters, lecture halls, offices, radio and television studios, laboratories, and even a subway station. There I could only paint that which corresponded to and was significant for the entire mass of producing citizens. (PA, 15–16)

Borrowing from the primary geometrical forms and bold lines of suprematist and constructivist styles, Rivera translated the commission's crossroads motif into a nexus of scientific and social representation (figure 2.31).Crossing the mural's diagonal axes, two elliptical planes comprised detailed imagery of, on the one hand, the microcosmic world of bacteria, tissue, and cell structures intersecting, on the other hand, the macrocosmic expanses of solar systems, comets, galaxies, and other heavenly bodies. More politically charged, however, was the fresco's polar visions of human destiny depicted through a contradictory visual collage of sociohistorical scenes. To the right of the central dynamo, symbolizing the new forces of industrial production, Rivera presented images of life under depression era capitalism: a decadent cabaret club; a labor rally disrupted by mounted police; an army moving into battle with fixed bayonets and gasmasks. On the left was a glimpse of the socialist alternative: a women's athletic festival; a Soviet mass demonstration based on the tenth annual celebration of the October Revolution that Rivera had witnessed in Red Square; and, more radically, a group of peasants and workers pledging allegiance in a collective handshake to their vanguardist leader, Vladimir Lenin.

2.31. Diego Rivera, *Man, Controller of the Universe*. Fresco. Museo del Palacio de Bellas Artes, Mexico City.

It was this last portrait, conceived only toward the conclusion of the project, that occasioned the historic conflict between the artist and his patrons. Nelson Rockefeller, who had heretofore given Rivera free reign in the execution of the work, simply refused to tolerate such an obvious tribute to the world's premier Marxist revolutionary in the Radio City foyer. But Rivera, who had been dogged for years by the charge that he had courted the bourgeois art market, saw in this turn of events a way of exonerating himself with the party, which had branded him as a Trotskyite sell-out. Pressured by their mutual constituencies on the right and the left, artist and patron were both unswerving in their positions. Both had made up their minds and, when it came, their head-on clash instantly became a global cause célèbre. On May 9, 1933, a squad of Rockefeller's men took possession of the walls by sheer force of arms, covering them from public view with stretched canvases. Such an unprecedented seizure of an artist's commissioned work sent shock waves throughout the country.

Having struck a nerve in the New York art market, Rivera could, at long last, move beyond a guerrilla aesthetics to launch a war of position against his capitalist patrons in the mainstream media. If relatively few would ever view his proletarian art on site, then he would exploit the communicative possibilities that this sudden media event presented. The spectacle of public controversy that the scandal had fomented would allow him to orchestrate a much grander intervention in American mass culture. Like the Constructivists, Rivera viewed his aesthetic as a praxis—one that exceeded the formal limits of painterly values. Fresco design as a social intervention, he theorized, should include reception and audience response as part of the art work. In New York City he had the kind of mass socioaesthetic laboratory for testing the political force of his craft. Not just a victim of patronage censorship, Rivera exploited his clash with the Rockefeller dynasty as a means for broadcasting the message of proletarian resistance to the masses. While "it is highly improbable that many of the seven million inhabitants of New York City would have seen the dangerous painting," he would later theorize,

> on the other hand, thanks to the valiant attack of Capitalism against the mural, the press, the radio, the movies, all of the modern mediums of publicity, reported the event in the greatest detail over the entire territory of a country peopled by 125,000,000. . . . Tens of millions of people were informed that the nation's richest man had ordered the veiling of the portrait of an individual named Vladimir Ilyitch Lenin, because a painter had represented him in a fresco as the Leader, guiding the exploited masses towards a new social order based on the suppression of classes, organization, love and peace among human beings, in contrast to the war, unemployment, starvation, and degeneration of capitalist disorder. (PA, 27)

Meanwhile, the New York counterculture was organizing its own inhouse defense of the work through the Artists' Action Committee headed by Hugo Gellert. Not only did Gellert lead mass demonstrations in support of the fresco, but along with William Gropper, Louis Lozowick, Ben Shahn, and others, he withdrew his art work from a municipal exhibition at Radio City in protest. But this symbolic show of solidarity, arriving after years of divisive infighting on the left, came as too little, too late. Unable to mount a popular campaign to save the frescos, the left was powerless to prevent the Rockefellers, six months later, from pulverizing the painting with sledgehammers.

Fordism and Americanism

The loss of Rivera's Rockefeller Center mural points up the party's inability to mobilize mass support against the dominant systems of cultural repre-

---

sentation shaping the depression era scene. This shortcoming, arguably, resulted from American proletcult's allegiance to the classist and economist reduction of the Third Period. Although Rivera was adept at subverting the depression era spectacle, the Old Left's refusal to support such popular interventions reflects its failure to wage what Gramsci was describing at the time as a *war of position* for the cultural mainstream. In his 1926 study *Notes on the Southern Question* and *Prison Notebooks,* begun that same year of his arrest under Mussolini, Gramsci looked forward to the Popular Front strategy of the next decade. These works lodged a decisive critique against the Second International belief that capital's mounting concentration, coupled with an increasingly exploited proletarian base, would necessarily fuel the revolutionary process. For such Second International theorists as, say, Karl Kautsky, social change was driven by the economy, not the force of political and ideological intervention.

Gramsci's cultural Marxism overturned Second International economism to broaden the Leninist push for willed, political struggle. Unlike Lenin, however, Gramsci did not view the party in an external relationship to its class bureaucracy and mass base. He campaigned against the Leninist subordination of populism to vanguardist politics. Instead, Gramsci theorized the specific national differences separating, on the one hand, the Russian experience of waging a frontal assault on the autocratic and repressive regime of tsarism and monopoly capitalism from, on the other, advanced capitalism's more diffused and nuanced terrain of cultural struggle in the West. The classist, and often militarist, representations of Soviet labor during the early 1920s, he argued, had little purchase on building broad ideological consensus within the American scene.

The Comintern's increasingly bureaucratic makeup throughout the 1920s, Gramsci observed, served to erode, rather than to foster, broad ideological consensus in mass society: "The prevalence of bureaucratic centralism in the State," he concluded in *Prison Notebooks,* "indicates that the leading group is saturated, that it is turning into a narrow clique which tends to perpetuate its selfish privileges by controlling or even by stifling the birth of oppositional forces.[94] Parties, according to Gramsci, draw whatever force or authority they possess, from the contingencies of specific "moments which are historically vital for their class" (PN, 211). There are no guarantees that a particular regime will adapt itself to the shifting tasks and challenges of the times. Consequently, it is important, Gramsci maintained, to draw sharp distinctions among a party's mass membership, the social groups it articulates, its leadership, and the tendency toward bureaucratization. "The bureaucracy," he held, "is the most dangerously hidebound and conservative force; if it ends up by constituting a compact body, which stands on its own and feels itself independent of the mass of members, the party ends up by becoming anachronist and at moments of acute crisis it is voided of its social content and left as though suspended in mid-air" (PN, 211).

The working class's frontal assault had been viable against an earlier version of monopoly capitalism. While moments of crisis like the Russian Revolution could still produce "charismatic 'men of destiny' " (PN, 210), by the 1930s the situation of advanced capitalism in the West called for an expansion of radical democracy beyond the proletarian party vanguard. Just as political leadership could no longer be won in a decisive coup de grâce, so party bureaucracy could not afford to "form the habit of considering politics, and hence history, as a continuous marché de dupes, a competition in conjuring and sleight of hand" (PN, 164). Instead, what the revolutionary process demands in the twentieth century, Gramsci argued, is a constant war of position waged across the total fabric of everyday life mediated as it is by advanced capitalism's sophisticated cultural apparatus. Class hegemony and state power could no longer be maintained through repression or through neutralizing antagonistic interests. Instead, power flowed to the party that proved itself capable of leadership—capable, that is, of articulating to its agenda a broad popular front powerful enough at once to reign over its constituent groups and to dominate the opposition.[95]

This revolutionary task, for Gramsci, would extend political democracy across a plurality of diverse, though allied, social elements. The challenge was to articulate disparate groups under a common hegemonic principle. What was needed was a politics responsive to the often conflicted and contradictory needs and agendas of an expanded social terrain. Not insignificantly, Gramsci was one of the first to consider such a revolutionary struggle as belonging necessarily to a cultural, not economic, sphere of textual praxis:

> To the extent that ideologies are historically necessary they have a validity which is "psychological"; they "organise" human masses, and create the terrain on which men move, acquire consciousness of their position, struggle, etc. . . . It is worth recalling the frequent affirmation made by Marx on the "solidity of popular beliefs" as the necessary element of a specific situation. . . . Another proposition of Marx is that a popular conviction often has the same energy as a material force or something of the kind, which is extremely significant. . . . From this one can deduce

the importance of the "cultural aspect," even in practical (collective) activity. An historical act can only be performed by "collective man," and this presupposes the attainment of a "cultural-social" unity through which a multiplicity of dispersed wills, with heterogeneous aims, are welded together with a single aim, on the basis of an equal and common conception of the world, both general and particular, operating in transitory bursts (in emotional ways) or permanently (where the intellectual base is so well rooted, assimilated and experienced that it becomes passion). (PN, 377, 349)

What is absent in American proletcult, read through Gramsci's critique of the Third Period, is precisely the kind of passionate, hegemonic principle that would articulate "popular beliefs" to a broad-based "cultural-social unity."

Gramsci's reservations about proletarian representations, however, would not be theorized in the American context until the mid-1930s. Not surprisingly, when Kenneth Burke at the 1935 meeting of the American Writer's Congress likewise questioned the *textual* efficacy of the worker as a revolutionary symbol, he was anathematized by the party faithful.[96] In the years leading up to the Rivera censorship, the Comintern's mistaken strategy pressured leftist artists and writers in the United States to simply reproduce a Soviet-style cultural revolution in the West. By promoting Russian proletcult and the aesthetics of socialist realism, groups like the John Reed Clubs had to compete for a mass audience with America's burgeoning culture industry, the spread of Madison Avenue advertising, and the spectacular resources of Hollywood.

Such a strategy was dubious at best given the sheer cultural momentum that capital had amassed during the "Roaring Twenties." Kitsch, popular journalism, radio, the film industry—along with the productive forces that drove the rest of America's nascent commodity culture—were much more deeply entrenched than they would ever be in the Soviet Union, whose more abrupt leap into the industrial era had never spawned a dominant consumer class. Moreover, the push for technical innovation, organized capital, and a planned economy in the United States—the social modernization that Gramsci described under the rubric of *Americanism*—did not have to contend with the conservative inertia of what he derided as Old Europe's feudal past. Such vestiges of Continental aristocracy functioned as "a whole series of checks (moral, intellectual, political, economic) incorporated in specific sections of the population, relics of past regimes which refuse to die out, which generate opposition to speedy progress and give to *every* initiative the equilibrium of mediocrity, diluting it in time and space" (PN, 20).

The advent in 1910 of the line production system at Henry Ford's Highland Park plant—coupled with the new techniques of managing factory labor pioneered by Frederick W. Taylor's time and motion studies—served as a catalyst not only for the stepped-up spread of America's industrial production but for dramatic shifts in cultural and interpersonal relations throughout the sociopolitical field. It was the genius of Ford's scientific management that meshed consumption, worker behavior, and ideological norms (such as sobriety, family life, health, moral and fiscal responsibility) with the factory system's productive apparatus. The pitfall of fetishizing Fordism's new technical rationality snared both communist and capitalist ideologues alike. As Max Eastman argued against the left, it was hardly a secret that Lenin and Stalin openly admired the dehumanizing regimen of the American factory.

Even more disturbing was the Soviet bureaucracy's rush to embrace the production line as a symbol for cultural output as such. "Such slogans," Max Eastman charged, "as 'the five year plan in poetry' . . . 'collective creation,' 'the art job,' the 'turning out of literary commodities,' 'poetry as socially responsible labor.' . . . have held the field for eight years in the Soviet Union without successful competition."[97] Similarly, Gramsci noted Trotsky's research on how Ford aligned the scientific management of new factory technologies to the shaping of workers' everyday lives. This capitalist model offered Trotsky an administrative solution to his failure to militarize the Russian trade unions in the name of War Communism during the early 1920s.[98]

Just as the Soviets embraced Fordism's accelerated pace of production, U.S. entrepreneurs such as *Life and Letters* editor E. Haldeman-Julius, were no less industrious in exploiting the factory metaphor to market American kitsch culture. "I Will 'Fordize' the Magazine Field Too" announced the headline to Julius' full-page ad in the 1923 volume of *Broom* (figure 2.32). "Mr. Haldeman-Julius' ambition to 'Fordize' the magazine field," the ad boasted, "coupled with a 100 percent automatic printing plant and presses that can print 25,000 magazines an hour, permits LIFE AND LETTERS to be sold at 25 cents a year. And still Mr. Haldeman-Julius can maintain around him an able editorial staff to make LIFE AND LETTERS distinctly a magazine of culture."[99] While the Russian futurists and Walter Benjamin welcomed the industrialization of the mind in the hope of expanding cultural production for the masses, the new technologies of mechanical production proved just as susceptible to

2.32. E. Haldeman-Julius, "I Will 'Fordize' the Magazine Field Too!" *Broom* (1923).

kitsch profiteering in the hands of Fordist factory owners like Haldeman-Julius.

However dehumanizing, Ford's adaptation of Taylorism—which regarded the worker as little more than a "trained gorilla"[100]—nevertheless merited serious analysis and critique mainly because it simply outstripped in its technical and ideological success any Soviet experiments in planned management. It had arrived, according to Gramsci, as "the biggest collective effort to date to create, with unprecedented speed, and with a consciousness of purpose unmatched in history, a new type of worker and of man" (PN, 302). While writers on the left fully expected that the new cultural order of social modernization would be shaped democratically by the workers, corporate America thought otherwise.

Beyond such oppressive strategies as harassing labor organizers, brutalizing demonstrators, shutting down plants, laying off strikers, and other Red Scare tactics, giant companies like Ford, General Motors, and General Electric had launched an ideological campaign to win over the hearts and minds of American workers for consumption. The design and orchestration of fresh markets and consumer demands would serve to govern the new masses of industrial workers not through forced coercion but by a manufactured consensus. Writing in the wake of the October Revolution, Frances Kellor, the director of the American Association of Foreign Language Newspapers would propose as early as 1919 in *Advertising and Selling* that advertising "is the answer to Bolshevism" in winning immigrant workers to American capitalism."[101]

The pressing corporate need to spur consumer desire for an exploding market of new products was met in the rise of advertising as a discipline in such trade journals as *Printers' Ink* and *Advertising and Selling*. Studies in popular persuasion ranged from general theories of mass psychology as in Edward Bernay's *Crystallizing Public Opinion* (1923) all the way to minute analyses of "Facial Expressions in Advertisements" (*Journal of Applied Psychology,* 1923). Similarly, economists such as Elizabeth Hoyt and Paul Nystrom theorized the psychosocial dynamics of exchange value that bestowed individuality, sensuality, status, taste, authority, and distinction on the otherwise "marginal utility" of the commodity form. Exploiting this body of theory in the commercial market, professional advertising and industry apologists such as Edward Filene and George Phelps lobbied to shift democratic values from the political sphere to the new public spaces of an emergent commodity culture. No longer invested in their roles as producers, the people would be "free" to exercise their choices as "individual" (yet serial) consumers within an ostensibly competitive (but centrally owned and managed) economy. Advertising's role within this corporate habitus would fetishize the pure exchange value of the commodity form so as to seduce a diversified buying public across traditional class, race, gender, and ethnic boundaries.[102]

As *Broom* editor Matthew Josephson had observed as early as 1922, the sheer financial power of this new culture industry, coupled with the general decline in government and private patronage, allowed commercial advertising to recruit some of America's brightest young artists and writers for commodification. But instead of stigmatizing the American popular milieu as mere "low-brow" entertainment—as did the contributors to *Civilization in the United States: An Inquiry by Thirty Americans* (1922)—Josephson offered a more productive reading of advertising's dialogue with high and mass cultures. Critics, he maintained should not repress the discourse of advertising in the name of high art but investigate how advertising functions within a "'material environment' moulding and launching the American type."[103] From his vantage point as an expatriate in Paris, Josephson observed that what America lacked in indigenous traditions of high art, it made up for in its popular culture, which was spreading apace worldwide. Europe, he noted, "is become fearfully Americanized what of the telephone, the trolley, the trolley-car, the department store, and the advertising press" (GAB, 305). Consequently, he judged any attempts to elide modernism in order to emulate, say, British romanticism, French realism, or Russian naturalism as aesthetic dead ends in the twentieth century. Instead, writers and artists should profit from advertising's discursive techniques and visual conventions.

The contemporary challenge to artists, writers, and intellectuals of the 1920s, as Josephson described it, was not to eschew the dadaist spectacle of American pop culture, but

> to plunge hardily into that effervescent revolving cacophonous milieu . . . where the Billposters enunciate their wisdom, the Cinema transports us, the newspapers intone their gaudy jargon; where athletes play upon the frenetic passions of baseball crowds, and sky-scrapers rise lyrically to the exotic rhythms of jazz bands which upon waking up we find to be nothing but the drilling of pneumatic hammers on steel girders. We must have poets who have dared the lightning, who come to us out of the heart of this chimera. (GAB, 305)

Josephson's manifesto was one of the first attempts to crack the subliminal codes of advertising discourse, as they both reflect and shape the chimerical signs of the modern spectacle. Through close readings of his moment's commercial semiotics—its verbal textures, visual icons, and typographical layouts—Josephson examined the ways in which '20s' advertising variously connoted industrial efficiency, corporate prestige, athletic virility, youth, fashion, and so on.[104] Josephson anticipated the theoretical revolution of the postwar era by calling for cultural studies of how advertising techniques have crept into both the fabric of modern aesthetics and the rhetoric of American nationalism.

For their part, writers on the depression era left were all too aware of the imminent conglomeration of the entire U.S. publishing scene by the same parent companies that presided over the rest of consumer society. Yet not unlike their counterparts on the right, who propped up the Western canon against the sprawl of mass culture, they too dismissed the contemporary spectacle of commodity exchange in favor of Soviet-style proletcult. Throughout the Third Period, they failed to heed Josephson's advice of working within the formal conventions of advertising discourse to rearticulate its rhetoric and visual signs for progressive social change. This socioaesthetic strategy would have to wait until the more sophisticated interventions of the postwar era. Following instead the orthodox Marxist line that in all class societies journalism, radio, film, and other media are shaped by the material interests of the dominant class, the Workers Cultural Federation pointed out in its 1931 program manifesto that "in the radio and movie we have reached the *industrialization of art,* under capitalism the mass production of bourgeois ideas" (AW, 11). Just as Gold, Freeman, and Cheney bemoaned the cultural gap separating revolutionary Russia from the United States, so the WCF complained:

> The greatest inventions for the spread of ideas, which in a socialist country like the Soviet Union are used to raise the cultural level of the masses, are used in the United States and other capitalist countries for the spreading far and wide lies about the extent of unemployment, lies about the economic crisis, lies about the preparations for war, lies about the tremendous socialist construction being carried out by the workers of the Soviet Union. (AW, 11)

Building on this institutional critique, Jack Conroy's 1932 editorial "Art Above the Battle?" described the restricted publishing opportunities for radical writings, noting that most bookstores refused to stock the Rebel Poets' *Unrest* anthologies. In response he called for breaking the bourgeoisie's "almost full control of the press, the screen, and the radio" through supporting the Workers Cultural Federation, John Reed Clubs, and *New Masses.*[105] At the onset of the depression, Jack Woodford suggested in his review of a 1929 booksellers convention for *New Masses,* "that publishers and booksellers get together to form an association for advertising *all* books."[106] Soon, he predicted quite accurately, "books will be sold like chewing gum through page ads, billboard signs, street car placards, direct-by-mail pieces, and the whole nauseating program of American high pressure advertising" (5). Woodford's critique was reinforced visually by William Siegel's lithograph cartoon, stereotyping urban readers as frivolous consumers of book culture (figure 2.33). Despite its

2.33. William Siegel, "Bigger and Better
Belles Lettres," *New Masses* (October
1929).

prophetic acumen, the Old Left was clueless in dealing with America's
conglomerate culture industry. In slamming the new entertainment flows
of the consumer society, Siegel's visual layout shows, symptomatically,
how difficult it was for the Old Left to position itself *within,* instead of
against, the popular imagery of mass culture.

Faced with the sheer cultural might of conglomerate advertising, how
was one to go about the business of swaying the masses away from corporate America to the cause of proletarian revolution? For its part, the
WCF responded to such market pressures by initiating its own Belles Lettres Service to stimulate the growth of proletarian literature.[107] But it was
one thing to study revolutionary verse at a Workers' School seminar;
amassing the needed capital, technical equipment, and talent to stage
popular theater productions, dance performances, and box office film hits,
however, was quite another matter. There was simply no way that the
Old Left's paltry budgets—scrimped together from radical magazine subscriptions, proletcult picnics, and other grass roots fundraisers—could
compete with the overflowing coffers of Hollywood media moguls and
newspaper monopolists like William Randolph Hearst.

Lenin, as Joseph Freeman had reported, was convinced that "cinema is the most important of all the arts" for "where the millions are, there serious politics begins" (VO, 228, 221). In Russia, Sovkino underwrote the production, sale, and worldwide distribution of such masterpieces as Eisenstein's *Potemkin* that, when broadcast in New York, met with rave reviews from the *New York Sun, Evening Telegram,* and the *Exhibitors' Daily Review.* Even Douglas Fairbanks, quoted in *Motion Pictures Today,* praised it, claiming, "The Russians have a more advanced understanding of the science of motion and movement than any other picture makers in the world" (VO, 217). But in America, how pathetic did proletarian agitators such as Whittaker Chambers and Hugo Gellert appear when they solicited support in *New Masses* for W.I.R. Film and Photo League docudramas: "Some cameras and equipment are at hand," they wrote, "but there is a shameful lack of money. The Advisory Board asks all who can to contribute to the Production Fund. Budget estimate is $4,500, a pitifully small sum compared to the cost of the commercial, usual Hollywood products."[108] The socialist campaign for mass cultural revolution depended, unfortunately, on such bankrupt enterprises as the Boston W.I.R. Solidarity Players. In mounting an ambitious plan for a large production spectacle, "the group learned the first lesson in proletarian dramaturgy: that proletarian playwrights must never forget the limits set by our lack of equipment and facilities. They must also remember that our organizations cannot spend too much money on dramatics. In learning this fundamental lesson the group paid a price. It fell into the slough of discouragement, and slowly disintegrated."[109]

In traveling to the United States, the ideological signs of Soviet-style proletcult met with a cultural terrain that resisted any revolutionary programs to change the world. This national difference was most poignantly registered by those like Joseph Freeman and Mike Gold who, as tourists of the Soviet Revolution, had developed an abiding faith in the Comintern's destiny throughout the 1920s. Freeman, for example, was ecstatic over his first glimpse of the Red Flag over Russia, which symbolized, he wrote, a "tribute to power, to the reality of a dream" (AT, 455). Similarly, the Soviet banner struck Gold with "a great stab of joy and wonder."[110] These idealized responses to Soviet symbols were, of course, reproduced in the subcultural imagery of progressive little magazines in the United States. Fred Ellis' poster "Two Civilizations," for example, drew a sharp contrast between, on the one hand, the pathos of America's depression era unemployed and, on the other, the utopian prospect of a worker's industrial paradise in the Soviet Union (figures 2.34 and 2.35). The Soviet

2.34/2.35. Fred Ellis, "Two Civilizations." Poster drawn for a Soviet exhibition, *New Masses* (June 1933).

reversal of capital's ownership of the means of production was similarly depicted in Hugo Gellert's lithography (figures 2.36 and 2.37). It was on behalf of this same idealized Promised Land that William Gropper agitated in cartoons like "Defend the Soviet Union" (figure 2.38). Such manic euphoria, however, was only matched in its intensity by the depressing letdown of capitalist America where, as Gold lamented, "you're a nut, a rebel, an outcast, a lone wolf, a green apple in the belly of things" ("Notes," 4).

Writing in the early 1930s, Ralph Cheney was similarly disheartened by the striking contrast between the popular success of the Russian cultural revolution and the failure of its American counterpart. "The Soviet Union is dotted with poetry societies throughout its vast land" he noted. "The poetry society in Moscow alone numbers approximately 3000 members. . . . This respect for poetry in Russia contrasts strongly with the scorn in which poetry is largely held throughout the United States."[111] This sharp disparity in cultural milieus led American rebels like Freeman to hope that Stalin's "iron determination would overcome the tremendous obstacles on the road to socialism" (AT, 626). Similarly, the successful fusion of critic and revolutionary that Gold first admired in Trotsky in the mid-1920s made the lack of an American counterpart nearly intolerable. "O Life," he pleaded, "send America a great literary critic. . . . Send us a man fit to stand up to skyscrapers. A man of art who can match the purposeful deeds of Henry Ford."[112] But when the proletarian messiah failed to arrive and the promised land of revolution receded into divisive Third Period purges and low-brow agitprop, it is small wonder that Freeman would characterize his New York JRC colleagues as "neither intellectuals nor workers nor professional revolutionists. . . . Most of the people in the writers' group," he grimly admitted, "do not write and cannot write; they do not read; they do not know what is going on in the intellectual field and it is impossible to struggle with them on the basis of ideas."[113]

For artists and writers like Freeman, Gellert, and Gold— whose identities were wholly invested in agitation—the failure of American leftism came as a profound psychic loss. Trapped in a culture that they never made, that largely ignored their utopian interventions, these Old Leftists experienced everyday life as at once a literal and psychic prison, where the business of social collaboration went on, both figuratively and literally, behind bars (figures 2.39 and 2.40). In a revealing dialogue from his *American Testament* Freeman staged the trauma of internal exile, pro-

2.36/2.37. Hugo Gellert, untitled lithograph of factory owner and
Soviet worker, from Karl Marx, *Capital: in Lithographs*.

2.38. William Gropper, "Defend the Soviet Union," *New Masses* (May 1932).

jecting it through the fateful prediction of a Bolshevik lover: "But America will be hard for you these coming years," she said:

> Everywhere it is the proletariat which steadies and guides the revolutionary artists, and the movement in your country is weak. In Russia the whole country breathes and feels socialism; in Germany we have millions organized and conscious. But you are only beginning; you will know what isolation means." She lit a cigarette and laughed softly. "Do you know," she went on, "I have a peculiar horror when I think of America. For some reason I see it in the shape of a devouring beast, when I think of the skyscrapers, those monoliths with the romantic palaces on top of thirty stories of steel and cement. That is America—the steel and cement is real, and the romantic palaces are *kitsch*." (AT, 664)

Given the "peculiar horror" of their political situation, it is hardly surprising that leftist artists and writers would invest symptomatically in the pro-

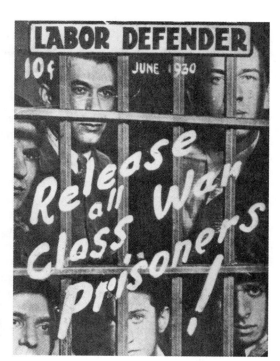

2.39. "Release All Class War Prisoners!" *Labor Defender* (June 1930).

2.40. Hugo Gellert, lithograph of prison handshake, from Marx: *Capital: in Lithographs.*

letarian aesthetic as a kind of cultural fetish—one that compensated for an American consumer society, envisioned here as a "devouring beast."

Left Androcentrism and the Male Dynamo

Recent feminist readings of proletcult have reminded us that the leading organs of working-class culture were all dominated by what Josephine Herbst dubbed as the period's literary "headboys": Eastman, Freeman, Gellert, Gold, and McKay.[114] Paula Rabinowitz, in particular, offers a cogent gender critique of how leftist androcentrism is inscribed in much of proletarian literature, namely through a masculine metaphorics of male vigor, possession, and penetration of virgin territories, as in Mike Gold's 1929 slogan "Go Left, Young Writers!" and V. F. Calverton's clever performative, "Leftward Ho!" (1932). Such citations, she notes, are tied to the kind of willful manifest destiny that we associate with such nineteenth-century American patriarchs as Horace Greeley.[115] By positioning leftist culture on a distinctively male terrain, these loaded metaphors served politically to exclude women's shaping role in American socialism.

But beyond pointing to Old Left androcentrism, feminist readings of this period have not provided an adequate explanatory account of such sexual politics, especially given the fact that women took an active hand in the everyday labor of coal mines, steel mills, lumber camps and factories. Why is it, exactly, that a discourse and semiology of male privilege held sway in leftist culture? The answer to this question lies, arguably, in the very political vulnerability of the proletarian enterprise. The Old Left's lack of real power is not only registered openly in the anxious dialogues of Freeman's *American Testament* but unconsciously acted out through compensatory fetish images of male authority everywhere encoding Third Period proletcult. Viewed against the era's actual context of political division and dissensus, the typical symbols of proletarian solidarity—the vertical red banner of class brotherhood, the assertive upraised fist (often clenching a weighty tool such as a wrench, sledgehammer, or sickle), the contractual handshake, the muscle-bound torso, the strained but determined visage—stand not so much as phallic icons of working-class hegemony but as uncanny symptoms of its absence (figure 2.41).

Vanguard artists such as, say, Hugo Gellert, who were intimately bound up in the moment's embattled politics of class representation, were especially prone to such male-gendered visual codes. Although Gellert was featured in the 1980s as one of the documentary informants in Warren Beatty's film *Reds* (1981), few now remember his contribution to the

2.41. Anton Refrigier, "Subway Model Sketch" (1939).

historical avant-gardes in America. The son of a Hungarian tailor, Gellert studied etching, lithography, and poster art at the National Academy of Design with Homer Boss. An early bohemian, Gellert in 1917 contributed exotic fin de siècle figures of nymphs, satyrs, and standing nudes to *The Masses,* reflecting the post-impressionist and primitivist influences of Gauguin and Matisse as well as the then widespread appeal of Arcadian mythology popularized by the Cambridge anthropologists. After the October Revolution and *The Masses* trial, however, his work took on a decidedly political cast. His cover lithograph for the inaugural issue of *The Liberator* (1918) portrayed a Russian peasant sowing the seeds of social change (figure 2.42). The following year Gellert traveled to Mexico with Mike Gold, who was emigrating to avoid the draft. Like Gold, Gellert toured the Soviet Union in 1927 and, in his tenure on the editorial board of *The Liberator* from 1918 to 1924, he struggled to move the journal to the left of the bohemian styles of fellow editors and contributors such as Max Eastman, Floyd Dell, Claude McKay, and the Baroness von Freytag-Loringhoven.

Gellert was at the center of a similar ideological clash with Ernest Walsh and John Dos Passos over the editorial direction of *New Masses,* which he helped found with Joseph Freeman and Mike Gold in 1926. *New Masses* offered Gellert a forum in which to debate such high modernists as Ezra Pound on, say, the work of Brancusi and to showcase his oppositional lithography.[116] Two years later Gellert and Gold conspired to revive the bankrupt magazine now as proletarian organ of the IURW. As a founding member of the New Masses Club, the New York John Reed

2.42. Hugo Gellert, cover illustration, *The Liberator*
(March 1918).

Club, and the W.I.R. Film and Photo League, Gellert was a visible figure
as a lecturer and teacher in the Greenwich Village intellectual scene.
Familiar with the spectacle of Soviet mass culture, Gellert imported proletcult to the United States in, among other projects, his 1929 labor fresco
for the Workers' Cafeteria at 28 Union Square. Under the auspices of a
cooperative Proletcos society, this socialist cafeteria served some 2,000
people daily. One of those who frequented this headquarters of the Communist Party of America, was the Chicago novelist Albert Halper. In his
memoir of the 1930s *Good-bye Union Square,* Halper recalled Gellert's
"gigantic murals, executed in the Soviet style, depicting heroic workmen
with huge muscular arms marching with banners toward victory" (15).

"On the walls," according to a *New Masses* review, "Gellert has painted a massive fresco of America labor—Negro workers, women workers, miners, the inside of a steel mill, Sacco and Vanzetti, John Reed, Lenin, Ruthenberg and other symbolic and real figures—ten feet tall. . . . It is the first large demonstration in this country of that union of art and labor which is the keynote of Soviet Russia."[117]

Not only did Gellert undertake mural compositions for the Workers' Cafeteria, Rockefeller Center, New Playwrights' Theater, and the Communications Building of the New York World's Fair, 1938–40, but his proletarian imagery circulated through such journals as *New Masses,* the *Daily Worker, Pagan,* the *New Yorker, Masses and Mainstream,* and the *New York Daily World,* among others. His portrait of Lenin from the Workers' Cafeteria mural, for example, appeared as an accompanying illustration to a *New Masses* review of "Lenin on Art" in its January 1929 issue. Moreover, in adopting the marketing strategies of the commercial press houses, *New Masses* offered Gellert give-aways as in its December 1931 subscription offer of a free Gellert 9×12-inch lithograph of Lenin (figure 2.43). Similarly, the *Daily Worker* advertised a subscription discount premium on Gellert's illustrated version of Marx's *Capital* with the purchase of a one-year subscription and a free copy of the text for a group of five yearly subs (figure 2.44). Such marketing ploys were part of Gellert's efforts to foster Marxist representations at the level of popular culture.

A remarkable, but now seldom-read volume, *Capital in Lithographs* reflects the Third Period doctrine of capitalism's imminent collapse before the triumph of international socialism: a prophetic faith personified in what Gellert hailed as the "new Prometheus" rising out of the East. "The Young Giant," of the new Soviet Union, he proclaimed "with his mighty hands builds the future of mankind and bright lights flare up in his wake." America, meanwhile, by sharp contrast was experiencing "a period of the greatest expropriation in history since we took the land from the Indian possessors." Symptomatic in its ethnocentrism toward Native Americans, Gellert's bid to build a Soviet America rested on an idealized proletariat that he lionized, following Marx, as the revolutionary class par excellence. "It is my hope," he wrote, "that in this abbreviated form the immortal work of Karl Marx will become accessible to the Masses: to the huge army of workers without jobs and farmers without land; to the workers in mills and mines, to all who toil with brain or brawn. This book is made for them. For my existence—and yours, depends upon *them.*"[118]

Yet after nearly two decades of editing radical magazines, and agitating in the W.I.R., WCF, and John Reed Clubs, Gellert was still frustrated in

2.43. Hugo Gellert, lithograph of V. I. Lenin, from Marx,
Capital: in Lithographs.

the vanguard task of educating the masses to their historic role of fomenting social change in the United States. Given his paradoxical situation in
1933—of having to agitate on behalf of a class supposedly preordained
to a revolutionary destiny but that, well into the depression era, still largely
ignored proletcult—Gellert's aesthetic stands out today as a utopian compensation for America's historic failure to follow the Russian lead of 1917.
Despite the almost religious rhetoric of Gellert's preface, his art betrays a
telling anxiety over capital's ability to thrive in a crisis economy. The new
productive forces spawned by the industrial revolution—machinery and
factory technology—while typically portrayed in this volume as vehicles
of working-class liberation are also depicted as sinister agents for intensifying the labor process. Marx, of course, had foretold that capital would
step up the pace of production through machine automation and other
technological advances in responding to organized labor demands for a

shorter work day and greater benefits. Capital's power of managing worker demands to its own advantage, in Gellert's work, literally locks labor into a technological strangle hold, as the machine (contrary to the usual proletcult depiction) becomes a source of radical alienation not emancipation (figure 2.45).

Nostalgic for a simpler moment of proletarian solidarity, before the alienating regimen of Taylorism, Fordism, and what Gramsci was then theorizing (unbeknownst to Gellert) as advanced technocapitalism, Gellert fetishizes the figure of the male proletarian body in the absence of the working class's actual hegemonic power. Gellert's most phallocentric images of proletarian mastery come in illustrating Marx's discussion of primary accumulation. In response to the rapid leaps in manufacturing and the complementary emergence of the working class's collective political agency, the nineteenth-century English Parliament repealed "laws against strikes and trade unions, after having for five centuries, with unblushing selfishness, itself played the part of a permanent trade union of capitalists directed against the workers" (11). In Gellert's visual depiction of this revolutionary turning point, however, the specific history of class struggle theorized in Marx's text is reduced to a universal allegory of primordial, masculine prowess (figure 2.46).

In Gellert's visual composition, the geometric planes defined by the crossed sledgehammers lend, in their clear and angular lines, a dynamic

2.44. Hugo Gellert, "Good News!" Advertisement, *New Masses* (March 1934).

2.45. Hugo Gellert, lithograph of machine strangling
worker, from Marx, *Capital: in Lithographs.*

abstraction to the more organic shaping of these brawny, bilateral figures.
More troubling, however, the representation of the proletariat in this stylized duo is at once literally stripped of any historical reference and
stamped with male essentialism. Brandishing their weighty tools and with
genitalia exposed, they flash the hierophantic high sign of masculine
authority and potency. But what does it mean, and whose interests are
served, in reducing the representation of race, gender, ethnic and transnational diversity of working-class people to a muscle-bound, white, male
torso? In light of the troubled context of American labor at the time, the
fetishistic display, in Gellert's visual images, of phallic tools, weapons, rigid
male body parts, and aggressively masculine posturing (figure 2.47) must
be read at once as a utopian investment in what Freeman beheld in the

Red Banner as a "tribute to power" *and* as an anxious symptom of its loss.

The psychoaesthetic investment in revolutionary Russia, industrial society, and proletcult that marks Gellert's visual art reflects modernism's broader fetishization of machine processes. As a mimetic sign of the times, the machine design signaled a cultural difference. It marked the boundary between what was radically inaugural in modern aesthetics and the conventionally démodé. William Carlos Williams, for example, defined the avant-garde in an early issue of Charles Henri Ford's magazine *Blues* (1929–30), through the metaphor of the machine. Avant-garde writing,

2.46. Hugo Gellert, lithograph of two nude workers with sledgehammers, from Marx, *Capital: in Lithographs.*

2.47. Hugo Gellert, lithograph of two workers with tools, from Marx, *Capital: in Lithographs.*

in his reading, outran velocities of obsolescence that relentlessly overtook language, whose "words (the parts) are getting old and out of date just as would be the corresponding parts of a motor car." Consequently, "literature, poetry especially, is to invent. It is not to invent emotions. . . . But it is to invent mechanisms of expression suitable to the keenest intelligence of the time, [which] struggling with emotion, finds the mechanisms formerly adequate to ensnare or vent them inadequate."[119] The glossy icon of the machine seemed to embody the modern impulse to break radically with the past so as, in Pound's dictum, "to make it new." Taking note of this tendency, William Phillips' *Dynamo* review of "Sensibility and Modern Poetry" observed that "perhaps the most pervasive . . . of poetic sensibilities is the sense of the machine, or of industrialization."[120]. Here Phillips analyzed Crane's experimental long poem sequences in *The Bridge* following from the poet's conviction in "Modern Poetry: An Essay" that "Unless poetry can absorb the machine . . . then poetry has failed of its full contemporary function" (22).

America's depression era celebration of the new machine age drew from the formal resources of Futurism and dadaist precursors of the previous two decades. The futurist imagery of American industry had served the New York Dadaists in the 1910s in their rebellion against the kind of European modernism exhibited at the 1913 Armory Show. "Almost immediately upon coming to America," recalled Francis Picabia, "it flashed on me that the genius of the modern world is in machinery, and that through machinery art ought to find a most vivid expression."[121] The visual fetishization of mechanical form was literally embodied in the new photographic equipment and techniques popularized by Alfred Stieglitz's journal *Camera Work* (1903–17), but it was also signified in such images as Picabia's *Mechanical Expression Seen Through Our Own Mechanical Expressions* (1913). The modern fascination with machine parts as *objets trouvés* variously marked Morton Schamberg's machine pastels of automatic mixers, wire book stitchers, hosiery winders, and various pulley, roller, and needle-bar-motion systems; the gadgetry and appropriated mass-produced objects that went into Marcel du Champ's "ready-mades"; and the sculptural transformation of industrial hardware as in Baroness Elsa Von Freytag-Loringhoven's *God* (1916)—literally a plumbing trap affixed to a miter box.

Meanwhile, following Marinetti's *Manifesto on the Foundation of Futurism* (1909), Continental figures such as Umberto Boccioni, Luigi Russolo, Luciano Folgare, Enrico Prampolini, and Gino Severini in Italy; Fernand Léger in Paris; Guillermo de Torre in Spain; Wyndham Lewis in England; and others such as Theo Van Doesburg, Hans Richter, El Lissitzky, Eggelin, and Janco in Russia, Germany, the Netherlands, Scandanavia, and Romania were importing industrial values and machine imagery into literature and the visual arts. Throughout the 1920s, the cultural celebration of industrial values was in turn broadcast to an American audience via such internationalist little magazines as *Blast, Broom,* and *transition*. In the pages of *Broom* one gleans the visual and linguistic semiotics of machinery, for example, in Enrico Prampolini's 1922 manifesto "The Aesthetic of the Machine and Mechanical Introspection in Art," published in the same issue as Louis Lozowick's constructivist review of Tatlin's futuristic "Monument to the Third International."[122] Here Prampolini proclaimed "the Machine to be the tutelary symbol of the universal dynamism, potentially embodying in itself the essential elements of human creation: the discoverer of fresh developments in modern aesthetics" (237).

Echoing Henry Adams' celebrated dichotomy of "The Dynamo and the Virgin," Prampolini likewise upheld the machine as the modern symbol par excellence, marking as it did modernism's break with the cultural icons of Western humanism. "The elements and the plastic symbols of the *Machine*," he wrote, "are inevitably much nearer to us (materially and spiritually) than any symbol of the past can be: symbols such as a god Pan, the taking down from the Cross or the Assumption of the Virgin, etc." (236). As a metaphor for the twentieth-century milieu, the machine reflected the new productive modes of industrial society that were changing the human order of things. In illuminating his manifesto with a visual ornament (figure 2.48), Prampolini offered a futurist portrait of a robotlike figure—a kind of human dynamo or cyborg—that, in its stylized visual composition, was not unlike the cubofuturist machine decorations that

2.48. Enrico Prampolini, "The Aesthetic of the Machine and Mechanical Introspection in Art," *Broom* (October 1922).

2.49. Louis Lozowick, *Machine Ornament 2* (1927).

Lozowick borrowed from Russian Constructivists such as El Lissitzky and Rodchenko (figure 2.49). "In agricultural societies," Lozowick theorized following the Russian avant-gardes, "ornament is based on vegetable and plant forms, and in contemporary industrial society, ornament should be based on machine parts and various technical aspects."[123] In the United States, Lozowick's machine ornaments were widely disseminated to an American audience through the pages of *New Masses,* where they illustrated brief imagist stylizations of the dynamo in works by MacKnight Black among others.

Little is now known about the poet MacKnight Black who, before his untimely death in 1931, had published his verse in *The Dial, The Saturday Review of Literature, The Nation, Harpers, The Bookman, New Masses,* and *Poetry.* In his two volumes of poetry *Machinery* (1929) and *Thrust at the Sky* (1932) he splices cubofuturist and proletcult styles in compressed vignettes of factory life, construction sites, and coal mines. His "Negro Foundation Gang," for example, stylizes construction workers through a series of striking, cubofuturist conceits: "Torsos / Dark triangles / Looming through sweated jeans . . . / Body-muscle of a nation, / Black Thaw / At the roots of new sky-lines."[124] Often his proletarian settings are marked by the semiotics of post-revolutionary agitprop as in his "Skyscrapers: Murky Morning," where "Giant laborers / Stare at the sun's red flag of revolt" (*Machinery,* 52). Building on the taut, chiseled language of imagist verse, Black celebrates a dynamic balance of natural and industrial forces in "Turbine Room"—one of five short lyrics originally published in *New Masses,* ornamented with one of Lozowick's machinery lithographs. At the heart of the dynamo's elegant violence, the poem depicts, paradoxically, a core of

> Peace
> Locked in thunders;
> Stillness
> like crystal,
> Shut in a roaring cube—
> Stealing words from the lips,
> Impact from movement—
> New Quiet that cages the blood,
> Nirvana
> Steam-born. (*Machinery,* 23)

Such futuristic, "steam-born" mechanisms of power, as they are depicted in Black's verse, appropriate the traditional landscapes, settings, and seasonal motifs of pastoral poetics. Poems like "In an Engine Room," for example, recode such naturalized tropes in terms of the phenomenological spaces of the machine age: "Here in this place, each morning is a new Spring / And powered splendor bursting from a sleep / Fires this city forever with April" (*Machinery,* 20).

In the expanded landscape of modernist visual culture, the play of abstract industrial shapes with architecture found formal expression in such avant-garde works as *Bridgebuilders* (1912), *Skyline* (1912), and *Metropolis* (1913) by Man Ray. Similarly, the bold assertion of the new urban skyscrapers—what in 1900 a Scottish journalist praised as the "simply astonishing manifestations of human energy and heaven-storming audacity"[125]—was captured in the urban surrealism of Black's "Ridden":

> Skyscrapers stand tethered at evening,
> Sinewy, dun.
> Against the sunset
> They show bloody flanks,
> As though fierce riders
> Had spurred them all day long. (*Machinery*
> 51)

The metropolitan skyline was similarly celebrated throughout the interbellum decades in the portraits of such monumental structures as Lozowick's lithograph of New York's Whitehall Building or Joseph Stella's cubo-futurist tribute to the Brooklyn Bridge. These visual representations found their poetic counterparts in expansive long poems such as Hart Crane's *The Bridge* and MacKnight Black's *Thrust at the Sky* (1932).

An unfinished version of Black's little-known and posthumously compiled long poem was published the year following the poet's death. In it Black takes as his central character an architect named Thomas Haig who, as the narrative unfolds, becomes obsessed with an ambitious design project for the monumental American Light and Power Building. Through the metaphor of urban architecture, the poet transcodes the abstract and dynamic values of the cubofuturist style from the visual arts to poetry. Pondering "[t]he bright spurt of a steel skyscraper," glimpsed in the blueprints for the structure, Haig is rendered "motionless":

> By verticals, the jut of lines, lean dimensions
> Straining upward to escape themselves; the countless deep
> Motions of his mind,
> Electron-swift, were drawn to patterns
> Of straightness reaching
> Up from the earth through fifteen hundred feet
> Of rivet-locked framework sheathed in blazing
> steel.[126]

Not unlike Tatlin's utopian model for his "Monument for the Third International," Haig's design, in its ambitious conquest of modernist space, reflects the austere visual elegance of vertical line captured in, say, Alfred Stieglitz's 1903 portrait of Daniel Burnham's Fuller (or "Flat Iron") Building of 1901–03. What Le Corbusier called the modern machine for living, the urban high rise boldly stood out in its "full sting of planes" and "edged nakedness" as, in Gorham Munson's phrase, a "skyscraper primitive": a grand objet d'art and emblem of the avant-garde imaginary.[127]

As a modern symbol of change, however, the dynamo was susceptible to a certain idealization. Responding to the supposed marvels of the machine age, *New Masses* published a series of articles throughout 1927 by Floyd Dell, Lewis Mumford, and Genevieve Taggard, among others, in an effort to stake out the positions of debate concerning the social and aesthetic significance of the new industrial technologies. Dell and Taggard indulged in somewhat utopian hopes for industry that ignored actual patterns of social modernization taking place in their midst. Theorizing the impact of the new machine age on traditional notions of self, family, and community, Floyd Dell productively underscored the social significance of industrialization "inasmuch as the machine is engaged in breaking down small groups and creating apparently a new human synthesis."[128] In this revolutionary period of industrial growth, he gleaned the chance at once for overturning the tyranny of monopoly ownership and for living out revisionary class, gender, and communal roles.

Six months later, however, *New Masses* staged a dispute between Mumford and Taggard that proved a salutary caveat against idealizing industry. Arguing against Taggard's rather naive embrace of the labor-saving technologies and creature comforts provided by modern machinery, Mumford demystified the exploitative economic underpinnings of what Taggard simply accepted at face value as technological progress. Subways and traffic systems, he pointed out, are not just efficient ways of shuttling people throughout the city, but manifest symptoms of social congestion: a "maladjustment, promoted by the price system."[129] Similarly, the skyscraper—what he maligned as "the chief fetish of the revolutionary boys and girls"—served mainly "the purpose of increasing the financial returns upon land and buildings" (23). Truly avant-garde architectural designs, he claimed, could be achieved on a smaller scale as "Sullivan did in his banks, as Wright does in his houses, as Goodhue did in the Los Angeles Public Library, as Saarinen did in the Helsingfors Railway Station, as Stein and Out and May and Taut do in workers' dwellings" (23).

Fetishized, however, in the period styles of art deco and cubofuturist signage, the social text of urban modernization was often obscured by what Phillips described as the "sharp and metallic patterns" (22) in, say, Williams' verse. For his part, the proletarian poet Joseph Kalar, in a review for *The Rebel Poet* of the 1931 *Unrest* anthology, warned against aestheticizing industrial processes. Kalar cautioned, in his critique of Sherwood Anderson's "Machine Song," that "It is not enough to chant the beauties of machinery without taking into account the realities of the 'new life' bred by the machine under capitalism."[130] In the course of his review, Kalar drew a keen distinction between a poem's representation of industrial design vs. the social processes entailed in the new industrial forces of production. He thus resisted any aestheticization of technology that would divorce machinery from its social contexts.

Despite the period's often naive enthusiasm for the machine age, industrialism for the *Dynamo* group did not merely connote an avant-garde aesthetic style as in some formalist versions of cubofuturism. The Dynamo circle included the several poets who published variously, throughout the Third Period and Popular Front years, not only in *Dynamo: A Journal of Revolutionary Poetry,* but also in such little magazines as *Anvil, Blues, Contempo, Laughing Horse, The Menorah Journal, New Masses, Partisan Review,* and *The Rebel Poet,* among others, as well as in alternative anthologies between the wars. Among the better-known poets of the Dynamo school were Kenneth Fearing, Sol Funaroff, Mike Gold, Horace Gregory, Joseph Kalar, H. H. Lewis, Lola Ridge, Edwin Rolfe, Muriel Rukeyser, Isidor Schneider, Herman Spector, and Genevieve Taggard.[131] Politicized in their renderings, the dynamo signified the entire ensemble of productive forces, conceived against the social background of the industrial era. These New York-based writers articulated the dynamo to a distinctively Marxist historical outlook. In their work machinery signified the new powers of industrial production as well as capital's contradictory relation to labor. According to this reading, capital creates the industrial base and exploitative social preconditions which prove indispensable, paradoxically, for the proletariat's communal destiny of seizing society's productive forces. In *The German Ideology* Marx argued that the complex, collective character of the new technological infrastructure, while temporarily dominated by individual owners, would in time necessarily transcend the competency of any single manager. Meanwhile, the actual workers, having already been alienated by mass production from their traditional craft roles, would be drawn into collective modes of social agency. Once positioned as a political bloc, they would appropriate capital's industrial base en masse.

This prediction, of course, has never arrived as capital has proved itself, in the twentieth century, far more resilient than Marxist historicism would allow. Instead, flexible techniques of intensifying an increasingly automated labor process, coupled with the culture industry's relentless promotion of consumer society, have removed the shaping of industry from the workers themselves and displaced proletarian class values in favor of commodity consumption. Far from inheriting industry's productive forces, those who actually produced each new wave of consumer goods, found themselves increasingly alienated from ever more automated systems of production, engineered and administered by a new class of technological experts. In our time, writes André Gorz, "the fragmentation of work, taylorism, scientific management and, finally, automation have succeeded in abolishing the trades and the skilled workers whose 'pride in a job well done' was indicative of a certain consciousness of their practical sovereignty."[132] While Marx's prognosis has never been borne out empirically, it seemed imminent to the poets of the depression era. History appeared at the time to be pressing them to come together as collective agents for hastening the proletarian revolution.

One way of resisting the aestheticization of the machine age was to infiltrate the moment's dominant discourses, thereby recoding the symbols of industrial society for the revolution, as in Ben Maddow's proletarian elegy "Remembering Hart Crane." Writing under the pseudonym David Wolff, Maddow laments the passing of the "Dead poet." While "bitter in the nighttime with our cheap fatigue," he nevertheless affirms an industrial vision of communal bonding, where

> . . . our rivets shock
> men into class among broad fierce
>   machines.
> True, to the world riveted, immutable
> till billions pass, Hart Crane, new
> bridge we project:
> O Party of the one weld, O living steel,
> arc whose first pier destroys the tenements!
> (*Proletarian Literature,* 202)

In such lines Maddow politicizes Crane's more mythic tribute to the monuments of American industry by rearticulating the poetic language of *The Bridge* to the discourse of class critique. In a more expansive mode, Sol Funaroff's "What the Thunder Said: A Fire Sermon"—illuminated with Herbert Kruckman's agitational cartoons in the August 1932 *New Masses*—similarly appropriates the alienated scene of modernism depicted in Eliot's *The Waste Land.* But unlike Eliot's verse epic, that voices a transcendental resolution to social fragmentation, Funaroff's poem rearticulates Eliot's "thunder" to a materialist vision of international class revolt, linking the unrest of pre-revolutionary Russia to depression era America.

Similarly, Funaroff's 1932 poem "Dnieprostroy" takes as its epigraph William Blake's opening stanza of "The Tyger." Funaroff's proletcult verse offers a dialogic response to Blake's rhetorical question—"What immortal hand or eye / Could frame thy fearful symmetry?"—blending the rhetoric of visionary romanticism with agitprop celebrations of Soviet industry:

> We perfect new and more vital symmetries,
> Burning oceans of motion,
> Tigers of our passion concrete lashed
> To expend no energy on parliamentary coquettes.
>
> While suns of photo-electric eyes petrify
> Barrack and bivouack, bullet and bayonet.
> . . . . .
> And new love burns with tigris eyes
> Billions of kilowatt hours.[133]

While such poetic interventions deflated any romantic transcendence of material culture, American proletcult, as a mouthpiece for orthodox Marxism, tended to promote its own brand of utopian representation. One pitfall, endemic to this tradition, idealized the industrial scene as a redemptive Promised Land somehow beyond the traumatic costs of its actual social and environmental historicity. Factory labor, however alienating, nevertheless gave tangible survival to starving workers and, accordingly, was venerated as a mystical essence underwriting whatever value life had to offer.

Thus, in "The Spider and the Clock" Funaroff asked "Where are the more magnificent, / the men with labor in their hands, / the hand's touch that renders things their meaning."[134] A worker's touch, for Funaroff, granted use value on things that were otherwise reified as sterile commodity fetishes. In contrast to the inaugural powers that labor bestowed, nothing seemed more demoralizing than the bleak spectacle of depression era bread lines, where unemployment sapped the world of its phenomenal vitality. The grim setting of a factory closing, as Joseph Kalar describes it in his widely published poem "Papermill" was "Not to believed hardly, this clammy silence":

> Where once feet stamped over the oily floor,
> Dinnerpails clattered, voices rose and fell
> In laughter, curses, and songs. Now the guts
> Of this mill have ceased their rumbling, now

The fires are banked and red changes to black,
Steam is cold water, silence is rust, and quiet
Spells hunger. Look at these men, now,
Standing before the iron gates, mumbling,
"Who could believe it? Who could believe it?"[135]

One of the few proletarian poets of the depression era who actually earned his living as a mill worker, Kalar was isolated on the iron range of northern Minnesota throughout his lifetime. Nevertheless, he published worldwide in *Red Flag* (official organ of the German CP), *Literature of the World Revolution* (Moscow), and *International Literature,* as well as in such domestic venues as *Anvil, The Daily Worker, Left, Morada, New Masses,* and *The Rebel Poet.* In fact, it was only through the literary network which little magazines kept alive that talents like Kalar's survived on the outskirts of provincial America. "*New Masses,*" he wrote in 1932, "kept me on the road, in this period, when the hallucinative fog of egotism . . . would ebb and I would write. Through *New Masses* I became acquainted with a number of fine fellows, Jack Conroy, H. H. Lewis, Walt Carmon, and others."[136] In introducing Kalar to a left audience in the 1933 anthology *We Gather Strength,* Mike Gold valorized him as "a young lumber worker and paper-mill mechanic of Minnesota":

> There is power in him that has not yet found words; but nobody can miss the ardor, the fierce proletarian groping for a clue to the world, the painful cheated sense of beauty. . . . He is a mystic, and he works in a papermill, sweating and starving. This is the contradiction, and this is the secret of his communism.[137]

From Gold's proletcult perspective, Kalar's strength lay in his everyday familiarity with working-class existence coupled with an understanding of Marxism and the Soviet Revolution. His proletarian credentials made him a native son of the American left, one who seemed to embody Gold's Soviet ideal of the worker correspondent.

Kalar's realistic style has the virtue of reflecting with exacting verisimilitude the barbarous side of capitalist production, as in, say, "Warm Day in Papermill Town," where

sulfur dioxide
burns the nose and wreathes the mind
with thoughts of beaters to be filled,
pumping jordans, swish swish of hot rolls,
paper to be made, the crash of spruce,

furred branches stabbing here and there,
the arm caught pulpy in the rolls,
the finger lost; faces young, floating in steam,
shouting, cursing, seen now,
haggard in the sun, remembering flowers. (JK, 52)

Echoing the "apparition" of faces in Pound's "In a Station of the Metro,"
Kalar's "faces young, floating in steam" lends a political inflection to modern imagist poetics. Beyond Pound's more cosmopolitan setting, the pastoral expectations set up in the poem's title are ironically undercut with
graphic scenes of abusive child-labor practices and industrial mutilation.

In addition to such disturbing portraits, Kalar also composed in the
agitprop manner, employing slogans, journalistic lampoon, and topical
parodies to critique American jingoism, red baiting, racism, and xenophobia, as in the "patriotic" mask of the "Flagwaver":

When I get patriotic, I go on the big drunk.
I cut Wesley Everest, I hang that black Injun
Frank Little from a bridge, I put Joe Hill
Against a wall and fill the lousy bastard
With hot jets of lead,
I break the foreign heads of strikers,
Them yella slackers, them chickenlivered
Bastards. (JK, 13)

Responding to the often violent scenes of depression era unrest, Kalar
artfully captures, in his grotesque personae, the reactionary vernacular of
the American midwest.

In dedicating their talents to the proletarian revolution, '30s poets did
not simply succumb to didactic formula writing or parrot Comintern slogans. For Edwin Rolfe, the poet's special handling of agitational forces in
the aesthetic dimension served, like the midwife's craft, to birth a new
social order beyond the mortifying milieu of the depression era, as in his
portrait of a successful Toledo trade union strike: "Not men alone / nor
women," he affirmed, "but cities also are reborn; not without labor, not
before the hour / when flesh feels lacerated, mangled, torn":

Not only men are resurrected. I have seen
dull cities bloom, grow meaningful
overnight. Wherever class war comes
awareness is its courier, a newer life[138]

The genesis of class solidarity that Rolfe commemorates in "Not Men Alone" borrows from the biblical imagery of crucifixion and resurrection to celebrate the advent of "new life" in the proletarian revolution. But under the ownership of finance capital, the industrial landscape for many depression era poets offered not so much a utopian vista as a scene of cruelty. Here one grew used to "Hearses along some streets, taking the bodies / Of men who failed, who were not cunning enough / To dodge the swift wheels in the sheds."[139]

While Funaroff's imagistic poem "Dusk of the Gods" celebrated the dynamo's "Violent blue leap of electric: / song of work and wheels, / of the motor's hum and charge of voltage" (SP, 57), for Stanley Burnshaw the powerplant turbine was not wholly divine, but "half-beast, half-god"— a demonic personification of alienated labor: "Slick unviolent robot whose pure voice / Tells no word of its daily murdering hands . . . The heart, the eyes, the flesh of men who feed / The flame for dynamos" (SP, 10). That workers literally fed the machine with their flesh and blood was recorded in vernacular ballad forms by poets such as John Beecher, who eulogized industrial victims like Henry Matthews: "He slung a sledge an he shovel san / Watch yo step, o watch yo step / Henry stepped in where de hot iron ran."[140] Similarly, Mike Gold's martyr Jan Clepak suffered more than just Matthews' "shoeful of steel" (CP, 3), toiling as he did "Where steel-mills live like foul dragons, burning, devouring man and earth and sky" (SP, 85). On the job one fateful day, he found himself suddenly caught in the path of a runaway torrent of molten metal: "Now three tons of hard steel hold at their heart the bones, flesh, nerves, the muscles, brains and heart of Jan Clepak" (SP, 86). In "A Strange Funeral in Braddock," Gold offers a kind of demonic parody of Whitman's "When Lilacs Last in the Dooryard Bloom'd." Here we witness the modern parade of Clepak's bizarre sarcophagus: as "on the great truck it is borne now to the great trench in the Graveyard" (SP, 86). Gold achieves a memorably uncanny spectacle by casting *the* element of America's industrial power into a cold funereal object: "Life is like a dirty joke, like Jan's funeral," thinks one of the bystanders before the open grave, "As a derrick lowers the three tons of steel that held Jan Clepak" (SP, 86–87).

In addition to these naturalistic scenes of industrial hazard, depression era poets presented the debilitating course of industrial disease in surrealistic lyrics such as Edwin Rolfe's "Asbestos." Here we meet a proletarian everyman whose "deathbed is a curious affair: / the posts are made of bone, the spring of nerves, / the mattress bleeding flesh. Infinite air / compressed from dizzy altitudes, now serves / his skullface as a pillow."[141]

The poem's closing epitaph—"that dead / workers are dead before they cease to be" (TMC, 10)—could just as easily stand as the motto for Rukeyser's "The Book of the Dead." But unlike these short lyrics that assert somewhat totalizing stances—either idealizing the proletariat as the privileged class of revolution or anathematizing capital's barbarous side—Rukeyser employs the expanded possibility of the long-poem format to lodge a more nuanced cultural critique of American industry.

3. The Feminist Vanguard in the Popular Front

Muriel Rukeyser and the Poetics of Specific Critique

It is an instructive paradox that in the divisive milieu of the Great Depression, the sign of a poem's cultural power lay not in its widespread acclaim, as it does today, but instead in the critical conflict it provoked. Indeed, entire careers of this period record in their twists and turns the historical pressures that writers were compelled to negotiate. Most notably, Archibald Macleish went the full gamut of interbellum political life. Graduating from Harvard Law School in the early 1920s, he was throughout the next two decades both vilified and valorized by such writers on the left as Mike Gold, Stanley Burnshaw, Malcolm Cowley, Rolfe Humphries, and Carl Sandburg. With the publication of "Invocation to the Social Muse" in 1932, the year he was awarded the Pulitzer Prize for *Conquistador,* Macleish became something of a lightning rod for the period's turbulent intellectual tempests. His anti-Semitic and anti-proletarian stereotypes portrayed in poems such as "Frescoes for Mr. Rockefeller's City" and "Comrade Levine" drew heavy fire from leftist poets and intellectuals at the time.[1] Yet in only one short year, as the Comintern's Popular Front began to court fellow travelers and bourgeois liberals like Macleish, his poetry was showcased in *New Masses* and *The Daily Worker,* journals that had so recently reviled him as a biggot and fascist. And while his support of the Spanish Civil War and other Popular Front positions made him a featured speaker at the party-dominated second Writers' Congress of 1937, he nevertheless became one of the CPUSA's more vocal antagonists in his pointed denunciations of the Hitler-Stalin pact of 1939—the year President Roosevelt appointed him Librarian of Congress.[2]

The rather wayward course of Macleish's career during these years stands out as only one of the many similar, though less celebrated, episodes in American cultural life of the 1930s. Significantly, the depression era's super-charged ambiance offers a kind of social laboratory for submitting to close scrutiny the worldly traces and effects of a work's textual power. For this period's insistent and often contradictory political forces made it that much more difficult to sustain the fiction of a poem's wholly intrinsic, disinterested, or ideal aesthetic status, especially so when such extrinsic demands themselves were often couched—both on the left and the right—in the name of intrinsic values and universal truths. What signals cultural power in the 1930s is a work's localized and contentious interpretive productivity, rather than any idealized "literary" merit we may assign to it. Not insignificantly, it is just such an aura of conflicted reception that we find enveloping the Popular Front writings of Muriel Rukeyser.

Throughout the decade, Rukeyser was dogged by a controversy that, however less remembered, is in some ways more intriguing than Macleish's. Fresh from Vassar College, where she shared literary lives with Elizabeth Bishop, Mary McCarthy, and Eleanor Clark, Rukeyser at the age of twenty-one had already arrived as a promising figure with the publication of her first book *Theory of Flight* (1935) in the Yale Series of Younger Poets. This volume's revolutionary blend of what Seldon Rodman described as "symbolism and socialism" was warmly received by such major reviewers as Kenneth Burke, Horace Gregory, F. O. Matthiessen, and John Crowe Ransom, among others.[3] Although the critics overwhelmingly testified to Rukeyser's poetic genius, she was soon swept up, like Macleish, in the period's heady currents of political debate.

Struggling over the body of her depression era writing, *Partisan Review* editors William Phillips and Philip Rahv clashed with F. O. Matthiessen and Rebecca Pitts in what came to be dubbed in the early 1940s as the "Rukeyser Imbroglio." Not surprisingly, what was at stake in this conflict was the status of Rukeyser's class allegiance and ultimately her commitment to proletarian revolution. In a sexist assault, the *Partisan Review* editors lampooned Rukeyser as a "poster girl" who "rode the bandwagon of proletarian literature"; her meteoric rise to fame, they quipped, made her eminently qualified to succeed Macleish in his post as Librarian of Congress.[4] For his part, Matthiessen refuted such charges, claiming that, far from a "slick careerist," Rukeyser had always been a staunch "anti-fascist and radical democrat." After all, he chided, hadn't Rahv and Phillips published her poetry in the early numbers of *Partisan Review?* Were not they the ones, rather than Rukeyser, who had hypocritically retired to "the now fashionable red ivory tower"?[5] Not so, they rebutted: Rukeyser's quest for "literary aggrandizement" was a telling "symptom of the backsliding so common among writers today." It was she, not they, who had abandoned Marxism for Americanism and, even worse, celebrated such "Stalinist organizers" as Ann Burlak.[6]

Underlying the rather prosaic stereotyping of these accusations and countercharges was a more provocative history of critical controversy that reached back to Rukeyser's second, and pivotal, volume *U.S. 1* (1938). In it Rukeyser featured her American long poem "The Book of the Dead," a modern tour de force in its experimental fusion of poetry with nonliterary languages drawn from journalism, Congressional hearings, biography, personal interviews, and other documentary forms. The revolutionary signifying practice mounted in this work effected a key displacement of "literature" itself as a bounded, disciplinary field. Rukeyser's bold language experiment touched off a subsequent critical debate that shook foundational assumptions on both the left and the right concerning the status of proletarian poetics, lyric form, documentary conventions, modernist representation, and poetry's proper audience. To begin with, the poem's subject—Union Carbide's ruthless mining practices at its Gauley Bridge hydroelectric project in West Virginia—was so controversial that it riveted national attention throughout the mid-decade. Here was a fast-breaking corporate scandal whose agitational power could not be contained, like typical labor disputes, to the 60,000 or so readers of *New Masses.* Broadcast as front page news and carried in such widely read journals as *Time, Newsweek, The Nation,* and *Science,* the Gauley Bridge story spread to millions of Americans. It offered a site for Rukeyser's poetic critique of industrial capitalism and, equally important, a chance for intervening in, and shaping, the era's public mind.

Briefly, the story began in 1929 when Union Carbide contracted through one of its local subsidiaries, the New Kanawha Power Company, to divert river water through a three-quarter mile tunnel to be dug from Gauley's Junction to Hawk's Nest, West Virginia, for a hydroelectric plant which, in turn, would sell the power generated to another Carbide subsidiary, the Electro-Metallurgical Company. While excavating the tunnel, the company came upon a mother lode of from 90 to 99 percent pure silica that Carbide eventually exploited as a precious by-product for Electro-Metallurgical's steel processing operation in Alloy, West Virginia. The accepted method of mining silica, based on existing research and technology at the time, was to employ hydraulic water drills, safety masks, and frequent relief teams so as to minimize worker exposure to the lethal silica dust. But in a greedy bid to cut costs, Carbide drilled the shaft dry without any prophylactic equipment, thus releasing tons of toxic dust that eventually led, according to subsequent congressional hearings, to the silicosis deaths of an estimated 476 to 2,000 miners. Particularly insidious were the conglomerate's methods of concealment that entailed bribing company doctors to misdiagnose silicosis as pneumonia, pleurisy, and tuberculosis and, even more outrageously, hiring the local mortician to bury the dead at "$55 / a head" quickly out of sight in the makeshift graves of a nearby cornfield.[7] What Carbide expected would quietly cost merely the lives of a few workers instead became a front page media event, every bit as horrific as its more recent industrial disaster of the mid-1980s in Bhopol, India.[8]

Intervening in this scene of corporate avarice and coverup Muriel Rukeyser boldly employed poetic discourse to recount these troubling signs of the time. Traveling to the site of the Carbide atrocity with friend and photographer Nancy Naumberg, Rukeyser seized this opportunity to gather informant narratives, interviews, and eyewitness testimony that she would later edit, cut, and mix into a radically new generic form. Rukeyser moved beyond Soviet-style proletcult by crossing verse and reportage, thereby giving a human face to the oppressive regime of industrial capitalism in the United States. Her poetic strategy rearticulated the ideological signs of class revolution to a more popular and decidedly feminist discourse. Reviewers on the right—although they could not politically dismiss Rukeyser's project *tout court*—resisted the work's partisan content as somehow unfit for poetry's more traditionally universal and timeless humanism. Thus, Willard Maas credited the poem's "ambitious inventiveness," but favored "Rukeyser's more subjective poetry rather than that modeled after leaflets," anathematizing the latter as "an immediate and transitory art as opposed to one which aims for permanence."[9] Such an idealized critique, based as it is on universal standards of aesthetic judgment, anticipated the later, New Critical divorce of formal lyricism from extrinsic history. But the more interesting pattern of reception of "The Book of the Dead" came from the left, where writers such as John Wheelwright also marshaled equally ideal and totalizing arguments against her work.

One symptom of Wheelwright's resistance to Rukeyser was his argument *ad feminine* attempt in his *Partisan Review* reading of *U.S. 1* to paint her as just another well-intentioned, but frivolous, female author. Deriding her first volume as theoretically naïve and démodé, his critical rhetoric lapsed into a chauvinistic impatience with Rukeyser's quest for sexual liberation. In rejecting the central metaphor of her first volume *Theory of Flight,* he complained that "The sensation of flight dreamily translates into fornicating. 'Yes,' she says, 'Yes,' she says, 'Do.' " Although placing Rukeyser in a female heritage that included Edna St. Vincent Millay—whom he nonetheless derisively stigmatized as the "sexual saint of the women's clubs"—he maligned Rukeyser's eroticism as merely "delayed adolescence."[10] Wheelwright's "fear of flying" (symptomatic in his scorn for feminist empowerment) paralleled the narrow classism of orthodox Marxism. Here he took an even harder line against the long poem's nuanced presentation of documentary languages, repudiating Rukeyser's focus on the contentious textual field of discourses that variously interpreted the community's struggle against the company. Her concern for the work of ideological representation was founded, he concluded, on an "unscientific socialism": "The poem attacks the excrescences of capitalism," he charged, "not the system's inner nature" (55).

Wheelwright's assumption that ideological "excrescences" merely express, but cannot intervene in, capital's "inner nature" resembles orthodox Marxism's base/superstructure binarism, where ideology merely reflects, and is powerless to change, a determining economic infrastructure. His desire to penetrate to capital's essence, and thus bypass the discursive war of representations mediating class struggle, is not unlike the Second International orthodoxy of such Communist ideologues as Karl Kautsky and George Plekhanov. Throughout the Third Period, ideological struggle was dismissed as unnecessary, given what was viewed at the time as fixed economic principles leading inevitably to a worldwide, proletarian revolution. In his own way, Wheelwright betrays—in his dogmatic appeals to capital's "inner nature" and to the (male) proletariat class as the privileged bearer of revolution—a theoretical position *every* bit as idealized as Maas' mystified gestures toward some timeless essence of bourgeois humanism.

Without resolving the tension among Rukeyser's, Wheelwright's, and Maas' positions, a more pertinent question to ask of this reception is *why* exactly did Rukeyser's long poem provoke such universal expressions of resistance on both the left and the right. Beyond the obvious sexism that marked Wheelwright's and later, the *Partisan Review* editors' attacks, Rukeyser's Popular Front poetics elicited such aggressive responses, arguably, because it embraced a revolutionary mode of political identity. In the '30s she inscribed a new subject position that departed from the late nineteenth- and early twentieth-century figurehead of what Michel Foucault would dub some forty years later as the "universal" intellectual: the one who "spoke and was acknowledged the right of speaking in the capacity of master of truth and justice."[11] As we know, this vestigial ideal of Enlightenment certainty has been dethroned by more localized writers and intellectuals "within specific sectors, at the precise points where their own conditions of work situate them (housing, the hospital, the asylum, the laboratory, the university, family and sexual relations)."[12]

Although Foucault dates the rise of the *specific* intellectual in the postwar era, this now dominant role was already emerging decades earlier in the work of such Popular Front figures as Rukeyser, whose local interventions were hotly contested on the left and right. Read through the vantage point of Foucault, the critical resistance that Rukeyser met in her local exposé of Union Carbide reflects symptomatically the struggle of universal stances—here those of the Old Left and bourgeois humanism—against the emergent powers of specific intellectual labor that would, in the postwar epoch, decisively overrun their flagging *régimes du savoir*.[13] However neglected today, Rukeyser's specific cultural critique in "The Book of the Dead," nevertheless marks a decisive displacement of both the affirmative poetics of the bourgeois academy and proletcult verse—a displacement that is inscribed in her long poem's situation and setting, in its narrative representation of the people, and in its dialogic mix of the period's representative discourses and rhetorical styles.

Rereading "The Book of the Dead"

To begin with, the poem's subject, social content, and regional setting depart from both the waste land of modernism's cosmopolitan milieu and proletcult's Soviet-style class representations. Instead, Rukeyser's verse epic migrates to America's local and liminal cultural spaces. As a kind of poetic travelogue "The Book of the Dead" opens onto an adventurous, centripetal passage beyond the "planned" and "central" culture of the urban present. "These are roads to take," she advises, "when you think of your country / . . . . Past your tall central city's influence, / outside its body" ("Book," 9). Rukeyser's foray into American place reflects what

Dixon Wecter described as the sudden "rise of the region" in depression era culture, due in part to the over 650,000 miles of new road construction undertaken between 1935–43 by the Works Progress Administration (WPA). One sign of this new interest in local histories, customs, and traditions was the 378 books and pamphlets published in the American Guide Series of the Federal Writers' Project. In addition to offering travelogues to each state and its major cities, towns, recreational areas, scenic drives, and historical points of interest, the series also featured a guide to *U.S. 1, Maine to Florida*. In her own version of *U.S. 1*, Rukeyser employs the depression era's regional diversity to lodge a specific, cultural critique. Not just a travelogue, "The Book of the Dead" as a critical documentary spliced together the generic conventions of photomontage, reportage, participant observer, and informant narrative modes that, supported and promoted by the Federal Art Project and other WPA programs, made up the definitive textual styles of the 1930s.[14]

Throughout the depression years, photodocumentary was widely broadcast as popular entertainment, enjoying a sizable readership through such feature series as *Fortune* magazine's "Life and Circumstances." While all of the documentaries of this period drew from the pictorial codes of depression era "human interest" reportage, the most theatrical exploitation of rural tenant farming, as William Stott has argued, was Erskine Caldwell and Margaret Bourke-White's 1937 study *You Have Seen Their Faces*. In order to convey, or rather *impose,* what Stott describes as the "primacy of feeling" underlying the empirical record of depression era poverty, Caldwell and Bourke-White presented romantic stylizations of sharecropper hardships that—in their encoding of a sentimental, stoical, and long-suffering heroism—tended to elide the sociopolitical contexts of class oppression. Photographers like Bourke-White and Arthur Rothstein, as Stott has shown, often composed their subjects in contrived situations guaranteed to capture the depression era's distinctively stylized *look* of sorrowful endurance. The emotive aura of such staged shots were then reinforced by writers like Caldwell through fictionalized quotes and sentimental captions. Here the "documented" shot of, say, a southern share cropper or dust bowl emigré arrived always already encoded by what we may describe, following Roland Barthes, as a more motivated, and ideologically loaded "second-order semiological system." Much of the photojournalism of the depression era, in fact, anticipates Barthes' postwar attention to the textual dimension inhabiting every visual image.[15]

Looking forward to Barthes' semiological reading of the postmodern spectacle, Rukeyser's critique of America's emergent visual culture employs the metaphor of the photographic eye in "The Book of the Dead" to explore the ideological powers of scenic representation that, however naturalized and effaced in the public mind, nevertheless shape (rather than reflect) the dominant world outlook in the social field. The spectacle of ideological representation, inverted as it is in the photojournalist's camera lens, literally turns the world on its head:

> Now the photographer unpacks camera and case
> surveying the deep country, follows discovery
> viewing on groundglass an inverted
>   image. ("Book," 10)

The camera obscura featured here is, of course, a somewhat pejorative figure for ideology in traditional Marxist literature. In *The German Ideology* (1845–47) Marx employed it as an explanatory metaphor in his critique of "false consciousness": "If in all ideology," he wrote, "men and their circumstances appear upside down as in a camera obscura, this phenomenon arises just as much from their historical life process as the inversion of objects on the retina does from their physical life process."[16] Under capitalism, according to this reading, the upside-down perspective that ideology casts at once hides the real conditions of material production and fosters illusory representations that serve to advance bourgeois class interests. Yet the camera obscura, as a critical metaphor, is not unproblematic, valorizing as it does a natural version of some "real," "true," or "objective" social reality beneath the distortions of ideology. Marx's failure in *The German Ideology* to consider ideology as a productive mode of social agency in its own right reflects his early investment in a universal and determining labor theory of value. Later, of course, he would go on in *A Contribution to the Critique of Political Economy* (1859) to argue a more neutral and autonomous status for ideology. There, insofar as the cultural sphere adjudicates class struggle through mediating systems of ideas, parliamentary processes, and institutions, ideology serves to constitute and empower subjects in material praxes that bridge the orthodox divide separating base and superstructure.[17]

Similarly, camera work, as a key metaphor for ideological representation in Rukeyser's verse, at once projects a visual image of middle class American prosperity *and* exposes it as the inverted "other" to Gauley Bridge's particular historicity of class conflict and ruthless labor relations. Contributing to the impression that "any town," as the poet says, "looks like this one-street town" ("Book," 16) is Gauley Bridge's local historical interest. Once a communication center for Union headquarters during the

Civil War, Gauley Bridge offers the casual tourist another roadside attraction in the state's network of historic sites. "The Road," the first of twenty poems comprising "The Book of the Dead," opens with a panoramic, establishing shot of Gauley Bridge, West Virginia and its surrounding landscape. History in the opening sections of "The Book of the Dead" belongs, as so much memorabilia, to the monumental past while the present reflects a gentrified scene of middle-class prosperity. Given the poem's proletarian subject, Rukeyser begins with a surprisingly luxurious vista of a "wealthy valley, resorts, the chalk hotel. / Pillars, and fairways; spa" ("Book," 9). But reflected through the lens of ideological representation— "on groundglass [as] an inverted image"—such affluent signs of high society are merely the upside-down versions of a classist mode of production. During the course of Rukeyser's long poem, this normalized setting is exposed and critiqued as a deceptively "inverted image"—one that distorts Gauley Bridge's actual history of gender, race, and class oppression. Mainstreet's facade of affirmative bourgeois culture only thinly masks what Marx would describe as the underlying historical "life-process" that everywhere negates its tranquil first impression.

The major trope for such cultural contradiction in "The Book of the Dead" is glass itself insofar as it signifies modernization, ownership, and the spectacle of consumerism everywhere moulding Gauley Bridge's social milieu. Downtown, for example, "in the commercial hotel (Switzerland of America) / the owner is keeping his books behind the public glass" that finds its counterpart in the "April-glass tinted" decor of the local bus station, where one notices on view a "coast-to-coast schedule on the plateglass window" ("Book," 16). The "many panes of glass" of this urban spectacle invite the viewer's gaze and thus solicit imaginary investment in the town's modern traffic in commodity fetishism. All of this is captured, of course, in the "ground glass" lens of the camera. But it is Rukeyser's purpose, as she says at a later moment in the work, to "widen the lens and see" ("Book," 71) with a greater depth of field into the production process underlying glass as such. Here the glass lens of the camera obscura functions as a metaphoric *pharmakon* at once to produce and "cure" powers of ideological representation.

On the one hand, as it showcases the distinctive signs and functioning of consumer society, glass serves in "The Book of the Dead" as a specular medium for reification and modern commodity exchange. On the other hand, however, insofar as the product glass (silicon dioxide) retains within itself the material history of America's abusive silica mining practices— documented policies that, according to Congressional investigations of the

1930s, had infected some half a million workers with silicosis, a fatal industrial disease—it is susceptible to Rukeyser's poetic critique. Here her strategy is to return glass to its specific "life-process" of industrial production. This local historicity is literally embodied in contaminated workers such as Vivian Jones whose personal narrative testifies in the poem to the horror of silica mining behind the facade of corporate public relations:

> There, where the men crawl, landscaping the grounds
> at the power-plant, he saw the blasts explode
> the mouth of the tunnel that opened wider
> when precious in the rock the white glass
> showed. ("Book," 18)

Thus, what in the poem first appears as a glossy medium for commodification is gradually redefined, through the accounts of figures such as Jones, as a symbol of corporate greed and gross industrial exploitation.

In the section "Alloy"—the West Virginia town where Carbide processed the mined silica—Rukeyser presents an estranged setting whose "audacious landscape" of "white / murdering snow" is nevertheless tied directly through its productive "life-process" to the manicured lawns of the power plant and further to the consoling glass facades of America's mainstreet. Drawing from the period's popular caricatures of capital with images of theft, brutality, and murder, the poet observes that "The gangster's / stance with his gun smoking and out is not so / vicious as this commercial field, its hill of glass" ("Book," 47). From this industrialized vantage point, every subsequent reference to glass in the work becomes a symbolic alloy, a polysemous sign that expresses both the ideology of social modernization and its "audacious" class history—a history, in this case, of having "filled [workers'] lungs full of glass" ("Book," 18).[18]

In its unflinching forays into capital's more barbarous settings, "The Book of the Dead" glosses the generic conventions of the proletarian elegy as employed in, say, Edwin Rolfe's "Asbestos" or Mike Gold's "A Strange Funeral in Braddock." Much of the leftist poetry that was written under the Marxist tutelage of mentors such as Mike Gold and Joseph Freeman, as Edwin Rolfe pointed out in his 1935 *Partisan Review* reading of proletcult verse, reflected the orthodoxy of the Second International that narrowly defined the historical roles of particular social classes—notably assigning the work of revolutionary agitation to the proletariat. This hegemonic task was broadened, of course, to liberals and fellow travelers of the Popular Front at mid-decade, but the ideological signs of the Third Period still persisted. In the verse of Alfred Hayes and Ben Maddow, such blind faith in the proletariat's imminent triumph over capital, Rolfe charged, led to a formulaic poetics laced with didactic slogans and stereotypes.[19] Similarly, as William Phillips and Philip Rahv argued in the founding issue of *Partisan Review,* the verbal impoverishment of political critique in poetry stemmed, from a "mechanical materialism." The tendency of Soviet-style proletcult under Stalin was to reduce the diversity of ideological representation to socialist realism's focus on the new industrial forces of production.[20]

The economism of traditional Marxism, as Phillips and Rahv described it, denied the active labor of ideology as a material power in its own right. It foreclosed any mutual interaction of the cultural sphere with its economic underpinnings. Such a "mechanical" outlook further blocked any theorizing of ideology's specific powers of textual representation. For Phillips and Rahv, however, ideology decisively crossed the bar separating base and superstructure so as to change the world's socioeconomic fabric. Similarly, it is precisely by working with ideology's local, discursive forces that Rukeyser avoids the universalizing pitfalls of leftist poetry. Instead of parading the usual proletarian slogans, Rukeyser employs the documentary mode of depression era reportage, laying bare the ways in which the Gauley Bridge tragedy involved a broader social panorama—a vista that collapsed the boundaries of racial, gender, and class experience. Unlike proletcult's rather predictable idealizations of the proletariat and its monologic tirades against capital, "The Book of the Dead" exploits the American long poem in order to lodge a more nuanced ideological contestation of corporate powers in the depression era. Rukeyser's depiction of the industrial workplace, for example, cuts across the grain of the more classist imagery of her contemporaries to focus on what M. M. Bakhtin would describe as the "heteroglossia" of discursive representations mediating the Gauley Bridge disaster.[21] Adopting the Popular Front strategy of representing not just workers but the people at large, Rukeyser provides a polyphony of personal voices and institutional discourses that together mediate the expressive life of the masses beyond proletcult's more univocal interpellation of labor.

In lodging a specific critique of corporate America, Rukeyser inmixes document and poetry to subvert formalism's aesthetic segregation from the worldly discourses of everyday life. Critics at the time praised Rukeyser's technical mastery in splicing document and poetry, but failed to theorize the specific ideological effects her writing advanced. Thus, Ben Maddow, writing under the pseudonym of David Wolff, welcomed "The Book of the Dead" as a triumph for the whole left movement, claiming that "it deserves our study and applause." Although he affirmed that "documents, skillfully cut do have a poetic force," he was unclear on what kind of power it was exactly.[22] Likewise, William Carlos Williams favorably compared Rukeyser's framing of congressional investigations, x-ray reports, and medical testimony to Ezra Pound's collage techniques in the *Cantos*. "She knows," he wrote, "how to use the *language* of an x-ray report or a stenographic record of a cross-examination. She understands what words are for and how important it is not to twist them in order to make 'poetry' of them."[23] But like Wolff, Williams was silent on the ways in which the poet's craft intervened in the representation of industrial disease.

In handling the documentary clash of personal accounts and public discourses that variously interpreted the grim reality of some half million silicosis victims nationwide, Rukeyser rests her poetic method on Marx's celebrated definition of ideology in *A Contribution to the Critique of Political Economy* (1859). There, Marx asserts that ideology as a material force actively shapes the contest of social forces through "the legal, political, religious, aesthetic or philosophic . . . forms in which men become conscious of this conflict and fight it out."[24] Not incidentally, because such ideological forms are linguistic, they are susceptible to the poet's acts of rereading and reinscription. Thus, engaging the competing heteroglossia of her moment, Rukeyser boldly collages informant narratives by infected miners, interviews with African-American tunnel workers from the neighboring black community of Vanetta; personal accounts by lovers, wives, and mothers of the dead and dying laborers; congressional testimony from Gauley Bridge social worker Philippa Allen and expert witness Emory R. Hayhurst, a U.S. Public Health Service and Bureau of Mines Hygenist. Intervening in the melee of interpretive contradictions thrown up by the silicosis scandal, Rukeyser foregrounds the struggle of professional opinion between company medical reports and outside evaluators. Moreover, she lays side by side legal correspondence, describing meagre disability benefits to diseased workers like Arthur Peyton, and stock market reports that show windfall dividends to Union Carbide stockholders: profits accruing from the hazardous but cost-cutting techniques which the company exploited in dry-drilling the silica-rich shaft. By exhibiting the parliamentary blockage of the congressional subcommittee's finding against Carbide together with x-ray reports of silica-obstructed lung tissues, Rukeyser notes the failure of the American body politic in meting out social justice. Moreover, she lodges a forceful moral indictment against Union Carbide by similarly contrasting the officious language of corporate coverup to Mrs. Jones' poignant testimony of having lost three sons and a husband to silicosis.

Rukeyser's focus on the poem's clash of narrative difference stems in part from her critical interest in photomontage and film editing. Throughout the late 1930s, she experimented with the construction of text and image not only in her photojournalism for *Life* and *Coronet,* but also in her later, collaborative poster art with Ben Shahn and others for the Graphics Division of the Office of War Information.[25] In addition to photomontage, Rukeyser viewed the cinematic techniques of film editing as an apt metaphor for the craft of formating the modern long poem. The cutting room's technical regimen confirmed her sense of the creative act as involving not so much a romantic outpouring of expressive life as a more modernist finesse in craft, assemblage, and disciplined construction. Moreover, the temporal sequencing of images in film provided her with new approaches to composing long poems. "The single image, which arrives with its own speed," she wrote, "takes its place in a sequence which reinforces that image. This happens most recognizably in films and in poetry."[26]

Parting company with the coherent narrative storyline and continuity editing techniques of classic Hollywood directing, Rukeyser adapted Sergei Eisenstein's discontinuous montage style to her verse compositions. Glossing Eisenstein's *Film Sense* in her prose volume *The Life of Poetry* (1949), she explains that in discontinuity editing, "one sequence will approach a main meaning, to be cut off by another sequence—about different people, in different circumstances" (*Life,* 17). Similarly, much of modern poetry is engineered for its shock value. "One characteristic of modern poetry," she observes, "is that arrangement of parts which strikes many people as being violent or obscure. It is a method which is familiar enough on the screen" (*Life,* 16). Rukeyser's long poem adopts Eisenstein's cinematic crosscutting of disjunctive images and sequences in order to stage a dialectical conflict of thematic and documentary elements. Cutting, splicing, and editing her documented accounts with poetic images, she achieves a shocking exposé of the ensemble of professional, corporate, and state discourses that together have served historically to protect the interests of capital before labor. Moreover, the gaps, breaks, and lacunae that punctuate the poet's presentation of documentary reportage permits her audience to collaborate in producing the poem's interpretive meaning.[27]

But perhaps Rukeyser's most stunning advance beyond proletcult and bourgeois aesthetics alike is her distinctively feminist rendering of social empowerment. To begin with, it is the mother's compassionate narrative in the "Absolom" section that augurs women's revisionary authority in "Power" and in the long poem's final title piece "The Book of the Dead." Mrs. Jones' poignant story of the loss of three sons to silicosis stands out as the poem's at once most desperate and heroic portrait. Failing to persuade the company doctor to examine or treat her sons for silicosis, she "went on the road and begged the X-ray money" ("Book," 28). As it happened, these x-ray pictures of damaged lung tissue were eventually presented as evidence in spearheading the first of many lawsuits brought against Union Carbide. Although successful in carrying out her son's last request to seek damages against the company, the mother, at the time of Rukeyser's interview, was woefully impoverished, having to hitchhike eighteen miles for the paltry subsistence settlement that only barely sustains her remaining family: "They asked me how I keep the cow on $2. / I said one week, feed for the cow, one week, the children's flour" ("Book," 29). In the mother's grim testimony of industrial disease and poverty, Rukeyser uncovers capital's hidden oppression of depression era families that, obscured in the domestic sphere, were not as visibly exploited as male workers.

However diminished by death and hardship, nevertheless the mother vows, in memory of her youngest boy Shirley, that "I shall give a mouth to my son" ("Book," 30). Likewise, as poet Rukeyser empowers the mother's pledge by supplementing her plain-spoken idiom with a more mythic discourse—one that voices a feminist rebirth:

> I open out a way, they have covered my sky with
> crystal,
> I come forth by day, I am born a second time,
> I force a way through, and I know the gate,
> I shall journey over the earth among the living. ("Book," 30)

The striking shift in tonal registers, achieved by crosscutting such italicized passages into the transcript of the mother's interview, effectively shatters the alienation and despair of silicosis, symbolized in the poem's crystal wall of glass sealing off the heavens. The mother forces "a way through" to a revolutionary, transpersonal resolve through her fusion with the invoked figure of the female messiah, here patterned after Isis, the Egyptian goddess of transmigration.[28] It is the power of the feminine in Rukeyser's revisionary mythology that transforms "the river of Death" at "the root of the tower and the tunnel's core" into the hydroelectric dam's "Pool of Fire" from which the world is reborn. Speaking in the persona of the goddess, the poet claims for herself "power over the fields and Pool of Fire, / Phoenix, I sail over the phoenix world" ("Book," 15).

Mythic feminism in "The Book of the Dead," however, is not privileged as a transcendent ideal but more as an avenue for reforming traditional gender roles. In "Power" the alienating reality of loss, death, and destitution that Rukeyser commemorates throughout "the Book of the Dead" serves as the precondition for the poem's revisionary presentation of women's roles in social change. Beyond America's industrial nightmare—where "Forced through this crucible, a million men" ("Book," 48) have been sacrificed to silicosis—the poet undertakes a feminist quest: a woman's way that returns to the "journey over the earth among the living" ("Book," 30). Not just a utopian investment, however, Rukeyser's feminist theology functions in the poem as a catylst for personal and political change. Departing from the third person objectivity of documentary reportage, Rukeyser addresses her reader in a more intimate second person voice: "The road to take when you think of your country," she writes, "is the midway between water and flame" ("Book," 49). Ultimately, this revolutionary path negotiates the dialectic between technological change and the environment's "green designs" that she celebrates as a personal "miracle yielding the sex up under all the skin, / until the entire body watches the scene with love" ("Book," 49). Unlike proletcult's almost homoerotic investment in the industrial workplace of men and machines, Rukeyser chooses a more holistic setting "midway" between nature and the dynamo. Here it is the valorized female subject who, through powers of feminine desire, actively transfigures a passive male other "on a brilliant / day when love sees the sun behind its man / and the disguised marvel under familiar skin" ("Book," 49).

The ecstatic force of the feminine—located "midway" as it is in Rukeyser' work between life and death, self and other, politics and the erotic, the personal and the collective, the dynamo and the garden—is the source of women's revisionary will to power, here mythically intoned through a divine poetic mask:

> I have gained mastery over my heart
> I have gained mastery over my two hands
> I have gained mastery over the waters
> I have gained mastery over the river. ("Book," 29)

Women's authority in "The Book of the Dead" bestows mastery not only over heart and hands but, equally important, over the element of water as such. Not incidentally, by laying claim to the river, Rukeyser's feminine muse moves beyond archetypal mystification, linking up to a collective politics. For it is the river that, in the poem's social context, drives the industrial forces of production—here the hydroturbine and its electric power—which are supremely at stake in Carbide's clash with America's working community.

The Visual Culture of the New Deal

Like the proletarian writers, Rukeyser does pay tribute to the gadgetry of the machine age—the "Wheels, control panels, dials, the vassal instruments" ("Book," 50) that she tours in the power-house's inner sanctum. And it is here that she celebrates "the independent figure of the welder / Masked for his work" who, as an industrial counterpart to the poet, artist and other intellectual laborers, "acts with unbearable flame. . . . from his writing torch" ("Book," 52). Yet such proletcult imagery is dwarfed by the poem's broader, popular tableau whose democratic vistas reflect the visual expanse of contemporaneous muralist art of the New Deal.

Published in 1938, *U.S. 1* was conceived in the heyday of the American muralist movement. The international notoriety that Diego Rivera received for his fresco work in Mexico and the United States throughout the late '20s and early '30s, coupled with a populist exhibition of thirty-five painters and fourteen photographers at the Museum of Modern Art in May 1932, provided the cultural catalyst the following year for a federal patronage program in America. It was George Biddle's successful lobbying of newly elected President Franklin Delano Roosevelt that led to the establishment of the Public Works of Art Program (PWAP) in December 1933. "The Mexican artists," wrote Biddle "have produced the greatest national school of mural painting since the Italian Renaissance." In his letter to the President, he argued that thousands of unemployed painters, sculptors, photographers, graphic and decorative artists "would be contributing to and expressing in living monuments the social ideals that you are struggling to achieve."[29] With the caveat that he would not welcome "a lot of young enthusiasts painting Lenin's head in on the Justice Building," Roosevelt nevertheless set up a one-year program of federal patronage under the Treasury Department from December 1933 through June 1934.[30]

By the time it expired, the PWAP had pioneered methods of decorating nonfederal government buildings and public parks. Federal patronage of the arts was kept alive through two new programs. The first was administered by the Treasury Department's Section of Painting and Sculpture and worked with the more gifted and reputable artists of the period. Receiving 1 percent of congressional funds allocated for public construction, the Treasury Department Section awarded 22 mural and 14 sculpture commissions for embellishing the newly built Justice Department and Post Office buildings in Washington D.C. The second, less competitive Federal Art Project of the Works Progress Administration provided art relief for less skilled or unknown talents, sponsoring some 2,500 murals nationwide (O'Connor, 29). Significantly, a year after the FAP was set up in the autumn of 1935, its political and ideological agenda was put on public display in a major Museum of Modern Art show entitled *New Horizons in American Art*.

In his introduction to the exhibition catalogue, Holger Cahill, national director of the Federal Art Project, rebuffed the purely formal techniques of Post-Impressionism and Cubism, calling for a return to America's populist scene. Because the more than 5,300 FAP artists were directly supported from commissions in local communities, they generally followed, he claimed, the "apparent trend toward social content in art."[31] Cahill eschewed fin de siècle art-for-art's sake, advocating a greater role for social representation in American art. But he also boldly challenged the bourgeois art market in its promotion of, and speculation in, the "great" works of individual talents. In contrast, the guiding assumption of the FAP held that the creative act is valued less in terms of the artist's signature status than its communal contexts of production and social exchange. "The organization of the Project," Cahill reported, "has proceeded on the principle that it is not the solitary genius but a sound general movement which maintains art as a vital, functioning part of any cultural scheme. Art is not a matter of rare, occasional masterpieces. The emphasis upon masterpieces . . . is a collector's idea" (18).

Not coincidentally, the demystification of the artwork, the interrogation of its disciplinary purity, and the erosion of its formal remove from everyday life (what Walter Benjamin was describing at the time in terms of the "deauraticization" of high culture)[32] was opening the doors of aesthetic opportunity for a whole generation of American women who, heretofore, had been excluded from the largely patriarchal networks and canons of patronage, museum culture, and the gallery market. During the New Deal era, the push for women's rights of the 1920s was consolidated in Franklin D. Roosevelt's appointment of the first woman cabinet member, Frances Perkins, as secretary of labor. Perkins secured under her tenure the landmark Fair Labor Standards Act of 1938—that prohibited wage discrimination by gender. Networking, moreover, with Labor Department colleague Mary Anderson and WPA appointees Ellen Woodward and Florence Kerr, she fostered equal access to government patronage in the arts as well. By the mid-decade, according to a 1935 survey, fully 41 percent of artists receiving federal assistance were women. But equally important, the Federal Art Project of the WPA was linked to a durable circle of influential women in the New York art community that empowered several notable female talents of the depression era. Figures such as Parnassus editor and College Art Association director Audrey McMahon, the Whitney Museum's Juliana Force, MOMA's Dorothy Miller, Hilla Rebay of the Guggenheim Museum and Frances Pollock were instrumental in bestowing federal commissions and public recognition on a number of aspiring women artists such as Berenice Abbott, Lucienne Bloch, and Marion Greenwood.[33]

Lucienne Bloch's fresco *The Cycle of a Woman's Life* for the New York Women's House of Detention exemplified Cahill's point that muralist art stemmed from the "active and often very human relationship" created out of the collaborative interplay between the federally supported artist and the local community (figure 3.1). The daughter of Swiss composer Ernest Bloch, Lucienne apprenticed to Diego Rivera during his Detroit Industry and Rockefeller Center projects before undertaking her own mural work sponsored by the WPA/FAP from 1935 to 1939. The New York Women's House of Detention commission emerged from her long consultations with the prison superintendent and discussions with

3.1. Lucienne Bloch, "Childhood," from *The Cycle of a Woman's Life* (1935). Fresco, Women's House of Detention, New York City.

inmates over her rough sketches for the fresco. Not just an autonomous aesthetic object, her mural in the production process infused art into the life of the prison community. "Many conversations with the inmates," wrote Bloch, "revealed with what sarcasm and suspicion the latter treated the mention of Art—as something 'highbrow,' indicating to what extent art had in the past been severed from the people and placed upon a pedestal for the privilege of museum students, art patrons, and art dealers."[34] In the mural's communal context, Bloch's creative role overflowed into the imaginative life of her audience, not a few of whom translated the mural subject into their literary themes, letters, and diary entries. Entering into this closely knit women's community also left its mark on Bloch's visual imagination as reflected in her work's decisive advance beyond Rivera's influence. In her 160-square-foot mural "Childhood," the only completed fresco of *Cycle of a Woman's Life,* Rivera's androcentric portraits of American industry recede into the background and are displaced by a revisionary tableau of an emerging, matrifocal society.

The same broadening of the popular meanings of America's working community happens in the muralist aesthetics of Marion Greenwood who, like Bloch, also apprenticed under Rivera. A native of Brooklyn, Greenwood received formal instruction at the Art Students League and the

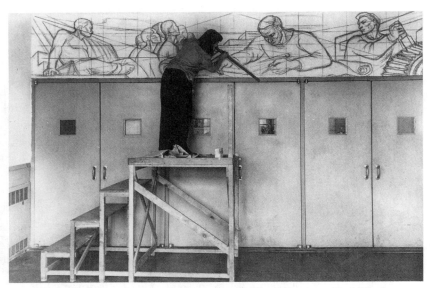

3.2. Marion Greenwood, standing on scaffold, working on Red Hook Housing Project mural (1940), Brooklyn, New York.

Grande Chaumière in Paris. Following her 1928 Paris single-artist exhibition, Greenwood traveled to the Southwest and Michoacàn where, in 1932 at the University San Nicolas Hidalgo, Morelia, she executed a monumental 750-square-foot fresco of Tarascan Indians. This work, followed by her 1,500-square-foot mural of camposino life in the Mercado Abelardo Rodriguez, Mexico City in 1934–36, made her the first female recipient of a federal mural commission from the Mexican government. Like Orozco, Rivera, and Bloch, Greenwood also employed the system of so-called Dynamic Symmetry, developed by the mathematician and artist Jay Hambidge. As shown in figure 3.2, Greenwood's compositional perspective for the *Blueprint for Living* mural—a fresco completed for the Red Hook Housing Project of her native Brooklyn (1940)—is overlaid on a map of framing rectangles and intersecting diagonal lines that recall the crossroads motif of Rivera's Radio City commission. In Greenwood's praxis, however, Dynamic Symmetry is articulated to the more organic models, sensuous forms, and sculptural figures of the emerging social realist style as seen in figures 3.3 and 3.4.[35] The utopian ideology that her work expresses here appears all the more poignant set in stark contrast with Red Hook's popular meanings today, whose social text of racial oppression and class exploitation are reflected, say, in Matty Rice's 1991 release *Straight Out of Brooklyn*.

The genuinely collaborative cast of American mural art, like that of its precursor syndicates in Mexico of the 1920s, came to fruition in such group efforts as the Williamsburg Federal Housing Project series undertaken collectively by eleven artists, including Stuart Davis and Paul Kelpe. In pursuit of a socialist aesthetic, FAP artists paid close attention to the local particulars of the American scene. "Art that is related to the history or the local color of a region," Cahill acknowledged, "has been encouraged where this has seemed a natural expression for the artist" (30). As an illustration of such regionalist and populist aesthetics, the MOMA/FAP show of 1936 included a selection of designs, sketches, models, and photographs of the 434 completed frescos and 55 murals in progress during the first year of the Project. Among the muralists exhibited were Charles Alston, Lucienne Bloch, Stuart Davis, William De Kooning, Philip Evergood, Jan Matulka, James Michael Newell, and Mitchell Siporin. Departing from the museum and gallery spaces of institutional art, these more site-specific works were bound up with the social contexts of their communal settings.

Charles Alston's panels for the Women's Wing of Harlem Hospital contrasted modern medicine with primitive magic; Francis Avery's *Mater-*

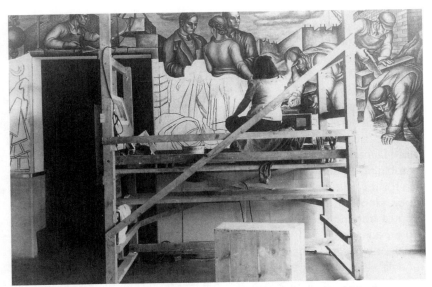

3.3. Marion Greenwood, seated on scaffold, working on Red Hook Housing Project mural (1940), Brooklyn, New York.

3.4. Marion Greenwood. Fresco, Red Hook Housing Project, Brooklyn, New York.

3.5. Walter Quirt, *The Pursuit of Happiness* (1937).

nity or the History of Obstetrics decorated the four walls of the doctors' library in Lincoln Hospital, Bronx; Philip Evergood's frescos for the Richmond Hill Branch Library, Long Island, depicted *The Story of Richmond Hill*; and Arshile Gorky's ten canvases devoted 1,530 square feet to the theme of *Aviation: Evolution of Forms Under Aerodynamic Limitations* for Newark Airport's administration building. Within the FAP's holistic art training and apprenticeship programs, such site-specific works pioneered new directions both in multicultural art education and, as was the case in Walter Quirt's surrealist murals for Bellevue Hospital, new techniques in art psychotherapy (figure 3.5). Following the earlier Harlem Renaissance agenda of breaking denigrating racial stereotypes, Vertis Hayes presents African-Americans in professional roles in medicine and the arts (figure 3.6). Although New Deal aesthetics typically downplayed racial difference, the heritage of black emancipation can nevertheless be gleaned in works such as Eitaro Ishijaki's Harlem Court House mural "Emancipation of the Negro Slaves" that articulates the coded sickle of proletarian revolution to images drawn from African-American history including the legacy of plantation slavery; the abolitionist tradition of John Brown, Frederick Douglass, and Abraham Lincoln; as well as the Tuskeegee work ethic (figure 3.7).

Typifying the social aesthetics of much FAP mural work, James Michael Newell's 1,400-square-foot fresco, *Evolution of Western Civilization*—five panels in the main reading room of the library at Evander Childs High School, Bronx—captured the monumental sweep of America's agricul-

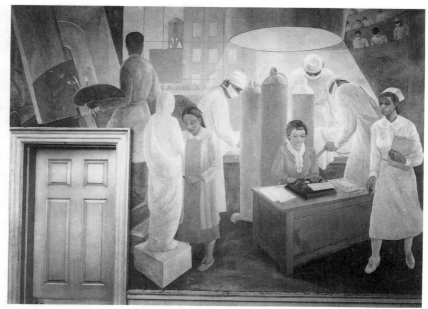

3.6. Vertis Hayes, *Growth of Medicine* (1937).

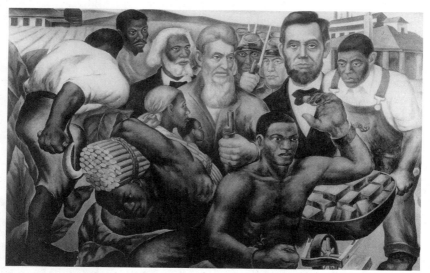

3.7. Eitaro Ishijaki, "Emancipation of the Negro Slaves," detail from *The Civil War* (no date). Harlem Courthouse, New York City.

3.8. Michael Newell, *Evolution of Western Civilization* (1938). Evander Childs High School. The Bronx, New York.

tural, industrial, and scientific heritage (figure 3.8). There Newell presented an epic tableau of the regional diversity of American working-class occupations by employing the dynamic, cubofuturist montage planes, monumental figures, heroic themes, and other visual techniques popularized by the Mexican Muralists. On his fresco's far left axis a line of miners enters a receding mine shaft, framed by Texas oil derricks that are in turn flanked by black migrant farm workers laboring in a Southern cotton field. Merging further to the center of the mural, these scenes give way to the energetic figures of Northern lumbermen and Western cowboys. Dividing the far right side of the panel, two more scenic motifs depict the harvesting of a sprawling midwest farm, converging diagonally with railworkers laying track before the dynamic advance of a giant locomotive.

Rukeyser was not only familiar with the visual conventions of depression era fresco design, but she would go on to collaborate with such major muralists as Ben Shahn in the Graphics Division of the Office of War Information. But it was especially in the work of the Mexican muralists Xavier Guerrero, David Alfaro Siquieros, Diego Rivera, and José Clemente Orozco that she found a "sight perfected and capable of many focuses and many perspectives" (*Life,* 143). As a feminist, moreover, she especially admired "the experiment in the South American vaulted hall where Siquieros made the shapes of women changing as you move through, in walking perspective" (*Life*, 144). It is just such a matrifocal vantage point on American history that Rukeyser achieves in the title piece section, concluding "The Book of the Dead." Not unlike the monumental visions of Mexican history that Rivera painted on the walls of the Ministry of Education building and National Palace, Rukeyser's final poem narrates the key events of the American heritage ranging from the pilgrim migration and colonial revolution, through frontier life and the westward expansion, climaxing in the urban sprawl of the modern American city.

Balancing the horror of industrial disease with a utopian vision of national resurrection, Rukeyser projects the United States into "arisen / fountains of life." Writing in this way, she follows the idealized commemoration of regional America in Popular Front muralists like Thomas Hart Benton, Lucienne Bloch, Marion Greenwood, and James Michael Newell. Unlike the more contentious signs of the Third Period, New Deal imagery tended to downplay racial, sexual, and class antagonisms in favor of an industrious vision of prosperity and optimism sustained by a populist solidarity. The poet likewise projects the United States in heroic dimensions through her verbal fresco:

> Before our face the broad and concrete west,
> green ripened field, frontier pushed back like river
>   controlled and dammed;
>
> the flashing wheatfields, cities, lunar plains
> grey in Nevada, the sane fantastic country
>   sharp in the south,
>
> liveoak, the hanging moss, a world of desert,
> the dead, the lava, and the extreme arisen
>   fountains of life,
>
> the flourished land, peopled with watercourses
> to California and the colored sea;
>   sums of frontiers ("Book," 68)

Such a Whitmanesque scene of adventurous, manifest destiny would be susceptible to the charge of ethnocentrism if it were not balanced by Rukeyser's specific critique of modern industry. Moreover, her vision of the "sums of frontiers" is articulated to a distinctively feminist understanding of cultural difference. Rukeyser's celebration of "the flourished land" mirrors the visual language Rivera employs in, say, his famous *Allegory of California* mural for the Luncheon Club of the Pacific Stock Exchange (figure 3.9). In this fresco it is the monumental figure of Gaea, the tradi-

3.9. Diego Rivera. *Allegory of California* (1931). Fresco,
Pacific Stock Exchange, San Francisco.

tional goddess of the earth that presides over California's bountiful cornucopia. The incarnation of the female messiah is not only celebrated in Rivera's scene of production, but also in Edna Hershman's depiction of leisure in her *Recreational Activities* mural for Riverside Hospital (figure 3.10). Likewise, spreading dominion over the poet's linguistic canvas is the "fertilizing image" of the goddess Isis, "a tall woman" who

Carries in her two hands the book and cradled dove,
on her two thighs, wings folded from the waist
cross to her feet, a pointed human
  crown. ("Book," 69)

As a counterpart to Rivera's and Hershman's utopian Gaea figure,
Rukeyser's regal muse reigns over the heavens, presaging women's ascent
to cultural power in the postwar epoch. But not just an idealized stereotype, Rukeyser's social muse charges her audience with changing the
world. Speaking with the prophetic authority of the feminine, the poet
employs direct address at once to beckon her readers toward a renovated,
populist horizon and to bestow a radically democratic challenge: "You
standing over gorges, surveyors and planners, / you workers and hope of
countries, first among powers / . . . and you young, you who finishing the
poem / wish new perfection and begin to make; / you men of fact, measure our times again" ("Book," 70). In reconstructing the age and taking
new soundings of its social currents, Rukeyser's Popular Front feminism
not only unflinchingly records the disturbing signs of the industrial workplace but, equally important, celebrates the heroic figures of the American
people.

Learning from the monumental designs of her moment, the poet likewise adjusts the metaphoric lens of her long poem to an expanded depth
of field: "Defense is sight," she advises "widen the lens and see / standing
over the land myths of identity, new signals, processes":

3.10. Edna Hershman, *Recreational Activities* (detail) (1937). Mural,
Riverside Hospital, New York.

Carry abroad the urgent need, the scene,
to photograph and to extend the voice,
     to speak this meaning.

Voices to speak to us directly. As we move.
As we enrich, growing in larger motion,
          this word, this power. ("Book," 71–72)

In such passages, Rukeyser urges a new social contract of solidarity among depression era intellectuals, writers, artists, and other cultural workers. Beyond the limits of Soviet proletcult, Rukeyser's long poem rearticulates the popular meanings of the American scene through the powers of visual and verbal representation. But equally important, her revolutionary mix of verse and reportage still has the potential for doing productive cultural work today. Through a dialogic blend of documentary discourses, informant narratives, revisionary myth, regional imagery, and native traditions, Rukeyser at once contests the industrial workplace as shaped by capital's public imaginary and, writing as a woman, witnesses to the plight and power of the American polis.

4. ● Transpersonal Poetics

L = A = N = G = U = A = G = E Writing and the Historical Avant-Gardes

The line of transpersonal aesthetics that joins the Russian futurists to such American vanguardists as Randolph Bourne and Max Eastman, and that connects the proletcult tendencies of, say, the Dynamo Group, to the Popular Front's sexual, racial, class, and ethnic solidarity, finds its post-modern text in the "post-individualist" poetics of the so-called *Language* movement.[1] The force of the *Language* project's recent intervention in contemporary poetics can best be gauged against the broader background of cultural critique carried out by the historical avant-gardes in the United States. Here the worldly aesthetic scene—preserved in such vanguard little magazines as *Anvil, Blues, Broom, Contact, Contempo, Crisis, Dynamo, Fire!!, Hound and Horn, Laughing Horse, Liberator, The Masses, New Masses, Opportunity, Others, The Rebel Poet, Secession,* and *transition*—offers a special vantage point on American poetry within an expanded social field, before its incorporation by the postwar academy. The sizable audience for these now mostly forgotten magazines read verse together with the languages of critical theory, reportage, radical journalism, and political manifestoes.

Today, it is difficult to grasp poetry's dialogue with society, in part, because the institutional and disciplinary settings where we first read verse tend to isolate it from the world. Typically, our formative encounters with American poetry take place in a university classroom where, as consumers, we study either a collection by a major writer or a packaged canon of anthologized poets. In the academy, traditional coverage boundaries dividing genres, periods, and "great" authors further reify verse as a "literary" commodity form, thus obscuring poetry's social text. The avant-gardes' communal alternative to the expressive life of the individual author—tied as it is to an institutional critique of the promotion, marketing, and distribution of the literary "star system"—finds its counterpart in the poststructuralist advance of the American *Language* movement. The postmodernism of the *Language* writers offers a contemporary analogue to what William Phillips welcomed as the "third generation" of avant-garde modernists associated with the *Partisan Review* circle of the depression era, notably Kenneth Fearing.

Dating from the early 1970s and fully blown with the 1978 publication of $L=A=N=G=U=A=G=E$ magazine, a new group of American poets including Charles Bernstein, Clark Coolidge, Tina Darragh, Lyn Hejinian, Bob Perelman, Ron Silliman, and Barret Watten, among others have theorized textual practices resistant to the discursive norms of affirmative bourgeois culture. Significantly, the *Language* poets have retrieved the avant-garde project of building, in Silliman's key term, a genuinely alternative *network* of literary exchange.[2] Resembling the historical avant-gardes, the *Language* movement emerged as a decentered confederacy of poets, collaborating in organic networks of home-grown journals and presses on the East and West coasts.

Since the early 1970s, they have exploited the small-scale resources of desk-top publishing to resist the centralized, market-driven press organs. Some of the biggest names in the contemporary poetry industry—such as, say, Robert Bly, Robert Creely, and Charles Olson—started this way. Most were quickly recruited into the university and conglomerate verse market that simply bought out the attractive socioaesthetic capital raked in from such notable little magazines as *The Black Mountain Review, The Fifties,* and *Origin.* Signs of such a takeover of the *Language* enterprise are already abundant. But it remains to be seen how these writers will negotiate the institutional pressures that often absorb emergent ventures on the margins of today's culture industry. For the moment, the

Language poets' project is aligned with the avant-gardes' leanings toward the group production of little magazines, small presses, and alternative anthologies.

Not insignificantly, like their precursors in the historical avant-gardes, the *Language* writers have also sought to close the gap dividing poetry from the world, while preserving the vital dialectic between political and cultural change. To begin with, their verse is lodged against the self-centered poetics of personal sensibility of the 1960s and 1970s. Such textual resistance to speech-based poetics is underwritten by a more theoretically sophisticated critique of the linguistic protocols and verbal habits reproduced throughout American consumer society. First and foremost, their oppositional aesthetics rest on a Marxist analysis of reification. Capital's social function in this reading, of course, levels the robust, full-bodied world of productive labor: replacing it with the one-dimensional spectacle of commodity exchange, where, as Georg Lukács puts it, "a relation between people takes on the character of a thing."[3] Without diluting the diversity of their individual projects, the *Language* writers hold in common the view that in the postwar era the stepped-up spread of commodity relations has reached into *every* corner of contemporary culture.

In our postindustrial era, they argue, the narrowing and normalizing of linguistic representation coincides with the triumph of reification. "The primary impact on language, and language arts, of the rise of capitalism," notes Ron Silliman, "has been in the area of reference and is directly related to the phenomenon known as the commodity fetish."[4] As Charles Bernstein argues in "The Dollar Value of Poetry," today's total orchestration of the world for consumption colonizes language at the syntactic level. The "use of the standard patterns of syntax and exposition," Bernstein explains, "effectively rebroadcasts, often at a subliminal level, the basic constitutive elements of the social structure—they perpetuate them so that by constant reinforcement we are no longer aware that decisions are being made; our base level is then an already preconditioned world view which this deformed language 'repeats to us inexorably' but not *necessarily*."[5] While mindful that the formal markers of a given discourse themselves often simply reproduce a society's dominant, ideological norms, Bernstein resists any necessary reduction of language to sheer mimesis. As far as he is concerned, discursive form is not fixed but polysemous. Consequently, the social relations language inscribes are always susceptible to acts of political intervention. Poetry is, for Bernstein, a medium for reconstructing, remolding, and reshaping the discursive surfaces that make up the world. In fact, the struggle against capitalist reification, for the *Language* poets, takes place on the terrain of textuality.

In subverting the linguistic habits fostered under commodity culture, the *Language* writers also revise the role of the individual subject as a source and consumer of poetic discourse. Writing after both Adorno's critique of lyric subjectivity in his benchmark essay "Lyric Poetry and Society" and later poststructuralist readings of the author's disciplinary function, the *Language* poets similarly examine the status of personal lyricism that has stood at the center of the postwar literary milieu. Since the 1960s, the major tendency of contemporary poetics in academia, in the conglomerate press market, and in its critical reception has been both to repudiate American New Criticism's strictures against the "intentional" fallacy and to valorize the private self as the proper source of lyric expression. At the close of the 1980s, for example, Bill Moyers' PBS video series on contemporary verse *The Power of the Word* (1989) popularized the view that "poetry is a dynamic, deeply personal process."[6]

Adorno, of course, interpreted such personal lyricism, especially in its neoromantic and pastoral versions, as a symptom of resistance to underlying social patterns of capitalist reification that have been spreading since the age of Baudelaire. Any nostalgia, for "the untouched virgin word," Adorno held

> is in itself social in nature. . . . The idiosyncrasy of poetic thought, opposing the overpowering force of material things, is a form of reaction against the reification of the world, against the rule of the wares of commerce over people which has been spreading since the beginning of the modern era—which, since the Industrial Revolution, has established itself as the ruling force in life.[7]

After Adorno and from the hindsight of such landmark essays as Michel Foucault's "What is an Author?" and Roland Barthes' "The Death of the Author," it should now be clear that the doctrine of the poet's introspective creativity, instead of serving as a fruitful source of literary expression, has constrained verse writing's verbal negotiations with history.[8] The personal confessionalism of a mostly white, middle-class, and male canon of postwar authors has further served to obscure the cultural differences that make up the social text of African-American, feminist, Chicano, and other ethnic poetics.

Crossing the Marxist and poststructuralist critiques of the author's disciplinary function, the *Language* movement has forcefully intervened in

American poetics to challenge the cult of personality dominating both the New Critical verse tradition and the various brands of the 1960s' "poetry of revolt": confessionalism, neo-surrealism, "deep" image poetics, Black mountain, and regional centers that feed the academic star system and anthology textbook markets. Unlike their immediate precursors in the postwar era who are more reliant on academic habits of personal lyricism, the *Language* poets have called attention to the ways in which expressive lyricism is discursively and institutionally mediated. "It's a mistake," writes Charles Bernstein, ". . . to posit the self as the primary organizing feature of writing. As many others have pointed out, a poem exists in a matrix of social and historical relations that are more significant to the formation of an individual text than any personal qualities of the life or voice of an author."[9] It is no accident that Bernstein's critique emerged in the 1970s—a decade when the demand for theory triumphed over the declining audience for verse and when poetry's incorporation into the academy had been completed.

Bernstein, like the rest of the *Language* group, took up his literary career at a time when the verbal resources of the confessional and "subjective image" schools of introspective poetics had succumbed, through sheer repetition, to an exhausted rhetoric of public cliché. Since the 1970s, he has contested traditional notions of individual talent and poetic vocation that, even now, dominate the reception and institutional makeup of postwar American poetry. But instead of jettisoning lyric privacy *tout court,* Bernstein redefined it in his 1980 essay "Thought's Measure" as a personal resistance to the kind of commodified discourse described in "The Dollar Value of Poetry." Writing against instrumental language's "formal requirements of clarity and exposition," Bernstein espoused in the 1980s a postindividualistic version of personal style where "confusion, contradiction, obsessiveness, associative reasoning, etc., are given fre(er) play" (*Content's* 80). It is this strategy of defamiliarizing "normal" discourse that, for Bernstein, underwrites such otherwise diverse projects as Jackson Mac Low's aleatory *Asymmetries*; the serial devices of Clark Coolidge's *Polaroid* and Ron Silliman's *Ketjak*; along with other postmodern poetics showcased in Lyn Hejinian's *Writing Is an Aid to Memory,* Kit Robinson's *Dolch Stanzas,* and Tina Darragh's *Pi in the Skye.* But Bernstein's promotion of such personally enigmatic, obscure, and difficult verse styles has not gone unchallenged within the *Language* movement. For example, in his critique of "Thought's Measure," Ron Silliman questioned its conflicted formulation of the author's role. Bernstein defined the author function, he observed, as both shaped by a communal scene of public discourse and yet grounded in autonomous and self-sufficient styles of private lyricism. Silliman read this impasse as a symptom of Bernstein's lingering tendency to idealize and dehistoricize the poet's core of personal identity.[10]

A similar rift unsettles such postmodern stagings of self as Lyn Hejinian's *My Life,* Clark Coolidge's *Mine,* David Bromige's *My Poetry,* Norman Fischer's *On Whether or Not to Believe in Your Mind,* and Jed Rasula's *Tabula Rasula.* Each of these works simultaneously negates instrumental discourse *and* asserts eccentric signatures of personal style. Hejinian's prose poem, for example, projects a dispersed vision of self across a spectrum of discursive modes. On the one hand, *My Life,* as the title suggests, pursues the kind of autobiographical reflections on childhood memory and formative spots of time that shape Wordsworth's *The Prelude* or Proust's *A la recherché du temps perdu.* Such neoromantic recollections of self in Hejinian's work, however, are both private and transpersonal. They are imbricated in familial and communal settings, where "You cannot determine the nature of progress until you assemble all of the relatives."[11] But more importantly, Hejinian's postmodernism radically disrupts such natural and humanizing scenes. Any semblance of a coherent personal identity is ruptured by her writing's highly metonymic and associative stream of images and musings. In addition to *My Life*'s fusion of reportage, lyric, and prose poem modes, its repetitive verbal character, for Marjorie Perloff, harks back to the indeterminate "tension between reference and compositional game" marking the accumulative, linguistic assemblages of Gertrude Stein.[12] Significantly, the Stein-Hejinian filiation foregrounds an alternative continuity of American poetry. Witnessed in their formal affinities is a new side of literary modernism—one that we now tend to associate with the distinctive symptoms of postmodern culture: the structural displacement of signified reference by the play of the material signifier, of the univocal "self" by the wayward agency of the letter, and of a work's unity and closure by textual jouissance.

But beyond Stein, Hejinian exploits the kind of serial forms popularized in, say, the postmodern compositions of Philip Glass. Specifically, in *My Life* she employs her age as a basis for serial sentence and paragraph construction: 37 paragraphs of 37 sentences each in her 1980 printing of *My Life,* moving to 45 in her second edition. Such numerical patterning is not unique to Hejinian, of course, but also structures Ron Silliman's *2197*—part of his tetralogy including *The Age of Huts, Chinese Notebook,* and *Sunset Debris.* This work, for example, is made up of 13 sections, each embodying 13 stanzas of 13 sentence units, the title *2197* equaling 13 cubed. Similarly, laying bare the literary device of serial form enables Hejinian to stage "repetitions, free from all ambition" (ML, 7). In this way *My Life* releases lyric modes from the often deadpan stylistics of bourgeois confessionalism into fresh, postindividualistic registers. "It is hard to know this as politics," she admits, "because it plays like the work of one person, but nothing is isolated in history—certain humans are situations" (ML, 10). But even if human subjectivity is situational, as Hejinian's poststructuralist dictum would suggest, her writing seldom situates it in the wordly realities of race or class experience. Indeed, it is a pressing question whether the *Language* movement's postmodern liberations of the personal actually subvert bourgeois confessionalism or merely remain oppositionally fixated on it at the expense of a wider dialogue with the languages of ethnic, black, Chicano, and other subaltern constituencies.[13]

Although one can identify a common commitment to deconstructing lyricism in the *Language* project, it is important, of course, not to lose sight of the local differences that distinguish regional groupings and individual careers. Hejinian's autobiographical decenterings of self, for example, are joined to a distinctively feminist constituency of *Language* writers, publishing in such woman-centered journals as *How(ever)*: Beverly Dahlen, Rachel Blau DuPlessis, Kathleen Fraser, Fanny Howe, Susan Howe, Frances Jaffer, Leslie Scalapino, and Rosemarie Waldrop, among others. Resembling Hejinian's work, and not unlike Hannah Weiner's *Clairvoyant Journal*—the psychic meditation of a latter-day New York intellectual—Fanny Howe's *Introduction to the World* (1986) presents a kind of postmodern diary format played off against Ben Watkins' striking photographs of metropolitan architecture. The aim of Howe's poetry journal from February-September 1985, she says, was "to participate in evolution as an esthetic adventure by using limited materials (those supplied from outside) in a process which had no goal."[14] As a poetic encounter with the postmodern sublime, *Introduction to the World* inscribes both a lyric intimacy and a more daring openness to today's multinational cityscape—something Fredric Jameson has described recently as an unimaginable "hyperspace": at once "exhilarating" and "terrifying."[15] Negotiating this new global habitat, which is for Howe also a densely coded linguistic terrain, entails a certain decentering of self before postmodernism's discursive perspective. "The taking of language from the outside," she writes, "was part of a general loss of myself to a new awareness, which I consider both a grace and a dangerous situation" (IW, 2). As Howe's trope of self-loss leading to grace suggests, the poet was steeped during the writing of the book in the intertext of *The Gospel of John* as part of her commitment to a "theology of liberation (Catholic and socialist)" (IW, 2).

Yet Howe's spiritual awakening, inflected politically as it is in her writing, resists any transcendence of history. Instead, the language of illumination, as she presents it in the following lines, is not ideal but entirely worldly—playfully grounded in work-place clichés, cut and mixed with the formulaic discourse of the Weather Channel:

> Sometimes the job gets you and sometimes
> You get the job. Jupiter, winking star:
> Physical knowledge is always off far
> And God the utter stranger
> Now a creature is free, now equal
> This is our history, vulnerable but grateful
> And thirty percent chance of showers
> For the unclean thing held to be holy
> The factor intrinsic to the Illuminati
> Is knowing that there is no inner life. (17)

Splicing her allusion to feminist emancipation—"Now a creature is free, now equal / This is our history, vulnerable but grateful"—with the mundane report of a "thirty percent chance of showers," Howe balances utopian desire against contemporary media strategies for regulating and normalizing our social climate.[16] Yet even more unsettling in Howe's *Language* writing, "physical knowledge" of the natural world in an age of interplanetary space probes, digital image enhancement, and microprocession no longer lends itself to neoromantic mystification. Instead, it is subject to what Jean Baudrillard has described as "the satellitization of the real" arriving "always off far" as Jupiter. Thus what traditionally would be held apart in rigorous distinction—here the "unclean thing" of mass telecommunication from the "inner life"—succumbs in Howe's *Introduction to the World* to a radical *implosion* of difference: "the factor intrinsic" to the "knowing" of the postmodern Illuminati.[17]

Howe's dialogic blend of vernacular idiom, media language, and the rhetoric of liberation theology has a greater purchase on estranging the verbal reproduction of consumer society, I would argue, than the more nonrepresentational *Language* poetics of, say, Alan Davies:

> Towards the latter days of the evening
> a kind of restored verbiage, a diligence
> came down within, towards us.

You can choose one for life
not exactly misunderstanding obeisance
inherent in subtraction from the crowd.

An agreement is radial in this part, or
a partial and agreed seating
that circumvents the permission to answer.

Swear perseverant patience hales our times
for deconstructing quest, for sense
mixes with this appetite that makes.[18]

Resembling John Ashbery's indeterminate verbal scapes, the first four tercets of Davies' "Shared Sentences" play first with coded fragments of situation and setting ("Towards the latter days of the evening"), then with direct address ("You can choose one for life), narrative emplotment ("An agreement is radial in this part"), as well as formal aspects of versification: stanza units, caesural pauses, alliteration, and occasional rhyme. Yet it is Davies' metapoetic tactic to raid such literary conventions so as to subvert and thus resist the standard categories of image, voice, symbolic depth, significant meaning, poetic closure, textual unity, and so on that we normally look for in a "well-wrought" poem. But a certain return of the repressed happens in these lines despite, or more properly occasioned by, Davies' exacting strategy of defamiliarization. In spite of the work's disrupted syntax and disorienting verbal character, it actually performs a rather monological message summed up in stanza four's conventional oath of allegiance to the "diligence" of deconstructive formalism: "Swear perseverant patience . . . / for deconstructing quest." However much they burlesques deconstruction, the now dominant theory that "hales our times," these lines in fact go little beyond an oppositional dependence on the poetic conventions they dismantle. Moreover, "Shared Sentences" seems disabled by its very status as a self-conscious version of deconstruction registered in the poem's somewhat clotted, latinate diction, posing as "a kind of restored verbiage." The socioaesthetic force of the even more minimalist, nonrepresentational poetics of, say, Bruce Andrews' "While" is similarly debatable. "Were I idiom," he writes, "and / the portray / what on / idiot you remarking / cessed to only up / opt hope this / was soundly action / more engineer / taut that the" (Messerli 126). Although this stanza playfully invites, even as it disorients, a normal positioning of shifters, subject ("I) and addressee ("you"), the political shock value of such virtually contentless, linguistic estrangement is dubious at best given the historical incorporation of earlier dadaist experimentation by American advertising.

The impasse of nonrepresentational formalism marking such works is unique neither to Davies' nor Andrews' brand of *Language* poetry but reaches back to the now virtually forgotten, but nevertheless crucial, aesthetic debates of the historical avant-gardes in both America and the Soviet Union. For Bernstein, it is the transrational poetics of Mayakovsky and Khlebnikov's *zaum* verse, aligned with Russian formalist theories of defamiliarization, that have a kind of foundational status for the *Language* movement's postmodern strategy of textual disruption.[19] Barrett Watten also links the *Language* project to the Soviet avant-gardes. In his key manifesto "Russian Formalism and the Present" Watten harks back to the work of Roman Jakobson and Osip Brik of the Moscow Linguistic Circle in 1915, as well as to the contemporaneous formalist theory of Boris Eichenbaum, Lev Jakubinsky, and Viktor Shklovsky that emerged from the Society for the Study of Poetic Language (OPOYAZ) in St. Petersburg. Watten offers a detailed and cogent dialogue between on the one hand Shklovsky's theories of textual estrangement (*ostranenie*) and on the other hand the poetry of such postmodern figures as Bruce Andrews, Clark Coolidge, Michael Palmer, Bob Perelman, and Ron Silliman, "whose work," he says, "might be characterized as showing an identity with technique."[20] But insofar as this nonrepresentational version of *Language* poetry rests on the Russian futurist and formalist projects, it is subject to the incisive critique made against both by the Bakhtin circle in the mid-1920s. Tying together the genesis of formalism and Russian futurism, Bakhtin and his collaborator P. N. Medvedev in *The Formal Method in Literary Scholarship* (1928) anathematized the latter as "a vaudeville movement" that "oriented on philistine views and practical utterances . . . strove to astound the bourgeoisie with its paradoxes by turning their petty merchant's logic inside out."[21] Bakhtin further excoriated formalism's ahistoric distinction between literature's "intrinsic" form and more worldly, "extrinsic" discourses. "Attempting to separate the work from the subjective consciousness," wrote Bakhtin, "the formalists at the same time sever it from the objective fact of social intercourse, with the result that the artistic work turns into a meaningless thing analogous to the commodity fetish" (FM, 151). Even more troubling, Russian formalism theorized poetry's oppositional dependence on practical language which, paradoxically, it sought to negate. Bakhtin not only repudiated Russian formalism's binary habits of thought but pursued a more dialectical understanding of how literature's intrinsic form is always already in dialogue with society's extrinsic spectrum of cultural discourse. "In the process of history," he maintained, " 'extrinsic' and 'intrinsic' dialectically change places, and, of course, do not remain unchanged as they do so" (FM 154).

The *Language* poets' reliance on textual defamiliarization, rooted as it is in Russian formalism, is susceptible arguably to Bakhtin's critique of ahistoricism. Both their rather cloistral reticence to speak to the full ethnic, racial, sexual, and economic diversity of America's social text and recent attempts in the academy to view them as heirs to American formalist poetics are symptoms of such ahistoricism.[22] Indeed, as Henry Sayre and Fred Pfeil have pointed out, *Language* poetry, by virtue of its extremely formal verbal techniques, functions in high, not mass, aesthetic registers.[23] Nevertheless, it would be a mistake to discount *Language* poetry's dialogic openness to reader collaboration and communal production. As reader-response criticism has shown, the verbal indeterminacy and narrative lacunae marking modernist and postmodernist experimental writing especially invites the reader's interpretive participation in the text. Moreover, as Ron Silliman has argued, in contrast to the individualist and anti-intellectual leanings of such so-called "actualist" poets as Darrell Grey and Andrei Codrescu, *Language* writers are engaged in "a far more collaborative project, a vision of literature as communitas."[24]

But equally important, we should not lose sight of the key sociocultural differences in the pre- and postwar contexts that necessitate contrasting verse strategies. No reconstructed Marxist would try to graft a 1920s Soviet critique of the Russian avant-gardes onto first-world postmodernism without a considered account of each period's distinctive historical, social, and cultural milieus. Not incidentally, the traditional avant-gardes could still hold out hope, in their historical moment, for reaching a popular audience that was by today's standards far less mediated by the then unfledged culture industry. Indeed, as Baudrillard has argued, any direct appeal to "the people" as such is no longer a viable option given not only the avant-garde's failure to sway the masses but, more radically, the *implosion* of the social itself as a stable referent, now saturated by the media's simulacral representations of *everyday* life (*Simulations,* 57).

Thus, in reading the textual poetics of the *Language* writers, what might seem a linguistic swerve from political engagement, appears, when focused through the lens of a more historicized account, a symptom of postmodernity. Here, no facet of contemporary experience—whether personal or public—is left unencoded by consumer culture. It is true that *Language* poetry is in the main difficult, formally rigorous, and (despite hundreds of titles now claimed under its rubric) hardly a mass aesthetic. Nevertheless, it would seem unproductive to deny its potential for political intervention both within the high aesthetic zones where Pfeil and Sayre locate it and in the more popular registers of mass culture. A reception more fully pertinent to the *Language* poets' own oppositional politics—and the one I would like to propose now—would read them through the analogous project of what William Phillips described as the "third" generation of the American avant-gardes: those poets who bridged the divide separating the populist styles of leftist agit-prop from the experimental techniques of the modern expatriots. It is in this new conjuncture, for example, that Bob Perelman's witty, dialogic critique of the postmodern condition finds its precursor in Kenneth Fearing's satiric interventions in the nascent media culture of the depression era.

Kenneth Fearing's Textual Recodings

Proletarian writers in the 1930s not only composed in democratic choral and vernacular verse modes but also delved into the linguistic resources of high modernism. Divisions thrown up within the depression era left by intellectual dissent from party-line positions were reflected in the *Partisan Review* circle of the mid-1930s. A literary organ of the New York John Reed Club in 1934, *Partisan Review* emerged three years later as an anti-Stalinist vehicle for showcasing sophisticated modernist aesthetics that surpassed the kind of "leftist" social realism featured in *New Masses*. Philip Rahv's and William Phillips' early editorial "Problems and Perspectives in Revolutionary Literature" (1934) looked ahead to their quarrel and contentious split with the Communist Party. Jettisoning any universal foundations of aesthetic form, they boldly declared that "The development of revolutionary literature is not unilinear . . . [but] a process unfolding through a series of contradictions, through the struggle of opposed tendencies."[25]

Renouncing the historical determinism of "mechanical Marxism," Rahv and Phillips cautioned writers "not to seek universals but usables" (8). "The Measure of a revolutionary writer's success," they asserted, "lies not only in his sensitiveness to proletarian material, but also in his ability to create new landmarks in the perception of reality" (9). For their part, Rahv and Phillips believed that the hegemonic task of revolutionary literature should forge pluralist alternatives to the status quo and not merely reflect the Second and Third Internationals' more simplified doctrine of class allegiance. This key recognition opened the way for sophisticated aesthetic critiques of late capitalism. In the work of what the *Partisan Review* critics would later describe as the "third generation" of progressive writers—those who synthesized the expatriate generation's experimental forms with "leftist" agit-prop—we find theoretically minded poetics that infiltrated and estranged the discursive reproduction of advanced consumer society.

Here the *Language* movement's postmodern critique of narrative commodification, grounded as it is in *ostranenie,* productively illuminates Kenneth Fearing's burlesque parodies of American advertising and other low brow discourses. Appearing as early as 1926 in such little magazines as *The Menorah Journal,* Fearing went on to publish widely in the poetry journals of his time and regularly penned film reviews, commentaries, and trenchant satirical pieces for *New Masses* and *Partisan Review*. Fearing's verse project in some ways anticipated Kenneth Burke's 1935 address to the American Writers' Congress, calling for revolutionary symbols which would ramify social realism's more parochial and classist representations. In "Revolutionary Symbolism in America," Burke argued that the depression-era writer should not mimic Soviet-style proletcult but "take an interest in as many imaginative, aesthetic, and speculative fields as he can handle—and into this breadth of his concerns . . . interweave a general attitude of sympathy for the oppressed and antipathy towards our oppressive institutions."[26]

As Burke pointed out in his *New Republic* comparison of Fearing's and E. E. Cummings' polemical verse modes, Fearing more than Cummings effected a powerful "fusion of ecclesiastic intonations (the lamentation) and contemporary cant (slang, business English, the imagery of pulp fiction, syndicated editorials, and advertising)."[27] Yet it is precisely because this nuanced discursive strategy was so doubly contested both on the left and right that it has now lapsed from our cultural memory. On the one hand, Fearing's populist fusions provoked attacks from party ideologues who held to classist representations of the proletariat. On the other hand, American New Critics like Robert Penn Warren successfully squelched the influence of such textual pastiches, relegating them to "the level near that on which the poet found them, the level of newspaper headlines."[28] Throughout the next decade, similar readings gave proletarian literature a bad name. But beyond New Criticism's crude reduction of such politicized poetics to mere journalism and propaganda—and from the hindsight of the *Language* poets' similar linguistic collages—we are now in a position to recover Fearing's sophisticated attention to the ideological work of advanced consumer capitalism.

Infiltrating the public discourse that serves to legitimate "oppressive institutions," Fearing anticipated poststructuralist analyses of how ideologies *interpellate* subjects by fostering imaginary investments in textual power.[29] His verse parted company with the less cosmopolitan poetics of proletarian agit-prop, focusing instead on advanced capitalism's relentless promotion of goods, services, and new consumer satisfactions. Paralleling the Frankfurt theorists' contemporaneous analyses of capitalism's *Kulturindustrie* (but in more populist and less elitist aesthetic registers), his poetry inhabited the dominant representations of consumer society. His textual praxis was lodged at once within *and* against the advertising and media imagery of a burgeoning pop culture. Thus, Fearing was not so much a propagandist of Communist humanism, although there is some of that in his work, but, more radically, a debunker of the commodity form as it pervades modern society.

His poem "Aphrodite Metropolis (2)," for example, broadens proletcult verse by playfully subverting the conventional boundaries that divide the traditionally pastoral lyricism of *carpe diem* poetics from the textuality of the modern mass media:

> Harry loves Myrtle—He has strong arms, from the
> warehouse,
> And on Sunday when they take the bus to emerald meadows
> he doesn't say:
> "What will your chastity amount to when your flesh withers in
> a little while?"
> No,
> On Sunday, when they picnic in emerald meadows they look at
> the Sunday paper:
> GIRL SLAYS BANKER-BETRAYER
> They spread it around on the grass
> BATH-TUB STIRS JERSEY ROW
> And then they sit down on it, nice.
> Harry doesn't say "Ziggin's Ointment for withered flesh,
> Cures thousands of men and women of moles, warts, red veins,
> flabby throat, scalp and hair diseases,
> Not expensive, and fully guaranteed."
> No,
> Harry says nothing at all,
> He smiles,
> And they kiss in the emerald meadows on the Sunday paper.[30]

The lovers' tryst depicted here is hardly ideal but thoroughly working class.

Not only does Fearing's pastoral scene parody the kind of romantic passion that, say, Keats glorifies as "forever panting, and forever young," but its "emerald meadows" are ironically set in dialogue with the tawdry headlines and tacky ads of the Sunday paper. But more importantly, in lampooning the English tradition of *carpe diem* poetics, Fearing also points to the print media as a discursive field that shapes even the most intimate moments of social life.

The kind of tabloid discourse that appears distanced and benign in "Aphrodite Metropolis (2)" more aggressively usurps the order of things in "Jack Knuckles Falters." Reflecting on Knuckles' plea of innocence before his execution, Fearing interrupts the prisoner's last words with the sensationalist headlines that report his electrocution:

How I
WISHES HE COULD HAVE ANOTHER CHANCE
Wish I could live my life over again. If I
Could only be given another chance I would show the world how to be
    a man, but I
"I AM AN INNOCENT MAN," DECLARES KNUCKLES
Declare before God gentlemen that I am an innocent man,
As innocent as any of you now standing before me, and the final sworn
    word I
POSITIVE IDENTIFICATION CLINCHED KNUCKLES VERDICT
Publish to the world is that I was framed. I
Never saw the dead man in all my life, did not know about the killing
    until
BODY PLUNGES AS CURRENT KILLS
My arrest, and I
Swear to you with my last breath that I
Was not on the corner of Lexington and Fifty-ninth Streets at
eight o'clock.
SEE U.S. INVOLVED IN FISHER DISPUTE
EARTHQUAKE REPORTED IN PERU. (CPF, 12)

These dialogic lines frame a life-and-death drama between Knuckles' desperate plea for life and the print media's impersonal captions. Fearing's verbal strategy effects an uncanny collapsing of the conventional difference between lived narrative and broadcast news. The poem's linguistic moment reverses the newsreport's normally belated reflection of events so that the word more assertively steps in to shape the world. Yet the tabloid's communicative power is itself susceptible to the poet's own manipulations of the full, linguistic staging of social existence. Thus in Fearing's writing, poetic discourse acts as a metacritique of the material powers of discursive form, dispersed as they are throughout the mass media, state and private institutions, folk customs, and social rituals generally.

High modernist precursors like Eliot and Joyce, of course, had perfected similar textual collage techniques, notably in *The Waste Land* and *Ulysses*. But when employed for politically progressive ends in Fearing's work, such formal devices, however valorized in the academic canon of modernist aesthetics, were dismissed as crude and banal by the New Critics and their ephebes. Yet even if we were to grant the vernacular character of much of Fearing's verse, the point in recovering his work in our moment would not be to judge it against Matthew Arnold's criterion of affirmative high culture ("the best that has been thought and said in the world"). Rather, our task would more properly situate his borrowings from the high modernist aesthetic within a broader analysis of the material institutions, discursive fields, and minute particulars of the depression era *régime du savoir*. From this perspective, we find in Fearing's vital exchange between poetry and the popular a pertinent anticipation and critique of the American culture industry that, while emergent in the interbellum period, would become a dominant force in the makeup of postmodern society.

Beyond New Criticism's reduction of such politicized poetics to mere journalism and propaganda—and from the hindsight of the *Language* poets' similar linguistic collages—we are now in a position to retrieve Fearing's sophisticated attention to the ideological work of advanced consumer capitalism. By focusing on print journalism as a technique of ideological domination, Fearing anticipates today's information society. While seemingly worldly and free, the discourse of the contemporary media mainly reproduce a more narrowly policed range of narratives that are culturally permitted by, in Edward Said's words, a global "disciplinary communications apparatus."[31] Decades before the theoretical revolution of the post-Vietnam era, Fearing looked forward to what Guy Debord and Jean Baudrillard would theorize as our postmodern society of the spectacle: "the moment when the commodity has attained the *total occupation* of social life."[32]

Fearing's work envisions our own cultural moment where everything that once stood against the commodity form—nature, the body, traditional social rituals and customs—has been recycled and disseminated by advanced capitalism's culture industry as a totalizing *scene* of consumption as in "X Minus X":

> Even when your friend, the radio, is still; even when
>   her dream, the magazine, is finished; even when
>   his life, the ticker, is silent; even when
>   their destiny, the boulevard is bare;
> And after that paradise, the dance-hall, is closed;
>   after that theater, the clinic, is dark,
>
> Still there will be your desire, and hers, and his
>   hopes and theirs,
> Your laughter, their laughter,
> Your curse and his curse, her reward and their reward,
>   their dismay and his dismay and her dismay and
>   yours—
>
> Even when your enemy, the collector, is dead; even when
> your counsellor, the salesman, is sleeping; even
> when your sweetheart, the movie queen, has spoken;
> even when your friend, the magnate, is gone. (CPF 51)

Desire in Fearing's poetry circulates through a highly orchestrated and technical habitus of radios, magazines, tickers, boulevards, dance-halls, theaters, and clinics that all are wholly rigged for commodity exchange. In such a setting, one's full social being is constantly deferred and dispersed across a network of alienating subject positions of collectors, salesmen, movie queens, and magnates. Into this dehumanizing scene, Fearing deploys the verbal techniques of black humor, parody, and burlesque to unmask the ways in which advanced capitalism solicits subjects ideologically. Employing anaphora, the poet's relentless direct address to "you," the reader, seizes on the language of sales advertising so as to subvert its all too familiar categories of textual representation.

In this vein, the discursive strategy in "Ad"—Fearing's lampoon of advertising discourse—is to disrupt capital's narrative hailing of the people. Composed on the eve of U. S. entry into the Second World War, the poem mimics the speaking of state propaganda as it recruits a few "good" men:

> WANTED: Men
> Millions of men are WANTED AT ONCE in a big field;
> NEW, TREMENDOUS, THRILLING, GREAT.

If you've been a figure in the chamber of horrors,
If you've ever escaped from a psychiatric ward,
If you thrill at the thought of throwing poison into wells,
  have heavenly visions of people, by the thousands,
  dying in flames—

YOU ARE THE VERY MAN WE WANT
We mean business and our business is YOU
WANTED: A race of brand-new men.

Apply: Middle Europe;
No skill needed;
No ambition required; no brains wanted and no
      character allowed;
TAKE A PERMANENT JOB IN THE COMING
PROFESSION
Wages: DEATH. (CPF, 103)

Resembling "X Minus X," Fearing's second person address here projects the reader into an even more radically ambiguous subject position—one that is at once seduced by untold opportunity and betrayed to unspeakable horror. The poet's political stance in "Ad" is akin to that of such communist ideologues as V. J. Jerome in, say, his 1940 manifesto *Intellectuals and the War,* but "Ad" actually launches an ethicopolitical critique of war as such. Jerome revived Bourne's earlier critique in quarreling with Archibald Macleish's repudiation of the Soviet-German Non-Aggression Pact of 1939. For his part, Jerome argued that American entry into World War Two, instead of serving the "anti-fascist" cause, would only advance the long-term interests of finance capitalism that "under the banner of false patriotism conscript the people's lives, despoil labor of its rights, and paralyze its organizations."[33]

Informed by this same historical subtext, "Ad" seems to follow the party position, but unlike Jerome's more dogmatic manifesto, Fearing's highly ironic poem preempts the rhetoric of capital, subversively reinscribing its call to arms. Writing in this way, the poet's verse parody recalls the black humor of American pacifism as you find it, say, in William Gropper's April 1927 cartoon for *New Masses,* "Join the Maroons" (figure 4.1). Like Fearing, Gropper also debunks the slogans and ad pitches that lure conscripts into war. Over against the army's age-old promises of health, wealth, and patriotic heroism—"Learn A Trade," "See the World," "Steady Employment," "Develop Physically"—Gropper presents the dark images of war's victims: a mutilated pencil seller and other variously indigent and dismembered veterans. Similarly splicing the codes of Madison Avenue advertising—"We mean business and our business is YOU"—with surrealist representations of war and genocide, Fearing offers a dialogic strategy of resistance to the communication industry's emergent techniques of mass cultural persuasion that would later culminate in what Baudrillard has described as today's increasingly *simulacral,* and global, telecommunity.

Even now, artists such as Sue Coe and Ilona Granet, who work within the postmodern spectacle, articulate the avant-garde yoking of image and text to critiques of nuclear proliferation and media representations of American adventurism in Vietnam and Central America. Bearing the cap-

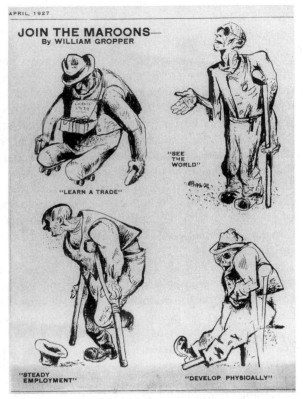

4.1. William Gropper, "Join the Maroons," *New Masses,* April 1927.

4.2. Sue Coe, *War Train* (1986).

tion "They Are in Such A Rush," Coe's mixed media work entitled *War Train* (1986) depicts a frenzied gang of male commuters struggling to board a subway marked "WAR" (figure 4.2). Like Gropper's earlier layout, Coe's visual composition ironically plays *Newsweek*'s glossy stylizations of war off against the figure of a homeless Vietnam vet, who solicits the viewer for a handout. While Coe demystifies the commercial promotion of militarism, Ilona Granet in *Bums Bomb* (1982) burlesques nuclear weaponry in comic book images of patriarchal malice (figure 4.3). Granet's visual semiology—that links nuclear profiteering to neofascism and the upscale look of American business—lodges a pop critique of the "bums" who administer the spectacle of the so-called new world order.

Similarly, in contemporary poetics, Bob Perelman's *Language* verse presents a more advanced, postmodern analogue to Fearing's trenchant critique of depression era media culture:

First sentence: Her cheap perfume
Caused cancer in the White House late last night.
With afford, agree, and arrange, use the infinitive.
I can't agree to die. With practice,
Imagine, and resist, use the gerund. I practice to live
Is wrong. Specify. "We've got to nuke em, Henry"
Second sentence: Inside the box is plutonium.
The concept degrades, explodes,
Goes all the way, in legal parlance.

"I can't stop. Stop. I can't stop myself."
First sentence: She is a woman who has read
Powers of Desire. Second sentence:
She is a man that has a job, no job, a car, no car,
To drive, driving. Tender is the money
That makes the bus to go over the bridge.
Go over the bridge. Makes the bus. Tender
Are the postures singular verbally undressed men and women
Assume. Strong are the rivets of the bridge. "I'm
not interested,

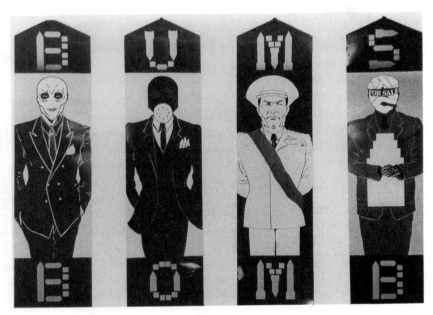

4.3. Ilona Granet, *Bums Bomb* (1982).

Try someone else" First sentence:
Wipe them off the face. Not complete. (Messerli, 116)

In these opening stanzas of "Seduced by Analogy," Perelman's "first sentence" employs the fetished codes of broadcast news—"caused cancer" and "in the White House last night"—at once to seduce the reader's investment in a typical news report and to estrange our conventional expectations of narrative emplotment. Not only do the poet's non sequiturs derail our habitual consumption of the simple sentence as a journalistic commodity form, but his playful quoting of grammatical rules foregrounds the *constructed* nature of discourse even as his primer examples—"I can't agree to die" and "I practice to live / Is wrong"—enact a certain angst from the poem's repetitious allusions to nuclear apocalypse: "Inside the box is plutonium"; " 'We've got to nuke em, Henry' "; and "Wipe them off the face." Yet the poem never "goes all the way" with this or any other story line.

While Fearing features anaphora to lay bare the tactics of interpellation at work in the nascent discourses of consumer society, Perelman uses repetition somewhat differently. Resembling the cinematic techniques of such neoavant-gardist film directors as Hollis Frampton, Peter Gidal, Sally Potter, Yvonne Rainer, and Michael Snow, Pereleman employs verbal repetition to expose the fetishistic character of representation within contemporary media culture. While the reiterated codes of traditional narrative cinema, as well as the closure of rhyme in poetry according to Freud, maintain the spectator's psychic unity, the disruptive signage of experimental cinema and poetry decenter one's mastery of narrative coherence.[34] Verbal repetition in Perelman's revised "first sentence" climaxes in stanza two with a narrative breaching of psychic drives—"I can't stop. Stop. I can't stop myself." Moreover, in another reiterated pattern, its "second sentence" defamiliarizes consumer society's gendered and fetishized codes of experience, here possessing or not having a job, a car, and so on: "She is a man that has a job, no job, a car, no car, / To drive, driving." Crosscutting disrupted citations of *Tender Is the Night*—"Tender is the money" and "Tender / Are the postures"—with everyday colloquialisms such as "I'm not interested, / Try someone else," Perelman's postmodern strategy exposes the representational signs and linguistic habits fostered under commodity culture as arbitrary, habitual, and simulacral rather than natural, expressive, or authentic.

Drawing on the verbal resources of subversion, satire, and estrangement, the dialogic strategy of resistance that joins Fearing's textual parody of depression media culture to Perelman's defamiliarizations of advanced capitalism more forcefully undermines the ideology of consumer society, I would argue, than the wholly anti-representational varieties of postmodernism. Indeed, as Jonathan Arac has recently argued, to deny representation *tout court* is to give up an important rhetorical weapon "where the power of representation is something sought, indeed passionately struggled for, by groups that consider themselves dominated by alien and alienating representations."[35] The strategic empowerment of alternative representations harks back, albeit in a more sophisticated theoretical register, to Fearing's dictum that "any writer who promotes the concept of freedom of thought and action for larger and still larger masses of the people is loyal to the democratic idea, while any who distorts, disrupts, or denies it is a traitor to it."[36]

Fearing's and Perelman's dialogic blend of literary and worldly discourses point out the political limits of the nonrepresentational formalism that marks a good deal of *Language* poetry. Today it is still an open question whether the *Language* poets' postmodern version of Shklovsky's *ostranenie* actually serves politically, as the Russian formalists claimed it would, to subvert the bourgeois world outlook—its rituals of social consumption and ideologies of the imperial self, introspective privacy, "voice," and so on—*or* if it merely reflects, symptomatically, capital's own fragmented spectacle of commodity exchange. While no serious Marxist critic would deny Huyssen's claim that "it was the culture industry, not the avant garde, which succeeded in transforming everyday life in the 20th century,"[37] we should also heed Jameson's recent argument that "proletarianization and the resistance to it in the form of class struggle" are once again, in the post-Reagan/Bush era, spreading "on a new and expanded world scale."[38] Within this new socioaesthetic horizon we still have much to learn from the transpersonal literary forms and collaborative scenes that once flourished in America's historical avant-gardes. For the moment, the dialogic recoding of popular discourse that we find in Fearing's textual parodies of depression era media culture and Perelman's defamiliarizations of advanced capitalism offers a pertinent strategy of resistance whose oppositional force will no doubt be the subject of continued, postmodern debate.

5. The New Times of Postmodernity

From Spectacle to Simulation

Midway through the Reagan era, the crossing of the Great Depression's communal aesthetics and the contemporary avant-gardes was theorized from the conservative right as a stigma of neo-Stalinism. In "Turning Back the Clock: Art and Politics in 1984," Hilton Kramer, the ideologue of painterly formalism, sought to discredit a number of gallery exhibitions mounted in resistance to the rapid gentrification of the New York art market. Not coincidentally, these oppositional shows culminated in a year charged with the political subtext of George Orwell's *1984*. Reviving Orwell's critique of the totalitarian state, the New Museum of Contemporary Art launched two exhibitions entitled "The End of the World: Contemporary Visions of Apocalypse" and "Art and Ideology." Meanwhile, the Edith C. Blum Art Institute of Bard College hosted a similar show whose theme "Art as Social Conscience" reinforced the New Museum initiatives. In addition to showings on the themes of "Women and Politics" at the Intar Latin American Gallery and "Dreams and Nightmares: Utopian Visions in Modern Art" at the Hirshhorn Museum in Washington, D.C., both the Graduate Center of the City University of New York and a network of private galleries affiliated with "Artists Call Against US Intervention in Central America" featured works that reflected on American imperialism in the third world.

Reacting against these progressive exhibitions, Kramer appealed to ideal canons of aesthetic "quality" in order to malign the politicized representations of "Artists Call." Kramer argued that art had somehow evolved, in the Age of Reagan, beyond ideology: that any explicit political allusion marked a work as a throwback to a now outdated cultural moment. But not satisfied with simply dismissing these shows as a mere recycling of some harmless and nostalgic version of 1960s leftism, Kramer tried to revive the more menacing specter that had expired three decades earlier with the scandal of McCarthyism, Red-baiting, and cold war paranoia that reigned over the 1950s. Tying the new 1980s-style critique to the "radicalism" of the 1930s, Kramer anathematized "social consciousness" as serving a "Stalinist ethos."[1] Through this historical framing, Kramer replayed the cold war era repression of antebellum populism: a period, in his reading, which "marked a great turning point not only in the history of American art but in the life of the American imagination" (72).

Like his formalist mentor Clement Greenberg, Kramer sought to displace partisan art works under the guise of disciplinary purity: that as Greenberg claimed "the essence of Modernism lies, as I see it, in the use of the characteristic methods of a discipline to criticize the discipline itself—not in order to subvert it, but to entrench it more firmly in its area of competence."[2] Tellingly, in Kramer's heavy-handed, ad hominem assaults on such critics as Benjamin H. D. Buchloch and Donald Kuspit, the campaign for a "neutral zone" of artistic purity—wrapped as it is in the neo-Kantian mantle of disinterested aesthetic judgment—proved a reactionary program. Under the guise of formalism, Kramer aimed to repress social representation *tout court*. His push for a resurgence of modern formalism "turned back the clock" to the eve of the cold war, rehearsing, albeit in a reductive version, Clement Greenberg's 1939 crusade for aesthetic autonomy against American kitsch culture and Soviet socialist realism.

While Greenberg is often set up as the strawman for contesting art's ontological remove from history, his actual version of high modernism rests (as does Adorno's) not on an ontic difference but a *relational* reaction to the spreading reign of kitsch.[3] Greenberg's privileging of avant-garde formalism over populist culture in his 1939 *Partisan Review* essay "Avant-Garde and Kitsch" imposes, rather than reflects, aesthetic distinction confronted by a moment where "one and the same civilization produces simultaneously two such different things as a poem by T. S. Eliot and a Tin Pan Alley song, or a painting by Braque and a *Saturday Evening Post* cover."[4] Greenberg's valuation of, say, Picasso over Norman Rockwell stems from disciplinary criteria that assert distinction, hierarchy, and the aura of aesthetic otherness against cultural modernity's more subversive play of high and low, classical and kitsch, within "one and the same civilization."

Genealogies of aesthetic taste, as Greenberg's own historicism acknowledges, are never fixed, as Kramer would later maintain, but always subject to contestation and change. The formal innovations of the traditional avant-gardes in Greenberg's 1939 reading are less ontic than occasioned by bohemia's resistance to affirmative bourgeois culture. Greenberg's historicism, while aligned with the anti-Stalinist program of *Partisan Review,* also credited Marxism's "superior consciousness of history" as the intellectual midwife for the birth of avant-garde aesthetics at the turn of the century.[5] But beyond the futurist task of deterritorializing the effete Alexandrianism and static academicism of the fin de siècle lay, in Greenberg's reading, another politicized agenda: one that would reterritorialize a privileged enclave of disciplinary self-reflection against the whole influx of twentieth-century kitsch culture.[6] The project of securing a *cordon sanitaire* of canonical formalism was for Greenberg, as it was for Wallace Stevens, a "necessary fiction." That Greenberg appreciated its contingent, not ideal, value followed from his Nietzschean credo that "All values are human values, relative values, in art as well as elsewhere" (AK, 104). That he nonetheless viewed nonobjective, abstract art as a modern necessity derived from his classist aesthetic theory.[7]

The contempt with which Greenberg greeted popular culture and its mass audience reflected symptomatically his historical situation that, in 1939, he anxiously viewed as imperiled by the triple threat of Nazism, Stalinism, and Americanism. The epochal shifts in technological reproduction, and collective systems of design, packaging, and distribution now delivered art to the masses making every reader a virtual writer, every viewer a potential *auteur,* and every audiophile a nascent composer. This modern development threatened, in Greenberg's reading, all semblance of hierarchy, distinction, and taste without which it was impossible to posit canonical value. Moreover, he regarded any democratization of cultural expression as a volatile formula for social unrest: "Every man, from the Tammany alderman to the Austrian house-painter," Greenberg warned, "finds that he is entitled to his opinion. . . . Here revolvers and torches begin to be mentioned in the same breath as culture. In the name of godliness or the blood's health, in the name of simple ways and solid virtues, the statue-smashing commences" (AK, 107).

Meanwhile, the materialist critic Walter Benjamin had theorized the same symptoms of massification in the shaping of cultural modernity. Unlike Greenberg, however, Benjamin articulated them to new aesthetic tendencies that questioned the authority of the individual genius, the canon, disciplinary autonomy, aesthetic purity, and so on. But equally important, he also resisted any reduction of popular culture to the vulgar display of monumental socialist realism, fascist spectacle, or kitsch consumerism.[8] The traffic in contemporary representation, for Benjamin, did not yet constitute a one-way flow, noting that "the newsreel offers everyone the opportunity to rise from passer-by to movie extra. In this way any man might even find himself part of a work of art."[9] Differing from Greenberg, Benjamin proposed cultural interventions that would reverse art's traditional social function, which "instead of being based on ritual . . . begins to be based on another practice—politics" (WMR, 241). Against fascism's "introduction of aesthetics into political life"—its kitsch stagings of nationalist mass spectacle imbued with the aura of archaic cult values—he proposed a counter-strategy of "politicizing art" as critique.

Revolutionary aesthetics must not only pursue progressive tendencies in form and content, Benjamin insisted, but should effect what Brecht theorized as a broader "functional transformation" (*Umfunktionierung*) of the institutional limits, sites, and modes of production that shape culture in the expanded social field.[10] In this vein, Benjamin cited Dadaism's experiments with the new techniques of mechanical reproduction which not only led to playful reframings of "masterpiece" art and other cultural icons, but also the appropriation of objects collaged from everyday life.[11] While Dadaism achieved a certain deauraticization of aesthetic cult values in the West, the Russian avant-gardes, according to Benjamin, mounted a broader strategy of sociocultural renovation in the early years of the Soviet Union. The example of the worker-correspondent, drawn from Soviet journalism, served in Benjamin's critique to deconstruct the oppositional roles that—under the bourgeois cult of specialization—separates writer and reader, expert and layman, poet and critic, scholar and performer.[12] Benjamin's materialist take on the avant-gardes, while surpassing the cloistral elitism of Greenberg's retreat from popular culture, nonetheless comes up against its own historical limits, particularly so in its allegiance to the classist and productivist ideologies of the 1930s.

Benjamin's proletcult credo—that "the author as producer discovers

. . . his solidarity with the proletariat'' (AP, 230)—is marked by one of the more visible fissures of the *coupure* severing the modern from postmodern epochs. The myth of an imminent proletarian revolution, that energized a range of utopian aesthetic projects between the wars, remains one of the definitive hallmarks of modernist culture. Yet despite the Third Period's diagnosis of a failing bourgeois order, and however much the depression era seemed at the time to confirm it, the hope for an international working-class revolution was, in any case, destined to founder on the underlying socioeconomic forces of modernization that were, even then, consolidating a global capitalist market. The unfolding of postwar history through the present has thoroughly discredited the orthodox Marxist faith in the working class as the front line in the communal appropriation of capital's new industrial and technological forces of production. Instead, the instrumental rationality shaping the productive apparatus has accelerated the labor process at once to the benefit of management and the detriment of labor. The new wave of computerization, containerization, and robotics in the 1960s did not so much ease as intensify the labor process. Such high tech advances, for the most part, stepped up the proletarianization and deskilling of workers, displacing them from lucrative, unionized jobs in the steel, automobile, and transportation industries into nonunionized and temporary service positions.[13]

While native traditions of socialism in America were forced underground by the Red-baiting and McCarthyism of the early 1950s, the bureaucratic state capitalism of Stalinist Russia propped up, under the guise of cold war logic, a brutal system of party privilege and popular repression throughout Eastern Europe. This political hegemony would not be unseated until the campaigns for radical democracy of the late eighties and the fall of the Soviet Union as such in the early nineties. Under these dire conditions, as Guy Debord and the Situationalists pointed out, the proletariat suffered a sea change as a vital social movement. Once the heroic subject of Marxism, the working class expired in the Soviet Union only to be resurrected as the diminished object of bureaucratic state representation. Far from eliminating the tyranny of commodity labor, the Bolshevik legacy (whose trajectory moves from Lenin through the Third International's undermining of popular revolution in Spain and on into the massive industrial exploitation of the Stalinist era) reduced the proletariat to its simulacral representation. This moment, for Debord, marks "the inauguration of the modern spectacle: the *representation of* the working class radically opposes itself to the working class."[14] Thus, the aestheticized politics of CP bureaucracy proved counterrevolutionary in simply substituting what had been exploitative property relationships in the pre-revolutionary period with its own brand of cultural capital: its new proprietorship of working-class representation.

In America, labor underwent a similar loss of political agency not through the administered repression of a Soviet-style bureaucracy but by capital's rapid advance beyond its traditional sites of modernist production into postmodern modes of consumption. Throughout the 1950s, as Ernest Mandel and more recently Fredric Jameson have observed, the sudden reserve of technological innovation in electronics, mass communication, and systems analysis and management—conceived during the war years and then coupled with accumulated surplus wealth—allowed capital to penetrate new markets through a constant turnover not only of services and commodity forms but of newly fabricated consumer needs and desires.[15] Capital was compelled, in this transition from a pre- to postwar economy, at once to deterritorialize its modern limits in the industrial workplace and to reterritorialize the entire fabric of everyday life for consumption. One symptom of this paradigm shift was the fragmentation of the proletarian community. No longer dwelling in the political and phenomenological spaces of extended social solidarity (the local neighborhood with its union hall, factory tavern, fraternal clubs, and so on) the postwar working class was radically decentered and dispersed along the new superhighways out into the netherworld of suburban America.

In the post-depression era the traditionally urban and ethnic working-class neighborhoods—like those, say, of the South Bronx—fell victim to the new generation of such metropolitan planners as Robert Moses. As New York State and City Parks Commissioner, Moses commandeered a huge "public authority" bureaucracy of federal, state, and private interests that backed the renovation of Central Park, Long Island's Jones Beach, Flushing Meadow fairgrounds—the site of the 1939–40 New York World's Fair—and 1700 recreational facilities. But Moses also oversaw the construction of such mammoth highway, bridge, and parkway systems as the West Side Highway, the Belt Parkway, and the Triborough Project. While labor was recruited to build these giant thoroughfares and spectacular, recreational spaces, it could not contain the momentum of social modernization that burst through the seams of the older metropolitan cityscape. The irresistible drive to accommodate the mounting traffic in consumer goods and services cut through the heart of the traditional, working-class community, leaving behind, in Marshall Berman's telling impressions of the Long Island Expressway, "monoliths of steel and cement, devoid of vision or nuance or play, sealed off from the surrounding city by great moats of stark empty space, stamped on the landscape with a ferocious contempt for all natural and human life.''[16]

Along these clotted arteries and by-passes, working America fled the decaying precincts of the postmodern city, seduced by the new suburban vision whose prototype mushroomed from a 1,500-acre Long Island potato farm bought-out by William J. Levitt in 1949. The first community to apply the logic of Fordism to home construction, Levittown overnight threw up some 17,500 virtually identical prefabricated four-room houses, followed by centrally designed plans for Levittown II, an eight-square-mile suburb on the Delaware River.[17] Ever more cloistered and privatized within such serial neighborhoods of single family track houses, American labor succumbed little by little to the postmodern regime of the commodity form. Madison Avenue's relentless fabrication of needs, desires, and sources of satisfaction, as Frankfurt School theorists Max Horkheimer and Theodor Adorno noted, spilled over into any number of pop cultural forms—Hollywood B films, Tin Pan Alley, and the pulp press market (westerns, romances, detective thrillers, biographies, all manner of trendy do-it-yourself manuals and self-help guides, shopping catalogues, and so on)—to the point where the entire ensemble of cultural practices meshed with mass commodity consumption.[18]

No longer limited to accumulating surplus value from its modern settings of industrial production—the factory, textile mill, powerplant, construction site, or agribusiness combine—capital now seized on the frontier markets of the nuclear household, the local neighborhood, and suburban strip with ever new generations of consumer goods, electrical appliances, gadgetry of all kinds, prepackaged foods, gas and restaurant franchises, accelerating rhythms of style, fashion, and popular trends in music, teen culture, and contemporary living. Here, the cement and steel hardscapes of the older urban environment were supplanted by the high-end, chi-chi-frou-frou softscapes of such mushrooming "edge cities" as Schaumburg, Illinois; Atlanta's Perimeter Center; California's Silicon Valley and Orange County; Bloomington, Minnesota; and the Washington D.C. beltway.[19]

As Henri Lefebre, Guy Debord, and the Situationists had predicted, the ideology of consumerism—reproduced throughout the omnipresent spectacle of modern advertising—came to dominate the total makeup of everyday life. Consumption thus eroded the older working-class values of industrious productivity, active creativity, and proletarian solidarity: replacing them with the ideals of possessive individualism and upward class mobility. Soon every conceivable site of consumption—ranging from one's TV room recliner to the corporate work station, from the hospital bed to the automated bank teller stall, from the supermarket register to the gas pump—was patched, faxed, and logged into an increasingly privatized, and centralized, grid of advanced telecommunication, information storage, and digital microprocession.

One symptom of this shift into the postmodern register of spectacular consumerism was what Lefebvre described as "the enormous amount of *signifiers* liberated or insufficiently connected to their corresponding signifieds (words, gestures, images and signs), and made available to advertising and propaganda."[20] Thus a cola's promise to deliver, say, "the real thing" or a sneaker's motto to "just do it" could now be evoked by an overdetermined multiplicity of signs and representations ranging from the sensuous caligraphy of a glossy logo to a hot rock-and-roll lick, to any number of more fetishized gestures (the driving NBA slam-dunk, the celebrity head shot, the sweaty "high five"). What desires the proferred "real thing" would actually satisfy were deferred through the linguistic slippage such contrived ensembles of transfers, subliminal messages, and polysemous signs put into play. Suddenly the world's entire semiotic fabric, from the sprawling signage of the suburban strip to a commercial's most intimate proxemic code, was now *readable*—laid out in textual praxes that framed everyday life through the discourse of mass advertising and the scene of spectacular display.[21]

Publicity in the postwar era, according to Lefebvre, moves from the margin to the center of social representation. It is installed as "the poetry of Modernity, the reason and pretext for all successful displays. It takes possession of art, literature, all available signifiers and vacant signifieds; it is art and literature, it gleans the leavings of the Festival to recondition them for its own ends" (EL, 107). Yet within what Lefebvre described as the "bureaucratic society of controlled consumption" it was capital that exploited the powers of textual representation at once to maintain a constant obsolence of *needs* as such, paradoxically, within a fixed framework of institutional durability. The task was to balance the necessity for a fast-paced turnover of cultural forms and trends in the consumer market in contradiction with the *class strategy* of preserving permanence, stability, and hierarchy amidst rapid cultural change. Of this double strategy underwriting Las Vegas strip messages, Robert Venturi has observed that "the most unique, most monumental parts of the Strip, the signs and casino facades, are also the most changeable; it is the neutral, systems-motel structures behind that survive a succession of facelifts and a series of themes up front" (LV, 32).

Throughout the 1980s, Jean Baudrillard supplemented this account of capital's relation to the postmodern spectacle. Not insignificantly, Baudrillard deconstructed Marxism's traditional distinction between the economic status of the commodity and the cultural register of the sign—theorizing both as mutually traversed by a "homological structure" of exchange.[22] In his reading, all fixed notions, ideas, and essences are no longer posited as prior to the more mundane traffic in material signification. Here, the myths, say, of scientific rationality, historical objectivity, literal reality, transcendent meaning, use value, and so on are actually produced out of the political economy of the sign. Each, in fact, "results from the complex play of interference of networks and codes—just as white light results from the interference of the colors of the spectrum" (PES, 158).

Such a poststructuralist reading of sign exchange moves beyond the Situationalists' theory of capital's manipulation of the social through the theater and circus of spectacular consumption. This somewhat outdated critique is still marked by the residue of naturalistic thinking, relying for its explanatory power on some recoverable world, utopian project, or valorized class somehow beyond, or prior to, the misrepresentations and "false" consciousness perpetuated by the dominant media industry. But in Baudrillard's descriptive account of recent decades, the naturalized and humanizing scene of commodity exchange—so familiar to us all in the conventional representations and cartoon-like stereotypes of consumer society—passes into a more rarefied and estranged dimension of contemporary simulation. Drawing from the Nietzschean critique of foundationalist metaphysics, Baudrillard argues that the cultural regime of the simulacrum emerges in the Renaissance, with the proliferation of bourgeois signs in excess of the feudal order's narrower and fixed system of allegorical signification.[23] The age of simulation proper, however, only attains hegemony through capital's "radical law of equivalence and exchange."[24]

In the twentieth century, the serial economy of the factory line—geared as it is to the mass reproduction of cultural forms, advertising, popular entertainment, the communications media, and so on—has liquidated traditional reference, signified meaning, and authentic use values. Postmodernity's regime of simulation is fueled by the Neo-Fordist saturation of the social field by the spreading systems and languages of the so-called "information" economy. Today, the pervasive scene of serial reproduction deauraticizes and flattens cultural meaning, reducing it to a one-dimensional surface expressed across a spectrum of postmodern forms ranging from pop art to monumental urban architecture: from Andy Warhol's simulacral silk screens of soup cans, movie stars, politicians, and other cult figures to the twin towers of the World Trade Center.

This new world order collapses any distinction between the social and its serial reproduction so that agent and object, model and copy, the real and its cultural representation *implode* into a postmodern system of circular causality—a Moebius strip of mutual and endlessly reversible determination. In this postmodern register, the MacLuhanesque slogan that the "medium is the message" reaches an estranging threshold. Here the physical *medium* of the telecommunication (mass)age infiltrates, mimics, mutates, and finally exterminates the Real like a virus or genetic code, in what Baudrillard describes as a global, "satellization of the real."[25] Within the horizon of the hyperreal, the instant *precession* of every conceivable interpretive model and representation around any historical happening or fact leaves in its wake an indeterminate, "magnetic field of events" (S, 32). Consequently, the difference between the signified event and its simulacrum implodes now in a global circulation/ventilation of contradictory signals, mutating codes, and mixed messages.

With the death of the referent, the social contract and political institutions conceived out of the universalist ideals of the Enlightenment are likewise thrown into crisis. "By treating as a *theatrical* performance the political scene and its actors," writes Baudrillard, the media reduces politics to the same spectacle staging TV game shows, sporting events, and other forms of popular entertainment.[26] Not coincidentally, the simulacral reproduction of the social erodes the proletariat's traditional class role as the subject of revolutionary liberation. Proletcult tropes and iconography have always betrayed, according to Paula Rabinowitz, a certain sexism in fetishizing the valorized figure of the white male worker while paying scant attention to those who labor in the service sector, in the domestic sphere, and on the subaltern margins of industrial society.[27] But more to the point, the presumption to speak now on behalf of the proletariat in some wholly unmediated fashion seems theoretically naïve after the pressing debates of postmodernity.

For example, during the 1985 Institute of Contemporary Arts forum on postmodernism, Jean-François Lyotard argued cogently against Terry Eagleton's orthodox nostalgia for the proletariat as the privileged agent for social change in the third world. Following Kant, Lyotard pointed out that in contradistinction to designating *specific* laborers in culturally diverse communites, the term proletariat, naming as it does a more properly universal "subject to be emancipated," is an ahistorical abstraction—

a "pure Idea of Reason" having little purchase today on the actual politics of everyday life. Indeed, some of the greatest atrocities, he cautioned, have been perpetuated under this very category error of pursuing a "politics of the sublime." "That is to say, to make the terrible mistake of trying to represent in political practice an Idea of Reason. To be able to say, 'We are the proletariat' or 'We are the incarnation of free humanity.' "[28] The Old Left faith in a global, working-class liberation seems especially dubious today after modernism's failed legacy of proletarian revolution world-wide.[29]

Against this outworn orthodoxy, the spectacle of postmodernism, for Baudrillard, positions mass society not so much as a valorized political agent but more as a passive medium or conductor for the cultural simulation of every representable social need, libidinal desire, political interest, or popular opinion. Relentlessly polled, solicited, and instructed by the print, television, and video media—whose corporate advertising budgets dwarf those of public and private education—the masses, in Baudrillard's descriptive account, are absorbed into a wholly commodified habitus. This seamless web of postmodern consumption joins the most intimate spaces of the domestic sphere to the giant, impersonal expanses of the mega-mall warehouse. But what is supremely at risk in this scene of simulacral exchange is the social *demand* for any fixed meaning, value, truth, or political platform that would serve to legitimate a dominant power structure. The revenge of the masses against such ideological, political, and psychosexual manipulation is expressed, for Baudrillard, as the sheer inertia of its silent majority: its tendency to consume in excess any message, code, or sign that is broadcast its way.

No longer constituting the proletarian class, a people, a citizenry, or any stable political constituency, the masses now mark the abysmal site of the radical equivalence of all value. Advanced consumer society, in one of Baudrillard's astrophysical metaphors, simply implodes like a collapsing star, drawing into itself "all radiation from the outlying constellations of State, History, Culture, Meaning" (SSM, 2). The postmodern *coupure* that breaks with the political utopias of modernism is marked precisely by the banal regime of everyday life, the status quo of its "silent" majority.[30] Such apolitical withdrawal from political struggle, Baudrillard notes, is usually read as a symptom of alienation (or worse, fascism). Yet when simulation has overrun the public sphere, then unnatural excess, parodic craving, and outrageous waste become viable tactics for stepping up the exchange and consumption of goods, services, information flows, and new technologies. The whole hyperreal economy of postmodern potlatch, Baudrillard argues, actually exhausts and debunks any vestige of use value, rationality, or authenticity serving to legitimate capital's cultural logic.

However one (dis)credits the paradoxical twists and turns that Baudrillard negotiates in theorizing a "silent" politics of hyperbolic consumption, what remains clear is that a postmodern resistance to the simulacral order of advanced capitalism cannot legitimately fall back on the now old-fashioned struggle for this or that modernist platform or unmediated political agenda, be it, say, Eliot's "idea" of a christian society, Pound's investment in Italian fascism, Charlotte Perkins Gilman's utopian "Herland," Edwin Rolfe's working-class "credo," or Mike Gold's allegiance to Russian proletcult. On the contrary, political intervention must be lodged from within today's omnipresent spectacle that denies any appeal to some "real" referent before the flow of signification. Indeed, as Henri Lefebvre grasped, in our contemporary moment, society as such can only be engaged through its prior inscription in a discursive field.

The Regime of Signs: Matt Mullican

The older reign of linguistic signs inaugurated by Gutenberg in the fifteenth century gives way in this postmodern domain to the contemporary regime of *signals*—the conventional, iconic codes everywhere directing one's hyperreal rite of passage on highways and in restaurants, airports, museums, corporate offices, public restrooms, and countless other sites and conduits of social traffic. Unlike either the Enlightenment's appeal to universal reason or what Habermas would locate in the uncoerced sphere of communicative rationality,[31] the rule of signals, according to Lefebvre, is based on the *manipulation* of social flows through compulsion and conditioning. "The signal," he writes, "commands, controls behaviour and consists of contrasts chosen precisely for their contradiction (such as, for instance, red and green); furthermore, signals can be grouped in codes (the highway code is a simple and familiar example), thus forming systems of compulsion" (EL, 62). It is this cosmopolitan commerce in signals and pictographs that Matt Mullican appropriates in a kind of second-order, metasimulation: one that foregrounds the coded organization of everyday life under advanced capitalism.

Upon graduating from the California Institute of the Arts in the early 1970s, Mullican began showing and performing his art, often under hypnosis, in such alternative galleries as The Kitchen and Artists' Space in New York with fellow CalArts alumni David Salle and Ross Bleckner. By

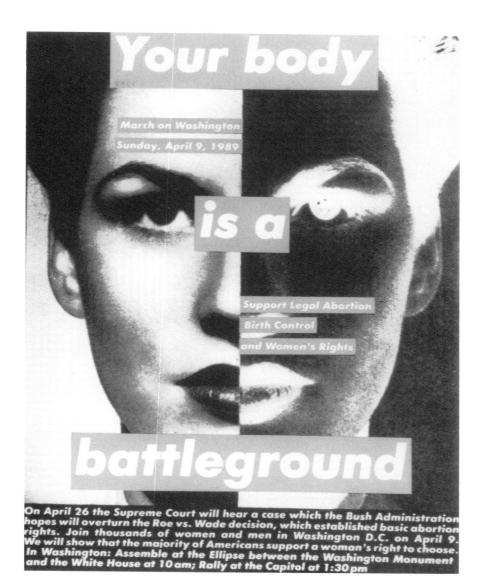

5.2. Barbara Kruger,
"Your body is a battleground" (1989).
Poster for 1989 March
on Washington, D.C.

5.3. Barbara Kruger, "You are an experiment in terror" (1983). Poster. Courtesy Barbara Kruger.

5.4. Barbara Kruger, "We won't play nature to your culture" (1983). Poster.

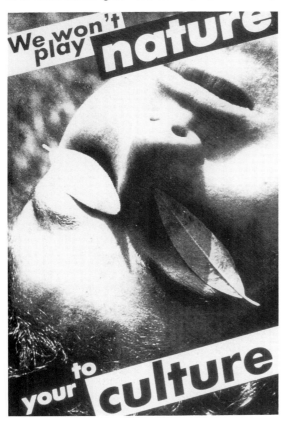

5.5. Barbara Kruger, "We are being made spectacles of" (1983). Poster.

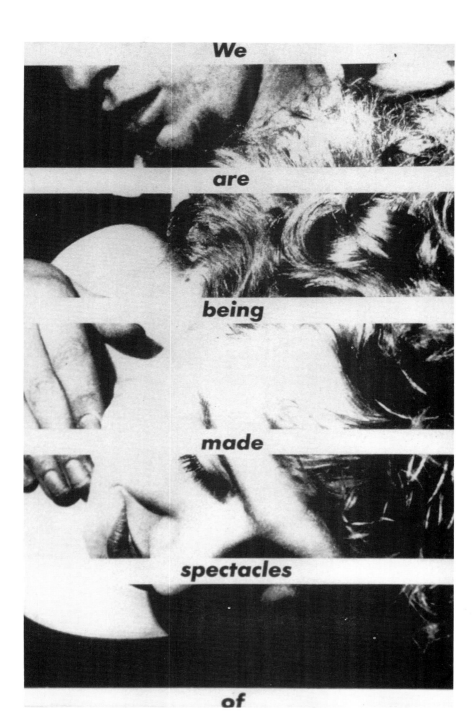

5.6. Barbara Kruger, "You construct intricate rituals which allow you to touch the skin of other men" (1983). Photograph.

5.7a. Jenny Holzer, selections from the "Survival" series (1984). Stickers.

5.7b. Jenny Holzer, selections from the "Survival" series (1984). Stickers.

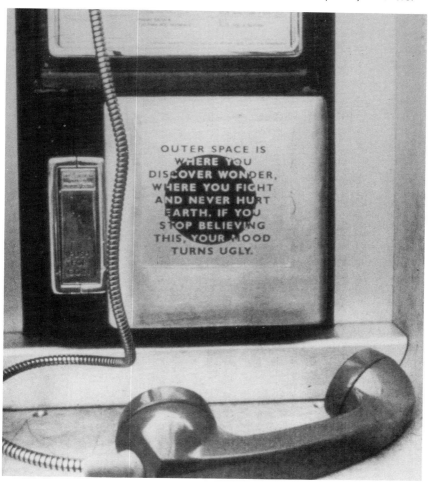

5.8. Jenny Holzer, *Private Property Created Crime* (1982).
L.E.D., Times Square, New York City.

5.9. Jenny Holzer,
Protect Me From What I Want (1986).
L.E.D., Caesar's Palace,
Las Vegas, Nevada.

5.10. Jenny Holzer,
Money Creates Taste (1986).
L.E.D., baggage carousels,
McCarran International Airport,
Las Vegas, Nevada.

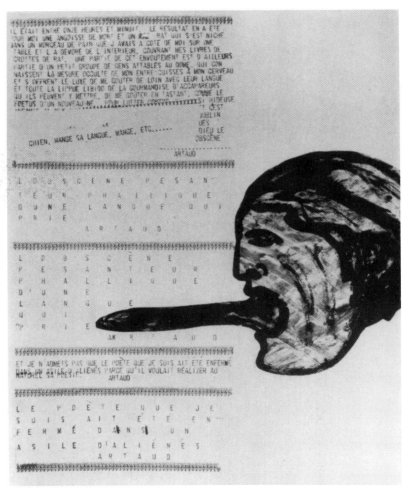

5.12. Nancy Spero,
Codex Artaud
XVII (detail)
(1971–72).
Josh Baer Gallery,
New York City.

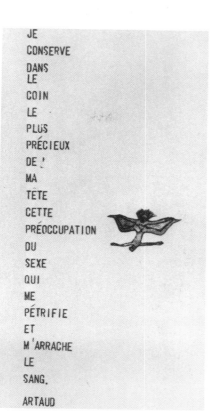

JE
CONSERVE
DANS
LE
COIN
LE
PLUS
PRÉCIEUX
DE !
MA
TÊTE
CETTE
PRÉOCCUPATION
DU
SEXE
QUI
ME
PÉTRIFIE
ET
M'ARRACHE
LE
SANG.

ARTAUD

5.13. Nancy Spero, *Codex Artaud IV* (detail) (1972). Josh Baer Gallery, New York City.

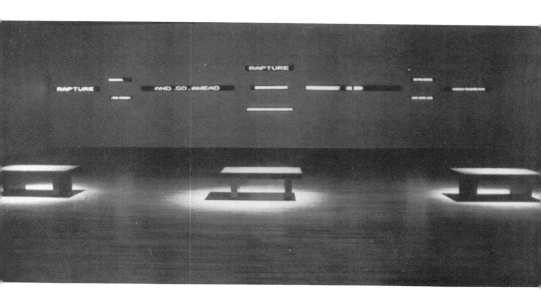

5.11. Jenny Holzer, *Under a Rock* (1987). Three L.E.D. electronic display signboards; three misty Black granite benches. Aspen Art Museum, Colorado.

5.14. Nancy Spero, *Let the Priests Tremble* (detail) (1984). Josh Baer Gallery, New York City.

5.15. Nancy Spero,
Sheela and the Dildo Dancer
(detail) (1987).
Josh Baer Gallery,
New York City.

5.16. Hans Haacke, *Taking Stock* (unfinished) (1983-84).

EXXON'S support of the arts serves the arts as a social lubricant.

And if business is to continue in big cities, it needs a more lubricated environment.

Robert Kingsley

5.17. Hans Haacke, *On Social Grease,* Plaque 6.

5.18. Hans Haacke,
The Chase Advantage
(1976).

The Chase Advantage

Give yourself

Even accountants put a money value on such intangibles as good will, and it is the conviction of Chase Manhattan's management that in terms of good will, in terms of staff morale and in terms of our corporate commitment to excellence in all fields, including the cultural, the art program has been a profitable investment.

David Rockefeller (Chairman of Chase Manhattan Bank, Vice Chairman of Museum of Modern Art) in *Art at the Chase Manhattan Bank*

David Rockefeller

Photo: William E. Sauro, *The New York Times*

The fundamental purpose, therefore, which must underlie any policy of publicity must be to induce the people to believe in the sincerity and honesty of purpose of the management of the company which is asking for their confidence.

Ivy L. Lee (public relations consultant, hired by John D. Rockefeller Jr., after «Ludlow Massacre», 1914) in *Publicity: Some of the Things it is and is not*, New York, 1926

CHASE

5.19. Hans Haacke,
The Chase Advantage
(detail) (1976).

5.20. Hans Haacke, *A Breed Apart* (1978).

5.21. Hans Haacke, *The Right to Life* (1979).

5.22. Adrian Piper, *Vanilla Nightmares #8* (1986).
John Weber Gallery, New York City.

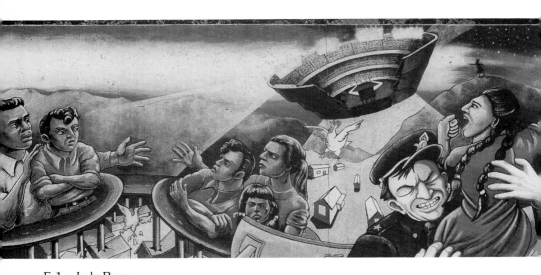

E.1. Judy Baca,
The Great Wall of Los Angeles
(detail: "Division of the Barrios") (1983).

E.2. Judy Baca,
The Great Wall of Los Angeles
(detail: "1940s: We Fight Fascism
Abroad and at Home") (1981).

E.3. Greenpeace Garbage Barge Protest,
banner on New York City garbage barge (1987).

E.4. Suzanne Lacy and Leslie Labowitz, *In Mourning and In Rage* (1977). Performance, Los Angeles.

E.5. Suzanne Lacy, *The Crystal Quilt* (1987). Performance at the Philip Johnson-designed IDS Building, Minneapolis.

E.7. Matt Herron,
"Rock Hudson Panel"
of *The Quilt*.
Washington, D.C.,
October 1987.

E.8. Matt Herron, The NAMES Project, *The Quilt*. Washington, D.C., October 1987.

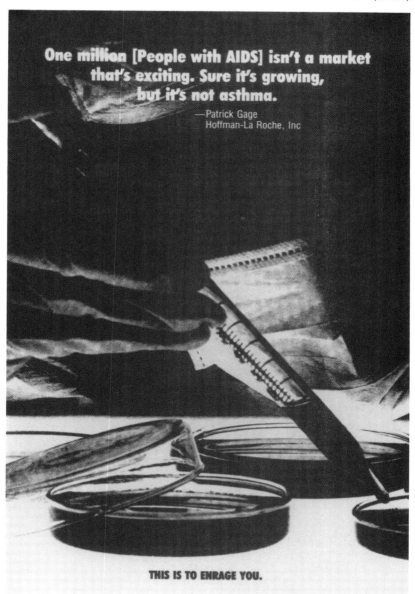

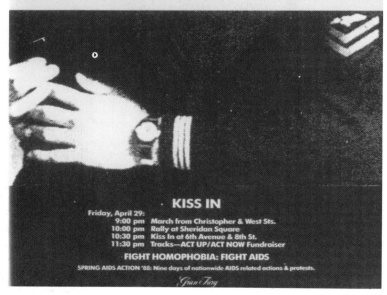

E.10. Gran Fury.
"Read My Lips (boys)"
(1988). Poster.

the 1980s, Mullican's art had adopted the distinctive look of the iconic signs, posters, placards, notices, logos, trademarks, and labels that, via capital's multinational network, have spread a common lexicon of visual symbols worldwide. Mimicking these informational and warning signs, Mullican's posters appropriated the distinctive format of familiar, everyday icons. In this postmodern turn, Mullican secularized an older, humanistic *lebenswelt* rooted in existential realities and theological values. Transcoding such metaphysically-freighted terms as "heaven," "hell," "angel," "demon," "life," "death," "fate," and so on into the flat visual surfaces and clear-cut icons of a slick advertising logo or functional traffic sign, Mullican drains each of these rubrics of whatever aura it might at one time have possessed (figure 5.1). Each is exposed as just another reified signal circulating in overdetermined networks of simulacral exchange. Mullican's uncanny yoking of word and image points to the arbitrary rather than "natural" system of signification that underlies and maintains the linguistic ordering of contemporary society.

Mullican has also parodied, within the commercial network of the New York art market, the sign value of the artist's signature and the cult of

5.1. Matt Mullican, "Untitled" (1982).

genius which it serves to prop up. Adopted by New York's Mary Boone gallery in the 1980s, Mullican exploited his new "acutely public image" to critique the glitzy promotion of "name" painters. By advertising his own name like a logo in block letters at the head of his posters, Mullican laid bare his work's fetishized status as a commodity form. "The names," he has said, "represented my emergence into the public arena. I was especially interested in artists like Julian Schnabel and the way a name could become so important."[32] By the end of the decade, Mullican's own name achieved commodity distinction in the world art market, with the artist giving shows in the New York Metropolitan Museum of Art and fetching $150,000 for large public commissions.

The indeterminate signs, posters, banners, stained-glass windows, and etched granite slabs of Mullican's installations often function to disorient and estrange the "normal" traffic in social communication. In a citational parody of the kind of commericalized museum banners that Thomas Hoving promoted during the 1960s–1970s as director of the Metropolitan Museum of Art, Mullican's 1986 installation in Brussels employed a large flag hung over the facade of the Palais des Beaux-Arts. This installation bore his own coded sign for "the world framed"—a black logo against a yellow background. Coincidentally, and unbeknownst to the artist, these happened to be the Flemish national colors, and they sparked a flare up of the traditional ethnic rivalry between Belgian and Flemish factions. Mullican's comment on the whole affair—"When I put an image on a flag, I found it meant something very different than when I put it on a piece of paper" (Clothier, 146)—underscores the unpredictable and site-specific contingencies of reception that any sign necessarily generates when released into a worldly social text.

Adrift on the postmodern welter of specialized languages and codes, any sign can be severed from its fixed moorings in foundational meaning and swept away in today's precession of simulacra. The new and properly unthinkable space of this indeterminate semiotic flux (which for Fredric Jameson is symptomatic of a broader social habitat—that of a global, postindustrial consumer society) occasions "a multidimensional set of radically discontinuous realities, whose frames range from the still surviving spaces of bourgeois private life all the way to the unimaginable decentering of global capital itself."[33] What Jameson finds at once bracing and politically disabling in the lived phenomenology of such postmodern heterogeneity is the sheer complexity of its international space of deployment, whose disorienting intensities are reflected in the dwarfing expanse of the contemporary cityscape.[34]

Answering, in some ways, to Jameson's call for an aesthetics of "cognitive mapping," Matt Mullican's postmodern topographies of urban space allude to today's metropolitan traffic in semiotic complexity even as they finesse the impasse of totality that marks the ideological limits of the modernist imaginary.[35] The artist's 1987 Dallas Project (an installation of 52 panels of personalized signs and cityscapes, ranging from urban to cosmological themes) has the look of a relief map, achieved through Mullican's compositional technique of rubbing blackoil stick on canvas over masonite templates. This presentation allows the artist to highlight his original signs, logos, and urban blueprints as inscribed traces. The bright primary and secondary acrylic backgrounds that color Mullican's pictographs are encoded by an eccentric sign system, as in his untitled eight-panel, 16-foot-square installation, narrating the history of the Paris Opera house (1986–87).

Since the early 1990s Mullican has branched out into computer art, undertaking a kind of postmodern mappemunde in his MOMA installation of an urban panorama drafted on a "Thinking Machine"—a Connection Machine-2 supercomputer designed at MIT. Composed under the auspices of NYNEX and with the collaboration of John Whitney Jr.'s Optomystic studio in Hollywood, Mullican's simulation of postmodern urban space, according to his technical consultant John Whitney Jr., maps a "massless, weightless . . . city of ideas and icons, archetypes and relationships—a whole metamorphosis of morphology."[36] Such advances in artificial intelligence enabled Mullican to project an urban topology in three-dimensional mathematical form, displayed via video screens and light boxes. This computerized microcosm of coded signs and architectural forms eludes totality through its self-reflexive understanding of its simulacral status. Not so much utopian (in Jameson's sense of charting some alternative aesthetic space at odds with reigning ideological representations), Mullican's supercomputer installation is, as he says, "an engine generating meaning" (Clothier, 147). It presents precisely what Baudrillard has described as postmodernism's "smooth operational surface of communication," where experience as such is "a pure screen, a switching center for all networks of influence."[37]

Tactics of Intervention

More politically engaged, perhaps, than Mullican's electronic reflections on a postmodern cosmology are the kind of specific tactics of aesthetic resistance that Baudrillard, given the totalizing and pessimistic nature of his critique, is driven to reject as hopelessly utopian. Beyond the scant attention that Baudrillard has devoted to subcultural resistance, theorists such as Michel de Certeau, Stuart Hall, and Dick Hebdige have offered more nuanced studies of micropolitical praxes of postmodern subversion.[38] New approaches in semiotics, gender theory, psycholinguistics, and cultural studies have ramified our understanding of the complex play of communication within advanced consumer society's exchange of signs as commodity forms and vice versa. In this vein, theoretical approaches to a postmodern politics of resistance have considered the multiple ways in which particular groups and individuals not merely consume but rearticulate to their own political agendas the dominant signs of social manipulation taken from the discourses of advertising, fashion, television, contemporary music, and pop culture in general.

Beyond content analyses, explications, or close readings of various textual praxes, a more productive approach to the micropolitics of postmodernism examines what audiences, viewers, readers, and shoppers produce with the texts, artifacts, and commodity forms they consume. "Thus, once the images broadcast by television and the time spent in front of the TV set have been analyzed," writes de Certeau, "it remains to be asked what the consumer *makes* of these images and during these hours."[39] What looks like a spectacle of passive consumerism actually yields a multiplicity of "tactics," options, and occasions for actively negotiating what Michel Foucault would describe as a "microphysics of power." Advancing Foucault's theory of disciplinary and institutional surveillance, de Certeau draws a cogent distinction between the established hegemonic regimes, or *strategies,* of power as opposed to the marginal and subaltern *tactics* of oppositional contestation and subversion that traverse them. Strategies, as de Certeau defines them, mark "a triumph of place over time" (PEL, 36). They transform the unreadable contingencies of history into a legible, *panoptic* space. Tactics, in contrast, cut across, raid, and out-maneuver, the logic, rules, and laws that govern such institutional and disciplinary sites of power. As the gambit of a weak force, a tactic relies on cunning, trickery, wit, finesse—what the Greeks described under the rubric of *metis,* or "ways of knowing" (PEL, xix).

The reproduction of consumerism, of course, relies on certain well-established strategies of representation that map the social field into a coded space of commodity exchange. The discourse of advertising, in particular—with its notorious manipulation of image and text—stands out as a ripe medium for the tactical subversion of dominant slogans and stereotypes. Throughout the 1970s and 1980s one specific site for intervening in the popular media has been its often sexist inscription of gender. Not insignificantly, in the work of such critical artists as Barbara Kruger, Jenny Holzer, and Nancy Spero, the subversion of sexism—as it is broadcast in everyday life through radio, television, and print journalism—has adopted tactics of quotation, citation, and appropriation that were pioneered some five decades earlier through Benjamin's examination of international Dada and the Russian Futurists in such essays as "The Work of Art in the Age of Mechanical Reproduction" and "The Artist as Producer." In particular, feminist critiques of the media representations perpetuated under capitalist patriarchy have benefited from Benjamin's earlier class-based analysis of aesthetic tactics that in the interbellum decades effected a functional transformation—a Brechtian *umfunktionierung*—of the then emerging apparatus of the bourgeois culture industry.[40]

To ignore or hope to transcend the new cultural logic of mechanical reproduction, in Benjamin's view, was simply to offer oneself up as a publicist for the status quo—a *hack* for an outmoded productive apparatus. The challenge that Benjamin laid down was for every author to become a producer, every artist a theorist, in the general remapping of generic boundaries, aesthetic traditions, and cultural conventions that the age demanded. Not incidentally, in photography this task entailed a subversion of "the barrier between writing and image. What we require of the photographer," Benjamin insisted, "is the ability to give his picture the caption that wrenches it from modish commerce and gives it a revolutionary useful value" (AP, 230). In thus linking photographic activity to language and signification, Benjamin's critique of photographic mimesis (that the photographic image *not* be taken as a literal, unmediated reflection of some "natural" signified reference, prepares for the antihumanist deconstruction of image and text in the writing of Roland Barthes.

In such early works of the 1950s as his seminal reading of "The Great Family of Man" exhibition in *Mythologies,* Barthes showed that "the conventions of photography . . . are themselves replete with signs."[41] Photographic codes and the cultural messages they broadcast, serve, in their signifying elements and discursive objects, what Barthes theorized as the secondary, metalinguistic operations of myth and ideological representation.[42] Myth "steals" from both written and pictorial languages in order to naturalize history according to the wholly motivated codes of its own "second-order semiological system." In the age of mass communication, as Barthes would go on to argue in the 1960s, every pictorial form is always already a linguistic text.[43] Barthes' sophisticated level of deconstructive reading, tied as it is to Benjamin's avant-garde concern for art's functional transformation of its enabling apparatus, provides a theoretical vantage point for reading contemporary feminist interventions in the contemporary media, such as those, say, of Barbara Kruger.

A one-time designer for Conde Nast during the 1970s, Kruger was thoroughly disciplined in the craft of commercial media design, whose graphic techniques, discursive codes, and semiotic protocals she appropriated in the 1980s for tactical reinscriptions of sexist, racist, and classist representations in the popular media. While her plates and posters have the look and feel of slick ads, the politics they inscribe cut across the grain of consumerist ideology. Indeed, her images frequently allude to the general violence, oppression, and humiliation entailed in the cultural logic of unequal exchange fostered under advanced capitalism. But equally important, her collages often serve various micropolitical agendas as in her participation in exhibitions like the *Disarming Images: Art for Nuclear Disarmament* (1984–86) show sponsored by Bread and Roses (the cultural organ of the National Union of Hospital and Health Care Employees, AFL-CIO). She also collaborates in any number of direct political actions, such as her poster "Your body is a battleground" advertising the 1989 March on Washington in support of Roe v. Wade (figure 5.2). (Figures 5.2–5.22 are in a photo insert following p. 222.)

Beyond such street-level praxes, however, one of Kruger's formal tactics is to open up the discursive field of advertising as such—what de Certeau would call its strategy—to unreadable gaps, contradictions, accusations, and dire judgments that interrupt our conventional responses and habits of consumption. "You are an experiment in *terror,*" for example, subverts the fetishized gesture of reaching out to touch, caress, and consume a typical commodity form (figure 5.3). Here she short-circuits our all-too-familiar grasp on things by displaying a hand flinching back from what looks like a booby-trapped beer can, exploding in an irrational and disarming act of malice. Yet the political intent of this terrorism remains undecidable. The image withholds any explicit ideological message beyond its own radical act of laying bare the fetishized scene of terrorism as itself a postmodern media code. For Baudrillard, any terrorist act—however it is later linked to this or that geopolitical agenda—functions first as a hyperreal performance. Terrorism is always already marked by a certain complicity with the culture industry that mediates its message and, more fundamentally, serves as the enabling ground of its spectacle. The terrorist act, he writes, "aims at that white magic of the social encircling us, that of information, of simulation, of deterrence, of anonymous and random control, in order to precipitate its death by accentuating it" (SSM, 51). Similarly deployed in Kruger's photography, media representation as such is defamiliarized as visual terrorism, especially so in its framing of gender relations.

The dominant coding of gender in the mass media—its repertoire of body language, facial expressions, styles of dress, and so on—positions the sexes differentially. Advertising, in particular, reproduces a semiotics of, on the one hand, patriarchal privilege, expertise, and authority vs. on the other hand, feminine passivity, sexual ingratiation, and infantalization. Photographic ads, as Erving Goffman has argued, broadcast a posed, "hyper-ritualization" of social situations, whose images are, more often than not, calculated to oppress women in subordinate roles to equally idealized male counterparts.[44] Much of Kruger's photographic appropriation of ad imagery and media slogans repudiate the sexist semiotic economy of capitalist patriarchy. For example, the use of personal pronouns to solicit the reader's investment in ads serves in Kruger's hands to heighten sexual antagonisms as in "We won't play nature to your culture" (figure 5.4). Here Kruger repudiates the dead letter of patriarchal stereotyping that, as Simone de Beauvoir theorized, reduces women's place to that of passive "Other": projected outside male civil order as nature, the unconscious, the exotic, what is either forbidden or taboo.[45]

Appropriating the glossy look of postmodern advertising—whose specular form solicits from the viewer a certain narcissism, a certain scopophilia—Kruger rebuffs the valorized male reader. She anathematizes this subject position with uncompromising, feminist refusals and such arresting judgments as:

> You thrive on mistaken identity.
> Your devotion has the look of a lunatic sport.
> You molest from afar.
> You destroy what you think is difference.
> I am your reservoir of poses.
> I am your immaculate conception.
> I will not become what I mean to you.
> We refuse to be your favorite embarrassments.
> We don't need another hero.
> Keep us at a distance.

While advertising exploits such "shifters" to ease consumption, Kruger's slogans maintain an urgent tension that throws into crisis any "normal" positioning of gendered pronouns. Her uncanny fusion of text and image, her impeccable craft, and her estranging wit resist any easy or complacent didacticism however. Several of her gendered appropriations, in fact, are calculated to deny decidable readings as in "We are being made spectacles of" (figure 5.5). Alluding to what Guy Debord dubbed as today's "society of the spectacle," Kruger's recoding of gender nevertheless voices an undecidable subject position. Who's speaking here? The male giving advice to a subordinated, feminine other? Not likely. The woman in a reversal of his advance? The artist in solidarity with women? Or are all of "us" addressed in a collective repudiation of the society of the spectacle?

More unsettling is Kruger's similarly ambiguous poster "You construct intricate rituals which allow you to touch the skin of other men" (figure 5.6). This work points up the homoerotic, libidinal economy that under patriarchy cements traditional social rituals of masculine bonding in sports, clubs, fraternities, and male cliques of all kinds. The generally progressive political stances that Kruger takes in her work make it very doubtful that she intends a critique of homoeroticism as such here. Obviously, she is not in league with the likes of, say, Jesse Helms. But does the fact that there is nothing in her fusion of text and image to disable such a reading be deemed a shortcoming in its execution? What is this poster's implied attitude toward homosexuality? Is this a "politically correct" representation or is it counterproductive? Does gender critique spill over into homophobia here? Tellingly, the vexed paradoxes that such undecidable collages pose are often domesticated in Kruger's reception through symptomatic acts of critical denial.[46]

More politically unsettled, perhaps, than Kruger's feminist critique of advertising discourse is Jenny Holzer's interventions within the electronic apparatus of the postmodern spectacle, particularly her appropriation of public light emitting diode (L.E.D.) boards. As an art student at the Rhode Island School of Design in the mid-1970s, Jenny Holzer came to New York via the Whitney Museum's Independent Study Program in 1976–77. After collaborating with a number of performance artists at the Whitney, she jettisoned painterly values. In 1977 she began to compose gnomic aphorisms that she collected in a series of "Truisms" formatted onto posters, stickers, handbills, hats, T-shirts, and other paraphernalia. Not unlike Daniel Buren's deconstruction of the gallery's conventional exhibition space, Holzer likewise took her placards to the streets of Soho and later throughout Manhattan. This aesthetic gambit allowed her to solicit a populist audience. But it also gave her work a certain shock value in its estrangement of everyday life. "From the beginning," she has said, "my work has been designed to be stumbled across when someone is just walking along, not thinking about anything in particular, and then finds these unusual statements either on a poster or on a sign."[47]

The verbal character of the "Truisms" themselves rely on the familiar slogans and one-liners common to tabloid journalism, the *Reader's Digest* headline, the TV evangelist pitch-line, campaign rhetoric, rap and hip-hop lyrics, bumper sticker and T-shirt displays, and countless other kitsch forms. In some ways the plainspoken vernacular of her midwest Ohio roots is, as Holzer admits, naturally suited to such tacky formats. What might redeem this risky project, possibly, is her avant-garde tactic of investing such predictable messages, and their all-too-familiar modes of mass distribution (posters, stickers, handbills, plaques, hats, T-shirts, and so on) with conflicted, schizophrenic, and at times politicized content. Her messages traverse the full spectrum of everyday life. They range from the reactionary complacency implied, say, in "AN ELITE IS INEVITABLE," or "ENJOY YOURSELF BECAUSE YOU CAN'T CHANGE ANY-THING ANYWAY," to the feminist essentialism of "A MAN CAN'T KNOW WHAT IT'S LIKE TO BE A MOTHER," to the populist credo that "GRASS ROOTS AGITATION IS THE ONLY HOPE," to the post-Marxist position that "CLASS STRUCTURE IS AS ARTIFICIAL AS PLASTIC." Foregrounding popular truisms as clichéd slogans, she play-fully deconstructs the humanist rhetoric of evangelism ("AWFUL PUN-ISHMENT AWAITS REALLY BAD PEOPLE"); pop psychoanalysis ("SOMETIMES YOUR UNCONSCIOUS IS TRUER THAN YOUR CON-SCIOUS MIND"); advice columns and self-help manuals ("EXPRESSING ANGER IS NECESSARY"); as well as the usual saws, platitudes, and hackneyed bromides that are with us everywhere:

A LITTLE KNOWLEDGE CAN GO A LONG WAY.
A LOT OF OFFICIALS ARE CRACKPOTS.
DON'T RUN PEOPLE'S LIVES FOR THEM.
GOOD DEEDS EVENTUALLY ARE REWARDED.
EVERY ACHIEVEMENT REQUIRES A SACRIFICE.
A SOLID HOME BASE BUILDS A SENSE OF SELF.

The political intent of some of her truisms are undecidably voiced. "GOVERNMENT IS A BURDEN ON THE PEOPLE," for example, is as serviceable to the reactionary right as the utopian left. Others, however, are more perversely drained of any meaning at all: "EVERYTHING THAT'S INTERESTING IS NEW."

Nonsensical, parodic, and ideologically loaded, such clashing platitudes, mottos, and non sequitors quickly caught on and won Holzer a popular audience as evidenced not only in the traces of graffitti left on her street posters, but in her window installations and exhibitions at Franklin Furnace (1978) and Fashion Moda in the South Bronx the following year. At this time Holzer undertook joint ventures such as the "Manifesto Show" that she helped organize with Colen Fitzgibbon and the Collaborative Projects group. Later, she would turn toward distinctively feminist collaborations with the female graffiti artist Lady Pink. Supplementing the poster art of "Truisms," Holzer in her 1980 "Living" series branched out into new materials. Holzer now inscribed her aphorisms in more monumental formats such as the kind of bronze plaques, commemorative markers, and commercial signs that everywhere bestow a kind of kitsch authority on offices, banks, government buildings, galleries, and museums.

One symptom of her work's emerging power was the resistance it met from patrons such as the Marine Midland Bank on Broadway that— responding to one of her truisms ("IT'S NOT GOOD TO LIVE ON CREDIT")—dismantled her window installation, consigning it to a broom closet. Not unlike Hans Haacke's celebrated expulsion from the Solomon R. Guggenheim Museum, such censorship testified to her work's site-specific shock value. In the mid-1980s, Holzer intensified her art's political content in her more militant "Survival" series (figure 5.7). At the same time, she undertook a bolder appropriation of a uniquely authoritative *and* spectacular medium—the light emitting diode (L.E.D.) boards installed worldwide in stock exchanges, urban squares, airports, stadiums, sports arenas, and other mass locales. The formal elements of this new high tech medium—its expanded memory of over 15,000 characters coupled with a built-in capacity for special visual effects and dynamic motion—advanced Holzer's poster aesthetics into the linguistic registers of poetics and textual performance art.

However Holzer's technique "naturalizes" the impersonal displays of her computerized texts, it shares in the Derridean, antihumanist deconstruction of the rhetorical presuppositions underwriting transcendental signified meaning, foundational thought, common sense—all ideal "truisms." The L.E.D. board's electronic mimicry of speech rhythms and inflection allows Holzer's mass art to solicit the humanist division between orality and inscription, logos and text, speech and writing. It puts into an uncanny, deconstructive play the margin of *différance* that normally separates, on the one hand, the intimacy and immediacy of a voiced presence from, on the other, the authoritative textual screens which function as the official media for postmodernism's high tech information society.[48] "A great feature of the signs," she has said, "is their capacity to move, which

I love because it's so much like the spoken word: you can emphasize things; you can roll and pause which is the kinetic equivalent to inflection in voice" (LG, 67). Typically, Holzer times her L.E.D. truisms to catch, like sound bites, the 2-to-3 second attention span of the average passerby.

As "an official or commercial format normally used for advertising or public service announcements" the L.E.D. signboard, Holzer maintains, is the medium par excellence of today's contemporary information society.[49] But more to the point, these high-tech boards are singularly positioned to reproduce the dominant codes and ideological myths that naturalize the reign of the commodity form. "The big signs," she has said, "made things seem official." In appropriating this public medium "it was like having the voice of authority say something different from what it would normally say."[50] Such interventions are pragmatically suasive, however, only if they hold in contradiction the dominant forms of the mass media and estranged, or radically ironic messages. In 1982, under the auspices of the Public Art Fund, Holzer went to the heart of America's mass spectacle, choosing selections from among her most succinct and powerful "Truisms" for public broadcast on the mammoth (20 × 40 ft) Times Square Spectacolor Board (figure 5.8). Commenting on the scandal-ridden political milieu of the Reagan era, slogans such as ABUSE OF POWER COMES AS NO SURPRISE were circulating suddenly at the very crossroads of American consumer society. Negotiating the official spaces of New York advertising demanded a reconsideration of the artwork beyond the limits of intrinsic form.

The formal composition of Holzer's spectacolor boards is mediated by site-specific forces in an expanded public field of legal, commercial, and political interests. For example, in mounting her own media blitz on Las Vegas—the American mecca of glitzy signage and neon kitsch—Holzer's choice of message, L.E.D. formats, and installation locales had to be adjudicated through a network of businesspersons, university managers, and political officials. Through these negotiations, and supported in part by the Nevada Institute of Contemporary Art, Holzer gained access to L.E.D. signs and poster installation sites in two shopping centers, the University of Nevada's sports center, the baggage claim areas of the Las Vegas airport, and the massive (20 × 40 ft) spectacolor publicity board outside of Caesars Palace (figures 5.9–5.10). Infiltrating the neon aura of the Caesars Palace logo, Holzer's playful L.E.D. display

> PROTECT ME
> FROM WHAT
> I WANT

laid bare the contradictory wager of consumerism at the heart of the post-modern spectacle.

Throughout the 1980s, Holzer mounted similar installations on the giant Alcoa Corporation L.E.D. sign outside Pittsburgh, on mobile truck signs in New York, and other sites nationwide. Moreover, as an intern for a Hartford television station, she purchased commercial time to broadcast her messages in 30-second commercial slots throughout the Northeast to a potential audience of millions. Here Holzer's textual praxis is guided by the same strategy of defamiliarization: mainlining the dominant arteries and electronic organs of the mass communications apparatus with post-modern ironies and heady, linguistic estrangements. "Again, the draw for me," she says, "is that the unsuspecting audience will see very different content from what they're used to seeing in this everyday medium. It's the same principle that's at work with the signs in a public place" (LG, 68). Whether Holzer's art remains oppositional to, rather than incorpo-rated by, the postmodern spectacle has become a more pressing question, given her rising star status in the late 1980s and '90s.

As a valorized figure in the world art market, Holzer enjoys regular gallery exhibitions in New York, Chicago, Los Angeles, Paris, Cologne, and other major art centers. In 1990 alone she not only undertook shows in the prestigious Solomon R. Guggenheim Museum and DIA Art Foun-dation, but served as the official U.S. representative to the Venice Bien-nial. When she made the jump from street agitation to international star-dom in the late 1980s, Holzer adjusted her presentation, paradoxically, to the more intimate and privatized nuances of commercial exhibition space. Installed in such settings as the Barbara Gladstone Gallery, the Grand Lobby of the Brooklyn Museum, the Rhona Hoffman Gallery, the Guggenheim, and the DIA Art Foundation, her new *Under a Rock* and "Laments" series inscribed her earlier truisms in granite and marble benches and sarcophagi quarried in Vermont near her summer residence in Hoosick, New York. Casting her truisms in stonework summoned an uncanny fusion of the monumental and the popular, at once glossing the medium of tombstones, anonymous war memorials, commemorative benches, and the kind of kitsch, public furniture found, say, in any bank lobby or shopping plaza (figure 5.11).

Departing from the spectacular spaces of Times Square and the Las Vegas strip, *Under a Rock* invoked the hushed atmosphere of a chapel by displaying files of stone benches, each illuminated by an overhead spot-light and arranged before a color L.E.D. display. Such an austere and shadowy layout—in its citation of church pews and stained glass iconography—employed a postmodern medium, paradoxically, to invoke a ritual aura of mourning, confession, and moral self-examination. This cult ambiance complemented the work's verbal content of unspeakable acts of torture, mutilation, and humiliation:

> CRACK THE PELVIS SO
> SHE LIES RIGHT. THIS
> IS A MISTAKE. WHEN
> SHE DIES YOU CANNOT
> REPEAT THE ACT.
> THE BONES WILL NOT
> GROW TOGETHER AGAIN
> AND THE PERSONALITY
> WILL NOT COME BACK.
> SHE IS GOING TO SINK
> DEEP INTO THE MOSS
> TO GET WHITE AND
> LIGHTER. SHE IS
> UNRESPONSIVE TO
> BEGGING AND SELF-ABSORBED.

While such terse, indeterminate narratives are not tied to any specific public agenda, they often adopt a feminist critique of male violence, misogyny, and machismo. Not unlike the matrifocal poetics of, say, Adrienne Rich, Holzer's *Child Text* created for her 1990 Venice Biennial negotiates between a personal phenomenology of mothering (as in "I AM SULLEN AND THEN FRANTIC WHEN I CANNOT BE WHOLLY WITHIN / THE ZONE OF MY INFANT. I AM NOT CONSUMED BY HER. I AM AN / ANIMAL WHO DOES ALL SHE SHOULD. I AM SURPRISED THAT I / CARE WHAT HAPPENS TO HER. I WAS PAST FEELING MUCH / BECAUSE I WAS TIRED OF MYSELF BUT I WANT HER TO LIVE") and a social critique of motherhood's institutional place under patriarchy.

Many of her "laments" are lyrical as in "I KEEP MY BRAIN ON SO I DO NOT FALL INTO NOTHING IF HIS CLAWS HURT ME." Others more broadly rely on the kind of fetishized coding of militarism, torture, and political assassination that, say, Leon Golub finds everywhere displayed in the contemporary media: "PEOPLE GO TO THE RIVER WHERE IT IS / LUSH AND MUDDY TO SHOOT CAPTIVES, / TO FLOAT OR SINK THEM. SHOTS KILL / MEN WHO ALWAYS WANT. SOMEONE / IMAGINED OR SAW THEM LEAPING TO / SAVAGE

THE GOVERNMENT. NOW BODIES / DIVE AND GLIDE IN THE WATER. SCARING / FRIENDS OR MAKING THEM FURIOUS.'' The spare and plainspoken language of ''Under A Rock'' is designed neither to shock the reader nor to subvert the linguistic medium, as in much of so-called Language writing. Rather, her work exhibits how the representation of such barbarism has moved to the center of the postmodern scene, whose routine horror is the daily stuff of the tabloid, the morning edition, and nightly update.

More subversive, perhaps, is the juxtaposition of linguistic elements and the arrangement of physical space that her installations exploit. In her DIA Foundation ''Laments'' series, for example, Holzer divides the exhibition space with thirteen sarcophagi variously carved in green and red marble, onyx, and black granite. These ritual objects are strangely illuminated with postmodern L.E.D. display boards that radiate vertically arrayed messages into the hushed and sepulchral air. The effect, however, of such a bizarre mix of antique caskets and high tech light grids is undecidable. Is it calculated to disrupt conventional oppositions between ancient artifacts and today's telecommunication medium, or to re-auraticize the L.E.D. medium as an object of contemporary veneration? Are the sarcophagi exposed as exhibition fetishes or simply updated in an aestheticized homage to the postmodern objet d'art? Undeniable, in any case, is the manic structure of feeling you get sitting on one of Holzer's granite benches beneath an electronic frieze of urgent, visually intense messages.

Yet however deconstructive of traditional gallery values, the political status of Holzer's recent installations—marked at once as objects of ritual ''lament'' and art market souvenirs—is debatable when one considers that these displays have themselves been conceived as commodity forms within the gallery exchange market, fetching up to $40,000 per L.E.D. sign, $30,000 per granite bench, and $50,000 per sarcophagus. It is not Holzer's purpose, of course, to deny or repress her work's commodity status but rather to exploit it: to de-auraticize art's remove from its commercial base. Holzer's truisms have always been up for sale but at the more populist rates of $15 per cap or T-shirt and $250 per set of 21 posters. Yet when she markets a granite slab for the price of a luxury car, her earlier truism—PRIVATE PROPERTY CREATED CRIME—necessarily returns with a vengeance. Indeed, Holzer does not flinch from such self-recrimination but pushes the difficult paradox of aesthetic critique and recuperation to its vexed limits: ''selling my work to wealthy people,'' she admits, ''can be like giving little thrills to the people I'm sometimes criticizing."[51] For all its honesty, such a frank acknowledgement of commodification, nonetheless, is a chilling echo of her onetime truism "AN ELITE IS INEVITABLE." It leaves Holzer susceptible to the critique of what Donald Kuspit has indicted as "Gallery Leftism": an aesthetic politics "calculated to make a certain impact, occupy a certain position, in the art world, whose unconscious ultimate desire is to produce museum art however much it consciously sees itself as having socio-political effect in the world."[52]

Part of what is at stake here is the difference between merely rehearsing the avant-garde critique of the museum—now itself a thoroughly stylized and recuperated gesture of protest—and committing art to social change. "The question is," as Kuspit poses it, "whether [a work] sensationalizes a socially important theme to make "advanced" art or whether it uses art to bring home on the level of personal sensation the socially relevant" (GL, 24). What remains undeniably productive in Holzer's praxis is her shrewd and decisive infiltration of today's dominant modes and technologies of mass persuasion. To her credit, Holzer's key precedent has unhinged the fixed status of today's communication apparatus, leaving it susceptible to more adventurous, more politicized interventions. Finding its roots in Benjamin's reading of the interbellum avant-gardes, her aesthetic strategy does not simply rest on socialist representation but aims for a broader, functional transformation of the electronic media as such. In achieving this end it deftly eludes the stigma and pitfalls of neoclassism.

Where art's social relevance spills over into the merely sensational is sometimes a hard call to make—contingent as it is on a work's staging, its reception, and audience response. Nevertheless, the overtly commercialized status of Holzer's "truisms" lends itself to gallery recuperation in a way that the more politicized feminism of Nancy Spero is calculated to disallow. In challenging women's historic exclusion from museum culture, Spero both critiques its sexist representations of the female body and blends a feminist mythology with women's contemporary experience. Her career is exemplary for women in the visual arts as it works through the painterly values of abstract expressionism and politicized textual collages to arrive at a nuanced celebration of the female tradition in expansive scroll formats.

In the so-called Black Paintings of the artist's early career (1959–64), her emerging feminist vision is obscured by the artist's concern for the formal craft of the oil medium. These works are marked by an essentialist aesthetics of expressionist surfaces that gesture toward a "deep" archetypal phenomenology. Veiled in the black spaces and dark zones of these canvasses, the goddess Ishtar presides, as she does in the contemporaneous poetry of Denise Levertov, as virgin, "great mother," and whore—a mythic figure at once of fertility, illicit sexuality, compassion, and ritual sacrifice. Such archetypal presences are as distanced and evanescent as shadowy photograph negatives, lost as they are from women's lived history under modern patriarchy. The mythic divide separating feminism from history, however, collapses in Spero's career under the pressing trauma of the Vietnam war. After a six-year stay in Paris, Spero returned to New York in 1966 where, in her "War Series," she undertook a more public reflection on the Holocaust, the arms race, and America's misadventure in Vietnam.

Not just an art of sociopolitical reference, however, Spero's new forays into the public violence of warfare were guided by a broader gender critique of patriarchal culture. In highlighting the coded signs of phallic power—as in the mushroom cloud of *Bomb and Victims* (1966); the vertical shaft and Nazi insignia of *Crematorium Chimney & Victims* (1968); the stylized cylindrical form of *Helicopter, Pilot, Eagle, Victims Being Thrown from Aircraft* (1968)—the "War Series" foreshadows Spero's later fusion of text and image in her celebrated "Codex Artaud Series" of the early 1970s. Spero's new concern for the visual image's linguistic coding of gender is reflected in her decisive move in the "War Series" away from expressionist oil painting to the medium of gouache, ink, and collage on Japanese rice paper. Unlike her practice in the Paris series of scrubbing, scratching, and blurring the oil medium, the rice paper surface did not lend itself to such painterly techniques. This formal shift to paper, collage, and inscription allowed Spero's art to occupy and unsettle the margins distinguishing text from image, art from writing, and aesthetics from politics.

But exceeding a simple deconstruction of such cultural binarisms, Spero's craft was tied to a progressive, institutional critique of the contemporary art market. "I was reacting to the self-importance of oil painting," she has said, "its value as a commodity and how I wanted to undermine this notion. It was important that I discard what I felt was an 'establishment' product and critique not only the art world by implication, but the politics of war."[53] Not coincidentally, it was at this time that Spero became involved in an activist protest against the widespread sexism that dominated the museum and gallery culture of the New York art market. As a member of the Women Artists in Revolution, a collaboration of the feminist Red Stockings group and Art Workers' Coalition, she participated in a 1969 delegation of eight women, petitioning MOMA's John Hightower

---

for equity in exhibition space for women. The next year Spero, along with Lucy Lippard and the other members of Committee of Women Artists, staged a picket around the Whitney Museum that proved successful in raising its number of women's exhibitions from four to twenty-five percent. It was also at this time that Spero became in 1971 a founding member of New York's first cooperative gallery space for women, the Artists in Residence gallery (A.I.R.). Yet however successful such explicitly politicized efforts proved in local instances, they hardly offset both the global exclusion women met in the art world and the fact of rampant sexism in the expanded social field.

Now at the height of her powers, Spero nevertheless was pushed to the margins of a gallery network, dominated by the cult of male originality and genius. Like Tillie Olsen, Spero found her work *silenced* by men. Resisting this threat to her artistic survival, Spero took a decisively feminist turn and anathematized such Victorian stereotypes as the self-effacing "angel of the house" and "dutiful daughter" of capitalist patriarchy. Not unlike the postwar poetics of, say, Sylvia Plath, Anne Sexton, or Adrienne Rich, Spero's work began to inscribe an "unspeakable" visual language in images of libidinal excess and sexual transgression—in mocking figures who literally stuck out their tongues at the spectacle of male authority. "For many years," she has said,

> when the work was not out, not acknowledged, I was silenced—lost my tongue, so to speak. Women talk but they do not speak insofar as they are, for the most part, historically silenced. So to speak, I stuck out my tongue (as in the disembodied heads with tongues sticking out that populated my "Artaud" paintings, "War Series," and "Codex Artaud" collages). Defiant gestures, obscene gestures, done in anger. This is not acceptable public behavior.[54]

In the 1970s, her "Codex Artaud" (1971–73) adopted the rebellious example of Artaud to wage a war of "unacceptable" violations against the art world's painterly values, its cult of artistic genius and canon of ideal masterworks (figure 5.12).

Not incidentally, the very rubric under which she drafted her work as a *codex*—an unbound sheaf of ancient manuscripts—translated her visual aesthetics into a linguistic medium. Moreover, the expanded visual space of these serial works (typically 20 inches in height by 125 to 210 feet in length) disallowed the viewer/reader any casual access or conventional consumption of the work. Resembling the "post-humanist" sprawl of Charles Olson's *The Maximus Poems,* the archival expanse of Spero's extended codices, scrolls, and mixed-media installations solicited her audience's collaboration in the work's unfolding textuality.

Beyond such formal dilations in the *lisible* space of conventional museum and gallery art, Spero also sought to foreground the material conditions that mediate artistic production under advanced capitalism. "In the Artaud series," she has said, "I wanted to view the artist's mental and physical condition in a Western bourgeois society that ignored the artist's message" (Siegel, 13). Following in the tracks of poststructuralism, Spero more broadly framed Artaud as a pioneering deconstructor of the whole edifice of representational mimesis that, historically in Western civilization, has reduced the aesthetic act to a mere repetition of a prior signified logos—whether political, philosophical, or religious. After Artaud, Spero would unsettle the conventional logic of Western metaphysics. Specifically, she challenged the economy of hierarchic divisions that discriminate the mind from the body, speech over writing, signified meaning before the play of the signifier, original from representation, model from copy, artist from viewer, writer from reader, art object from interpretation, book from text, the aesthetic sublime from realpolitik.

Positioned in this way, Spero's project lends itself to the kind of reception that poststructuralist theorists have performed on Artaud in such well-known essays as "La Parole Soufflée" and "The Theater of Cruelty and the Closure of Representation" (1967) by Derrida and later in Julia Kristeva's dissertation *La Revolution du langage poetique* (1973). For Derrida, Artaud sought a hallucinatory, hieroglyphic, and incarnate language of a dangerous, Nietzschean *becoming*. He pursued a discourse "whose clamor has not yet been pacified into words."[55] Artaud achieves such dramatic spontaneity in his so-called "theater of cruelty," whose actors, as he described them, "on stage are not afraid of the true sensation of the touch of a knife and the convulsions—*absolutely* real for them—of a supposed birth."[56] This level of intensity would be reduced in various ephebes to absurdist theater and other brands of ideological, interpretive, and didactic drama. But Artaud did not view writing as a transparent medium for communication or "thought." Instead, it should function, analogously, to the more delimited role that Freud ascribes to language in dream-work. In *The Interpretation of Dreams* and in the *Metapsychological Supplement to the Theory of Dreams,* Freud theorized that dream language is gestural and hieroglyphic: less a script than a "thing-presentation" (TC, 241). Mediated by the disorienting rebus of a dream, words appear less linguistic than pictorial and sculptural. Here, "gesture and speech have not yet been separated by the logic of representation" (TC, 241). Rather, such a discourse is properly *illegible,* where "in the night that precedes the book, the sign has not yet been separated from force."[57] Supplementing Artaud's critique of conventional representation in Derrida's poststructuralist reading, Julia Kristeva's *La Revolution du langage poetique* (1973) advanced Artaud's text into psychoanalytic registers.

Kristeva retrieves Artaud's writing as a prototype for the avant-garde's subversive rejection of patriarchy's symbolic order, the unified subject, scientific objectivity, the conventional status quo, and rationality as such. She positions Artaud's sensuous fusion of sign and force, signification and bodily drives, language and jouissance in the pre-symbolic, pre-oedipal register of the *semiotic* (la semiotique). Here "signifying unity itself vanishes into glossolalia."[58] For Kristeva, the transrational linguistic textures of the semiotic—its pulsations, rhythms, and play of sound-sense—derives from the libidinal economy of the infant's relation to the mother. This primary cathexis, she stresses, is more primordial than the child's later entry, via the oedipal stage, into the symbolic order of the word, the *nom du père.* It is the pre-oedipal domain of the semiotic that Spero invokes through her citations of Artaud's text. At the level of content, her appropriations of Artaud, as in, for example, *Codex Artaud IV*—"In the most valuable corner of my mind I harbor that preoccupation with sex which petrifies me and stops my blood"—solicit primordial drives (figure 5.13). Yet Spero resists a mere thematic representation of the semiotic. On the contrary, she inscribes Artaud's discourse as a gestural, "thing-presentation" of signs. Not only does she employ enjambment to format her citations as "concrete" poetry, but individual words are set off against ecstatic, surrealistic visual figures in stunning gold metallic paint and black borders.

Many of these hieroglyphic forms are gendered as female and some hyperbolically so in mythic portraits of multiheaded and multibreasted goddesses. Such matrifocal images look forward to her 1981 series *The First Language* that employs stylized poses of women in pregnancy and active labor to explore a gestural discourse of the body. In the mid-decade, Spero entered into an intertextual dialogue with the writing of Hélène Cixous and the French feminist group *Psychanalyse et politique.* Here she retrieved an alternative sexuality (one based in the empowered "otherness" of women's embodied experience) to the male phallocentric order dominating Western thought. In her 1985 composition *Let the Priests Tremble,* for example, Spero joins the prepatriarchal figure of the "great mother" (a frontal display of a nude female torso) to a polemical citation from Cixous's "The Laugh of the Medusa": "Let the priests tremble, we're going to show them our sexts! Too bad for them if they fall apart upon discovering that women aren't men, or that the mother doesn't have one" (figure 5.14).[59] Overturning women's role as the passive bearer of cultural meaning, Cixous's intertext actively interrupts the phallocentric reproduction of woman as either a fetish of visual pleasure or a stigma of failure, denigration, and loss. Likewise, Spero's revisionary images push the iconic representation of women beyond an androcentric visual economy based in male voyeurism and scopophilia: one that reads biological difference—the absence of the penis—through the male anxiety of castration.[60]

Spero's tactic is to foreground the look of female difference in a sexual politics that empowers women's sexuality *in excess* of its reproductive framing within patriarchy's *uterine* economy of conception, gestation, and birth. Instead, she celebrates—in figures such as the Celtic goddess "Sheela-na-gig and the Dildo Dancer" from her "Notes on Women" (figure 5.15)—what Gayatri Spivak has described as a *clitoral* social organization. This mode of sexuality is based on "the theme of woman's *norm* as clitorally ex-centric from the reproductive orbit . . . *before* the reproductive coupling of man and woman, *before* the closing of the circle whose only productive excess is the child, and whose 'outside' is the man's 'active' life in society."[61] Although Spero's art releases powers of female sexuality, her matriarchal imagery, in a number of ways, deftly eludes the problematic charge of idealism and essentialism lodged against *l'écriture féminine* and feminist praxes informed by psychoanalytic theory.

Beyond the so-called new French feminism's ties to the phallocentric order of Freudian and Lacanian psychoanalysis, the whole notion of enjoying a direct relation to the body, according to the editorial collective of *Questions féministes*, by-passes the social and historical contexts that necessarily mediate embodied experience, whether repressive or emancipatory.[62] It is this essentialist logic that, according to Spivak, leads in Kristeva's version of the *semiotique* to "a set of directives for class- and race-privileged literary women who can ignore the seductive effects of identifying with the values of the other side while rejecting their validity; and, by identifying the political with the temporal and linguistic, ignore as well the micrology of political economy" (136). Not insignificantly, Spero's policiticized version of *l'écriture féminine* undertakes precisely the kind of nuanced attention to the specific historicity mediating the feminine body that Spivak espouses.

To begin with, her art seldom lapses into the kind of ahistorical or utopian version of matriarchal culture that marks, say, the Victorian stereotypes of "mother-right" in the Bachofen tradition. In contrast, Spero's meticulously documented series *The Torture of Women* (1974–76) brings primordial rituals of female oppression into dialogue with contemporary accounts of violence against women. Displaying the kind of documentary material she had employed earlier in *Torture in Chile* (1974), Spero relates mythic accounts of the torture of women—as in the ritual disembowelment of the female goddess Tiamat—to actual case histories gleaned from such popular sources as the *New York Times, Time, The Nation,* and Amnesty International. Formatted in the impersonal bulletin type of contemporary journalism, these disturbing narratives of interrogation, torture, mutilation, and military-style execution, possess a cool, computerized look. By contrasting this discourse with the classical lines and graceful forms of Spero's feminist iconography, *The Torture of Women* links today's information age to patriarchy's historic repression of feminine jouissance.

Spero's mixed-media presentations of patriarchal violence dispel any ideal or ahistorical versions of women's lived experience. Her dialogic citations, drawn from a gamut of aesthetic traditions, resist any essentialist reduction of women's cultural diversity. Employing over 100 zinc plates of feminist poses and body language, she cites such figures as Venus of Willendorf, Helen of Egypt, Shela-na-gig, anonymous Paleolithic goddesses, as well as images of women drawn from Greek, Roman, Celtic, African, Vietnamese, and countless other traditions. Spero presents these images of "female bodies" she explains, "to speculate on what is possible and to comment upon immediate events and rites of passage—political, sexual, personal" (SG, 105). But equally important, Spero's compositional strategies of citation, appropriation, and postmodern "plagarism" of text and image deny any universal definition of woman as such. "I ransack art history," she admits, "and photographic sources. I usually change the images in some way. But I do unashamedly appropriate from found images" (Siegel, 12). Such an "unashamedly" collaged field of textuality presents feminine identity mediated by an expanded field of cultural representation.

Glossing figures as diverse as Isis and Abigail Adams, Ishtar and Hilda Doolittle, Pliny and Nietzsche, Marduk and Barry Goldwater, Spero negotiates a "thick" palimpsest of quotations. Her citations from other print and visual media illustrate the artist's 1979 intertext from Derrida in

"Notes in Time on Women II" that "there is no essence of woman . . . / there is no truth about woman." Echoing this poststructuralist take on essentialist feminism, Spero insists that:

> In representations of women, I examine difference—to make manifest, to put them to work, to signify how we envision the body. For me as a feminist artist, to depict the female body is to depict ranges of difference. Not to set up an ideal or universal . . . but particulars, a kind of naming. Ideal types of the past—Greek, goddesses, prehistoric or Hittite fertility figures—jostle or intersect, come up against Vietnamese peasants or veiled Arab women, porn queens, etc.—all to be clarified through their specificity and their refusal of closure. (SG, 105)

Spero's differential cultural feminism, set as it is in dialogue with contemporary news bulletins on today's global violence against women, successfully denies any aesthetic transcendence of sexual politics or fetishized versions of women's essence. Although her art presents an elegant, semiotic language of the female body, the expanded format of her codices and scrolls disallow their "masterpiece" status. Similarly, her appropriated imagery and serial citations resist the claim of canonicity. Spero's shocking journalistic accounts and graphic images of patriarchal violence are less recuperable to "gallery leftism" than the slogans and slick visuals of Holzer or Kruger. Yet they are susceptible, nonetheless, to a certain aestheticizing of political representation for commercial exchange within the contemporary art market. Some degree of institutional assimilation is desirable, of course. After all, the market provides access to a broad audience. Moreover, such exposure allows one to create key precedents for other artists to adopt in lodging further critiques within, yet against, the regimen of the art establishment and wider culture industry.

Soliciting Censorship

The true mark of a work's oppositional power, perhaps, is its capacity to solicit its own censorship by affirmative museum culture. On the vanguard of such revolutionary aesthetics, the work of Hans Haacke has more than once been banned by noteworthy museums for its deconstructive readings of the ostensibly divorced but, in fact, complicit relationship between "high" art and the economic, cultural, and political interests of the state, private investors, and today's multinational corporate sector. Critical of the valorized status of masterpiece art, Haacke exercises a more radical subversion of aesthetic representation than Holzer, Kruger, or Spero, who all preserve some trace of a recognizable art object (however estranged, parodied, or subverted).

Haacke, however, reverses art's "normally" extrinsic and social modes of production as the "intrinsic" concern of his installations. "Here what survives the extinction of the 'work',", comments Fredric Jameson, "is not its materials or components, but rather something very different, its *pre-suppositions, its conditions of possibility.*"[63] One of the frequently over-looked but nonetheless enabling preconditions of gallery art is its prag-matic relation to an audience. Haacke's early works such as *Gallery-Goers Birthplace and Residence Profile* (1969), his MOMA *Information* (1970) exhibit, and similar shows throughout the early 1970s at the Mil-waukee Art Center, *Documenta 5,* and the John Weber Gallery in New York, simply polled museum goers on demographic, cultural, and political topics. This strategy transformed the flaneur's normally silent and passive witnessing of masterpiece art into a more active and participatory role. The exhibition of the viewer's response as such functioned, in Haacke's work, to rupture the museum's "natural" subordination of the spectator to the privileged, canonical artifact. Displaying the tabulated responses to polls at later installations, Haacke ruptured the hermetic canon of valor-ized art, opening it to a broader social text.

Although Haacke shook the structural logic of canonicity that elevates the "intrinsic" value of gallery art over its "extrinsic" production and audi-ence reception, he did not become a cause célèbre until his single-artist show *Hans Haacke: Systems* (1971) was censored by Thomas Messer, the director of the Solomon R. Guggenheim Museum. At the heart of the controversy lay some 142 photographs and accompanying documenta-tion installed under the title *Shapolsky et al. Manhattan Real Estate Holdings.* In it Haacke meticulously recorded the pattern of family-owned dummy corporations and cross-held real estate mortgages through which Shapolsky and some dozen other slum lords "had controlled," according to a 1966 investigation carried out by New York radio station WMCA, "500 tenement buildings housing 50,000 persons buying and selling—or foreclosing—among each other in deals that increased rents and prof-its."[64] Installing the scandal of sleazy urban rent-gouging at the center of a museum renowned for its collection of early modernist abstract art (whose very edifice, designed by Frank Lloyd Wright, stands as an eloquent synecdoche of modernism's futuristic spiral beyond everyday life), Haacke aimed to deconstruct the formalist remove of this privileged cultural enclave.

Through a meticulous strategy worked out with his legal team, the artist not only anticipated the museum's censorship but exploited it as part of his intervention. Employing subsequent exchanges in art journals and the wider public media, Haacke stretched the formal art object to include reception as part of its spectacular makeup. Thus the work as such emerged only through manipulating an institutional process bent on censoring its presentation. That the Guggenheim was compelled to silence its own complicity in New York's shady real estate market belied art's remove from social praxis.

Traditionally, the modern museum has been regarded as a politically disinterested and largely custodial institution, one that subscribes to the highest canons of artistic genius, formal integrity, and disciplinary self-sufficiency. It aims for an aesthetic transcendence of the more worldly networks of valuation based in corporate patronage, critical reception, and audience response. In other words, the museum represses art's ideological role in shaping social distinction and class legitimation. While this is the official line for public consumption, close ties have always bound museum and gallery culture to an elite patronage circle of first families.

Increasingly in the postwar era the role of promoting and speculating in high art has passed from the Ford, Rockefeller, Whitney, Getty, and other dynasties to a more anonymous, institutional network of corporate sponsors. Responding, in part, to his own censorship at the Guggenheim, Haacke began in the mid-1970s to target the institutional nexus joining contemporary museum culture to the corporate interests of multinational conglomerates like Alcan, Alcoa, American Cyanamid, British Leyland, Exxon, Mobil, Philip Morris, and the Rembrandt Group, among others. By documenting the business interests represented in the board of trustees of the Solomon R. Guggenheim Museum, Haacke's 1974 installation at the Stefanotty Gallery traced a pattern of corporate affiliation linking key board members—among them trustee president and family member Peter O. Lawson-Johnston, son of Barbara Guggenheim—to such companies as Kennecott Copper, Pacific Tin, Feldspar, Anglo Company and numerous subsidiaries. Not incidentally, Kennecott Copper was subpoenaed to appear before a 1973 Subcommittee on Multinational Corporations of the U.S. Senate Committee on Foreign Relations over its alleged role in unseating President Salvador Allende in Chile. In fact, Kennecot received the handsome sum of $68 million from the Pinochet regime as remuneration for the Chilean parliament's earlier nationalization of the company in 1971.

Not insignificantly, Haacke's cultural critique exposed a telling classism tying the Guggenheim trustees' first world promotion of a sanitized aesthetic formalism to its third world exploitation of cheap labor markets. By laying bare the corporate role in masterpiece art, Haacke underscored the materialist critique of canonicity, summed up in the seventh of Walter Benjamin's "Theses on the Philosophy of History":

> Whoever has emerged victorious participates to this day in the triumphal procession in which the present rulers step over those who are lying prostrate. According to traditional practice, the spoils are carried along in the procession. They are called cultural treasures, and a historical materialist views them with cautious detachment . . . There is no document of civilization that is not at the same time a document of barbarism. And just as such a document is not free of barbarism, barbarism taints also the manner in which it was transmitted from one owner to another. A historical materialist therefore dissociates himself from it as far as possible. He regards it as his task to brush history against the grain. (*Illuminations*, 256–57)

Satisfied to let the facts speak for themselves, Haacke did not lodge any overt political judgment against the Guggenheim beyond exposing an overlapping genealogy of corporate and cultural holdings. Later that year Haacke's Manet-PROJEKT '74, a work solicited by the Wallraf-Richartz Museum in Cologne, applied a similar strategy of tracing the lineage of ownership that mediates the reception and status of the art object itself. But Haacke's avant-garde tactic of simply presenting what Benjamin describes above as a cultural treasure's barbarous transmission from owner to owner shook the art establishment. The proposed installation would have displayed Manet's *Bunch of Asparagus* (1880), held in the collection of the Cologne museum, with ten accompanying panels presenting "the social and economic position of the persons who have owned the painting over the years and the prices paid for it" (Haacke, 118). Scandalized by such a straightforward documentation, the directors of the PROJECT '74, like the Guggenheim trustees, voted to censor it. Moreover, when Daniel Buren smuggled a facsimile of Haacke's work into his own installation, they went so far as to paper over the Manet panels, hiding them from public view.

As a critical artist, Haacke holds that any museum or gallery as an "institution should be challenged if it refuses to acknowledge that it operates under constraints deriving from its sources of funding and from the authority to which it reports" (Haacke, 66). Throughout the late 1970s and 1980s, Haacke advanced this institutional critique, examining how museum culture is shaped by and in turn reproduces the forces of conglomerate ownership, corporate politics, and marketing strategies. Within a post-Marxist horizon of cultural critique, Haacke's installations interrogate the political economy of "naturalized" standards of distinction, taste, and high culture as they are tied to corporate speculation in the art market. What remains perhaps Haacke's most caustic intervention into the commodification of gallery art is his oil painting of Margaret Thatcher entitled *Taking Stock* (unfinished) (1984), first exhibited in the Tate Gallery (figure 5.16). In it the artist offers a biting commentary on Thatcherism, whose conservative nostalgia for the Victorian age is captured in the citational portrait of Queen Victoria adorning the back of a chair held in the collection of the Victoria and Albert Museum. Not incidentally, Thatcherism as a cultural ideology comprises, in Stuart Hall's analysis, an active yoking of free market laissez faire and organic Toryism with a conservative "return to the old values—the philosophies of tradition, Englishness, respectability, patriarchalism, family, and nation."[65] In articulating Thatcherism's conservative nostalgia for empire to a specific gallery aesthetic, the painting's kitsch bric-a-brac alludes, in its portraits of Maurice and Charles Saatchi inscribed on broken plates (appropriated from Julian Schnabel), to the corporate shaping of the commercial art market.

Through a number of buy-outs and takeovers of U.S. firms in the 1980s, Saatchi & Saatchi emerged as the leading advertising firm worldwide. In the political arena, the Saatchi's backed Thatcher in her successful election campaigns of 1979 and 1983. Likewise in their roles as Patrons of New Art of the Tate Gallery and trustees of England's Whitechapel Gallery, they have promoted a stable of pseudoexpressionist painters such as Sandro Chia, Francesco Clemente, and Julian Schnabel. Not coincidentally, the Saatchi's have bought heavily into these artists as lucrative investments. Under their far from disinterested patronage, the corporate politics of Thatcherism decisively intersects with the aesthetic ideology of *la mode retro*. Schnabel's fetishized citations from the "great" tradition (tied as they are to the art market's valorized medium of oil painting) are further propped up by his fashionable signature of personal creative genius. Together they reinstate the formal regime of museum culture, whose reign is so lucrative for corporate investment in the arts. At the level of both content and form, Haacke's oil portrait of Maggie Thatcher, like his equally subversive painting of Ronald Reagan in *Oelgemaelde, Hommage a Marcel Broodthaers* (1982), takes as its subject precisely what is so rigorously silenced in the "normal" presentation of "fine" art—its ideological complicity with state politics and the corporate profit motive.

Theorizing institutional art as itself a kind of "consciousness industry," Haacke further assumes that those who orchestrate the public imagery of today's giant multinational conglomerates understand "sometimes better than the people who work in the leisure suits of culture, that the term 'culture' camouflages the social and political consequences resulting from the industrial distribution of consciousness."[66] Museum culture, in fact, often serves as a medium (or more crudely, in the words of Robert Kingsley—former manager of Urban Affairs within Exxon's Department of Public Affairs—as a "social lubricant") for big business's penetration of new markets (figure 5.17). In fact, many of his exhibitions—such as, say, *On Social Grease* (1975), *Mobilization* (1975), *The Chase Advantage* (1976), *The Road to Profits Is Paved with Culture* (1976), and *MetroMobiltan* (1985)—recode multinational public relations documents so as to tease out the socioaesthetic ties binding corporate sponsorship of the arts and advertising (figures 5.18 and 5.19).

Haacke seizes on the promotional relations linking capital to canvas as the postmodern aesthetic object par excellence, whether quoting on the corporate side from David Rockefeller ("From an economic standpoint, such involvement in the arts can mean direct and tangible benefits")[67] or from the promotional brochures of the Metropolitan Museum:

> Many public relations opportunities are available through the sponsorship of programs, special exhibitions and services. These can often provide a creative and cost-effective answer to a specific marketing objective, particularly where international, governmental or consumer relations may be a fundamental concern.[68]

His installations document how advertising discourse invests a company's public image with the museum's "civilized" aura, thus obscuring otherwise barbarous corporate practices in third world locales like Chile, Angola, and South Africa.

As a historical materialist in Benjamin's sense, Haacke brushes tradition against the grain. In what Fredric Jameson describes as a homeopathic intervention, he mainlines the otherwise unspeakable reality of corporate race, class, and gender oppression into advertising's simulacral medium. For example, Haacke appropriates the glossy, high-tech look, say, of a Jaguar's luxurious cockpit and articulates it—through an ad caption format quoting the U.K. Parliamentary Select Committee on African Wages, 1973—to British Leyland's repressive labor policies, based throughout the '70s in South African Apartheid (figure 5.20):

An employee may have an incentive to remain with his employer, no matter how he is treated, in order to qualify for urban residence: and it has been argued that contract workers' rights to work in urban areas are so tenuous that, regardless of how uncongenial their employment or how poor their pay, they are forced to stay in their job for fear of being endorsed out of their area and back to the homelands.

Haacke's ironic fusion of image and text demystifies the Jaguar's commodity status by returning it to its barbarous scene of production. The same metasimulation of advertising discourse guides his scathing exposé of American Cyanamid, where he signifies on the reified fetish image of the Breck "girl" (figure 5.21). Postmodern irony serves here in what Foucault would describe as a *specific* critique of Cyanamid's sexist and classist labor practices. What looks like a slick promotional ad for a company "Where Women Have a Choice" actually uncovers—again in its print text layout—Cyanamid's heinous policy of pressuring female employees of childbearing age to submit to sterilization:

> **American Cyanamid** is the parent of BRECK Inc.. maker of the shampoo that keeps the Breck Girl's hair clean, shining and beautiful.
> **American Cyanamid** does more for women. It knows: "We really don't run a health spa."
> And therefore those of its female employees of child-bearing age who are exposed to toxic substances are now given a choice.
> They can be reassigned to a possibly lower paying job within the company. They can leave if there is no opening. Or they can have themselves sterilized and stay in their old job.
> Four West Virginia women chose sterilization.

Not insignificantly, Haacke advances the political agenda of the historical avant-gardes into postmodern registers by estranging our traditional expectations of advertising iconography. His art's shock effects spring from the sharp discontinuity of reified image and social text—a defamiliarized ensemble that returns the fetishized commodity sign to its actual scene of production.

While Haacke articulates advertising's formal language mainly to economic and class issues, Adrian Piper's interventions into the discursive field of consumer culture are lodged within the registers of race and gender critique. Her *Vanilla Nightmares* series of the mid '80s, in particular, recode mainstream advertising images so as to unsettle the racist and sexist visual economy of American consumer culture. Her metasimulation of Bloomingdale's full-page *New York Times* ad for Christian Dior's "Poison," for example, intrudes upon the stylized, glossy stereotype of the youthful white "enchantress" by introducing an anonymous gang of black figures etched in grainy charcoal (figure 5.22). In Piper's revisionary reading, "Poison" serves as a visual pharmakon. It displays at once the source and cure for capitalist patriarchy's racial, sexual, and class dualisms that privilege rich over poor, men over women, white over black, the first over the third world. Piper's ludic, visual layout injects the ad's print text—"A Mysterious Encounter Defying Description"—with heady postmodern ironies, playing as it does on white ethnocentrism and outworn taboos on interracial sexuality. But what on one level simulates the "vanilla nightmare" of white xenophobia, also comes as a toxic shock for the black subaltern, whose forehead is indelibly stamped with the logo of the postmodern apocalypse. For Piper, today's global consumption of the reified fetish images and high-end status symbols of American glamour describes a spectacle of commodity vampirism, where crowds of zombies spend an "Eternity, a Thousand and One Journeys" in pursuit of consumer culture's "mysterious" signage. In such postmodern subversions of advertising discourse, Mullican, Kruger, Holzer, Spero, Haacke, and Piper have employed the formal resources of image and text to solicit and deconstruct the margin separating institution art from popular culture. But equally important, their pioneering techniques, as I detail in my epilogue, have provided important models for several collaborative projects that, in the post-Vietnam era, intervene politically in the spectacular makeup of everyday life.

Epilogue

In rereading the Old Left push for a Soviet-style cultural revolution in the United States, one is struck by our own moment's uncanny reversal of precisely that earlier dream of social utopia. That the actual Soviet Union never offered a Promised Land for American labor—just as there may never have existed true matriarchal precursors for contemporary feminism—does not necessarily lessen the force of either as a revisionary forerunner of social critique. With or without the USSR, the revolutionary tradition *imagined* by the American Old Left lives on as a rich resource in the struggle for social guarantees and communal satisfactions that are not driven by individual consumption and the profit motive. New social movements, in fact, have advanced the American tradition of cultural critique into postmodern registers by articulating the class-based representations of the Old Left to a broader, multicultural discursive field.

Contemporary muralist syndicates such as, say, the Citywide Mural Project in Los Angeles and Artmakers in New York have added a distinctively *inter*national perspective to the Constructivist inheritance of class critique, passed on as it was through Diego Rivera from Russia to the United States. Unhindered, however, by Rivera's contradictory ties to corporate benefactors and party ideologues, these group efforts are more collective and site specific in terms of both production and reception. For example, the Great Wall of the San Fernando Valley and the La Lucha murals of La Plaza Cultural part company with the universalizing, master narratives that shape Rivera's Marxist historicism as well as the New Deal themes of manifest destiny and industrial optimism typifying WPA mural work.

The largest fresco in the world, *The Great Wall* was organized by Judy Baca in collaboration with 250 youth and 70 artists through a collective process of negotiation with the Army Corps of Engineers and countless government agencies, community organizations, local businesses, labor unions, and arts councils. Across its expansive, half-mile-long surface are inscribed specific narratives of struggle undertaken by African-American, Chicano, Asian-American, and Native-American peoples against racism, classism, and sexism in the United States. One witnesses in the mural's depiction of California's local historicity the genealogies of dust bowl émigrés and Japanese internment camp detainees, the Chicano "zoot suit" riots, black protests against south central Los Angeles's restrictive covenant housing laws, and the division of the L.A. barrio which, like the South Bronx, was cleaved by the postwar freeway (figures E.1 and E.2). (Figures E.1–E.5 and E.7–E.10 are in a photo insert following p. 222.) Conceived as an alternative to the centrally administered imagery of the culture industry, "the mural," Baca has said, "is not just a big picture on a wall. The focus is on cooperation in the process underlying its creation. . . . With what the historians bring in we develop images to put back into public consciousness information that has been lost."[1] *The Great Wall*'s communal mode of production joins aesthetics with cultural history to recover the social images and local stories that have been erased by the consumer media.

Baca's interventionist agenda is summed up in her recent L.A. billboard slogan: "Be Skeptical of the Spectacle. Respect Your Own Perspective." The same suspicion is inscribed in the oppositional representations of New York's La Lucha mural project of the mid-eighties—a spinoff of the "Artists Call Against Intervention in Central America" and "Art Against Apartheid" exhibitions as well as shows protesting the rapid gentrification of the East Village, mounted by Political Art Distribution/Documentation (PADD). Positioned between 8th and 9th Streets at Avenue C in the Lower East Side, the twenty-four murals of the La Lucha project covers 6,310 square feet of wall space. Across its expanse are depicted images of feminist liberation in South Africa and Central America, the police killing of graffiti artist Michael Stewart in 1985, and the displacement of Asian-American, Latino, and African-American artists by urban renewal. Gentrification happened as the Lower East side was developed in the 1980s from its 160-year history as a working-class neighborhood into what art pundits hailed at the time as the New York Montmartre and American Bateau Lavoir.

Over forty new gallery entries such as 51X, Nature Morte, Civilian Warfare, Gracie Mansion, and the Fun Gallery made up the cutting edge of New York's lucrative $2-billion art industry. This irresistible lobbying force, with ties to the mayor's office and housing development boards, simply carved up the Lower East Side's twelve square blocks into "assemblages" for public auction. Through tax abatement incentives, developers retrofitted affordable housing into luxury condominiums, driving up storefront square footage by more than 600 percent overnight. Not coincidentally, such upscale gentrification went hand-in-hand with a commercial crusade for a neoexpressionist, painterly canon. "This doctrine," according to Rosalyn Deutsche and Cara Gendel Ryan,

> is embodied in . . . a system of rigid and restrictive beliefs: in the primacy of the self existing prior to and independently of society; in an eternal conflict, outside of history, between the individual and society; in the efficacy of individualized, subjective protest. The participants in the East Village scene serve this triumphant reaction.[2]

In representing the social consequences of Lower East Side gentrification, Artmakers' communal, nonprofit muralist syndicate resisted the promotion of 80s-style neoexpressionism at the levels of content, form, mode of aesthetic production, and audience reception.

Such collaboration underscores the multicultural recoding of the American spectacle in New York's La Lucha murals and Los Angeles' *Great Wall*. Moreover, group solidarity has also served in the struggle over the popular meanings of environmentalism, particularly in the guerrilla aesthetics of Greenpeace. This antinuclear/ecological network was founded in 1971 when a group of activists, guided by Marie Bohlen's Quaker philosophy of "bearing witness," attempted to sail the *Phyllis Cormack* into an American nuclear test site located on Amchitka island, a bird sanctuary in the Aleutian chain. Over its twenty-year history, Greenpeace has grown into a proactive, environmental-defense organization with over five million members worldwide. The association is perhaps most well known for its daring protests of international whaling on the high seas. By placing its own small navy of inflatable dinghies between the whales and harpoon guns, Greenpeace has thrown a monkey wrench into the corporate machine, reducing whaling during the past two decades by 84 percent. "Our agenda, however," writes Peter Dykstra, "has constantly evolved. . . . We had to expand to stop ocean dumpers and plutonium producers; fight acid rain and driftnetters; and put a halt to clearcutting and landfiller owners. The list, alas, goes on."[3]

Throughout the Reagan/Bush era, however, politicians stepped up their own damage control efforts to "greenwash" devastating environmental policies through slick public relations campaigns. Becoming an "environmental" mayor, governor, or president has less to do with conservation than the fine art of staging pastoral photo opportunities against All-American backdrops straight out of *Field and Stream* or the L. L. Bean catalogue. Consequently, Greenpeace has had to respond precisely at the level of the image to recode such ideologically-loaded spectacles to its own progressive agenda. "Greenpeace believes," says Steve Loper, the Action Director for Greenpeace, U.S.A, "that an image is an all-important thing. The direct actions call attention to the issues we're involved in. We put a different point of view out that usually ends up on the front page of the paper . . . If we just did research and lobbying and came out with a report it would probably be on the 50th page of the paper."[4]

The creation of compelling images, however, is a rigorously site-specific process. Although articulated to politicized positions on, say, nuclear arms escalation, deforestation, and toxic dumping, each intervention is radically contingent on the particular, conjunctural forces and pragmatic demands of a given moment. One of Greenpeace's tactics is to seize on popular news reports such as the scandalous New York City garbage-barge story of 1987. In the absence of a dump site, the eyesore sailed up and down the eastern seaboard for several months. Appropriating this object of sustained public embarrassment, Greenpeace linked it to the theme of recycling through unfurling a giant banner across the length of the vessel reading: "NEXT TIME . . . TRY RECYCLING" (figure E.3). Greenpeace's better-known gambit is to go to the heart of America's national heritage. This tactic recodes the popular meanings of such monumental icons as, say, South Dakota's Mount Rushmore or New York's Statue of Liberty to Greenpeace's own agenda.

Such was Greenpeace's strategy in its 1987 attempt to place a giant surgical mask over the mouth of Rushmore's George Washington reading "WE THE PEOPLE SAY NO TO ACID RAIN." Another subversive action involved hanging an antinuclear banner—"Give Me Liberty from Nuclear

Weapons, Stop Testing"—like a giant stripped-in caption on the Statue of Liberty for the 1984 commemoration of the U.S. atomic bombing of Hiroshima and Nagasaki. Although Greenpeace works with a yearly budget equal to about four hours of General Motors' revenues, what is at stake in its agitational praxis is nevertheless vital. Writes Judy Christup:

> We frame the environmental debate in moral terms. This means saying some obvious but unpopular things. It's wrong to turn healthy rivers into industrial sewers; it's wrong to turn a profit at the expense of people's health; it's wrong to destroy the habitats of endangered animals. Human beings seem to be able to rationalize every conceivable form of planetary destruction. Our job is to punch holes in the rationalizations and point to the truth.[5]

As we move from the interbellum to postwar decades—from, say, Louis Lozowick's idealized portraits of New Jersey blast furnaces to the menacing cooling towers of Three Mile Island and Chernobyl—the popular meanings of the industrial landscape undergo a radical reversal, shifting from utopian hope to apocalyptic angst.

Similarly, the politics of gender identity have undergone a remarkable sea change since the Third Period. The kind of hard guys that Hugo Gellert was prone to celebrating, when depicted in contemporary mass culture, are fraught with postmodern irony—staged as they are through such pumped and grotesque cyborgs as Arnold Schwarzenegger. The Old Left coding of workers as muscle-bound white males—toiling for the so-called dictatorship of the proletariat—not only clashes with the more democratic iconography of the Popular Front years but is particularly alienating after the feminist mass spectacles of postmodernity. On the vanguard of such revisionary displays of gender, Susan Lacy's media art has since the early 1970s pioneered interventionist strategies for rearticulating women's place in mass culture. Significantly, Lacy's 1977 collaboration with Leslie Labowitz in *Three Weeks in May,* a public informational campaign on the representation of women in advertising, the news media, and pornography, led to the founding of Ariadne: A Social Network.

Lacy's most forceful work of this period, her 1977 performance piece *In Mourning and In Rage,* resisted the sensationalist media coverage of the Hillside Strangler murders (figure E.4). According to Lacy, the project took "this culture's trivialized images of mourners as old, powerless women and transformed them into commanding seven-foot-tall figures angrily demanding an end to violence against women."[6] Lacy staged the performance during a city council session on the steps of the Los Angeles

City Hall. Timed to capture the attention of television reporters already on site, it mainlined a powerful icon of feminist solidarity into the broadcast news medium. In the 1980s, Lacy directed a series of spectacles that relied less on feminist critique and more on what Elaine Showalter would describe as a gynocritical examination and recovery of women's lived experience across racial, national, and generational boundaries.[7]

Two notable works of this decade, *Whisper, the Waves, the Wind* (La Jolla, 1984) and *The Crystal Quilt* (Minneapolis, 1987) brought together senior women to explore and express the meanings and experience of aging in America (figure E.5). The Minneapolis project, in particular, staged Lacy's developing understanding of public spectacle, theorized in the late '80s (figure E.6). Unlike painterly aesthetics—that receive authority from the signature value of the privatized, individual artist—public art happens through a constant process of negotiation of material resources

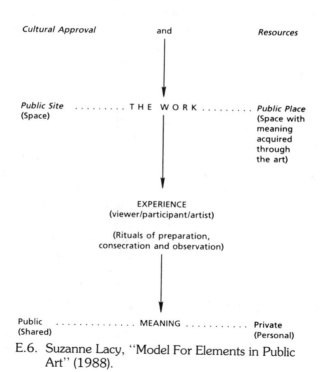

MODEL FOR ELEMENTS IN PUBLIC ART

| Cultural Approval | and | Resources |

Public Site (Space) .... T H E   W O R K .... Public Place (Space with meaning acquired through the art)

EXPERIENCE (viewer/participant/artist)

(Rituals of preparation, consecration and observation)

Public (Shared) .... MEANING .... Private (Personal)

E.6. Suzanne Lacy, "Model For Elements in Public Art" (1988).

that depends on some degree of cultural approval in the form, say, of grants-in-aid, patronage, zoning authorization, copywrite permissions, and so on. Ideally, the work should exist in an organic relationship to the social values and traditions of its site.

The actual meaning of such site-specific installations is never fixed in advance but depends on a process of negotiating the experience of the audience—always to some extent unpredictable—and the artist's intention—always already mediated by the communal process of its production. Lacy's performance pieces differ from the ideological spectacles of modernity, whose meanings are shaped by prior metanarratives of one kind or another (heroic communism, Americanism, German National Socialism, etc.). Instead, her sites attempt to capture the kind of phenomenological openness found, say, in such postmodern public monuments as Maya Lin's Vietnam Veteran's Memorial. "It is quite possible," Lacy writes of Lin's work "that no one knew for sure exactly what the nature of that meaning would be; rather, it was the knowledge that a relationship *would* occur among the work, its place and the viewer." Government resistance to the installation, for Lacy, belied "the fear of unmediated, unpredictable, authentic experience, for out of such response ethics are sharpened, and action might ensue."[8]

Lacy achieved such an indeterminate space of aesthetic disclosure in *The Crystal Quilt,* paradoxically, through a meticulous, two-year process of institutional cultural approval. This collective project was adjudicated through various local agencies and state funding sources including the feminist theater group "At the Foot of the Mountain," Hubert H. Humphrey Institute of Public Affairs, the Minneapolis College of Art and Design, and Minnesota Board on Aging. Such a populist network gave her the necessary budgetary resources and personnel to perform a distinctively feminist aesthetic ritual. Lacy's work allowed those who are most marginalized under capitalist patriarchy—a group of 430 senior women—to come together at the heart of its cosmopolitan space: Phillip Johnson's IDS Building foyer. Her installation took this postmodern agora—whose public status is normally tied to business interests—and opened it to the dialogic exchange (or, in Lacy's metaphor, the living quilt) of a distinctively matrifocal community.

Quilting as a metaphor for recovering the role of gender in society also informs the more urgent, more politically inflected, work of the NAMES Project. This cultural network has launched crucial aesthetic interventions into the popular meanings, public perceptions, and institutional regulation of the AIDS epidemic. Conceived during a 1985 candlelight vigil for slain San Francisco Mayor George Moscone and Harvey Milk, the NAMES Project mushroomed from a mere 40 quilted panels devoted to AIDS victims, displayed at San Francisco's Lesbian and Gay Freedom Day Parade in June 1987, to 1,920 exhibited the following October for the National March for Lesbian and Gay Rights in Washington, D.C. By the time the Project tour reached New York the following year, that number had tripled. Since the late '80s, the NAMES Project has grown apace from the local quilting bees of small groups organized by Cleve Jones and Mike Smith in San Francisco into a nationwide aesthetic ritual.

Moving beyond the formal limits of the fabric arts medium, the NAMES Project organizers, like the Constructivists before them, embrace audience response and public spectacle in the makeup of the aesthetic object. In its 1988 New York installation, for example, the NAMES Project drew on the collective resources of over 25 AIDS service organizations. The Project ran a gamut of agencies from the Gay Men's Health Crisis to the Association for Drug Abuse Prevention and Treatment, staging AIDS awareness through a grass roots network not only of professional quilters, bobbin-mavens, and fabric designers but countless lay volunteers. Similar to Maya Lin's powerful fusion of personal naming and public spectacle in the Vietnam Veterans Memorial, the NAMES Project creates a cultural arena where the private suffering, grief, rage, and mourning of individuals touched by the AIDS crisis can find broad, popular expression and support. But more to the point, by articulating the AIDS epidemic to the communal tradition of quilting, the NAMES Project lends civic pride and cultural diversity to an illness that has otherwise been repressed in the mainstream media as a stigma of social deviance. In 1989, at a time when the number of People With Aids (PWA) in America had passed the 100,000 mark, the NAMES Project was widely broadcast in an Academy Award-winning documentary, narrated by Dustin Hoffman.

The broad spectrum of contributors to the NAMES Project, coupled with the variety of their design contributions, bears poignant, but eloquent, witness to the alarming spread of AIDS across, gender, racial, and class boundaries (figures E.7 and E.8). According to Cindy Ruskin:

> The disease's undiscriminating nature is easily seen in the range of the people memorialized. They include a Colorado stockbroker, a mother of four teenagers in Atlanta, an Olympic athlete, a prize-winning Chicago journalist, a biker from Nevada, and a Stanford University profes-

sor. Some quilt panels name celebrities like Rock Hudson and Liberace. Others name people who were living on welfare, struggling to keep off the streets. There are policemen, school teachers, farmers, doctors, playwrights, ministers, chefs, lawyers, artists and politicians.[9]

Consistently since the late '80s, the NAMES Project has been positioned against the reigning narratives that frame the AIDS crisis as a gay, white disease. The dominant ideological representations in the broadcast media, print journalism, as well as museum and gallery culture have limited popular perceptions of the epidemic so as to obscure glaring lapses in public policy. Such distortions are hardly innocent but function, arguably, to maintain dominant racial and class interests.

Although AIDS in New York City, for example, is the leading cause of death in women from ages 25 to 34 (with the Centers for Disease Control reporting some 2,000 cases of AIDS among American women by the late 1980s), and while Newark, New Jersey, has an HIV rate of 1 in every 20 live births, AIDS is typically presented as a disease that afflicts white males in so-called high risk groups: gay men and intravenous drug users.[10] In both the broadcast media and gallery culture, scant attention is paid to people of color even though they are both proportionately more at risk for the heterosexual spread of AIDS and, in the absence of a national health care system, are more often denied adequate medical treatment. Adding to these misperceptions, major photographic exhibitions dealing with AIDS such as, say, Nicholas Nixon's MOMA installation "Pictures of People" (1988) and Rosalind Solomon's *Portraits in the Time of AIDS* (1988), as Douglas Crimp has argued, mirror the strategies of visual containment inscribed in such TV documentaries as *Sixty Minutes'* "AIDS Hits Home" and *Frontline*'s "AIDS Victim."

Whether vilifying PWAs as social deviants or idealizing them as martyrs to transcendent human suffering, the media typically privatizes AIDS by wrenching patients out of the context of their everyday lives in a willful repression of the epidemic's social politics. "The portrayal of these people's personal circumstances," Crimp writes,

> never includes an articulation of the public dimension of the crisis, the social conditions that made AIDS a crisis and continue to perpetuate it as a crisis. People with AIDS are kept safely within the boundaries of their private tragedies. No one utters a word about the politics of AIDS, the mostly deliberate failure of public policy at every level of government to stem the course of the epidemic, to fund biomedical research into

effective treatments, provide adequate health care and housing, and conduct massive and ongoing preventive education campaigns.[11]

Since the mid-'80s, however, the graphic resources pioneered by such visual/text artists as Hans Haacke, Jenny Holzer, and Barbara Kruger have been appropriated from the New York art market and articulated, at street level, to the social text of AIDS. On the vanguard of such post-modern agitational work, "queer" guerrilla collectives like Gran Fury, Little Elvis, and Wave Three of the AIDS Coalition to Unleash Power (ACT UP) have mastered the fine art of interventionist critique.[12]

Conceived in 1987, ACT UP emerged from community dissatisfaction with the failure of New York's Gay Men's Health Crisis in lobbying agencies such as the Food and Drug Administration and National Institutes of Health. What was needed was the timely development, testing, and approval of antiviral drugs such as ampligen, ribavirin, AL-721, and azidothymidine (AZT). It was patently obvious to AIDS activists at the time that foot-dragging at FDA and NIH reflected the Reagan administration's six-year silence on the epidemic.

But more to the point, what drugs were released, most notably AZT, betrayed a class strategy that placed profits before people. The institutional history of AZT offers a particularly scandalous instance of federal collusion with big business to reap windfall corporate profits. Developed in 1964 as a cancer-fighting drug and later adapted by Dr. Samuel Broder of the National Cancer Institute in 1985 as an antiviral agent against HIV, AZT was tested by the Burroughs Wellcome pharmaceutical corporation in the mid '80s. In 1987 the FDA granted Burroughs Wellcome sole rights to market AZT along with a seven-year tax credit to offset production costs. With an exclusive monopoly to AZT, Welcome set an inflated price of $10,000 cost per year per patient, making AZT the most expensive pharmaceutical to date. In a 1988 FDA ACTION HANDBOOK, ACT UP laid out a stinging critique of the Reagan administration's classist federal drug policy: "To add to the company's coffers, already bulging with tax credits and a lucrative monopoly, Congress appropriated $30 million to buy the drug for indigent PWAs. Thus, the drug, originally developed at federal expense, now soaks up tax dollars to subsidize a secretive, profit-hoarding pharmaceutical monopoly."[13]

Two years later, Gran Fury, a collective of ACT UP graphic artists borrowed from Hans Haacke's pioneering subversion of advertising signage to refocus public attention on corporate profiteering from the AIDS crisis. Gran Fury's tactic followed Haacke's uncanny fusions of slick advertising visuals set off against texts exposing the often brutal work settings and ruthless industrial practices such imagery normally deflects. But unlike Haacke's point of subversion, positioned as it is within museum culture, Gran Fury's mode of distribution targeted a potentially much wider audience—the readership of the New York Times. In "New York Crimes," Gran Fury produced a meticulous four-page simulacrum of the print layout and masthead design of the New York Times that documented the Koch administration's cuts to hospital facilities servicing AIDS. Moreover, the art collective exposed New York's failure to address the housing needs of the city's homeless PWAs and its cutbacks to drug treatment programs by shifting them to shrinking state budgets. Finally, "New York Crimes" publicized the state's withholding of condoms and medical support to the 25 percent of its prison inmates tested positive for HIV infection.

On the morning of ACT UP's March 28, 1989, mass demonstration at City Hall, Gran Fury opened Times vending boxes and wrapped the paper in their own "NY Crimes" jacket. For those who would simply ignore the stories, Gran Fury also included a slick clash of text and image that articulated the visual iconography of painstaking antiviral research to outrageous corporate greed summed up in an unguarded quote from Patrick Gage of Hoffman-La Roche, Inc. (figure E.9). "One million [People with AIDS]," Gage mused, "isn't a market that's exciting. Sure it's growing, but it's not asthma." Such callous disregard for life is played off Gran Fury's polemical caption that plainly lays out its agitational mission: "This is to Enrage You."

More subversive, perhaps, is Gran Fury's counter-narrative to the homophobic hegemony of the American military displayed in its Read My Lips lithograph for a Spring 1988 AIDS Action Kiss-in to protest against gay bashing (figure E.10). Read My Lips employs a camp image of two '40s-style sailors in a loving embrace, thereby recoding the national image of military service to a bold, homoerotic sexuality. But beyond this obvious agenda, Gran Fury employs the look of Kruger's graphics in an allusive critique of George Bush's 1988 campaign vow to slash tax supports for domestic social programs.

Such sophisticated metasimulations of the advertising sign's formal inmixing of image and text in the work of ACT UP and Queer Nation collectives challenge today's largely homophobic world outlook to make us think twice about what Adrienne Rich has defined as compulsory heterosexuality.[14] As we pass beyond the twentieth-century scene into the new millennium, it will surely be in the collaborative aesthetic praxes of such new social movements—articulated as they are to class, environmental, racial, feminist, gay rights, and public health issues—that America's avant-garde legacy of cultural critique will live on, its political edge cutting through the semiosis of everyday life and going to the heart of the postmodern spectacle.

Notes

Introduction

1. See Marjorie Perloff, "Pound/Stevens: Whose Era?" in *The Dance of the Intellect: Studies in the Poetry of the Pound Tradition* (New York: Cambridge University Press, 1985), 1–23.

2. See Hayden White, *Tropics of Discourse: Essays in Cultural Criticism* (Baltimore: Johns Hopkins University Press, 1978), 69–70 (hereafter cited in the text as T).

3. Cary Nelson, *Repression and Recovery: Modern American Poetry and the Politics of Cultural Memory, 1910–1945* (Madison: University of Wisconsin Press, 1989), 4 (hereafter cited in the text as RR).

4. On the theory of tropology as a constitutive ground for historical inscription, see Hayden White, *Metahistory: The Historical Imagination in Nineteenth-Century Europe* (Baltimore: The Johns Hopkins University Press, 1973), 31–38.

5. See Kenneth Burke, *A Grammar of Motives* (Berkeley: University of California Press, 1969), 3–20.

6. Robert Scholes, *Textual Power: Literary Theory and the Teaching of English* (New Haven: Yale University Press, 1985), 17.

7. Fredric Jameson, *Postmodernism; or, The Cultural Logic of Late Capitalism* (Durham: Duke University Press, 1991), 324 (hereafter cited in the text as P).

8. Jameson's take on postmodernism is, in fact, oppositional to the interbellum period, which he dismissed *tout court* under the sweeping rubric of "nostalgia" as early as his 1971 study *Marxism and Form*. Writing on leftist culture of the 1930s, Jameson allows as how "the burning issues of those days—anti-Nazism, the Popular Front, the relationship between literature and the labor movement, the struggle between Stalin and Trotsky, between Marxism and anarchism—generated polemics which we may think back on with nostalgia but which no longer correspond to the conditions of the world today." *Marxism and Form: Twentieth-Century Dialectical Theories of Literature* (Princeton: Princeton University Press, 1971), ix. Although serving Jameson's Neo-Marxist agenda, such a reductive version of the Great Depression simply represses the complex, socioaesthetic linkages between postmodern culture and the interbellum avant-gardes.

9. The neo-Gramscian notion and praxis of "articulation" has been forwarded recently by Stuart Hall, Ernesto Laclau, Chantal Mouffe, and in the study of modern poetry by Cary Nelson. "In England," writes Hall, " the term has a nice double meaning because 'articulate' means to utter, to speak forth, to be articulate. It carries that sense of language-ing, of expressing, etc. But we also speak of an 'articulated' lorry (truck): a lorry where the front (cab) and back (trailer) can, but need not necessarily, be connected to one another. The two parts are connected to each other, but through a specific linkage, that can be broken. An articulation is thus the form of the connection that *can* make a unity of two different elements, under certain conditions. . . . The theory of articulation, as I use it, has been developed by Ernesto Laclau, in his book *Politics and Ideology in Marxist Theory*. His argument there is that the political connotation of ideological elements has no necessary belongingness, and thus, we need to think the contingent, the non-necessary, connection between different practices—between ideology and social forces, and between different elements within ideology, and between different social groups composing a social movement, etc. He uses the notion of articulation to break with the necessetarian and reductionist logic which has dogged the classical marxist theory of ideology." Stuart Hall, " On Postmodernism and Articulation: An Interview with Stuart Hall," L. Grossberg, ed. *Journal of Communication Inquiry,* 10, 2 (1986), 53.

10. On the Frankfurt School's failure to distinguish between popular aesthetics and mass culture see Tania Modleski, "Introduction," *Studies in Mass Entertainment,* ed. Tania Modleski (Bloomington: Indiana University Press, 1986), ix–xix.

11. For a discussion of the tension between the cultural and the political avant-garde traditions from the French Revolution through Russian Cubofuturism see Andreas Huyssen, *After the Great Divide: Modernism, Mass Culture, Postmodernism* (Bloomington: Indiana University Press, 1986), 3–5 (hereafter cited in the text as AGD).

12. See Raymond Williams, *Keywords: A Vocabulary of Culture and Society* (New York: Oxford University Press, 1976), 80.

13. See Pierre Bourdieu, *Distinction: A Social Critique of the Judgement of Taste,* tr. Richard Nice (Cambridge: Harvard University Press, 1984). For a

discussion of the significance of institutional analysis in the study of cultural regulation, see Tony Bennett, "Putting Policy into Cultural Studies," in *Cultural Studies,* ed. Lawrence Grossberg, Cary Nelson, and Paula A. Treichler (New York: Routledge, 1992), 23–37.

14. T. S. Eliot, "Tradition and the Individual Talent," *Selected Essays* (New York: Harcourt, Brace and World, 1960), 6.

15. See Jean-François Lyotard, "Defining the Postmodern, etc." tr. G. Bennington, in *Postmodernism* (London: ICA Documents 4 & 5, 1986), 6–7 (hereafter cited as ICA).

16. Homi K. Bhabha, "Introduction: Narrating the Nation," in *Nation and Narration* (New York: Routledge, 1990), 3.

17. See Gerald Graff, *Professing Literature: An Institutional History* (Chicago: University of Chicago Press, 1987).

18. The term "postindividualistic" is Fredric Jameson's usage from his essay "Imaginary and Symbolic in Lacan: Marxism, Psychoanalytic Criticism, and the Problem of the Subject," in *Literature and Psychoanalysis: The Question of Reading: Otherwise,* ed. Shoshana Felman (Baltimore: Johns Hopkins University Press, 1982), 338–95. For a definitive discussion of subject positions in post-Marxist theory, see Ernesto Laclau and Chantal Mouffe, *Hegemony and Socialist Strategy: Towards a Radical Democratic Politics,* trs. Winston Moore and Paul Cammack (London: Verso Press, 1985). For an applied discussion of subject positions to modernist poetic discourse, see Cary Nelson, *Repression and Recovery: Modern American Poetry and the Politics of Cultural Memory.*

19. Jürgen Habermas, *Legitimation Crisis,* tr. Thomas McCarthy (Boston: Beacon Press, 1975), 85.

20. Walter Benjamin, "The Work of Art in the Age of Mechanical Reproduction," *Illuminations,* tr. Harry Zohn (New York: Schocken Books, 1960), 234. T. W. Adorno, to Walter Benjamin, March 18, 1936, "Letters to Walter Benjamin," in *Aesthetics and Politics,* tr. Ronald Taylor (London: NLB, 1977), 123 (hereafter cited in the text as AP).

21. Whatever pleasure one might take in Chaplinesque slapstick, he held, "is anything but good and revolutionary; instead, it is full of the worst bourgeois sadism" (AP, 123).

22. See Herbert Marcuse, "On the Affirmative Character of Culture," *Negations: Essays in Critical Theory,* tr. J. J. Shapiro (Boston: Beacon Press, 1968), 88–133; and *The Aesthetic Dimension: Toward a Critique of Marxist Aesthetics* (Boston: Beacon Press, 1978).

23. Briefly, in Bürger's historical reading the increasingly urbanized art market of the Renaissance ushers in bourgeois aesthetics by displacing art's traditionally "feudal" role as court handicraft and ecclesiastical ritual. The philosophy of aesthetic autonomy, as a disciplinary formation, coincides with the empowerment of the bourgeoisie in the eighteenth-century, coming into its own in Immanuel Kant's *Critique of Judgment* (1790) and Friedrich Schiller's *Letters on the Aesthetic Education of Man* (1795). The uncoupling of art from the world, undertaken by Kant and Schiller, culminates in the "art-for-art's-sake" milieu of the fin de siècle,

where the doctrine of aesthetic autonomy shapes the distinctive content of the art work.

24. Thomas Crow argues provocatively that the avant-garde in the twentieth century actually serves as "a kind of research and development arm of the culture industry: it searches out areas of social practice not yet completely available to efficient manipulation and makes them discrete and visible." Thomas Crow, "Modernism and Mass Culture in the Visual Arts," in *Modernism and Modernity,* ed. S. Guilbaut and D. Solkin (Halifax, N. S.: Press of the Nova Scotia College of Art and Design, 1983), 253.

25. See Hans Magnus Enzensberger, "The Industrialization of the Mind" (3–14) and "Constituents of a Theory of the Media" (46–76) in *Critical Essays,* Reinhold Grimm and Bruce Armstrong, trs. (New York: Continuum, 1982).

26. As one example, Marjorie Perloff's *The Futurist Moment* (1986), like her study *The Dance of the Intellect* (1985), tends to valorize Ezra Pound in the reception of the Futurist project in the West. Aside from sweeping generalities concerning the fate of the Russian avant-gardes under Stalinism, Perloff elides the sociohistorical context of the Russian Revolution and its internationalist lines of reception and ideological support in the United States to focus on the level of linguistic, stylistic, and generic *rupture* undertaken by the Russian Futurists. But canonizing Pound's role in the reception of Futurism obliges her to ignore such seminal exhibitions as the New York Armory Show of 1913 as well as the rich participation of the American left in the Soviet cultural revolution, as if the United States was a cultural tabula rasa throughout the 1910s: "For political and social reasons," she writes, "the American response to Futurist poetic was delayed by at least a decade, and by then, Futurist elements had been inextricably altered by their contact with Dada. . . . Pound's Vorticist poems and manifestos are a special case: because Pound was living in London in the early 1910s, he came into direct contact with the Italian, German, and French avant-garde." *The Futurist Moment: Avant-Garde, Avant Guerre, and the Language of Rupture* (Chicago: University of Chicago Press, 1986), xx–xxi.

27. For a detailed reading of the postwar institutional settings of recent American literature, see Walter Kalaidjian, *Languages of Liberation: The Social Text in Contemporary American Poetry* (New York: Columbia University Press, 1989).

28. See Houston Baker, *Modernism and the Harlem Renaissance* (Chicago: University of Chicago Press, 1987), 76–77.

29. Michael Gold, "A Word as to Uncle Tom," in *Negro: An Anthology,* ed. Nancy Cunard (London, 1934), (rpt. New York: Frederick Ungar Publishing Co., 1970), 136.

30. "In the age of nascent socialism *and* the first major women's movement in Europe," writes Huyssen, "the masses knocking at the gate were also women, knocking at the gate of a male-dominated culture. It is indeed striking to observe how the political, psychological, and aesthetic discourse around the turn of the century consistently and obsessively genders mass culture and the masses as feminine, while high culture, whether traditional or modern, clearly remains the priv-

ileged realm of male activities" (AGD, 47). Such high-cultural misogyny, as Janice Radway has argued, continues in the critical reception of the Book-of-the-Month Club by old-line New England literary critics in late 1920s: "As frequently as the [critical] discourse branded the Book-of-the-Month Club anathema to the cause of democracy and the fate of the individual, so too did it metaphorically connect the Club with the organic lack of differentiation associated with the feminine and the maternal. By associating the Club again and again with forced feeding, pabulum, and indiscriminate consumption, the Club's critics were once again unconsciously evoking traces of the scandalous, grotesque body and its earthy, material nature believed capable of engulfing everything from below. . . . The people's body the critics labored to repress, however, was not so much the carnivalesque body discussed by Peter Stallybrass and Allon White after Bakhtin, but the live, militarized body of the mass assembled by fascism and bolshevism on the Continent and by labor unions and people's parties in the United States." Janice Radway, "Mail-Order Culture and Its Critics," in *Cultural Studies*, 523, 522.

31. Antonio Gramsci, *Selections from the Prison Notebooks,* ed. and trs. Quintin Hoare and Geoffrey Nowell Smith (New York: International Publishers, 1971), 302.

32. For a discussion of the growth of what Daniel Bell, B. Bruce-Briggs, Everett Carll Ladd, Jr., Norman Podhoretz, and others have discussed as the postwar "new class," see B. Bruce-Briggs, ed., *The New Class?* (New York: McGraw Hill, 1979), and Alvin W. Gouldner, *The Future of Intellectuals and the Rise of the New Class* (New York: Oxford University Press, 1979).

33. "During the period in which we largely increased wages," Ford wrote, "we did have a considerable supervisory force. The home life of the men was investigated and an effort was made to find out what they did with their wages." Henry Ford, *My Life and Work* (New York: Garden City Publishing Co., 1926), 263.

34. Michel Aglietta, *A Theory of Capitalist Regulation: The US Experience,* tr. David Fernbach (London: NLB, 1979), 116–17.

35. Building on Gramsci's analysis, Aglietta writes that "not content to create a space of objects of daily life, as supports of a capitalist commodity universe, it [Fordism] provided an image of this space by advertising techniques. This image was presented as an objectification of consumption status which individuals could perceive outside themselves. The process of social recognition was externalized and fetishized. Individuals were not initally interpellated as subjects by one another, in accordance with their social position: they were interpellated by an external power, diffusing a robot portrait of the 'consumer' " (161).

36. Thus Neil Larsen in "Postmodernism and Imperialism: Theory and Politics in Latin America," *Postmodern Culture* 1, 1 (Sept. 1990), borrows from Lukács' assault on Nietzsche in *The Destruction of Reason,* to lodge the blunt accusation that "Postmodern philosophy receives Nietzsche through the filters of Deleuze, Foucault, and Derrida, blending him with similarly mediated versions of Heidegger and William James into a new irrationalist hybrid. . . . The fact that the 'third path' calls itself 'radical democracy,' draping itself in the 'ethics' if not the epistemology

of Enlightenment, the fact that it outwardly resists the 'fixity' of any one privileged subject, makes it, in a sense, the more perfect 'radical' argument for a capitalist politics of pure irrationalist spontaneity" (4). Larsen dismisses the so-called metropolitan theory of the postmodern left as empty, irrational, and politically inadequate to its revolutionary task. Besides Laclau and Mouffe, among the postmodern metropoles whom Larsen rejects for having lapsed into "the most threadbare sorts of political myths and fetishes" are Fredric Jameson, Edward Said, Laura Kipnis, and George Yudice. What is unacceptable for Larsen, as for Ellen Meiksins Wood, is the poststructuralist displacement of social agency by discursive praxes, and of class struggle by hegemonic politics. "Laclau and Mouffe," writes Wood, "also require us to believe that while there is a smooth and non-contradictory continuity between the various forms of 'democratic struggle,' there is a rigid boundary between class struggles on the economic 'level' and struggles in the political sphere. This means that political movements motivated by liberal-democratic discourse bring us closer to socialism than do class struggles impelled by material interests directly antagonistic to the interests of capital." *The Retreat From Class* (London: Verso, 1986), 71. Laclau's and Mouffe's work, she concludes, does not offer "an analysis of contemporary society and the conditions of its transformation; it is little more than a verbal conjuring trick" (Wood, 70).

37. Angela Davis quoted in Max Elbaum "De-Stalinizing the Old Guard," *The Nation* February 10, 1992, 158.

38. In a 1935 *Art Front* exposé, Mary Randolph accused Rivera of being "a willing prostitute who makes his work pay." Mary Randolph, "Rivera's Monopoly," *Art Front* (December 1935), 12. Reflecting back on Rukeyser's socialist impulses during her Popular Front period, *Partisan Review* editors Philip Rahv and William Phillips lampooned Rukeyser as a "poster girl" who "rode the bandwagon of proletarian literature." See Rahv, Phillips, and Matthiessen, "The Rukeyser Imbroglio," *Partisan Review,* 11 (Winter 1944), 125–129; and *Partisan Review,* 11 (Spring 1944), 217–18.

39. Henry Sayre, *The Object of Performance* (Chicago: University of Chicago Press, 1989), xi (hereafter cited in the text as OP).

40. For a discussion of de- and re-territorialization, see Gilles Deleuze and Félix Guattari, *A Thousand Plateaus: Capitalism and Schizophrenia,* tr. Brian Massumi (Minneapolis: University of Minnesota Press, 1988).

41. "The socialization of consumption implied by Neo-Fordism," Aglietta writes, "will make absolutely necessary and unavoidable new types of social control for regularizing a consumption norm very different from that which prevailed after the Second World War and is now in crisis. Neo-Fordism, however, can only become the future principle of intensive accumulation if it bears with it qualitatively new productive forces. Such productive forces imply a far greater degree of unification of the proletariat. The material conditions of the maintenance cycle of labour-power will probably have to be embodied in an urban development that is no longer compatible with the maintenance of the ghettos. An increase in relative surplus-value by a revolutionization of the production processes of means of collective consumption seems possible without massive unemployment only by a sig-

nificant shift in the frontier between working time and leisure time, in the direction of a reduction of working hours. The development of collective consumption would remove every objective basis from the discrimination against woman's work. It is clear that all these forces point in the direction of a gathering threat to capitalism as a whole" (TCR, 173–74).

42. Quoted in David Rocks, "Life Becomes a Commercial Exchange," *In These Times* 16 (November 20–26, 1991), 9.

43. New Times Project, "From the Manifesto for New Times," in *New Times: The Changing Face of Politics in the 1990s,* ed. Stuart Hall and Martin Jacques (London: Lawrence & Wishart in association with *Marxism Today,* 1989), 36.

44. "To try to represent and visualize the boardroom and the ruling class," Jameson writes, "is uncool because it involves an old-fashioned commitment to content in a situation in which only form as such—the most formalistic of all types of law or regularity, the profit motive (which clearly outweighs even such more vivid ideological slogans as 'efficiency')—counts, and in which the commitment to form, the tacit presupposition of the profit motive, is assumed in advance and not subject to reexamination or to thematization as such" (351). Yet it is precisely within the advertising sign's own register of formal sophistication that many oppositional movements such as ACT UP and GREENPEACE, following interventionist artists like Barbara Kruger and Hans Haacke, level critique.

45. "There is increasing class division and differentiation," West writes, "creating on the one hand a significant black middle class, highly anxiety-ridden, insecure, willing to be co-opted and incorporated into the powers that be, concerned with racism to the degree that it poses constraints on upward social mobility; and, on the other, a vast and growing black underclass, an underclass that embodies a kind of *walking nihilism* of pervasive drug addiction, pervasive alcoholism, pervasive homicide, and an exponential rise in suicide. Now, because of the deindustrialization, we also have a devastated black industrial class. We are talking here about tremendous hopelessness." Anders Stephanson, "Interview with Cornel West," in *Universal Abandon?: The Politics of Postmodernism,* ed. Andrew Ross (Minneapolis: University of Minnesota Press, 1988), 276.

1. Revisionary Modernism

1. Randolph Bourne, *The History of a Literary Radical and Other Papers,* ed. Van Wyck Brooks (New York: S. A. Russell, 1956), 303 (hereafter cited in the text as HLR).

2. See Werner Sollors, *Beyond Ethnicity: Consent and Descent in American Culture* (New York: Oxford University Press, 1986).

3. Max Eastman, *The Enjoyment of Living* (New York: Harpers, 1948), 409.

4. Mabel Dodge Luhan. *Movers and Shakers.* Vol. 3 of *Intimate Memories* (New York: Harcourt Brace, 1936), 83; quoted in Rebecca Zurier, *Art for the Masses* (Philadelphia: Temple University Press, 1988), 105.

5. Sara N. Cleghorn, "Golf Links," in *An Anthology of Revolutionary Poetry,* ed. Marcus Graham (New York: Active Press, 1929), 168.

6. See Zurier, *Art for the Masses,* 96.

7. Quoted in Joseph Freeman, *American Testament: A Narrative of Rebels and Romantics* (New York: Farrar & Rinehart, 1936), 101 (hereafter cited as AT).

8. Max Eastman, *Max Eastman's Address to the Jury in the Second Masses Trial* (New York: Liberator, 1919), 12.

9. For discussions of this transaction see Draper, 107–08; and Daniel Aaron, *Writers on the Left: Episodes in American Literary Communism* (New York: Harcourt, Brace & World, 1961), 43 (hereafter cited in the text as WL).

10. Lincoln Steffens, *The Autobiography of Lincoln Steffens* (New York: Harcourt, Brace, 1931), 799; quoted in Draper, 115.

11. Beyond such ecclesiastical classicism, the move toward a modern rapprochement between art and life dates from Nikolai Chernyshevsky's 1855 manifesto *The Aesthetic Relations of Art to Reality* and the subsequent Society of Wandering Exhibitions of the 1870s, whose major artists—Ivan Kramskoi, Vasilii Surikov, and Ilya Repin—drew inspiration from the realist modes of Courbet and Daumier. During this time wealthy industrialists and aristocrats such as Savva Mamontov and Princess Mariya Tenisheva established artist colonies and estates at Abramtsevo and Talashkino.

12. The "Blue Rose" group—Pavel Kuznetsov, Nikolai Sapunov, Martiros Saryan, Mikhail Larionov, and Natalya Goncharova—emerged from the Union of Russian Artists (1903) and, through the financial backing of Nikolai Ryabushinsky, launched the noted review *The Golden Fleece* in 1906. In this journal they espoused the artist's subjective freedom of creative impulse and the doctrine of art's ideal, spiritual wholeness—its symbolic "reflection of the Eternal." Nikolai Ryabushinsky, "Preface" *The Golden Fleece* (1906), in *Russian Art of the Avant-Garde: Theory and Criticism, 1902–1934,* ed. and trans. John E. Bowlt (New York: Viking Press, 1976), 8 (hereafter cited in the text as RA). In some ways, the mystified idealism expressed in *The Golden Fleece* and in exhibition catalogue statements such as David Burliuk's "The Voice of an Impressionist: In Defense of Painting" (1908) for his "Link" exhibition served to repress the devastating history of the Russo-Japanese War and its attendant domestic unrest. For his part, Vasilii Kandinsky sought to overcome the era's turbulent material forces through an idealized aesthetic—one that would reflect the dawn of a "great epoch of Spirituality." Kandinsky, "Content and Form" (1910) (RA, 21). The desire for transcendence, achieved through the formal elements of art, led Kandinsky to theorize, in his 1910 essay "Content and Form," that "two elements—*paint and line*—constitute the essential, eternal, invariable language of painting" (RA, 22).

13. Learning from the "color tension, density, and depth" of Cezanne's sensuous visual canvases, Picasso's cubistic synthesis and analytic decomposition of geometric planes, and the attention to speed and mechanical dynamics of Italian Futurism, Larionov theorized a rayonist aesthetic that would depict "the combination of colors, their saturation, the interrelation of colored masses, depth, and texture . . . the sum of rays reflected from the object." Mikhail Larionov, "Rayonist Painting" (1913) (RA, 99, 98). Rayonist theory was most fully realized in such works as *Cats* (1912) by Goncharova and *Glass* (1912–13) by Larionov.

14. Kazimir Malevich, "From Cubism and Futurism to Suprematism: The New Painterly Realism (1915)" (RA, 126). Malevich's early works, exhibited in the "Knave of Diamonds," "Donkey Tail," and "Blaue Reiter" gallery shows from 1909–1912, were marked by neo-primitive elements and visual compositions based on Cezanne, as well as the formal techniques of Cubofuturism, reaching remarkable sophistication in his rayonist composition *The Knife Grinder* (1912). But the new forces of Modernism, he wrote, "have awakened the soul, which was suffocating in the catacombs of old reason and has emerged at the intersection of the paths of heaven and earth. . . . The rapid interchange of objects struck the new naturalists—the futurists—and they began to seek means of transmitting it. Hence the construction of the futurist pictures that you have seen arose from the discovery of points on a plane where the placing of real objects during their explosion or confrontation would impart a sense of time at a maximum speed" (RA, 126, 127).

15. "I have transformed myself *in the zero of form*," he proclaimed, "*and have fished myself out of the rubbishy slough of academic art*" (RA, 118).

16. "Cubism and futurism," Malevich maintained, "were revolutionary movements in art anticipating the revolution in the economic and political life of 1917." Kazimir, Malevich, *O novykh sistemakh v iskusstve* (Vitebsk, 1919), 10. Quoted in Bowlt, "Introduction," *RA*, xxxiii.

17. "Miting ob iskusstve" ("A meeting about art"), *Iskusstvo kommuny*, 1918, no. 4, 2.), quoted in Mikhail Anikst, ed., *Soviet Commercial Design of the Twenties* (New York: Abbeville Press, 1987), 15 (hereafter cited in the text as SCD).

18. Quoted in RoseLee Goldberg, *Performance Art: From Futurism to the Present* (New York: Harry N.Abrams, 1988), 41.

19. See Nina Baburina, "The Soviet Political Poster," in *The Soviet Political Poster*, ed. Mikhail Anikst, tr. Boris Rubalsky (New York: Penguin Books, 1985), 3.

20. Dating from 1913, the Russian Futurists had experimented with collaborative performance art and guerrilla theater, wearing bizarre and colorful costumes, jewelry, art fetishes, and face paint, literally to body forth their art to the streets. In "Why We Paint Ourselves: A Futurist Manifesto" (1913), Ilya Zdanevich and Mikhail Larionov declared, "We have joined art to life. After the long isolation of artists, we have loudly summoned life and life has invaded art, it is time for art to invade life. The painting of our faces is the beginning of the invasion" (RA, 81). After completing a tour of seventeen cities, Burliak and Mayakovsky produced two films to document the group's aestheticized life styles: *Drama in Cabaret No.13,* featuring the rayonist painters Larionov and Goncharova, and *I Want to be a Futurist* with Mayakovsky playing opposite to the State Circus clown, Lazarenko. By the end of that year, the joint efforts of poets and painters climaxed in two "Union of Youth" productions staged in St. Petersburg's Luna Park Theater: *Vladimir Mayakovsky, A Tragedy,* against a backcloth designed by Pavel Filonov, and Alexei Kruchenikh's libretto for Mikhail Matyushin's futurist opera *Victory Over the Sun,* with decor, costumes, and papier-mache masks fashioned by Malevich.

21. Osip Brik, "Drenash iskusstu" ("Drainage to Art"), in *Iskusstvo kommuny* 1918, no. 1, 1. Quoted in *Soviet Commercial Design,* 14.

22. Quoted in Camilla Grey, *The Russian Experiment in Art, 1863–1922* (New York: Harry N. Abrams, 1970), 250–51.

23. Anotolii Lunacharsky and Yuvenal Slavinsky, "Theses of the Art Section of Narkompros and the Central Committee of the Union of Art Workers Concerning Basic Policy in the Field of Art" (1920), (RA, 185).

24. Differing from the European avant-gardes, that privileges the artist's personal signature of authenticity, the Soviet conception of faktura, according to Benjamin H. D. Buchloh, "emphasizes precisely the mechanical quality, the materiality, and the anonymity of the painterly procedure from a perspective of empirico-critical positivism." Buchloh, "From Faktura to Factography," *October* 30 (Fall 1984), 87. But equally important, the faktura of the constructivist art work also referred to its social positioning and its relation to the audience. Thus, Modernism for the Constructivists did not merely mark a crisis in representation but also a crisis in aesthetic communication: "In the early '20s the Soviet avant-garde (as well as some members of the de Stijl group, the Bauhaus, and Berlin dada) developed different strategies to transcend the historical limitations of Modernism. They recognized that the crisis of representation could not be resolved without at the same time addressing questions of distribution and audience. Architecture, utilitarian product design, and photographic factography were some of the practices that the Soviet avant-garde considered capable of establishing these new modes of simultaneous collective reception" (Buchloh, 95).

25. Vladimir Mayakovsky, *Polnoe Sobranie Sochinenii v 13-ti tomakh* (Complete Collected Works, in 13 Volumes) (Moscow: GIKhL, 1955–61), vol. 13, 57. Quoted in *Soviet Commercial Design,* 23.

26. Yakov Chernikhov, "The Construction of Architectural and Machine Forms" (1931) (RA, 261).

27. Max Eastman, *The Colors of Life: Poems and Songs and Sonnets* (New York: Knopf, 1918), 13 (hereafter cited in text as CL).

28. Aleksandr Bogdanov, "The Proletarian and Art" (1918) (RA, 181).

29. Max Eastman, *Artists in Uniform: A Study of Literature and Bureaucratism* (New York: Knopf, 1934), 13.

30. Mike Gold, "Towards Proletarian Literature," in *Mike Gold: A Literary Anthology,* ed. Michael Folsom (New York: International Publishers, 1972), 67.

31. Mike Gold, "America Needs a Critic," (1926) in *Mike Gold,* 136 (hereafter cited in the text as ANC).

32. Joseph Freeman, "Past and Present," in *Voices of October: Art and Literature in Soviet Russia,* eds. Joseph Freeman, Joshua Kunitz, and Louis Lozowick (New York: Vanguard Press, 1930), 21 (hereafter cited in the text as VO).

33. Walter Benjamin, "The Artist as Producer," *Reflections,* tr. Edmund Jephcott (New York: Schocken Books, 1986), 300 (hereafter cited in text as AP).

34. "Resolution on Literature Adopted by the Political Bureau of the Communist Party" (1924), quoted in VO, 63.

35. Max Eastman, *Artists in Uniform: A Study of Literature and Bureaucratism* (New York: Knopf, 1984), 144.

36. Louis Lozowick, "Soviet Painting and Architecture" (VO, 265).

37. Louis Lozowick, "The Americanization of Art" in *The Machine Age Exposition* (New York: Little Review, 1927); quoted in Janey A. Flint, *The Prints of Louis Lozowick: A Catalogue Raisonné* (New York: Hudson Hills, 1982), 18–19.

38. Edwin Rolfe, "Poetry," *Partisan Review* 2 (April-May 1935), 36, 38.

39. *New Masses* 1 (May 1926), 1.

40. *New Masses* 4 (June 1928), 2.

41. *New Masses* 4 (July 1928), 2; quoted in Aaron, *Writers on the Left,* 205.

42. *New Masses* 5 (January 1930), 21.

43. See Eric Homberger, *American Writers and Radical Politics, 1900–1939: Equivocal Commitments* (New York: St. Martin's Press, 1986), 129.

44. Randolph Bourne, "To the Friends of The Seven Arts," *Seven Arts* 2 (October 1917), n.p.

45. "Modernist poetics (along with its New Critical offspring)," writes Schwartz, "is part of a major intellectual development that produced significant changes in philosophy, the arts, and other fields as well." *The Matrix of Modernism: Pound, Eliot, and Early Twentieth-Century Thought* (Princeton: Princeton University Press, 1985), 3–4. Arguing for modernism as a "matrix," or field of knowledge, Schwartz would supplement its prior reception that fails to go beyond "atomistic" studies of "individual influences or affinities" among poets and philosophers (3). Yet insofar as this project rests on "intellectual" foundations segregated from the period's full social text, it marks not so much an expansion of the modernist terrain as its further, disciplinary confinement.

46. Ralph Cheney, Jack Conroy, Lucia Trent et. al. "Manifesto," *The Rebel Poet* 1 (January 1931), 1.

47. Ralph Cheney and Lucia Trent, "Introduction." *An Anthology of Revolutionary Poetry,* ed. Marcus Graham (New York: Activist Press, 1929), 36–37.

48. Quoted in Rolfe, "Poetry," *Partisan Review* 2 (April-May 1935), 33.

49. See for example, Marjorie Perloff, "Pound/Stevens: Whose Era?" in *The Dance of the Intellect: Studies in the Poetry of the Pound Tradition* (New York: Cambridge University Press, 1985), 1–23.

50. Isidor Schneider, "Proletarian Poetry" in *American Writers' Congress,* ed. Henry Hart (New York: International Publishers, 1935), 116, 117.

51. Ralph Cheney and Lucia Trent, *More Power to Poets!* (New York: Henry Harrison, 1934), 56.

52. Mike Gold, "Forward" to "Strike!: A Mass Recitation." *New Masses* 1 (July 1926), 10.

53. Jack Haynes, "Scottsboro Boys Chant" *The Rebel Poet* 1 (August 1932), 4.

54. V. J. Jerome, "A Negro Mother to Her Child," *The Rebel Poet* 1 (August 1932), 1.

55. See Sollors, *Beyond Ethnicity: Consent and Descent in American Culture.*

56. Joseph Freeman, "They Find Strength," *New Masses* 10 (March 1936), 23.

57. Edwin Rolfe, "Credo," *To My Contemporaries* (New York: Dynamo, 1936), 11.

58. Jerome McGann defines the aesthetics of sincerity "as one of the touchstones by which Romantic poetry originally measured itself. In a poem's sincerity one observed a deeply felt relation binding the poetic Subject to the poetic subject, the speaking voice to the matter being addressed. Romantic truth is inner vision, and Romantic knowledge is the unfolding of the truths of that inner vision. . . . [T]hey are the positions that will dominate the theory of poetry for 150, 175 years more, even to our own day." "Private Poetry, Public Deception," in *The Politics of Poetic Form: Poetry and Public Policy,* ed. Charles Bernstein (New York: Roof Books, 1990), 121, 141.

59. On this point, see Jean-Francois Lyotard, "Complexity and the Sublime," tr. G. Bennington, in *Postmodernism* (London: ICA Documents 4 & 5, 1986), 11.

60. See Barbara Herrnstein Smith, *Contingencies of Value: Alternative Perspectives for Critical Theory* (Cambridge: Harvard University Press, 1988).

2. War of Position and the Old Left

1. For a discussion of Bukharin's report see Theodore Draper, *American Communism and Soviet Russia, the Formative Period* (New York: Viking Press, 1960), 302–3.

2. See Donald Drew Egbert, *Socialism and American Art* (Princeton: Princeton University Press, 1967), 75.

3. "In 1924," writes Harvey Klehr, "the Fifth Comintern Congress identified three different types of united front. One, the united front from above, made by Communist leaders with leaders of other organizations, was 'categorically rejected.' A second, 'unity from below and at the same time negotiations with leaders,' was acceptable only where Communists were weak and social democracy strong. The only type to receive unqualified endorsement was the united front from below. This meant a united front with the rank and file of socialist or labor parties or unions, without—or over the heads of—their leaders." Harvey Klehr, *The Heyday of American Communism: The Depression Decade* (New York: Basic Books, 1984), 13.

4. "The Charkov Conference of Revolutionary Writers," *New Masses* 6 (February 1931), 7.

5. See International Union of Revolutionary Writers, "Resolution on the Work of the *New Masses* for 1931," *New Masses* 8 (September 1932), 20–21.

6. Dick Hebdige defines this term, following Paul Willis, as the "symbolic fit between the values and lifestyles of a group, its subjective experience and the . . .

forms it uses to express or reinforce its focal concerns." Dick Hebdige, *Subculture: The Meaning of Style* (New York: Methuen, 1979), 113; see also Paul Willis, *Profane Culture* (London: Routledge & Kegan Paul, 1978).

7. "The 'culture' of a group or class is the peculiar and distinctive 'way of life' of the group or class, the meanings, values and ideas embodied in institutions, in social relations, in systems of beliefs, in *mores* and *customs,* in the uses of objects and material life. Culture is the distinctive shapes in which this material and social organisation of life expresses itself. A culture includes the 'maps of meaning' which make things intelligible to its members. These 'maps of meaning' are not simply carried around in the head: they are objectivated in the patterns of social organisation and relationship through which the individual becomes a 'social individual.' " See John Clarke, Stuart Hall, Tony Jefferson, and Brian Roberts, "Subculture, Culture and Class," in *Resistance Through Rituals,* eds. S. Hall et al. (London: Hutchinson, 1976), 10.

8. Richard Wright, "Richard Wright," in *The God That Failed,* ed. Richard Crossman (New York: Harpers, 1949), 118 (hereafter cited in the text as GF).

9. "The earliest Ragtime songs," wrote Johnson, "like Topsy, 'jes' grew.' Some of these earliest songs were taken down by white men, the words slightly altered or changed, and published under the names of the arrangers. They sprang into immediate popularity and earned small fortunes . . . The reader might be curious to know if the 'jes' grew' songs have ceased to grow. No, they have not; they are growing all the time." James Weldon Johnson, "Preface to the First Edition," in *The Book of American Negro Poetry,* ed. J. W. Johnson (New York: Harcourt, Brace 1922, rpt. 1931), 13–15.

10. See Mark Naison, *Communists in Harlem During the Depression* (Urbana: University of Illinois Press, 1983), 279–80 (hereafter cited in the text as CH).

11. Symptomatic of the party's resistance to the organic, subcultural organization of black political life was its intervention in Harlem during the early 1930s. In an effort to break up the indigenous political groups formed in Harlem during the mass agitation surrounding the Scottsboro trial, the Central Committee of the CPUSA authorized James Ford, as Harlem's chief party organizer, to crack down on the local leadership of Richard Moore and Cyril Briggs, reorganizing Harlem under the bureaucratic domination of the CP rather than the cause of black cultural nationalism. See Naison, "James Ford Comes to Harlem—The Central Committee Reasserts Control," in *Communists in Harlem,* 95–114.

12. "Not only did the Party face formidable competition in the electoral arena from local black elites," writes Naison, "but its whole mode of organization clashed with the cultural traditions of much of Harlem's population. Had the Party expressed its message in the language of black religion and incorporated religious rituals into its meetings, had it allowed all-black branches or cultural organizations to form when demography dictated it, or the membership requested it, then working-class blacks might have felt more comfortable in the Party. But in a Party forged in the image of the Russian Revolution, and distinguished, in its growth, by an interracial solidarity unparalleled in its time, the deepest convictions of its leading

cadre, black as well as white, prevented them from suggesting such changes" (CH, 283).

13. James Weldon Johnson, "Preface," *God's Trombones* (New York: Viking Press, 1927), 2.

14. Lawrence Gellert, "Negro Songs of Protest," *New Masses* (January 1931) and (May 1932), rpt. in *Negro,* 232.

15. Henry Louis Gates, Jr., *The Signifying Monkey: A Theory of Afro-American Literary Criticism* (New York: Oxford University Press, 1988), 75–76. In Ishmael Reed's postmodern novel *Mumbo Jumbo,* African artifacts play a double life as both drained art objects for Caucasian museum culture and vital signs of primitive worship, whose authenticity, however parodied in Reed's "neohoodoo" satire, is nevertheless preserved as a valuable subcultural resource of resistance.

16. Alaine Locke, "1928: A Retrospective Review," *Opportunity* 7 (January 1929): 8.

17. On Van Vechten's role in the Harlem Renaissance see Leon Coleman, "Carl Van Vechten Presents the New Negro," in *The Harlem Renaissance Re-examined,* ed. Victor A. Kramer (New York: AMS Press, 1987) and Bruce Kellner, *Carl Van Vechten and the Irreverent Decades* (Norman: University of Oklahoma Press, 1968).

18. See David Levering Lewis, *When Harlem Was in Vogue* (New York: Knopf, 1981), 183–84.

19. *Borzoi Broadside,* August 1926, 8 (New York: Knopf, 1926). Quoted in Charles Scruggs, "Crab Antics and Jacob's Ladder: Aaron Douglas's Two Views of Nigger Heaven," in *The Harlem Renaissance Re-examined,* 150. This blurb, as Scruggs points out, was accompanied by a depiction of Harlem as "mythical city" (162). Scruggs offers a discerning reading of how racial difference is inscribed in the two visual designs Douglas composed for Knopf's advertising campaign. Scrugg's claim is that Douglas' drawings reveal the "craftsmanship and thematic complexity of *Nigger Heaven*" (150).

20. Robert Bone, *The Negro Novel in America* (New Haven: Yale University Press, 1958), 60.

21. W. E. B. Du Bois, "Books," *Crisis* 33 (December 1926), 81–82.

22. James Weldon Johnson, "Romance and Tragedy in Harlem—A Review," *Opportunity* 4 (October 1926), 316. The differential strategy Johnson reads in the book seems lost, for example, on Mabel Dodge Luhan, who in a letter to Van Vechten complimented him not on his rendering of Harlem's "Niggerati" but rather on the book's frank eroticism, its portrait of the "archaic real nigger being able to do the deed." Luhan to Van Vechten, August 11, 1926, quoted in Lewis, 188.

23. Max Eastman, "Point-Black: Poems on the Negro, 1933–1970," typescript, ed. Al Cartusciello, Schomburg Center for Research in Black Culture, 357; quoted in James De Jongh, *Vicious Modernism: Black Harlem and the Literary Imagination* (New York: Cambridge University Press, 1990), 37.

24. James Weldon Johnson, "Preface to the First Edition," *The Book of American Negro Poetry* (New York: Harcourt Brace, 1922, rev. ed. 1931), 9 (hereafter cited in the text as ANP).

25. Alain Locke, "The New Negro," in *The New Negro,* ed. Alain Locke (New York: Albert and Charles Boni, 1925), 6 (hereafter cited in the text as NN).

26. Anonymous editorial statement published in *Black Opals* 1 (Spring 1927), n.p.

27. According to U.S. Bureau of the Census figures, New York City's black population rose from 33,888 to 327,706 between 1890 and 1930. While black men earned from $1.10 to $2.50 a day in the South, they could expect a rate of $3.75 for comparable work in the North. Similarly, black women could expect to make $2.50 per day in the North, which in the South would constitute a weekly wage. See Cary D. Wintz, *Black Culture and the Harlem Renaissance* (Houston: Rice University Press, 1988), 14–15.

28. Charles S. Johnson, "Black Workers and the City," *Survey Graphic* (March 1925), 643.

29. W. E. B. Du Bois, "Worlds of Color: The Negro Mind Reaches Out," in *The New Negro,* 408.

30. C. L. R. James, *A History of Negro Revolt* (New York: Haskell House, 1938; reprt. 1969), 66.

31. In contrast to Locke's framing of Pan-Africanism as a grass roots movement, Langston Hughes posed the telling question "how could a large and enthusiastic number of people be crazy about Negroes forever? But some Harlemites thought the millennium had come. . . . I don't know what made any Negroes think that—except that they were mostly intellectuals doing the thinking. The ordinary Negores hadn't heard of the Negro Renaissance. And if they had, it hadn't raised their wages any. As for all those white folks in the speakeasies and night clubs of Harlem—well, maybe a colored man could find *some* place to have a drink that the tourists hadn't yet discovered." *The Big Sea* (New York: Hill and Wang, 1940), 228.

32. Houston A. Baker, Jr. has described the anthology's cultural ambitions through the revolutionary figure of the black maroon, "a person not only possessed of the skills and knowledge of a 'master culture' but also motivated by a firm understanding of African modes of existence." *Modernism and the Harlem Renaissance* (Chicago: University of Chicago Press, 1987), 76.

33. Henry Louis Gates, Jr., *Figures in Black: Words, Signs, and the "Racial" Self* (New York: Oxford University Press, 1987), 184–85.

34. W. E. B. Du Bois, "Our Book Shelf," *Crisis* 31 (January 1926), 141.

35. "The appearance of such poetry," writes Honey, "was made possible, in part, by the support of Alain Locke and Countée Cullen who were themselves gay and committed to frank expression of sensuality in verse . . . Alain Locke's intellectual leanings were, perhaps, even more instrumental in creating a tolerant atmosphere for lesbian writing." Maureen Honey, *Shadowed Dreams: Women's Poetry of the Harlem Renaissance* (New Brunswick, N.J.: Rutgers University Press, 1989), 22–23. Gloria Hull's take on same sex relationships in Harlem stresses how the literary politics of gay male "negrotarians" worked against their lesbian and feminist counterparts: "Locke's behavior," she claims, "becomes even more problematic because of his obvious partiality toward young males, to whom he was sexually attracted. Locke, in fact, functioned within a homosexual coterie

of friendship and patronage that suggests that literary events were, in more than a few instances, tied to 'bedroom politics' and 'sexual croneyism'—as they no doubt may have been in the heterosexual world also. The point here, though, is that women were definitely excluded from Locke's beneficence and this particular sphere of favoritism." Gloria T. Hull, *Color, Sex, & Poetry* (Bloomington: Indiana University Press, 1987), 8.

36. Countée Cullen, "Foreword," *Caroling Dusk: An Anthology of Verse by Negro Poets,* ed. Countée Cullen (New York: Harpers, 1927), x.

37. In comparing African-American poetics of the 1920s to the black postmodernism of Ishmael Reed, Gates concludes: "Although the Harlem Renaissance did succeed in the creation of numerous texts of art and criticism, most critics agree that it failed to find its voice, which lay muffled beneath the dead weight of convention of romanticism, which most black writers seemed not to question but adopted eagerly." *Figures in Black,* 257.

38. "The semiotic activity," writes Kristeva, "which introduces wandering or fuzziness into language and *a fortiori,* into poetic language is, from a synchronic point of view, a mark of the workings of drives (appropriation/rejection, orality/anality, love/hate, life/death) and, from a diachronic point of view, stems from the archaisms of the semiotic body. . . . Language as a symbolic function constitutes itself at the cost of repressing instinctual drive and continuous relation to the mother." *Desire in Language: A Semiotic Approach to Literature and Art,* ed. Leon S. Roudiez, and tr. Thomas Gora et al. (New York: Columbia University Press, 1980), 136.

39. Langston Hughes, "The Twenties: Harlem and Its Negritude," *African Forum* 1 (Spring 1966): 18–19; quoted in *Propaganda and Aesthetics,* 78.

40. Interview, Charles Michael Smith, "Bruce Nugent: Bohemian of the Harlem Renaissance," *In the Life: A Black Gay Anthology,* ed. Joseph Beam (Boston: Alyson, 1986), 214.

41. Quoted in Richard Bruce (Bruce Nugent), "Smoke, Lilies, and Jade, A Novel, Part I," *Fire!!* 1 (November 1926), 35.

42. Bruce Nugent, "Beyond Where the Stars Stood Still" (New York: Warren Marr II Agent, n.d.), 25.

43. For a discussion of coming out as a performative speech act, see Eve Kosofsky Sedgwick, *Epistemology of the Closet* (Berkeley: University of California Press, 1990).

44. Countée Cullen, "Tableau," *Color* (New York: Harpers, 1927), 12.

45. Building on the work of Malachi Andrews, Paul T. Owens, J. L. Dillard, William Labov, William A. Stewart, Jim Haskins, Hugh F. Butts, Harold Wentworth, and Stuart Berg Flexner, among others, Henry Louis Gates, Jr. elaborates signifying as a verbal praxis that "turns on the sheer play of the signifier. It does not refer primarily to the signified; rather, it refers to the style of language, to that which transforms ordinary discourse into literature. Again, one does not Signify some thing; one Signifies in *some way.* . . . Signifyin(g) is the black rhetorical difference that negotiates the language user through several orders of meaning. In formal literature, what we commonly call figuration corresponds to Signification.

Again, the originality of so much of the black tradition emphasizes refiguration, or repetition and difference, or troping, underscoring the foregrounding of the chain of signifiers, rather than the mimetic representation of a novel content." *The Signifying Monkey,* 78–79.

46. See Wallace Thurman, "A Stranger at the Gates," *Messenger* 8 (September 1926), 279.

47. Benjamin Brawley, "The Negro Literary Renaissance," *The Southern Workman* 56, 4 (April 1927), 178.

48. George S. Schuyler, "The Negro-Art Hokum," *Nation* 122, no. 3180 (June 16, 1926), 662.

49. James Weldon Johnson, "Preface to the First Edition, *The Book of American Negro Poetry* (New York: Harcourt Brace, 1922: rev. ed. 1931), 41. In the preface to the revised edition (1931), Johnson distinguished "genuine folk stuff in contradistinction to the artificial folk stuff of the dialect school" (6) but failed to unpack their specific differences in close readings of actual texts.

50. Mike Gold, "Where the Battle Is Fought," *Nation* 123 (July 14, 1926), 37 (hereafter cited in the text as WBF).

51. Langston Hughes, "The Negro Artist and the Racial Mountain," *The Nation* 122 (June 23, 1926), 692.

52. Aaron Douglas, "The Negro in American Culture," *First American Artists Congress* (New York: 1936), 16.

53. The definitive study of the trial is Dan T. Carter, *Scottsboro: A Tragedy of the American South* (Baton Rouge: Louisiana State University Press, 1969) (hereafter cited in the text as S).

54. Eugene Gordon, "The Negro's New Leadership," *New Masses,* 7 (July 1931), 14–15; quoted in Carter, 86; New York *Daily Worker,* June 9, 1931, quoted in Carter, 86.

55. Quoted in "Seven Negro Editors on Communism," *The Crisis* (April 1932), 117 (hereafter cited in the text as *Crisis*).

56. Quoted in "Seven More Negro Editors on Communism," *The Crisis* (May 1932), 156.

57. Langston Hughes, "Park Bench," *New Masses* 10 (March 6, 1934), 6.

58. Langston Hughes, "Good Morning Revolution," in *Good Morning Revolution: Uncollected Social Protest Writings,* ed. Faith Berry (New York: Lawrence Hill, 1973), 3–4 (hereafter cited in the text as GMR).

59. Quoting Albert Murray, for example, Charles H. Rowell describes "the blues musician as 'fulfilling the same fundamental existential requirement that determines the mission of the poet, the priest, and the medicine man. He is making an affirmative and hence exemplary and heroic response to that which André Malraux describes as *la condition humaine.'* " Charles H. Rowell, "Sterling A. Brown and the Afro-American Folk Tradition," in *The Harlem Renaissance Re-examined,* ed. Victor A. Kramer (New York: AMS Press, 1987), 324.

60. See Langston Hughes, *Good Morning Revolution: Uncollected Social Protest Writings by Langston Hughes.*

61. Raymond Smith, "Langston Hughes: Evolution of the Poetic Persona," in *The Harlem Renaissance Re-examined,* 242.

62. "Draft Manifesto of the John Reed Clubs," *New Masses* 7, (June 1932), 1.

63. "Art as a Weapon: Program of the Workers Cultural Federation," *New Masses* 6 (August 1931), 11 (hereafter cited in the text as AW).

64. See Mike Gold's glowing review of Trotsky's *Literature and Revolution* in "America Needs a Critic," *New Masses* 1 (October 1926), rpt. in *Mike Gold: A Literary Anthology,* ed. Michael Folsom (New York: International, 1972), 129–39.

65. "Resolution on the Work of the New Masses for 1931," 20.

66. For a discussion of Elistratova's position, see Aaron, WL, 437. On the official adoption of "socialist realism" in the Soviet Union, see Donald Drew Egbert, *Social Radicalism and the Arts* (New York: Knopf, 1970), 302.

67. See Max Eastman, "Artists in Uniform," *The Modern Monthly,* 7 (August 1933), 397–404; rpt. in *Artists in Uniform: A Study of Literature and Bureaucratism* (New York: Knopf, 1934).

68. Max Eastman, "Artists in Uniform," *The Modern Monthly* 7 (August 1933), 399.

69. Joshua Kunitz, "Max Eastman's Hot Unnecessary Tears," *New Masses* 8 (September 1933), 15. See also Joshua Kunitz, "Choose Your Uniform," *New Masses* 8 (August 1933), 14–15; rpt. in *Proletarian Literature In the United States,* eds. Granville Hicks, Michael Gold, Isidor Schneider, et al. (New York: International, 1935), 361–67.

70. Ralph Cheney and Lucia Trent, "Introduction," *An Anthology of Revolutionary Poetry,* ed. Marcus Graham (New York: Activist Press, 1929), 36–37.

71. Untitled editorial, *Anvil* 1 (May 1933), 4.

72. Wallace Phelps, Charles Henry Newman (Sol Funaroff), and Herman Spector, "Sensibility and Modern Poetry," *Dynamo* 1, 3 (Summer 1934), 30 (hereafter cited in the text as SMP).

73. Untitled editorial, *Contempo* (May 5, 1932) 2.

74. Herbert Solow, "Minutiae of Left-Wing Literary History," *Partisan Review* 4 (March 1938), 59. Solow summarized his findings with the following chart:

No.	Items Contributed	Total	"Enemies of Mankind"	% "Enemies of Mankind"
I.	1 item	106	6	5.5
II.	2 to 4 items	34	8	26.5
III.	5 or more items	10	3	33.33
IV.	Members of executive board	15	3	20.0
V.	Editors	6	2	33.33
	10 or more items Editor, also on board	2	1	50

75. Irving Howe and Lewis Coser, *The American Communist Party, A Critical History (1919–1957)* (Boston: Beacon Press, 1957), 296.

76. Freeman's references to Trotsky were anathema to the Comintern which,

through Earl Browder's American influence, negotiated with Freeman to remove the book from circulation, to cancel his speaking tour, and to abandon other promotional activities on behalf of the work. For an account of this party intervention, see Aaron, WL, 368–69.

77. Joseph Freeman, "Six Poems," *Dynamo* 1, 1 (January 1934), 11.

78. Diego Rivera, "The Guild Spirit in Mexican Art." (As related to Katherine Anne Porter), *Survey Graphic* 5, 2 (May 1, 1924), 175, 174.

79. Diego Rivera, "The Revolutionary Spirit in Modern Art," *The Modern Quarterly* 6, 3 (Autumn 1932), 52 (hereafter cited in the text as RS).

80. John Dos Passos, "Diego Rivera Murals," *New Masses* 2 (March 1927), 15.

81. See Bertram D. Wolfe, *The Fabulous Life of Diego Rivera* (New York: Stein and Day, 1963), 216–17.

82. Diego Rivera, "What is Art For?" *The Modern Monthly* 8 (June 1933), 275 (hereafter cited in the text as WAF).

83. Robert Evans, "Painting and Politics: The Case of Diego Rivera," *New Masses* 7 (January 1932), 25.

84. "Diego Rivera and the John Reed Club," *New Masses* 7 (February 1932), 31.

85. Albert Halper, *Good-Bye Union Square, A Writer's Memoir of the Thirties* (Chicago, Quadrangle Books, 1970), 96.

86. Mary Randolph, "Rivera's Monopoly," *Art Front* (December 1935), 12.

87. "October—Association of Artistic Labor Declaration (1928)," in *Russian Art of the Avant-Garde: Theory and Criticism, 1902–34*, 277.

88. Diego Rivera, "Introduction," in Bertram Wolfe, *Portrait of America* (New York: Covici-Friede, 1934), 13 (hereafter cited in the text as PA).

89. See Wolfe, 301–2.

90. For a discussion of Rivera's use of archaic Mexican icons see Betty Ann Brown, "The Past Idealized: Diego Rivera's Use of Pre-Columbian Imagery," in *Diego Rivera: A Retrospective* (New York: Detroit Institute of Arts and W. W. Norton, 1986), 143.

91. See Maurice Sugar, "Bullets—Not Food—for Ford Workers," *The Nation* 134 (March 23, 1932), 334 (hereafter cited in the text as Sugar).

92. Herbert L. Cruden, "An Open Letter to Edsel Ford," *New Masses* 7 (April 1932), 23.

93. See Wolfe, 312–13 for a discussion of Rivera's reception in Detroit.

94. Antonio Gramsci, *Selections from the Prison Notebooks,* Quintin Hoare and Geoffrey Nowell Smith, ed. and tr. (New York: International, 1971), 189 (hereafter cited in the text as PN).

95. In a note on the Risorgimento entitled "Class political leadership before and after attaining governmental power," Gramsci writes that "a class is dominant in two ways, i. e. 'leading' and 'dominant.' It leads the classes which are its allies, and dominates those which are its enemies . . . there can and must be a 'political hegemony' even before the attainment of governmental power, and one should not count solely on the power and material force which such a position gives in

order to exercise political leadership or hegemony." See *Prison Notebooks,* note 5, p. 57.

96. See Kenneth Burke, "Revolutionary Symbolism in America," in *American Writers' Congress,* ed. Henry Hart (New York: International, 1935), 87–94. "In 1935," writes Frank Lentricchia, "Burke was saying to America's radical left not only that a potentially revolutionary culture should keep in mind that revolution must be culturally as well as economically rooted, but, as well, and this was perhaps the most difficult of Burke's implications for his radical critics to swallow, that a revolutionary culture must situate itself firmly on the terrain of its capitalist antagonist, must not attempt a dramatic leap beyond capitalism in one explosive, rupturing moment of release, must work its way through capitalism's language of domination by working cunningly within it, using, appropriating, even speaking though its key mechanisms of repression. What Burke's proposal in 1935 to America's intellectual left amounts to is this: the substance, the very ontology of ideology—an issue that Marx and Engels engaged with little clarity, to put it charitably—in a broad but fundamental sense is revealed to us *textually* and therefore must be grasped (read) and attacked (reread, rewritten) in that dimension." *Criticism and Social Change* (Chicago: University of Chicago Press, 1983), 24.

97. Max Eastman, "Artists in Uniform," 397.

98. For a critique of Trotsky's attempts to restructure the Soviet labor force, see *Prison Notebooks,* 301–02.

99. Advertisement, *Broom* 4 (January 1923), n.p.

100. "This work," boasted Taylor of pig-iron handling, "is so crude and elementary in its nature that the writer firmly believes that it would be possible to train an intelligent gorilla so as to become a more efficient pig-iron handler than any man could be." *The Principles of Scientific Management* (New York: Harpers, 1911), 40.

101. *Advertising and Selling* (July 5, 1919), 2; quoted in Stuart Ewen, *Captains of Consciousness: Advertising and the Social Roots of the Consumer Culture* (New York: McGraw-Hill, 1976), 88.

102. For a definitive discussion of the rise of American advertising during the 1920s and its critical reception, see Stuart Ewing, *Captains of Consciousness,* 51–109. Not coincidentally, the growth in advertising revenues from 58.5 million in 1918 to 196.3 million by 1929, according to Ewing, paralleled the increasingly centralized ownership of the burgeoning print media industry and giant information monopolies such as the Hearst syndicate (32).

103. Matthew Josephson, "The Great American Billposter," *Broom* 3 (November 1922), 304 (hereafter cited in the text as GAB).

104. In considering how advertising appropriated avant-garde styles, Josephson analyzed the marketing campaign for the 1923 Buick Roadster as it exploited futurist motifs to convey speed, power, and mechanical streamlining. Similarly, he pointed to common alliterative devices linking high- and low-brow texts, subversively comparing Keats' "Ode to a Nightingale" ("beaded bubbles winking at the brim") with the more prosaic prosody of "Meaty Marrowy Oxtail Joints."

105. Conroy also noted that *New Masses* had doubled its circulation in 1931 and was aiming to boost it to 50,000 in 1932. See Jack Conroy, "Art Above the Battle," *The Rebel Poet* 13 (March 1932), 3.

106. Jack Woodford, "Bigger & Better Belles Lettres," *New Masses* 5 (October 1929), 8.

107. See *The Rebel Poet,* 15 (August 1932), 2.

108. "Workers' Films and Photos," *New Masses* 7 (December 1931), 27.

109. "Boston—Solidarity Players," *New Masses* 7 (December 1931), 26.

110. Mike Gold, "Notes from Kharkov" *New Masses* 6 (March 1931), 4.

111. Ralph Cheney and Morris Spiegel, "Poetry and Revolution: A Study of Poetry in the USSR," *The Rebel Poet,* 1, 6–7 (June-July 1931), 3.

112. Mike Gold, "America Needs a Critic," *New Masses,* 1 (October 1926), 9.

113. Joseph Freeman, "Memo," quoted in Aaron, WL, 228.

114. Josephine Herbst, quoted in *Proletarian Writers of the Thirties,* ed. David Madden (Carbondale: Southern Illinois University Press, 1968), xxi. See also Paula Rabinowitz, "Women and U.S. Literary Radicalism," in *Writing Red,* ed. Charlotte Nekola and Paula Rabinowitz (New York: Feminist Press, 1987), 2.

115. See Mike Gold, "Go Left, Young Writers!" *New Masses* 4 (January 1929), 3–4; and V. F. Calverton, "Leftward Ho!" *Modern Quarterly* 6 (Summer 1932), 26–32. Such gendered coinages, Rabinowitz explains, "suggested that the Left, like the West, was a wild place—brutal, rugged, and certainly no place for a lady" (3).

116. See "Pound vs. Gellert," *New Masses* 4 (June 1928), 27.

117. Untitled, anonymous review, *New Masses* 4 (January 1929), 4.

118. Hugo, Gellert, "Preface," to Karl Marx, *Capital in Lithographs* (New York: Ray Long and Richard R. Smith, 1934), n. pag.

119. William Carlos Williams, "For A New Magazine," *Blues* 2 (1929), 32.

120. William Phillips (Wallace Phelps), "Sensibility and Modern Poetry," *Dynamo* 1 (Summer 1934), 22.

121. Francis Picabia, quoted in "French Artists Spur on an American Art," *New York Tribune* October 24, 1915, sec. 4, 2.

122. See Louis Lozowick, "Tatlin's Monument to the Third International," *Broom* 3 (October 1922), 232–34; and Enrico Prampolini, "The Aesthetic of the Machine and Mechanical Introspection in Art," *Broom* 3 (October 1922), 235–37.

123. Louis Lozowick, quoted in Janet Flint, *The Prints of Louis Lozowick* (New York: Hudson Hills Press, 1982), 17; and in William C. Lipke, *Abstraction and Realism, 1923–1943: Paintings, Drawings, and Lithographs of Louis Lozowick* (catalogue of an exhibition held in the Robert Hull Fleming Museum, University of Vermont, Burlington, March 14–April 18, 1971), 5.

124. Macknight Black, *Machinery* (New York: Horace Liveright, 1929), 45.

125. Quoted in William Jordy, *American Buildings and Their Architects: Progressive and Academic Ideals at the Turn of the Twentieth Century* (Garden

City, N.Y.: Doubleday, 1976), 44–45; and in Cecelia Tichi, *Shifting Gears: Technology, Literature, Culture in Modernist America* (Chapel Hill: University of North Carolina Press, 1987), 141.

126. Macknight Black, *Thrust at the Sky* (New York: Simon and Schuster, 1932), 38–39.

127. See Gorham Munson, "The Skyscraper Primitives." *The Guardian* 1 (March 1925): 164–78.

128. Floyd Dell, "Some Gifts of the Machine Age," *New Masses* 2 (March 1927), 23.

129. Lewis Mumford and Genevieve Taggard, "That Monster the Machine," *New Masses* 2 (September 1927), 23.

130. Joseph Kalar, "Review of Unrest 1931," *The Rebel Poet* 1 (October–December 1931), 11.

131. See Estelle Gershgoren Novak, "The Dynamo School of Poets," *Contemporary Literature* 11, 4: 526–39.

132. André Gorz, *Farewell to the Working Class,* tr. Michael Sonenscher (Boston: South End Press, 1982), 46.

133. Sol Funaroff, "Dnieprostroy," *New Masses* 8 (November 1932), 20.

134. Sol Funaroff, "The Spider and the Clock," in *Social Poetry of the 1930s, A Selection,* ed. Jack Salzman and Leo Zanderer (New York: Burt Franklin, 1978), 56 (hereafter cited in the text as SP).

135. Joseph A. Kalar, "Papermill," *Joseph A. Kalar . . . Poet of Protest,* ed. Richard G. Kalar (Blaine, Minn: RGK Publications, 1985), 32 (hereafter cited in the text as JK). "Papermill" was published in 1931 in the April issue of *Front* and in *Unrest*; during the 1930s, it was also reprinted in *We Gather Strength* (1933) and *Proletarian Literature in the United States* (1935).

136. Joseph Kalar, "Letter to Warren Huddleston," September 4, 1932, in *Joseph A. Kalar . . . Poet of Protest,* 147.

137. Mike Gold, "Introduction," *We Gather Strength* (New York: Liberal Press, 1933), 7–9.

138. Edwin Rolfe, "Not Men Alone," *Anvil* (October-November 1935), 10.

139. Stanley Burnshaw, "Variations on a Baedecker," in *Socialist Poetry of the 1930s: A Selection,* eds. Jack Salzman and Leo Zanderer (New York: Burt Franklin, 1978), 17.

140. John Beecher, "Report to the Stockholders," *Collected Poems, 1924–1974* (New York: Macmillan, 1974), 3.

141. Edwin Rolfe, "Asbestos," *To My Contemporaries* (New York: Dynamo Press, 1936), 10.

3. The Feminist Vanguard in the Popular Front

1. The nadir in Macleish's reception by such writers on the left came in 1933 with Mike Gold's *New Republic* tirade "Out of the Fascist Unconscious," followed

by Margaret Wright's scathing *New Masses* review "Der Schone Archibald" the following year. See Daniel Aaron, WL, 264–67, 429.

2. Similarly, Mike Gold had lambasted Ernest Hemingway in 1928, calling him "heartless as a tabloid." "Hemingway will soon exhaust the illusion that he is a brainless prize-fighter," Gold declared, "and since he is too bourgeois to accept the labor world, I predict he will [seek] Nirvana in the Catholic Church." But by 1937, Hemingway, like Macleish, was a keynote speaker at the second American Writers' Congress. See Herbert Solow, "Minutia of Left Wing Literary History," *Partisan Review* 4 (March 1938), 60.

3. Seldon Rodman quoted in Louis Untermeyer, "The Language of Muriel Rukeyser," *Saturday Review,* August 10, 1940, 12. Stephen Vincent Benét, who bestowed the Yale award, welcomed Rukeyser's first book as an "accomplishment which ranks her among the most interesting and individual of our younger poets." "Foreword," Muriel Rukeyser, *Theory of Flight* (New Haven: Yale University Press, 1935), 6. Three years later, Louis Untermeyer affirmed that this first effort "is still the most distinguished in the annual Yale Series of Younger Poets," (11). Similarly, William Rose Benét called her "the most interesting of the younger women poets." "Four American Poets," *The Saturday Review,* April 30, 1938, 16. By the end of the decade, Horace Gregory cited Rukeyser as one of the very few poets of her generation who would survive as a major talent beyond the 1930s. See Gregory, "American Poetry 1930–40," *Decision,* 1 (January 1941), 24–29. For a more recent discussion of Rukeyser's early career, see Louise Kertesz, *The Poetic Vision of Muriel Rukeyser* (Baton Rouge: Louisiana State University Press, 1979).

4. William Phillips and Philip Rahv, "Grandeur and Misery of a Poster Girl," *Partisan Review* 10 (September-October 1943), 471.

5. F. O. Matthiessen, "The Rukeyser Imbroglio (cont'd)," *Partisan Review* 11 (Spring 1944), 217.

6. William Phillips and Philip Rahv, "The Rukeyser Imbroglio (cont'd)," *Partisan Review* 11 (Spring 1944), 218.

7. Muriel Rukeyser, "The Book of the Dead," *U.S. 1* (New York: Covici-Friede, 1938), 43 (hereafter cited in the text as "Book").

8. Union Carbide's contempt for safety was not untypical of the dominant corporate attitude toward depression era workers. An equally noteworthy case was labor's four-year battle against the Six Companies who contracted to build the Hoover Dam: Utah, Morrison-Knudsen, J. F. Shea, Pacific Bridge, MacDonald & Kahn, and Bechtel-Kaiser-Warren Brothers. After a much-publicized legal struggle, fifty plaintiffs settled out of court with the Six Companies based on allegations that the contractors had failed to adopt adequate safety measures in protecting tunnel workers against carbon monoxide poisoning. "Six Companies," writes Joseph E. Stevens, "knew that carbon monoxide was a potentially lethal hazard, but to protect a $300,000 investment in gasoline-fueled trucks and avoid a costly delay while electric motors were installed, it was willing to circumvent state legal restrictions on the use of internal-combustion equipment underground and put its employees

at risk. Then, when the bill for this decision was rendered in the form of a long casualty list and at least half a hundred lawsuits, the company tried to cover up and evade responsibility in a manner that was at best odious and at worst criminal." Joseph E. Stevens, *Hoover Dam: An American Adventure* (Norman: University of Oklahoma Press, 1988), 214.

9. Willard Maas, "Lost Between Wars," *Poetry* 52 (May 1938), 102.

10. John Wheelwright, "Review of *U.S. 1*," *Partisan Review* 4 (March 1938), 54.

11. Michel Foucault, *Power/Knowledge: Selected Interviews and Other Writings, 1972–1977,* Colin Gordon, ed. and tr. (New York: Pantheon, 1980), 126 (hereafter cited in the text as *Power*).

12. "This has undoubtedly given them," writes Foucault, "a much more immediate and concrete awareness of struggles . . . This is what I would call the 'specific' intellectual as opposed to the 'universal' intellectual" (*Power*, 127).

13. In theorizing the dynamic effects of *specific* intellectual labor, Foucault observed that such new micrological praxes necessarily set in motion institutional counterforces. "And for the first time, I think, the intellectual was hounded by political powers, no longer on account of a general discourse which he conducted, but because of the knowledge at his disposal: it was at this level that he constituted a political threat" (*Power*, 128).

14. Following the documentary pairing of word and image in such precursor works as Jacob Riis' *How the Other Half Lives* (1890), Lewis Hine's six-volume *Pittsburgh Survey* (1901–14), Rexford Tugwell and Thomas Munro's *American Economic Life and the Means of Its Improvement* (1925), and Yale University's fifteen-volume *Pageant of America* (1925–29), photodocumentary studies of the depression era ranged all the way from the affluent life-styles of the White House as witnessed in Pare Lorentz's *The Roosevelt Year: A Photographic Record* (1934) and Don Wharton's *Roosevelt Omnibus* (1934) to the impoverished victims of the Dust Bowl captured in M. Lincoln Schuster's *Eyes of the World: A Photographic Record of History-in-the-Making* (1935). For a detailed discussion of depression era photodocumentary styles, see William Stott, *Documentary Expression and Thirties America* (New York: Oxford University Press, 1973), 110–11, 211–13.

15. "Today," he would argue in the 1960s, "at the level of mass communications, it appears that the linguistic message is indeed present in every image: as title, caption, accompanying press article, film dialogue, comic strip balloon." Roland Barthes, *Image/Music/Text,* Stephen Heath, tr. (New York: Hill and Wang, 1974), 38.

16. Karl Marx, *Writings of the Young Marx on Philosophy and Society,* Loyd D. Easton and Kurt H. Guddat, eds. and trs. (New York: Doubleday, 1967), 414.

17. Advancing Marx's mature understanding of ideology, contemporary theorists such as Althusser, Eagleton, Jameson, and others have variously ramified and refined the early empiricist metaphor of the "camera obscura," by interrogating its unmediated vision of social reality. In particular, W. J. T. Mitchell has

proposed a cogent reinterpretation of this spectacular icon that is central to so many provocative Marxist critiques of visual representation in film, photography, and other media discourses. On the one hand, Mitchell grants the figure's reliance on ideology as false consciousness—whose potential for critique he does not wholly reject. On the other hand, he reminds us that the camera obscura, far from passively reflecting a distorted image of an underlying sociohistorical referent, records the full "historical life process" of production and exchange that local ideologies actively negotiate. Thus, instead of simply exposing ideology as an expression of false consciousness, the camera obscura, as Mitchell stresses, calls attention to the way in which the material historicity of any specific ideology is always available for interpretive reconstruction and critique: "The camera obscura plays a deeply equivocal role, then, as a figure for both the illusions of ideology and for the 'historical life-process' that generates those illusions and provides a basis for dispelling them. In this light, the camera obscura is both the producer and the cure for the illusions of ideology." *Iconology: Image, Text, Ideology* (Chicago: University of Chicago Press, 1986), 178. Mitchell's rereading of the camera obscura as a *pharmakon*—at once projecting and revealing ideology's shaping role in history—is pertinent to Rukeyser's own presentation of photography's powers of cultural representation.

18. Rukeyser's deconstruction of glass's symbolic value in "The Book of the Dead" is only part of her long poem's broader subversion of conventional oppositions. In the account of "George Robinson," a black tunnel worker, silica's "white glass" unsettles the social boundaries that divide the miners by race. "As dark as I am," he recounts, "when I came out at morning after the tunnel at night, / with a whiteman, nobody could have told which man was white. / The dust had covered us both, and the dust was white" ("Book," 34). In Robinson's account, the silica dust serves symbolically to rearticulate racial differences to an overarching recognition of solidarity in class oppression. Throughout the poem, Rukeyser overturns America's conventional color hierarchy by linking whiteness not to racial privilege but to Union Carbide's exploitative mining operations and its silica by-product of "white / murdering snow" ("Book," 47). At the site of the dam, for example, the rapids' "fern and fuming white" that "ascends in mist of continuous diffusion" ("Book," 55) mirrors the "skin-white" generating plant whose turbines they drive. Moreover, the poem's "river Death"—channeled as it is by the labor of Carbide's tunnel workers—is literally translated through the "valley's work, the white, the shining" ("Book," 57) into electric currents that haunt the eerily illumined "white cities" of depression era America.

19. "Simply," wrote Rolfe, "the formula is to describe an event in verse, add a second part of interpretation (generally pseudophilosophical), and wind up with a third part which, instead of tying the first two parts together as it is meant to do, introduces a prophecy or a call to action, very often bombastic and in the barest, worst sense, didactic. Such formula-writing, from which Maddow and Hayes have suffered, is always ineffective. Another danger in revolutionary verse is the tendency to sloganize. Many of us recognized long ago that the use of slogans was entirely valid in revolutionary poetry, but that this validity depended on two factors:

the slogan's meaning in actual life and struggle, and its integration with the poem." Edwin Rolfe, "Poetry," *Partisan Review* 2 (April–May 1935), 40.

20. "In philosophy," they claimed, "mechanical materialism assumes a direct determinism of the whole superstructure by the economic foundation, ignoring the dialectical interaction between consciousness and environment, and the reciprocal influence of the parts of the superstructure on each other and on the economic determinants. The literary counterpart of mechanical materialism faithfully reflects this vulgarization of Marxism. But its effects strike even deeper: it paralyzes the writer's capacities by creating a dualism between his artistic consciousness and his beliefs, thus making it impossible for him to achieve anything beyond fragmentary, marginal expression." William Phillips and Philip Rahv, "Problems and Perspectives in Revolutionary Literature," *Partisan Review* 1 (June–July 1934), 6.

21. M. M. Bakhtin, *The Dialogic Imagination,* Michael Holquist, ed., and Caryl Emerson and Michael Holquist, trs. (Austin: University of Texas Press, 1981), 272.

22. David Wolff (Ben Maddow), "Document and Poetry," *New Masses* 26 (February 22, 1938), 21.

23. William Carlos Williams, "Muriel Rukeyser's *U.S. 1,*" *New Republic* (March 9, 1938), 141.

24. Karl Marx, *A Contribution to the Critique of Political Economy* (Chicago: Charles H. Kerr, 1913), 12.

25. Noting the polysemous play of meaning in poster art, Rukeyser asserted that "when we see the fierce and vivid and constructive image—a face of the war— before us, we have, too, a point of conflict if we are not yet agreed on the issues of the war. . . . We have an emotional image, *reinforced* from another direction by words." Muriel Rukeyser, "Words and Images," *The New Republic* (August 2, 1943), 140–41 (hereafter cited in the text as "Word").

26. Muriel Rukeyser, *The Life of Poetry* (New York: Current Books, 1949), 152 (hereafter cited in the text as *Life*).

27. Not incidentally, the poet viewed the formal regimen of cutting and splicing document and image as serving a distinctively communal function. Here, she claims, the poem has no existence apart from what she theorized, after the semiotic theory of Charles Sanders Peirce, as a "triadic" communicative relationship among the sign, its object, and its interpretant. In Rukeyser's humanistic reading of Peirce, the formal, constructive aspect of any poem, like the sign itself, is inherently incomplete apart from its involvement in a "triadic" communicative framework. What Rukeyser understands as the full life of poetry is its double mediation at once by the author's assemblage of poetic discourse and the reader's interpretive act that supplements and forwards the poem's semiotic production. "The artist," she writes, "has performed upon his experience that work of acknowledging, shaping, and offering which is the creative process. The audience, in receiving the work of art, acknowledges not only its form, but their own experience and the experience of the artist" (*Life,* 51).

28. As Philip Blair Rice pointed out in his *Nation* review, Rukeyser's "road is also the Osiris way described in the Egyptian *Book of the Dead*. The tunnel is the

underworld, the mountain stream is the life-giving river, the Congressional inquiry is the judgment in the Hall of Truth." Philip Blair Rice, "The Osiris Way," *Nation* (March 19, 1938), 336. Yet, as M. L. Rosenthal argued in supplementing Blair's reading, Rukeyser stages the myth of death and transfiguration through the persona of Isis, not Osiris. "It is, incidentally, as the prophet of Isis, not Osiris, that the poet utters these 'magic' lines. This is another example of the translation 'into feminine' of revolutionary and heroic themes. The translation is aided by the echoes of a whole tradition of female protagonists from the great mythological earth-mothers through the heroines of Euripides to the modern self-discovering women of Lawrence and the working-class mothers of such novels as Gorky's *Mother,* Steinbeck's *The Grapes of Wrath,* and Wright's *Native Son.*" M. L. Rosenthal, "Muriel Rukeyser: The Longer Poems," *New Directions in Prose and Poetry,* James Laughlin, ed., 14 (1953), 218.

29. Quoted in Ralph Purcell, *Government and Art* (Washington, D.C.: Publlic Affairs Press, 1956), 48–49; and Francis O'Connor *Federal Support for the Arts* (Greenwich, Conn: New York Graphic Society, 1971), 17–18.

30. Franklin Delano Roosevelt, quoted in George Biddle *An American Artist's Story* (Boston, 1939), 273; quoted in Purcell, 75, n.12 and O'Connor, 18.

31. Holger Cahill, ed., *New Horizons in American Art* (New York: Metropolitan Museum of Art, 1936), 29.

32. See Walter Benjamin, "The Work of Art in the Age of Mechanical Reproduction," *Illuminations,* tr. Harry Zohn (New York: Schocken Books, 1985), 217–51.

33. For a definitive discussion of women's contribution to the visual culture of the 1930s, see Karal Ann Marling, "American Art and the American Woman," in Karal Ann Marling and Helen A. Harrison, *7 American Women: The Depression Decade* (Poughkeepsie, N.Y.: Vassar College Art Gallery, 1976), 7–16.

34. Lucienne Bloch, "Art for Use," quoted in O'Conner, *Art for the Millions,* 76.

35. For a critical biography of Greenwood, see Helen A. Harrison's entry in *7 American Women: The Depression Decade,* 28–29.

4. Transpersonal Poetics

1. See Jameson's use of the term "postindividualistic" in "Imaginary and Symbolic in Lacan: Marxism, Psychoanalytic Criticism, and the Problem of the Subject," *Literature and Psychoanalysis: The Question of Reading: Otherwise,* 382.

2. Ron Silliman, "The Political Economy of Poetry," $L=A=N=G=U=A=G=E$ (*Open Letter* 5:1) 4, 60–65.

3. Georg Lukács, *History and Class Consciousness: Studies in Marxist Dialectics,* tr. Rodney Livingstone (Cambridge: MIT Press, 1971), 83.

4. Ron Silliman, "Disappearance of the Word, Appearance of the World,"

The L=A=N=G=U=A=G=E Book, eds. Bruce Andrews and Charles Bernstein (Carbondale: Southern Illinois University Press, 1984), 122.

5. Charles Bernstein, *Content's Dream* (Los Angeles: Sun & Moon Press, 1986), 59–60.

6. Bill Moyers, "The Simple Acts of Life," in *The Power of the Word,* videotape PBS, 1989.

7. Theodor W. Adorno, "Lyric Poetry and Society," tr. Bruce Mayo, *Telos* 20 (1974), 58.

8. The author, writes Foucault, "does not precede the works, he is a certain functional principle by which, in our culture, one limits, excludes, and chooses; in short, by which one impedes the free circulation, the free manipulation, the free composition, decomposition, and recomposition of fiction." Michel Foucault, "What Is an Author?" *Textual Strategies: Perspectives in Post-Structural Criticism,* ed. Josué V. Harari (Ithaca: Cornell University Press, 1979), 159. See also Roland Barthes, "The Death of the Author," *Image—Music—Text,* tr. Stephen Heath (New York: Hill and Wang, 1977), 142–48.

9. Charles Bernstein, "Interview with Tom Beckett," *The Difficulties: Charles Bernstein Issue* 2 (Fall 1982), 41.

10. See Silliman's and Bernstein's exchange following the endnotes of "Thought's Dream," in *Content's Dream,* 85–86.

11. Lynn Hejinian, *My Life* (Los Angeles: Sun & Moon Press, 1987), 85–86 (hereafter cited in the text as ML).

12. Marjorie Perloff, *The Poetics of Indeterminacy: Rimbaud to Cage* (Princeton: Princeton University Press, 1981), 72.

13. On the issue of the political force of *Language* writing see Jameson, "Postmodernism and Consumer Society," *The Anti-Aesthetic,* Hal Foster, ed. (Port Townsend, Wash.: Bay Press, 1985), 111–25; and George Hartley, *Textual Politics and the Language Poets* (Bloomington: Indiana University Press, 1989).

14. Fanny Howe, *Introduction to the World* (Berkeley: The Figures, 1986), 1 (hereafter cited in the text as IW).

15. Fredric Jameson, "Postmodernism or the Cultural Logic of Late Capitalism," *New Left Review* 146 (July–August 1984), 77.

16. Similarly, in "The Work of Nature in the Age of Electronic Emission," Andrew Ross speculates that "in an imagined national community, the weather plays nature to the culture of our social and political life while it manages the symbolic relations that help us to make sense of that social and political life." Ross, "The Work of Nature in the Age of Electronic Emission," *Social Text* 18 (Winter 1987–88), 123.

17. See Jean Baudrillard, "The Ecstasy of Communication," "The Anti-Aesthetic, ed. Hal Foster (Port Townsend: Bay Press, 1983), 128; and "The Precession of Simulacra," *Simulations,* trs. Paul Foss, Paul Patton, and Philip Beitchman (New York: Semiotext(e), 1983), 57.

18. Alan Davies, "Shared Sentences," in *"Language" Poetries,* ed. Douglas Messerli (New York: New Directions, 1987), 159.

19. See Bernstein, *Content's Dream,* 75.

20. Barret Watten, "Russian Formalism and the Present," *Hills* 6–7 (Spring 1980), 62.

21. M. M. Bakhtin and P. N. Medvedev, *The Formal Method in Literary Scholarship,* tr. Albert J. Wehrle (Baltimore: Johns Hopkins University Press, 1978), 103 (hereafter cited in the text as FM).

22. For example, Perloff's discussion of the *Language* School in *The Dance of the Intellect* safely incorporates the political activism of the group within the stylistic hegemony of the Pound tradition, thus reproducing high modernism's swerve from social engagement now on the postmodern terrain. Unlike Perloff, Jerome J. McGann's "Contemporary Poetry and Alternative Routes"—his theoretical map of the poetry scene since 1946—does productively discuss black and feminist writing within his guiding period opposition between the 1960s' poetry of revolt and the 1970s' *Language* movement. See Marjorie Perloff, *The Dance of the Intellect: Studies in the Poetry of the Pound Tradition* (New York: Cambridge University Press, 1985); and Jerome J. McGann, "Contemporary Poetry and Alternative Routes," *Critical Inquiry* 13 (Spring 1987): 624–47.

23. See Henry M. Sayre, "The Avant-Garde and Experimental Writing," *The Columbia Literary History of the United States,* Emory Elliott, ed. (New York: Columbia University Press, 1988), 1178–99; and Fred Pfeil, "Postmodernism as a 'Structure of Feeling'," *Marxism and the Interpretation of Culture,* eds. Cary Nelson and Lawrence Grossberg (Urbana: University of Illinois Press, 1988), 381–403.

24. Ron Silliman, "Interview," *The Difficulties* 2 (1985), 37.

25. Philip Rahv and William Phillips, "Problems and Perspectives in Revolutionary Literature," *Partisan Review* 1 (June–July 1934), 4.

26. Kenneth Burke, "Revolutionary Symbolism in America," 91.

27. Kenneth Burke, "Two Kinds of Against," *The New Republic,* June 26, 1935, 198 (hereafter cited in the text as "Two").

28. Robert Penn Warren, "The Present State of Poetry in the United States," *The Kenyon Review* 1 (August 1939), 393 (hereafter cited in the text as "Present").

29. This is Louis Althusser's term from his famous piece "Ideology and the State" where he describes the ways in which ideology transforms individuals into subjects through a communicative act of "hailing" or "interpellation." See Louis Althusser, *Lenin and Philosophy,* tr. Ben Brewster (Bristol: Western Printing Services, 1971), 162.

30. Kenneth Fearing, *The Collected Poems of Kenneth Fearing* (New York: Random House, 1940), 14 (hereafter cited in the text as CPF).

31. Edward Said, "Permission to Narrate," *London Review of Books,* February 16–29, 1984, 13–17.

32. Guy Debord, *Society of the Spectacle* (Detroit: Black and Red, 1983), 42.

33. V. J. Jerome, *Intellectuals and the War* (New York: Workers Library, 1940), 34.

34. Reading the compulsion to repeat in film through Freud's *Beyond the*

Pleasure Principle, Stephen Heath and Jean-François Lyotard note the contradictory work of repetition. On the one hand, it functions as a shoring up or binding (*Bildung*) of the ego by mapping what is unfamiliar, unrecognizable or threatening onto the regime of the same. On the other hand, however, repetition in service to the *death drives* signals what is outside of, or unconscious to, the maintenance of the ego: the "very essence of drives tending beyond the pleasure principle to absolute discharge, to the total dispersal of unity." Stephen Heath, "Repetition Time: Notes Around 'Structural/Materialist' Film," *Wide Angle* 2, 3: 6–7. See also Jean-François Lyotard, "Acinema," *Wide Angle* 2, 3: 52–59.

35. Jonathan Arac, "Introduction," *Postmodernism and Politics* (Minneapolis: University of Minnesota Press, 1986), xxi.

36. Kenneth Fearing, "The Situation in American Writing: Seven Questions," *Partisan Review* 6, 4 (Summer 1939), 35.

37. Andreas Huyssen, *After the Great Divide: Modernism, Mass Culture, Postmodernism,* 15.

38. "Periodizing the Sixties." *The Sixties Without Apology,* ed. Sohnya Sayres (Minneapolis: University of Minnesota Press, 1982), 209.

5. The New Times of Postmodernity

1. Hilton Kramer, "Turning Back the Clock," *The New Criterion* (April 1984), 72.

2. Clement Greenberg, "Modernist Painting," *The New Art,* ed. Gregory Battock (New York: Dutton, 1973), 101 (hereafter cited in the text as MP).

3. On this point see Rosalind Krauss, *The Originality of the Avant-Garde and Other Modernist Myths* (Cambridge: MIT Press, 1985), 1; Andreas Huyssen, *After the Great Divide: Modernism, Mass Culture, Postmodernism* 57; Thomas Crow, "Modernism and Mass Culture," in *Modernism and Modernity,* eds. Benjamin H. D. Buchloch, Serge Guilbaut, and David Solkin (Halifax: Press of Nova Scotia College of Art and Design, 1983), 215–264; and T. J. Clark, "Clement Greenberg's Theory of Art," *The Politics of Interpretation,* ed. W. J. T. Mitchell (Chicago: University of Chicago Press, 1983), 203–20.

4. Clement Greenberg, "Avant-Garde and Kitsch," *Partisan Review* 6 (Fall 1939), 34–49; rpt. in *Mass Culture,* ed. Bernard Rosenberg and David Manning White (Chicago: Free Press, 1957), 98 (hereafter cited in the text as AK).

5. Radical critical theory, for Greenberg, forwarded the aesthetic rebellion against bourgeois cultural norms, though the avant-garde would never completely sever its dependence on capital's "umbilical cord of gold" (AK, 101). Nevertheless, the avant-garde task, in his view, was to "keep culture *moving* in the midst of ideological confusion and violence" (AK, 99).

6. For a discussion of de- and re-territorialization, see Gilles Deleuze and Félix Guattari, *A Thousand Plateaus: Capitalism and Schizophrenia,* tr. Brian Massumi (Minneapolis: University of Minnesota Press, 1988).

7. In the absence of absolute values, it is the "minority of the powerful"—

according to Greenberg's genealogical take on medieval and Renaissance art—that perfect formal culture, relegating the "great mass of the exploited" to the ignorance of rudimentary subcultures, folk art, and kitsch. Modernism, however, with its techniques of mass communication and mechanical reproduction, poses a problematic blurring of distinctions that deconstructs this neat binarism. In the twentieth century, he complains, "the axioms of the few are shared by the many; the latter believe superstitiously what the former believe soberly" (AK, 106).

8. For Benjamin, art was inseparable from its particular technological evolution, reaching back from the primitive origins of man-made fetish objects and the ancient craft guilds of founding and stamping bronzes, terra cottas, and coins through modern techniques of woodcut graphics, engraving, etching, movable type printing, and lithography. Such advances, in Benjamin's historicist reading, culminate in our own century's developments in photography, sound recording, and film that at once deauraticize art objects—stripping them of traditional cult values—and, as in Greenberg's more pessimistic account, disperse what were once central icons of artistic distinction and cultural power to the margins of popular entertainment.

9. Walter Benjamin, "The Work of Art in the Age of Mechanical Reproduction," *Illuminations,* tr. Harry Zohn (New York: Schocken Books, 1985), 231 (hereafter cited in the text as WMR).

10. Walter Benjamin, "The Author as Producer" in *Reflections,* tr. Edmund Jephcott (New York: Schocken Books, 1986), 228 (hereafter cited in the text as AP).

11. For example, Marcel Duchamp's whimsical *Fountain* (1917), his infamous exhibition of a urinal as an *objet trouvé* decisively recast the institutional space of the gallery; similarly his shameless signature inscribed like graffiti in the moustache and goatee over Da Vinci's Mona Lisa, (L.H.O.O.Q., 1919) laid bare the formal protocols and promotional systems of aesthetic distinction and taste as arbitrary, not ideal: "And thereby the public was shown, look, your picture ruptures time; the tiniest fragment of everyday life says more than painting. Just as the bloody fingerprint of a murderer on the page of a book says more than the text" (AP, 229). Dadaism's purchase on a functional transformation of the visual arts relied on the shock effects of defamiliarization: finding within the cultural apparatus precise zones and specific sites of privilege, hierarchy, and power in which to stage heretical displays that reversed dominant aesthetic conventions.

12. Unlike the capitalist press that reproduces dominant bourgeois class interests, newspaper publication in Russia, Benjamin argued, offered a "theater of literary confusion," that nevertheless broadcast the political concerns of the writer as producer, and more widely, "the man on the sidelines who believes he has a right to see his own interests expressed" (AP, 300).

13. Consider the dehumanizing regimen, say, of a McDonald's kitchen. In this postmodern sweatshop, employees are trained by video disks to perform the tedious, predesigned regimens for twenty-odd work stations that when meshed together make each franchise a highly efficient fastfood production machine. Each of the twenty-four burgers one cooks in any given batch is part of a completely

Taylorized process: from the premeasured beef patties to the computerized timers for heating each bun, to the automatic catsup, mustard, and special sauce dispensers, to the formulas for the exact measurements of onion bits, pickles, and lettuce each Big Mac receives. Far from possessing even the autonomy of a short-order cook, one serves here purely as a cog in a ninety-second burger assembly line. Moreover, from the monitored soft-drink spigots to the fully automated registers, from the computerized formulas for hiring, scheduling, and organizing workers to the centrally administered accounting systems, every aspect of a McDonald's franchise is organized and scrutinized in minute detail by the panoptic Hamburger Central in Oak Brook, Illinois. A thoroughly postmodern institution, McDonald's presides at any given time over a temporary workforce of some 500,000 teenagers; by the mid-1980s nearly 8 million Americans, had earned their living under the sign of the Golden Arches. See John F. Love, *McDonald's Behind the Golden Arches* (New York: Bantam, 1986) and Barbara Garson, *The Electronic Sweatshop* (New York: Simon and Schuster, 1988), 19.

14. Guy Debord, *Society of the Spectacle* (Detroit: Black and Red, 1983), 100.

15. See Ernest Mandel, *Late Capitalism* (Atlantic Highlands, N.J.: Humanities Press, 1975).

16. Marshall Berman, *All That is Solid Melts in Air: The Experience of Modernity* (New York: Simon and Schuster, 1982), 308.

17. Levittown II, in William Manchester's description, comprised "schools, churches, baseball diamonds, a town hall, factory sidings, parking lots, offices for doctors and dentists, a reservoir, a shopping center, a railroad station, newspaper presses, garden clubs—enough, in short, to support a densely populated city of 70,000, the tenth largest in Pennsylvania." William Manchester, *The Glory and the Dream: A Narrative History of America, 1932–1972* (New York: Bantam Books, 1980), 432.

18. Max Horkheimer and Theodor Adorno, *Dialectic of Enlightenment*, tr. John Cumming (New York: Herder and Herder, 1972), 163.

19. "Edge cities," writes Joel Garreau, "represent the third wave of our lives pushing into new frontiers in this half century. First we moved our homes out past the traditional idea of what constituted a city. This was the suburbanization of America, especially after World War II.

"Then we wearied of returning downtown for the necessities of life, so we moved our marketplaces out to where we lived. This was the malling of America, especially in the 1960s and 1970s.

"Today, we have moved our means of creating wealth, the essence of urbanism—our jobs—out to where most of us have lived and shopped for two generations. That has led to the rise of Edge City." *Edge City: Life on the New Frontier* (New York: Doubleday, 1991), 4.

20. Henri Lefebvre, *Everyday Life in the Modern World*, tr. Sacha Rabinovitch (New York: Harper and Row, 1971), 56 (hereafter cited in the text as EL).

21. See, for example, Robert Venturi's analysis of the Las Vegas Strip: "The zone *of* the highway is a shared order. The zone *off* the highway is an individual

order. The elements of the highway are civic. The buildings and signs are private. In combination they embrace continuity *and* discontinuity, going *and* stopping, clarity *and* ambiguity, cooperation *and* competition, the community *and* rugged individualism. . . .There *is* an order along the sides of the highway. Varieties of activities are juxtaposed on the Strip: service stations, minor motels, and multimillion-dollar casinos. Marriage chapels ("credit cards accepted") converted from bungalows with added neon-lined steeples are apt to appear anywhere toward the downtown end. . . . The rate of obsolescence of a sign seems to be nearer to that of an automobile than that of a building. The reason is not physical degeneration but what competitors are doing around you. The leasing system operated by the sign companies and the possibility of total tax write-off may have something to do with it." Robert Venturi, Denise Scott Brown, and Steven Izenour, *Learning from Las Vegas* (Boston: MIT Press, 1972), 31–32 (hereafter cited in the text as LV).

22. "[T]oday consumption . . . defines precisely *the stage where the commodity is immediately produced as a sign, as sign value,* and where signs (culture) are produced as commodities." Jean Baudrillard, *For a Critique of the Political Economy of the Sign,* tr. Charles Levin (St. Louis: Telos Press, 1981), 147 (hereafter cited in the text as PES).

23. Not just a postmodern condition, the regime of simulacrum—today's proliferation of serial copies, reproductions, and images of all kinds—reaches back to the campaigns of medieval iconoclasts against the worldly representations of the sacred, grounded in the Platonic critique of mimetic art. In Socrates' dialogue with Ion, for example, the repudiation of the rhapsode's art rests on a critique of poetry's third remove from the Real, imitating as it does merely the art, say, of the charioteer, cowherd, or carpenter. Such crafts, in turn, take their models—for example, the design for a particular table, bed, or chair—from ideal and transcendent forms. Insofar as simulacra—what Socrates in *The Sophist* distinguishes as false claimants over true, or iconic, copies—break the lineage of resemblances ranging from the Idea through the worldly appearances of its Essence, to aesthetic copies of the Same, their incorporation of dissimulation, internal difference, and otherness appears sacrilegious, heretical, and demonic within the order of Platonic mimesis. Yet in the Nietzschean inversion of this paradigm, according to Gilles Deleuze, the differential logic that orders the binary pairs Idea/imitation, Essence/appearance, and Model/copy is susceptible to the simulacrum's structural reversal and displacement of all foundational systems of meaning and valuation based in the order of resemblance, repetition, and mimesis. In this deconstructive move, it is the "positive power" of the simulacrum—its nomadic *effondement*—"which negates *both original and copy, both model and reproduction*" in a vertiginous play of difference, unhinged from the regime of hierarchy. "The simulacrum," writes Deleuze, "in rising to the surface, causes the Same and the Like, the model and the copy, to fall under the power of the false (phantasm). It renders the notion of hierarchy impossible in relation to the idea of the order of participation, the fixity of distribution, and the determination of value. It sets up the world of nomadic distributions and consecrated anarchy. Far from being a new foundation, it swallows up all foundation, it assures a universal collapse, but as a positive and joyous

event, as the de-founding (*effondement*): 'Behind every cave [writes Nietzsche]. . . . there is, and must necessarily be, a still deeper cave: an ampler, stranger, richer world beyond the surface, an abyss behind every bottom, beneath every foundation.' " Gilles Deleuze, "Plato and the Simulacrum," tr. Rosalind Krauss, *October* 27 (Winter 1983), 53.

24. Jean Baudrillard, *Simulations,* Paul Foss, Paul Patton, and Philip Beitchman, tr. (New York: Semiotext(e), 1983), 43 (hereafter cited in the text as S).

25. "We must think of the media," he advises, "as if they were, in outer orbit, a sort of genetic code which controls the mutation of the real into the hyperreal, just as the other molecular code controls the passage of the signal from a representative sphere of meaning to the genetic sphere of the programmed signal" (S, 55).

26. Jean Baudrillard, *In the Shadow of the Silent Majorities,* trs. Paul Foss, Paul Patton, and Philip Beitchman (New York: Semiotext(e), 1983), 37 (hereafter cited in the text as SSM).

27. See Paula Rabinowitz, "Women and U.S. Literary Radicalism," in *Writing Red,* eds. Charlotte Nekola and Paula Rabinowitz (New York: Feminist Press, 1987), 2.

28. Jean-François Lyotard, "Complexity and the Sublime," tr. G. Bennington, in *Postmodernism* (London: ICA Documents 4 & 5, 1986), 11 (hereafter cited as ICA). "What kind of thought," Lyotard queries in an echo of Adorno's radical pessimism, "is able to sublate (*Aufheben*) Auschwitz in a general (either empirical or speculative) process towards a universal emancipation." Lyotard, "Defining the Postmodern, etc." in ICA, 6.

29. "Workers' capacity," writes André Gorz, "to recognise the difference between their objective position as cogs in the productive machine and their latent potential as an association of sovereign producers is not inherent in the proletarian condition. The question is under what circumstances this capacity is likely to emerge and develop. Up to now, marxist theory has been unable to produce an answer to this problem. Worse, its predictions have been belied by the facts." André Gorz, *Farewell to the Working Class: An Essay on Post-Industrial Socialism,* 44.

30. "This can be seen in the shift in value from history to the humdrum, from the public sphere to the private sphere. Up till the 60's history leads on the downbeat: the private, the ordinary is only the dark side of the political sphere. . . . Today, there is a reversal of the downbeat and the upbeat: one begins to forsee that ordinary life, men in their banality, could well not be the insignificant side of history—better: that withdrawing into the private could well be *a direct defiance of the political,* a form of actively resisting political manipulation" (SSM, 38, 39).

31. See Jürgen Habermas, *The Theory of Communicative Action,* Vol. I: *Reason and the Rationalization of Society,* tr. Thomas McCarthy (Boston: Beacon Press, 1984), 392.

32. Quoted in Peter Clothier, "Sign Language," *Art News* 88 (Summer 1988), 146.

---

33. Fredric Jameson, "Cognitive Mapping" in *Marxism and the Interpretation of Culture* (Urbana: University of Illinois Press, 1988), 351.

34. Reading this urban terrain through Kevin Lynch's *The Image of the City,* Jameson argues, by way of analogy, that just as today's metropolitan maze of architectural forms and period styles (not to mention more subaltern enclaves of social diversity) virtually disallows any unified "cognitive mapping" of one's urban habitus, likewise the attempt to navigate politically within capital's global spectacle of fragmented commodity exchange (to coordinate, that is, a specific, regional, or grass roots agenda with some more properly macroscale, national or internationalist blueprint for social empowerment) has proved, in the postwar era, historically inconceivable. Nevertheless beyond a simple critique of advanced consumer society, the now utopian project of charting some alternative, multilayered, and cosmopolitan terrain, however limited to the aesthetic dimension, would seem indispensable in negotiating one's way through the postmodern condition. "An aesthetic of cognitive mapping in this sense," Jameson insists, "is an integral part of any socialist political project" (CM, 353).

35. Mullican, writes Kathy O'Dell, "engages in a kind of mapmaking by exploring the terrain of the unconscious through hypnosis, commandeering the imagination on fantasy voyages into perspectival space and maneuvering the viewer-reader across the distance between signs and their meanings." Kathy O'Dell, "Through the Image Maze," *Art in America* 76 (January 1988), 119.

36. Quoted in Clothier 147.

37. Jean Baudrillard, "The Ecstasy of Communication," in *The Anti-Aesthetic,* ed. Hal Foster (Port Townsend, Wash.: Bay Press, 1985), 127, 133.

38. A great deal of study, of course, has supplemented the Frankfurt school's postwar critique of the culture industry, the conglomerate print and telecommunications media, global networks of mass satellite distribution, and the social policy issues and questions these new developments compel. See, in particular, Herbert I. Schiller, *Culture, Inc.: The Corporate Takeover of Public Expression* (New York: Oxford University Press, 1989).

39. Michel de Certeau, *The Practice of Everyday Life,* tr. Steven Rendall (Berkeley: University of California Press, 1984), 31.

40. It was the influence of Sergei Tretyakov and the postsynthetic cubist collaborations of the Russian Supremamatists, Constructivists, and Laboratory Period figures that guided Benjamin's thinking on the avant-garde turn (brought about by photography, film, and other mechanically reproducible media) away from the modernist paradigm of aesthetic representation—its cult of artistic genius and the *aura* of the unique work of art. By taking into account an artwork's material conditions of exhibition, distribution, and audience reception, as part of its productive apparatus, the Russian Constructivists decisively challenged the abstract and self-reflexive values of modern formalism in favor of the more critical representations of documentary photomontage and photocollage. The new cultural logic of mechanical reproduction, occasioned by photography and film, not only unsettled the traditional divide between high and low aesthetics but deconstructed conven-

tional oppositions separating art from advertising, agitation, and propaganda. No longer invested with the aura of a ritual object, the artwork as such was opened to the vital dialectic between intrinsic form and the politics of mass persuasion.

41. Roland Barthes, *Mythologies,* tr. Annette Lavers (London: Jonathan Cape, 1972), 92 (hereafter cited in the text as M).

42. Thus in his famous example from "Myth Today" the *Paris-Match* image of the black soldier who stands at attention before the French tricolour, as a signifier, suffers a certain *deformation.* Here the specific historicity of post-colonial domination is drained from the stereotyped figure who salutes the myth of French empire. Appropriated by the ideological code of French imperialism, the black subject of colonial rule is distorted to communicate, in Barthes' reading, the patronizing message *"look at this good Negro who salutes like one of our own boys"* (M, 124).

43. "Today, at the level of mass communications, it appears that the linguistic message is indeed present in every image: as title, caption, accompanying press article, film dialogue, comic strip balloon." Roland Barthes, *Image/Music/Text,* tr. Stephen Heath (New York: Hill and Wang, 1977), 38. While Barthes' early theory of the mythic imaginary followed the traditional Marxist view of ideology as a "false" cultural inversion of history that, through the "science" of semiology, deserved to be demystified and somehow "righted," he later espoused a more fundamental deconstruction of the sign ("semioclasm") and a more rigorous description of the linguistic ensemble of "reference, citation, stereotype" that constitutes a given *sociolect.* See Steven Ungar, *Roland Barthes: The Professor of Desire* (Lincoln: University of Nebraska Press, 1983), 168.

44. See Erving Goffman, *Gender Advertisements* (Cambridge: Harvard University Press, 1979).

45. See Simone de Beauvoir, *The Second Sex,* tr. H. M. Parshley (New York: Knopf, 1957), 132.

46. Craig Owens, for example, betrays a certain critical defensiveness in delimiting the work's communicative meaning when he claims that it alludes "not, I think, to repressed homosexuality, but rather to the fact that physical contact has itself become a social ceremony." Craig Owens, "The Medusa Effect or, The Spectacular Ruse" in *We Won't Play Nature to Your Culture, Barbara Kruger* (London: ICA, 1983), 7.

47. Jenny Holzer, "Jenny Holzer's Language Games," interview with J. Siegel *Arts Magazine,* 60, 4 (December 1985), 67 (hereafter cited in the text as LG).

48. "If, by hypothesis," Derrida writes, "we maintain that the opposition of speech to language is absolutely rigorous, then *différance* would be not only the play of differences within language but also the relation of speech to language, the detour through which I must pass in order to speak, the silent promise I must make; and this schemata, of message to code, etc. (Elsewhere I have attempted to suggest that this *différance* in language, and in the relation of speech and language, forbids the essential dissociation of speech and language that Saussure, at another level of his discourse, traditionally wished to delineate. The practice of a language or of a code supposing a play of forms without a determined and

invariable substance, and also supposing in the practice of this play a retention and protention of differences, a spacing and a temporization, a play of traces— all this must be a kind of writing before the letter, an archi-writing without a present origin, without archi-. Whence the regular erasure of the archi-, and the transformation of general semiology into grammatology, this latter executing a critical labor on everything within semiology, including the central concept of the sign, that maintained metaphysical presuppositions incompatible with the motif of *différance*.)'' Jacques Derrida, "Différance," *Margins of Philosophy,* tr. Alan Bass (Chicago: University of Chicago Press, 1982), 15.

49. Jenny Holzer, "Wordsmith, An Interview with Jenny Holzer," with Bruce Ferguson, *Art in America,* 74 (December 1986), 113.

50. Paul Taylor, "We are the Word: Jenny Holzer sees aphorism as art," *Vogue* 178 (November 1988), 390.

51. Quoted in Colin Westerbeck, *Jenny Holzer.* Rhona Hoffman Gallery, Chicago *Artforum International Magazine* 25 (May 1987), 155

52. Donald Kuspit, "Gallery Leftism" *Vanguard* 12, 9 (November 1983), 24 (hereafter cited in the text as GL).

53. Jeanne Siegel, "Nancy Spero: Woman as Protagonist," *Arts Magazine* 62 (September 1987), 12.

54. Nancy Spero, "Sky Goddess, Egyptian Acrobat," *Artforum* 26 (March 1988), 104 (hereafter cited in the text as SG).

55. Jacques Derrida, "The Theater of Cruelty and the Closure of Representation," in *Writing and Difference,* tr. Alan Bass (Chicago: University of Chicago Press, 1978), 240 (hereafter cited in the text as TC).

56. Antonin Artaud, "Letter to Roger Blin," September 1945, quoted in TC, 244.

57. Jacques Derrida, "La Parole Soufflée," in *Writing and Difference,* 189.

58. Julia Kristeva, *Revolution in Poetic Language,* Margaret Waller, tr. (New York: Columbia University Press, 1984), 186. For a critique of l'écriture féminine see Gayatri Chakravorty Spivak, *In Other Worlds: Essays in Cultural Politics* (New York: Methuen, 1987), 134–53; and Editorial Collective, "Variations sur des thèmes communs," in *Questions féministes.* 1 (November 1977), tr. Yvonne Rochette-Ozzello; rpt. "Common Themes," in *New French Feminisms: An Anthology,* eds. Elaine Marks and Isabelle de Courtivron (New York: Schocken Books, 1981), 213.

59. Hélène Cixous, "The Laugh of the Medusa," in *New French Feminisms,* 257.

60. Laura Mulvey's seminal essay "Visual Pleasure and Narrative Cinema" adapts Freud's theory of scopophilia in *Three Essays on Sexuality* and Lacan's model of the imaginary stage to a feminist reading of how women are objectified as an erotic spectacle for male voyeurism and scopophilia: "But in psychoanalytic terms, the female figure poses a deeper problem. She also connotes something that the look continually circles around but disavows: her lack of a penis, implying a threat of castration and hence unpleasure. Ultimately, the meaning of woman is sexual difference, the absence of the penis is visually ascertainable, the material

evidence on which is based the castration complex essential for the organization of entrance to the symbolic order and the Law of the Father . . . This second avenue, fetishistic scopophilia, builds up the physical beauty of the object, transforming it into something satisfying in itself. The first avenue, voyeurism, on the contrary, has associations with sadism: pleasure lies in ascertaining guilt (immediately through punishment or forgiveness)." Laura Mulvey, "Visual Pleasure and Narrative Cinema," *Art After Modernism: Rethinking Representation,* ed. Brian Wallis (New York: The New Museum of Contemporary Art, 1984), 368.

61. Gayatri Spivak, *In Other Worlds,* 151.

62. "It is at times said that woman's language is closer to the body, to sexual pleasure, to direct sensations, and so on, which means that the body could express itself directly without social meditation and that, moreover, this closeness to the body and to nature would be subversive. In our opinion, there is no such thing as a direct relation to the body. To advocate a direct relation to the body is therefore not subversive because it is equivalent to denying the reality and the strength of social mediations, the very same ones that oppress us in our bodies. At most, one would advocate a different socialization of the body, but without searching for a true and eternal nature, for this search takes us away from the most effective struggle against the socio-historical contexts in which human beings are and will always be trapped. If there is one natural characteristic of human beings, it is that human beings are by nature social beings" (219).

63. Fredric Jameson, "Hans Haacke and the Cultural Logic of Postmodernism," in *Hans Haacke: Unfinished Business,* ed. Brian Wallis (Cambridge: MIT Press, 1986), 42.

64. Peter Kihss, "Liability is Fixed in New Slum Bill," *New York Times,* February 10, 1966, quoted in Rosalyn Deutsche, "Property Values: Hans Haacke, Real Estate, and the Museum," *Hans Haacke, Unfinished Business,* 31.

65. Stuart Hall, "The Toad in the Garden: Thatcherism Among the Theorists," *Marxism and the Interpretation of Culture,* Cary Nelson and Lawrence Grossberg, eds. (Urbana: University of Illinois Press, 1988), 39.

66. Haacke, "Museums, Managers of Consciousness," in *Hans Haacke, Unfinished Business,* 65.

67. Hans Haacke, "On Social Grease," in *Hans Haacke, Unfinished Business,* 154.

68. Hans Haacke, *Hans Haacke, Unfinished Business,* 70–71.

Epilogue

1. Judy Baca, "Our People are the Internal Exiles," in *Cultures in Contention,* eds. Douglas Kahn and Diane Neumaier (Seattle: Real Comet Press, 1985), 73.

2. Rosalyn Deutsche and Cara Gendel Ryan, "The Fine Art of Gentrification," *October* 31 (1984), 106.

3. Peter Dykstra, "Twenty Years: No Time Off for Good Behavior," *Greenpeace Magazine* (January/February/March 1991), 2.

4. December 1987 interview quoted in Steve Durland, "Witness: The Guerrilla Theater of Greenpeace," *Art In the Public Interest,* ed. Arlene Raven (Ann Arbor: University of Michigan Research Press, 1989), 35.

5. Judy Christrup, "Our Twentieth Anniversary," *Greenpeace Magazine* (January/February/March 1991), 13.

6. Suzanne Lacy and Leslie Labowitz, "Feminist Media Strategies for Political Performance," in *Cultures in Contention,* 129.

7. See Elaine Showalter, "Feminist Criticism in the Wilderness," in *The New Feminist Criticism* (New York: Pantheon Books, 1985), 243–70.

8. Suzanne Lacy, "Fractured Space," in *Art in the Public Interest,* 299.

9. Cindy Ruskin, *The Quilt: Stories from the Names Project* (New York: Pocket Books, 1988), 12.

10. See Douglas Crimp and Adam Rolston, *AIDSDEMOGRAPHICS* (Seattle: Bay Press, 1990), 39, 54.

11. Douglas Crimp, "Portraits of People with AIDS," in *Cultural Studies,* 120.

12. On Queer Nation and "queer theory," see Lauren Berlant and Elizabeth Freeman, "Queer Nationality," *Boundary 2* 19 (Spring 1992), 149–80; and Teresa de Laurentis, ed., "Queer Theory: Lesbian and Gay Sexualities" issue of *Differences,* vol. 5, no. 2 (1991).

13. ACT UP, FDA ACTION HANDBOOK, quoted in Douglas Crimp and Adam Rolston, *AIDSDEMOGRAPHICS,* 115.

14. Adrienne Rich, "Compulsory Heterosexuality and Lesbian Existence" in *Blood, Bread, and Poetry* (New York: Norton, 1986), 23–75.

Picture Credits

Introduction: The Vision Thing

0.1. Courtesy Hans Haacke.

1. Revisionary Modernism

1.5–1.14. Courtesy John Calmann and King, Ltd.
1.15–1.20. Courtesy Adele Lozowick.

2. War of Position and the Old Left

2.10. Beinecke Library, Yale University.
2.19. Courtesy Fisk University Collections, Nashville, Tennessee.
2.24. Courtesy Louisiana State University Press.
2.27. Courtesy San Francisco Art Institute.
2.28, 2.29. Courtesy Detroit Institute of Arts.
2.31. Museo del Palacio de Bellas Artes.
2.41. Archives of American Art, Smithsonian Institution.
2.49. Courtesy Adele Lozowick.

3. Feminism in the Popular Front

3.1–3.8, 3.10. WPA photograph collection, Archives of American Art, Smithsonian Institution.

3.9. San Francisco, Pacific Stock Exchange.

4. Transpersonal Poetics

4.2. Copyright © 1986 Sue Coe. Courtesy Galerie St. Etienne, New York.

4.3. Courtesy Ilona Granet.

5. The New Times of Postmodernity

5.1. Courtesy Michael Klein, New York.

5.2–5.6. Courtesy Barbara Kruger.

5.7–5.8. Courtesy Jenny Holzer and Barbara Gladstone Gallery, New York City.

5.9–5.10. Courtesy Jenny Holzer and Barbara Gladstone Gallery, New York City.

5.11. Courtesy Jenny Holzer and Barbara Gladstone Gallery, New York City.

5.12–5.15. Courtesy of the artist and Josh Baer Gallery, New York City.

5.16–5.21. Courtesy Hans Haacke.

5.22. Courtesy John Weber Gallery, New York City.

Epilogue: Acting Up

E.1, E.2. Courtesy Judy Baca.

E.3. Courtesy Greenpeace.

E.4–E.6. Courtesy Suzanne Lacy.

E.7, E.8. Courtesy Matt Herron.

E.9, E.10. Courtesy Donald Moffett.

Index

Aaron, Daniel, *Writers on the Left: Episodes in American Literary Communism,* 272n9

Abbott, Berenice, 177

Abernethy, M. A., 108

ACT UP, 94, 271n44

Adams, Henry, 148

Adorno, Theodor, 5–6, 298n28; on advertising, 217; "Letters to Walter Benjamin," 267n20; "Lyric Poetry and Society," 191

African-American aesthetic (also black aesthetic), 55, 66–68, 71–72, 73, 86, 103

Aglietta, Michel, 12; consumerism, 269n35; on neo-fordism, 270n41

AIDS, 18, 258–61

Alston, Charles, 179

Althusser, Louis, "Ideology and the State," 293n29

Altman, Natan, "The Storming of the Winter Palace," 32

Americanism, 11, 122–38

Anderson, Mary, 177

Anderson, Sherwood, 46

Andrews, Bruce, 196–97

Anti-Stalinism, 17, 105–6

Aptheker, Herbert, 13–14

Arac, Jonathan, 210

Arens, Egmont, 46

Arnold, Matthew, 203

Ashbery, John, 196

Astaire, Adele, 70

Atkins, J. Alston, 99

Avant-garde, 3, 35; aesthetics, 38; American, 188, 199, 210; American, Russian, European compared, 8; cross-cultural boundaries, 55; interbellum, 3; *Language* movement, 189; modernists, 189; Russian, 28, 31, 45, 197–98, 214; styles, 45; Soviet, 274n24; traditional, 198

Avery, Francis, *Maternity or the History of Obstetrics,* 180–81

Baca, Judy, 253
Baker, Houston, 10
Bakhtin, Mikhail, 170, 197
Barthes, Roland, 166; "The Death of the Author," 191; on deconstructionism, 227; *Image/Music/Text,* 300n43
Baudrillard, Jean, 11, 195, 203, 225, 198; cultural simulation, 221; postmodernism, 219; terrorism, 228
Bell, Daniel, postwar "new class," 269n30
Bell, Josephine, 24
Benet, Stephen Vincent, 287n3
Benet, William Rose, 287n3
Benjamin, Walter, 5–6, 14, 105; analysis of aesthetics, 22; "The Artist as Producer," 38; canon formation, 247; cultural modernity, 214; cultural production, 126; deauraticization, 176; Russian avant-gardes, 214
Bennet, Gwendolyn, 78, 91
Bennett, Tony, "Putting Policy into Cultural Studies," 267n13
Benton, Thomas Hart, 184
Berman, Marshall, 216
Bernay, Edward, *Crystallizing Public Opinion,* "Facial Expressions in Advertisements," 128
Bernstein, Charles, 189; on Russian formalist theories, 197; "The Dollar Value of Poetry," 190; "Thought's Measure," 192
Bhabha, Homi K., 5
Biddle, George, 175
Bishop, Elizabeth, 161
Black, MacKnight, 149
Blake, William, "The Tyger," 155
Bloch, Lucienne, 177, 184
Bloom, Harold, 1
Bly, Robert, 189
Boccioni, Umberto, 147
Bogdanov, Aleksandr, 30, 36
Bohlen, Marie, 254
Bone, Robert, 73
Boss, Homer, 139
Bourdieu, Pierre, 4
Bourke-White, Margaret, 166

Bourne, Randolph, 24, 27, 36, 51, 188, 205; "Trans-National America," 19; "The War and Intellectuals," 20
Brawley, Benjamin, 86, 95
Brecht, Bertolt, 14, 214
Briggs, Cyril, 277n11
Brik, Osip, 33, 197
Bromige, David, *My Poetry,* 193
Brooks, Gwendolyn, 85
Brooks, Van Wyck, 44, 46
Browder, Earl, 283n76
Brown, Sterling, 55, 96, 103
Bruce-Briggs, B., *The New Class?,* 269n32; postwar "new class," 269n30
Buchloch, Benjamin H. D., 212; "From Faktura to Factography," 274n24
Buren, Daniel, 230, 247
Bürger, Peter, *Theory of the Avant-Garde,* 6, 267–68n23
Burke, Kenneth, 2, 14, 36, 125; "Revolutionary Symbolism in America," 200
Burlak, Ann, 162
Burliak, David, 29, 46, 91, 273n20; "The Voice of an Impressionist: In Defense of Painting," 272n12
Buttita, A. J., 108
Burnshaw, Stanley, 158; on Macleish, 160

Cahill, Holger, 176
Caldwell, Erskine, *You Have Seen Their Faces,* 166
Calverton, V. F., 105, 108
Canon formation, 51, 53, 103, 191, 213, 245
Carmichael, Stokeley, 75
Chagall, Marc, 29, 33, 40
Chambers, Whittaker, 132
Chase, Stuart, 46
Cheney, Ralph, 52; contrast of Russian and American culture, 134
Chernyshevsky, Nikolai, *The Aesthetic Relations of Art to Reality,* 272n11
Chia, Sandro, 248

Christup, Judy, 256
Cixous, Hélène, 88, 161, 241; "The Laugh of the Medusa," 242
Clark, Eleanor, 161
Clark, T. J., "Clement Greenberg's Theory of Art," 294n3
Cleghorn, Sarah, "Golf Links," 21
Clemente, Francesco, 248
Clements, Travers, 108
Codrescu, Andrei, 198
Coe, Sue, 206
Communism, 9–10, 13; "heroic," 30, 32
Conroy, Jack, 52, 107, 156; "Art Above the Battle?" 130
Constructivism, 28–35, 39, 115, 259, 299–300n40
Coolidge, Clark, 189, 197; *Mine,* 193; *Polaroid,* 192
Covarrubias, Miguel, 68–70
Cowley, Malcolm, 160
Creely, Robert, 189
Crimp, Douglas, 260–61
Crow, Thomas, *Modernism and Modernity,* 268n24; 294n3
Cullen, Charles, 78; illustrations in *Ebony and Topaz,* 80, 81; "Tableau" (drawing), 94
Cullen, Countee, 55, 70, 84, 86–87, 279n35; *Caroling Dusk,* 86
cummings, e.e., 200

Dadaism, 3, 28, 147, 197, 214, 227, 295n11
Dahlen, Beverly, 194
Dali, Salvadore, 70
Dana, Henry Wadsworth Longfellow, 36
Darragh, Tina, 189; *Pi in the Skye,* 192
Davidson, Jo, 28
Davies, Alan, 195–96
Davis, Angela, 13–14
Davis, Frank M., 100
Davis, John, 91
Davis, Stuart, 46, 179
de Beauvior, Simone, 229

Debord, Guy, 11, 203, 215, 217; "society of spectacle," 230
de Certeau, Michel, 16, 226
Dehn, Adolph, 46
De Kooning, William, 179
Deleuze, Gilles: "Plato and the Simulacrum," 297n23; *A Thousand Plateaus: Capitalism and Schizophrenia,* 270n40
Dell, Floyd, 44, 46, 139, 152; "Education and Art in Soviet Russia," 27
Derrida, Jacques, 300–301n48; on Artaud, 240
Deutsche, Babette, 46
Deutsche, Rosalyn, 254
Diaghilev, Sergei, *"Mir Iskusstva,"* 28
Dodge, Mabel, 21
Dos Passos, John, 36, 46, 108; on Rivera, 111
Douglas, Aaron, 70, 91, 96, 97, 102; ad for *Nigger Heaven,* 74; *Aspects of Negro Life,* 65–66
Dreiser, Theodore, 70, 95
Du Bois, W. E. B., 74, 86, 97; in *The New Negro,* 81
Duchamp, Marcel, 147; "Fountain," 295n11
Dunbar-Nelson, Alice, 86–87
Dunjee, Roscoe, 100
DuPlessis, Rachel Blau, 194
Durland, Steve, "Witness: The Guerrilla Theater of Greenpeace," 303n4
Dykstra, Peter, 255

Eastman, Crystal, 20
Eastman, Max, 20, 21, 26–27, 39, 46, 75, 105, 139, 108, 188; *The Colors of Life,* 35–36; on dehumanization of Fordism, 126; on proletcult values, 106
Ehrenbourg, Ilya, 109
Eichenbaum, Boris, 197
Eisenstein, Serge, 4, 39; *Film Sense,* 172
Eliot, T. S., 4, 53, 213, 222; *The Waste Land,* 154, 203
Ellis, Fred, 50; "Two Civilizations" (poster), 133

Enzensberger, Hans Magnus, 7
Evan, Robert, "Painting and Politics: The Case of Diego Rivera," 112
Evergood, Philip, *The Story of Richmond,* 179

Fairbanks, Douglas, 132
Faucet, Jessie, 84, 87
Fauset, Arthur Huff, 78; "Intelligentsia," 94–95
Fearing, Kenneth, 153, 189, 199; on parodies of advertising, 200; works: "Ad," 204; "Aphrodite Metropolis (2)," 201; "Jack Knuckles Falters," 202; "X Minus X," 204
Filene, Edward, 128
Fischer, Norman, *On Whether Or Not to Believe in Your Mind,* 193
Fisher, Rudolph, 84
Fitzgerald, F. Scott, 70
Folgare, Luciano, 147
Ford, Edsel, 117
Ford, Henry, *My Life and Work,* 269n33
Ford, James, 277n11
Fordism, 11, 15, 20, 122–38
Foucault, Michel, 165; "What Is an Author?" 191; and "microphysics of power," 226
Frampton, Hollis, 209
Frank, Waldo, 46, 108
Frankfurt School of Social Research, 3, 5, 266n10
Fraser, Kathleen, 194
Freelon, Allan Randall, 78, 82
Freeman, Joseph, 27, 36, 41, 45, 56, 108–9; on touring the Soviet Union, 132; *Voices of October,* 37
Freud, Sigmund, *The Interpretation of Dreams,* 240; *Metapsychological Supplement to the Theory of Dreams,* 240
Funaroff, Sol, 52, 153; on visionary romanticism, 155; on Williams, 107–8; works: "Dusk of the Gods," 158; "The Spider and the Clock," 155; "What the Thunder Said: A Fire Sermon," 10, 154

Futurism, 28, 147, 268n26; Italian, 116, 272n13; Russian, 126, 227

Gan, Alexei, 33
Garreau, Joel, 296n19
Garson, Barbara, *The Electronic Sweatshop,* 296n13
Garvey, Marcus, 83
Gates, Henry Louis, Jr., 66, 84, 88, 280n45
Gay literature, 258–63
Gellert, Hugo, 45, 46, 99, 139, 140, 256; defense of counterculture, 122; founding *New Masses* with Freeman and Gold, 139; idealized proletariat, 141; lithographs, 135; on male-gendered visual codes, 138; support for advertising, 132
Gender critique, 227–44, 250
Gershwin, George, 69
Gilman, Charlotte Perkins, 222
Giovanitti, Arturo, 46
Glaspell, Susan, 46
Glass, Philip, 193
Glintenkamp, Henry, "Physically Fit," 24–25
Goffman, Erving, 229
Gold, Michael, 10, 39, 41, 45–46, 53, 60, 86, 95, 101, 107, 153, 222; ideal of worker correspondent, 156; on Macleish, 160; parody of Whitman, 158; on touring in the Soviet Union, 132; works: "American Ideals of Poetry," 36–37; "A New Program for Writers," 47; "A Strange Funeral in Braddock," 169; "Towards Proletarian Literature," 36
Goncharova, Natalya, 29, 272n12, 273n20
Gorky, Arshile, *Aviation: Evolution of Forms Under Aerodynamic Limitations,* 181
Gorz, Andre, 154; *Farewell to the Working Class: An Essay on Post-Industrial Socialism,* 298n29
Gouldner, Alvin W., *The Future of Intellectuals and the Rise of the New Class,* 269n32

Graff, Gerald, 5
Graham, Marcus, *An Anthology of Revolutionary Poetry,* 21–22
Gramsci, Antonio, 3, 11, 12, 14; on Americanism, 125; cultural sphere, 124–25; war of position, 123
Gran Fury, 18, 94, 261; on Haacke, 261–62
Granet, Ilona, 206
Greenberg, Clement, 212; on Picasso over Norman Rockwell, 213
Greenpeace, 254–56, 271n44
Greenwood, Marion, 177, 184
Gregory, Horace, 153; praising Rukeyser, 287n3
Grey, Darrell, 198
Grimké, Angelina Weld, 84, 86–88
Gropper, William, 46, 60; "Defend the Soviet Union" (cartoon), 136; on antiwar ads, 205; withdrawl from art exhibition, 122
Guattari, Félix, 270n40
Guerrero, Xavier, 110, 183

Haacke, Hans, 3, 15, 244–51, 271n44; expulsion from museum, 232; works being banned, 242
Habermas, Jürgen, 5, 222
Haldeman-Julius, E., 126–27
Hall, Gus, 13
Hall, Stuart: neo-Gramscian articulation, 266n9; on postmodern subversion, 226; "Thatcherism," 248
Halper, Albert, 112; recalling Gellert, 140
Harlem Renaissance, 4, 75, 181
Hayes, Alfred, 169
Hayes, Vertis, 181
Hayford, Gladys May Casely, 87–89
Haynes, Jack, "Scottsboro Boys Chant," 53–54
Hearst, William Randolph, 131
Heath, Stephen, on repetition, 294n36
Hebdige, Dick, 276n6; on postmodern subversion, 226
Hejinian, Lyn, 192; *My Life,* 193; *Writing Is an Aid to Memory,* 189

Hemingway, Ernest, 287n2
Herbst, Josephine, 138
Hershman, Edna, *Recreational Activities* (mural), 185
Hine, Lewis, 21, *Pittsburgh Survey,* 288n14
Holzer, Jenny, 15, 230–37, 251; censorship issues, 244; subversion of sexism, 227
Honey, Maureen, 86
Horkheimer, Max, 217
Hoving, Thomas, 224
Howe, Fanny, *Introduction to the World,* 194
Howe, Irving, 48, 108
Howe, Susan, 194
Hoyt, Elizabeth, 128
Hughes, Langston, 44, 70, 74, 84, 91, 95–96, 100; *Fine Clothes to a Jew,* 68; "Park Bench," 102; *The Weary Blues,* 68
Hull, Gloria, 86, 279–80n35
Hume, David, 103
Humphries, Rolfe, 160
Hurston, Zora Neale, 68, 70, 84, 91, 102
Huyssen, Andreas, 7–8, 210, 294n3; *After the Great Divide: Modernism, Mass Culture, Postmodernism,* 266n11; on gender, 268n30

Industrial Workers of the World (IWW), 20, 48
Irigaray, Luce, 88
Ishijaki, Eitaro, "Emancipation of Negro Slaves," 181

Jakobson, Roman, 197
James, C. L. R., 82–83
Jameson, Fredric, 2–3, 18, 194, 216, 270n36; on class struggle, 210; on global consumer society, 224; on Haacke, 245; homeopathic intervention, 249; "postindividualistic," 267n18
Jeffers, Robinson, 46

Jerome, V. J.: "A Negro Mother to Her Child," 54–55, 205; *Intellectuals and the War,* 205
Johnson, Charles S., 79–80
Johnson, Georgia Douglas, 84
Johnson, Hall, 102
Johnson, Helene, 87
Johnson, James Weldon, 55, 63, 70, 74–75, 87, 89, 96, 103; *The Book of American Negro Poetry,* 86; *God's Trombones,* 65; "Let My People Go," 65; preface to *The Book of American Negro Poetry,* 77
Jones, Cleve, 259
Josephson, Matthew, 36; on financial power of advertising, 128–29
Joyce, James, *Ulysses,* 203

Kalaidjian, Walter, *Languages of Liberation: The Social Text in Contemporary American Poetry,* 268n27
Kalar, Joseph, 52, 107, 153; industrial design and social processes, 152; works: "Flagwaver," 157; "Papermill," 155–56; "Warm Day in Papermill Town," 156–57
Kandinsky, Vladimir, 33; "Content and Form," 272n12
Kant, Immanuel, *Critique of Judgment,* 267n23
Kautsky, Karl, 56; orthodox communism, 164
Keats, John, 202; "Ode to a Nightingale," 284n104
Kellogg, Paul V., 20
Kenner, Hugh, *The Pound Era,* 1, 51
Kerlin, Robert, *Negro Poets and Their Poems,* 86
Kerr, Florence, 177
Khlebnikov, Velimir (Victor), 91; transrational poetics, 197
Kingsley, Robert, 249
Kipnis, Laura, 270n36
Klehr, Harvey, 276n3
Knopf, Alfred A., 70
Kramer, Hilton, "Turning Back the Clock: Art and Politics in 1984," 211
Krauss, Rosalind, *The Originality of the Avant-Garde and Other Modernist Myths,* 294n3
Kristeva, Julia, 88; *La Revolution du Langage Poetique,* 241
Kruger, Barbara, 15, 227–30, 251, 271n44; in censorship issues, 244; *Disarming Images: Art of Nuclear Disarmament,* 228; subversion of sexism, 227
Kunitz, Joshua, 39, 60
Kuspit, Donald, 212, 237
Kuznetsov, Pavel, 272n12

Labowitz, Leslie, 256
Laclau, Ernesto, 12–13, 15; and Chantal Mouffe, *Hegemony and Socialist Strategy: Towards a Radical Democratic Politics,* 267n18; neo-Gramscian articulation, 266n9
Lacy, Susan, 18, 256–58; *The Crystal Quilt,* 258; and Leslie Labowitz, 256
Ladd Jr., Everett Carl, postwar "new class," 269n30
Larionov, Mikhail, 29, 272nn12, 13, 273n20
Larsen, Neil: "Postmodernism and Imperialism: Theory and Politics in Latin America," 269n36; rejection of Laclau and Mouffe, 270n36;
Lawrence, D. H., 46
Lefebvre, Henri, 217–18, 222
Lenin, Vladimir, 34; Letter to the American Workingmen, 27
Lentricchia, Frank, 284n96
Lewis, David, 73
Lewis, H. H., 52, 153, 156
Lewis, Sinclair, 95
Lewis, Wyndham, 147
Lin, Maya, 258–59
Lippard, Lucy, 239
Lissitzky, Eliezer, 31, 33, 39, 40, 147; "Drive Red Wedges into White Troops!," 32
Little Elvis, 261

Locke, Alain, 78, 80, 84, 86, 89, 102, 105, 279n35; "1928: A Retrospective Review," 67
Loper, Steve, 255
Lorentz, Pare, *The Roosevelt Year: A Photographic Record,* 288n14
Love, John, *McDonald's: Behind the Golden Arches,* 296n13
Lowell, Amy, 87
Lozowick, Louis, 39–40, 46, 48–49; articles and essays, 40; idealized portraits, 256; on Russian avant-gardes, 149; withdrawl from art exhibition, 122; works:"Brooklyn Bridge," 40, 43; "Buy a Poppy," 41; "Lynching," 41; "New York," 40, 41; "Strike Scene," 41, 44; "Tanks #1," 40, 42; "Tear Gas," 41; "Thanksgiving Dinner," 41, 45
Luhan, Mabel Dodge, 278n22
Lukács, Georg, one-dimensional spectacle, 190
Lynch, Kevin, *The Image of the City,* 299n34
Lyotard, Jean-François, 4, 57, 220; on repetition, 294n36

Maas, Willard, 163
McCarthy, Mary, 161
McDougald, Elise Johnson, "The Double Task: The Struggle of Negro Women for Sex and Race Emancipation," 89
McGann, Jerome, 276n58; "Contemporary Poetry and Alternative Routes," 293n22
McKay, Claude, 36, 46, 84, 102, 139; *Home to Harlem,* 68
McKeon, Richard, 36
Macleish, Archibald, "Comrade Levine," 160; "Frescoes for Mr. Rockefeller's City," 160; on World War II, 205
Macleod, Norman, 52
Mac Low, Jackson, *Asymmetries,* 192
Maddow, Ben, 169; "Remembering Hart Crane," 154; review of Rukeyser, 170–71
Magil, A. B., 60

Malevich, Kazimir, 29, 33; "From Cubism and Futurism to Suprematism: The New Painterly Realism," 29; on modernism, 273n14
Mandel, Ernest, 216
Marcuse, Herbert, 6
Marinetti, F. T., 3
Marling, Karal Ann, "American Art and the American Woman," 291n33
Marx, Karl: *A Contribution to the Critique of Political Economy,* 167, 171; *The German Ideology,* 167
Mason, Charlotte, 101
Matthiessen, F. O., 161; and "Rukeyser Imbroglio," 161
Mayakovsky, Vladimir, 39, 43–44, 91, 273n20; "Agitation and Advertisement," 34; "Shrine or Factory?" speech, 31; transrational poetics, 197
Medvedev, P. N., *The Formal Method in Literary Scholarship,* 197
Mencken, H. L., 70, 95
Metahistory, 2
Minor, Robert, 22–23
Mitchell, W. J. T., *Iconology: Image, Text, Ideology,* 288–89n17
Modernism, 1, 2, 4, 5, 212, 295n7; high, 9; historical limits of 274n24; literary, 51
Modleski, Tania, *Studies in Mass Entertainment,* 266n10
Mouffe, Chantal, 12–13, 16; *Hegemony and Socialist Strategy,* 267n18; neo-Gramscian articulation, 266n9
Moyers, Bill, *The Power of the Word (TV),* 191
Mullican, Matt, 15, 222–25, 251
Mulvey, Laura, "Visual Pleasure and Narrative Cinema," 301–302n60
Mumford, Lewis, 46, 152
Munson, Gorham, 152
Murray, Albert, 281n59

Naison, Mark, 63
Naumberg, Nancy, 163

Negri, Ramon P., 112
Nelson, Cary, 2; *Repression and Recovery: Modern American Poetry and the Politics of Cultural Memory,* 52, 55, 266n18; neo-Gramscian articulation, 266n9
Newell, James Michael, 184; *The Evolution of Western Civilization,* 179
Nugent, Bruce, 68, 84, 86, 91, 92–94; "Drawing for Mulattoes—Number 2," 71; "Drawing for Mulattoes—Number 3," 72; "Carus" (drawing), 93
Nystrom, Paul, 128

O'Dell, Kathy, "Through the Image Maze," 299n35
O'Neill, Eugene, 46
Olsen, Tillie, 239
Olson, Charles, 189; *The Maximus Poems,* 239
Orozco, José Clemente, 110, 179, 183
Orwell, George, *1984,* 211
Owen, Chandler, 75
Owens, Craig, "The Medusa Effect; or, The Spectacular Ruse," 300n46

Peirce, Charles Sanders, 290n27
Perelman, Bob, 189, 197; postmodern critique, 199; "Seduced by Analogy," 207–9
Perkins, Frances, 176
Perloff, Marjorie: *The Dance of the Intellect,* 268n26, 293n22; *Futurist Moment: Avant-Garde, Avant Guerre, and the Language of Rupture,* 268n26; on Hejinian, 193; "Pound/Stevens, whose era?" 1
Pfeil, Fred, 198, 199
Phelps, George, 128
Phillips, William, 189, 199; disagreement with Matthiessen and Pitts in "Rukeyser Imbroglio," 162–62, 270n38; "mechanical Marxism," 199; mechanical materialism, 170; on poetic sensibilities, 146–47; "Problems and Perspecitves in Revolutionary Literature," 199

Picabia, Francis, 147
Picasso, Pablo, 29, 109, 272n13
Piper, Adrienne, 15, 250–51
Pitts, Rebecca, and "Rukeyser Imbroglio," 161
Plath, Sylvia, 239
Podhoretz, Norman, postwar "new class," 269n30
Postmodernism, 7, 198, 210, 218–20; beyond spectacle, 263; high-tech society, 232; subversion of advertising, 251
Potter, Sally, 209
Pound, Ezra, 52, 87, 222, 268n26; "In a Station of the Metro," 57
Prampolini, Enrico, 147; machine as symbol, 148
Proletariat, 138; after postmodernity, 220; agitation, 169; classist representations of, 200; imagery, 141; literature, 154, 162; writers in the 1930s, 199
Proletcult, 11, 33, 36, 47, 58, 60–61, 101, 105, 123, 138, 156; Benjamin's credo on, 214–15; Burke's advice on, 200; new form by Rukeyser, 163; reductionist under Stalin, 170, 290n20; Rukeyser's advancement, 172; tropes of, 220; writers, 9

Queer Nation, 94, 262
Quirt, Walter, 49, 181

Rabinowitz, Paula, 138; on the Left, 285n114; on sexism and fetishism, 220
Radway, Janice, 11; "Mail-Order Culture and Its Critics," 269n30
Rahv, Philip: disagreement with Matthiessen and Pitts in "Rukeyser Imbroglio," 162–62, 270n38; "mechanical Marxism," 199; mechanical materialism, 170; "Problems and Perspecitves in Revolutionary Literature," 199
Rainer, Yvonne, 209

Randolph, A. Philip, 75
Randolph, Mary, 112; "Rivera's Monopoly," 270n38
Ransom, John Crowe, 161
Rasula, Jed, *Tabula Rasula,* 193
Ray, Man: "Bridgebuilders," "Skyline," "Metropolis," 150
Rebel Poets, 52; *Contempo,* 52; *The Rebel Poet,* 52; "Unrest," 52
Reed, Ishmael, 278n15, 280n37; *Mumbo Jumbo,* 63
Reed, John, 36, 47
Reiss, Weinold, 89, 97; "African Phantasy Awakening," 67; "The Brown Madonna," 84–85
Repin, Ilya, 272n12
Reznikoff, Charles, 107
Rhodes, E. Washington, 100
Rice, Elmer, 46
Rice, Philip Blair, 290–91n28
Rich, Adrienne, 88, 93, 239; compulsory heterosexuality, 262
Richter, Hans, 147
Ridge, Lola, 45–46, 153
Rivera, Diego, 12, 14, 179, 183; aesthetics of, 109–22; notoriety of, 175; on Russian futurist and socialist realists, 111; works: *Allegory of California* (mural), 184; *Detroit Industry* (mural), 11, 115–16; *The Making of a Fresco, Showing the Building of a City* (mural), 113–14; *Man, Controller of the Universe"* (mural), 121
Robeson, Paul, 70, 97
Robinson, Boardman, 46
Robinson, Kit, *Dolch Stanzas,* 192
Rockefeller, John D., 113
Rockefeller, Nelson, 121
Rodchenko, Alexander, 33–35
Rodman, Seldon, 161
Rolfe, Edwin, 42–43, 52, 153, 161; birth of a new social order, 157–58; on formulaic verse, 170, 289–90n19; works: "Asbestos," 158–59, 169; *To My Contemporaries,* 56–57

Rorty, James, 108
Rosenthal, M. L., "Muriel Rukeyser: The Longer Poems," 291n28
Ross, Andrew, 292n16
Rukeyser, Muriel, 14, 153; beyond the proletcult, 187; critical reception of, 161; critique of American visual culture, 166–67; deconstruction, 289n18; as Popular Front author, 161; reactions to "The Book of the Dead," 162–63, 165; works: "The Book of the Dead," 160; "Words and Images," 290n25
Ruskin, Cindy, 259–60
Ryan, Cara Gendel, 254

Saatchi, Maurice and Charles, 248
Said, Edward, 203, 270n36
Salle, David, 222
Sandburg, Carl, 27, 46; on Macleish, 160
Sayre, Henry, 15, 198
Scalapino, Leslie, 194
Schiller, Friedrich, *Letters on the Aesthetic Education of Man,* 267n23
Schnabel, Julian, 224, 248
Schneider, Isidor, 52, 53, 153
Scholes, Robert, 2
Schuster, M. Lincoln, *Eyes of the World: A Photographic Record of History-in-the-Making,* 288n14
Schwartz, Sanford, *The Matrix of Modernism,* 52
Sexton, Anne, 239
Shahn, Ben, 172, 183; collaboration with Rukeyser, 172; withdrawl from art exhibition, 122
Shklovsky, Viktor, 197, 210
Showalter, Elaine, 257
Siegel, William, 64, 118–19; "Bigger and Better Belles Lettres" (drawing), 131
Silliman, Ron, 189–90, 197; on Bernstein, 192; works: *The Age of Huts,* 193; *Chinese Notebook,* 193; *Ketjak,* 192; *Sunset Debris,* 193; *2197,* 193

Siquieros, David Alfara, 110, 183
Smith, Mike, 259
Smith, Raymond, 103
Snow, Michael, 209
Soglow, Otto, 46
Sollors, Werner, 55
Solow, Herbert, 108
Spector, Herman, 52, 107, 153
Spencer, Anne, 84, 87
Spero, Nancy, 15, 237–44, 251; censorship issues, 244; subversion of sexism, 227
Spivak, Gayatri, 242
Stalin, Joseph, 59–60
Steffens, Lincoln, 27–28
Stein, Gertrude, 193
Stella, Joseph, 151
Stenberg, Vladimier and Georgii, 35
Stepanova, Varvara, 33, 35
Stephanson, Anders, "Interview with Cornel West," 271n45
Stevens, Wallace, 53, 213
Stieglitz, Alfred, 4; Camera Work: Mechanical Expression Seen Through Our Own Mechanical Expressions, 147
Stott, William, 166
Strong, Anna Louise, 36

Taggard, Genevieve, 46, 152–53
Tatlin, Vladimir, 29, 33
Thurman, Wallace, 86, 91; "Fire Burns," 94
Toomer, Jean, 46, 84, 97
Trent, Lucia, 52
Trotsky, Leon, 41, 46, 59–60, 105, 108; Literature and Revolution, 60

Untermeyer, Louis, 46, 70; praising Rukeyser, 287n3

Van Vechten, Carl, 73, 278n22; promoter of black literature, 68; literary party host, 69–70; Nigger Heaven, 68
Venturi, Robert, 218
Vorse, Mary Heaton, 46

Waldrop, Rosemarie, 194
Warhol, Andy, 219–20
Warren, Robert Penn, 200
Washington, Booker T., 83, 95
Waters, Ethel, 70
Watkins, Ben, 194
Watten, Barrett, 189; "Russian Formalism and the Present," 197
Wave Three of the AIDS Coalition to Unleash Power (ACT UP), 94, 261–62
Wecter, Dixon, 166
Weiner, Hannah, Clairvoyant Journal, 194
Wheelwright, John, 164
White, Hayden, 2
White, Newman Ivey, An Anthology of Verse by American Negroes, 86
White, Walter, 68, 70, 99
Whitman, Walt, 87; "When Lilacs Last in the Dooryard Bloom'd," 158
Williams, William Carlos, 46; defining avant-garde, 145; on Funaroff, 107; praise of Rukeyser, 171
Wilson, Edmund, 46, 108
Wood, Ellen Meiksins, The Retreat from Class, 270n36
Wright, Richard, 61–63
Wylie, Elinor, 70

Young, Art, 46; "Having Their Fling," 24, 26
Yudice, George, 270n36

Zdanevich, Ilya, "Why We Paint Ourselves: A Futurist Manifesto," 273n20
Zukofsky, Louis, 107

Designer: Teresa Bonner
Text: Souvenir Light
Compositor: Impressions, *a division of* Edwards Brothers
Printer: Edwards Brothers
Binder: Edwards Brothers